Pioneer Reminiscences of Puget Sound

PIONEER REMINISCENCES

OF

PUGET SOUND

THE TRAGEDY OF LESCHI

AN ACCOUNT OF THE COMING OF THE FIRST AMERICANS AND THE
ESTABLISHMENT OF THEIR INSTITUTIONS; THEIR ENCOUNT-
ERS WITH THE NATIVE RACE; THE FIRST TREATIES
WITH THE INDIANS AND THE WAR THAT FOLLOW-
ED; SEVEN YEARS OF THE LIFE OF ISAAC I.
STEVENS IN WASHINGTON TERRITORY;
CRUISE OF THE AUTHOR ON PUGET
SOUND FIFTY YEARS AGO;
NISQUALLY HOUSE AND
THE HUDSON BAY
COMPANY.

FROM PERSONAL OBSERVATION DURING FIFTY YEARS RESIDENCE,
CONTEMPORARY PIONEER REMINISCENCES AND
OTHER AUTHENTIC SOURCES.

BY EZRA MEEKER
SEATTLE, WASH.
1905

LOWMAN & HANFORD
STATIONERY AND PRINTING CO.
SEATTLE, WASH.

DEDICATION

To the intrepid pioneer men and women of the Northwest,

this work is respectfully dedicated.

Seattle, Washington, 1905.

EZRA MEEKER

ILLUSTRATIONS

FRONTISPIECE.

TABLE OF CONTENTS

CONTENTS.

CHAPTER IV.

CRUISE ON PUGET SOUND.

CHAPTER V.

CRUISE ON PUGET SOUND.—*Continued.*

CHAPTER VI.

CRUISE ON PUGET SOUND.—*Continued.*

CHAPTER VII.

CRUISE ON PUGET SOUND.—*Continued.*

CHAPTER VIII.

CRUISE ON PUGET SOUND.—*Continued.*

CHAPTER IX.

FROM COLUMBIA RIVER.

CHAPTER X.

THE SECOND CABIN.

CHAPTER XI.

TRIP THROUGH THE NATCHESS PASS.

CHAPTER XII.

TRIP THROUGH THE NATCHESS PASS—*Continued.*

CHAPTER XVII.

FIRST IMMIGRANTS THROUGH THE NATCHESS PASS, 1853.

CHAPTER XVIII.

BUILDING OF THE NATCHESS PASS ROAD.

CHAPTER XIX.

BUILDING OF THE NATCHESS PASS ROAD.—*Concluded.*

CHAPTER XX.

THE MUD WAGON ROAD.

CHAPTER XXI.

THE FRASER RIVER STAMPEDE.

CHAPTER XXVI.

THE MORNING SCHOOL.

CHAPTER XXVII.

CHARACTERISTICS OF LESCHI.

CHAPTER XXVIII.

THE OUTBREAK.

CHAPTER XXIX.

THE PRIMITIVE PEOPLES.

CHAPTER XXX.

THE MEDICINE CREEK TREATY.

CHAPTER XXXI.

MEDICINE CREEK COUNCIL REVIEWED.

CHAPTER XXXII.

CAUSE OF GOVERNOR STEVENS' FAILURE.

CHAPTER XXXIII.

POINT ELLIOTT AND OTHER TREATIES.

CHAPTER XXXIV.

DEFECTS AND RESULTS OF TREATIES.

CHAPTER XXXV.

GATHERING WAR CLOUDS.

CHAPTER XXXVI.

BEGINNING OF THE WAR.

CHAPTER XXXVII.

THE WHITE RIVER MASSACRE.

CHAPTER XXXVIII.

THE FLIGHT OF SETTLERS.

CHAPTER XXXIX.

BATTLE OF WHITE RIVER.

CHAPTER XLIX.

CONTROVERSY BETWEEN STEVENS AND WOOL.

CHAPTER L.

TROUBLES IN PIERCE COUNTY.

CHAPTER LI.

MARTIAL LAW.

CHAPTER LII.

MARTIAL LAW.—*Concluded.*

CHAPTER LIII.

GOVERNOR STEVENS' CHARACTERISTICS.

CHAPTER LIV.

GOVERNOR STEVENS' TRIAL.

CHAPTER LV.

THE UNRELENTING FOE.

CHAPTER LVI.

THE TWO TRIALS OF LESCHI.

CHAPTER LVII.

HEARING BEFORE SUPREME COURT.

CHAPTER LVIII.

DEFEAT OF THE EXECUTION OF LESCHI.

CHAPTER LIX.

THE OTHER SIDE.

CHAPTER LX.

DR. TOLMIE'S PLEA.

CHAPTER LXI.

FINAL SENTENCE AND EXECUTION OF LESCHI.

CHAPTER LXII.

REBURIAL OF LESCHI.

CHAPTER LXIII.

AN AFTER-WORD.

CHAPTER LXIV.

IN THE BEGINNING.

INTRODUCTORY

THE HISTORY OF A HISTORY.

Four years ago to-day I arrived at the ripe age of three score years and ten, supposed to be the limit of life. Finding that I possessed more ambition than strength, and that my disposition for a strenuous life was greater than my power of physical endurance, I naturally turned to other fields of work, that condition of life so necessary for the welfare and happiness of the human race.

Many years before it had been my ambition to write our earlier experiences of pioneer life on Puget Sound, and not necessarily for the printer, but because I wanted to, but never could find time; and so when the change came and my usual occupation was gone, what else would I be more likely to do than to turn to my long delayed work, the more particularly being admonished that it must be done soon or not at all. And so, in a cheerful, happy mood, I entered again into the domain of pioneer life, and began writing. But this is not history, you will say. True, but we will come to that by and by.

I had, during the summer of 1853, with an inexperienced companion, in an open boat—a frail skiff built with our own hands—crossed the path of Theodore Winthrop, spending more than a month on a cruise from Olympia to the Straits and return, while that adventurous traveler and delightful writer had with a crew of Indians made the trip from Port Townsend to Fort Nisqually in a canoe. I had followed Winthrop a year later through the Natchess Pass to the Columbia River and beyond, alone, except a companion pony that carried my sack of hard bread for food, the saddle blanket for my bed and myself across the turbulent rivers, and on easy grades. If Winthrop could write such a beauti-

ful book, "The Canoe and the Saddle," based upon such
a trip, with Indians to paddle his canoe on the Sound,
and with an attendant and three horses through the
mountains, why should not my own experience of such a
trip be interesting to my own children and their children's children? And so I wrote these trips.

Did you ever, when hungry, taste of a dish of fruit,
a luscious, ripe, highly flavored apple for instance, that
seemed only to whet but not satisfy your appetite? I
know you have, and so can appreciate my feelings when
these stories were written. I craved more of pioneer life
experience, and so I went back to the earlier scenes, a
little earlier only—to the trip in a flat boat down the
Columbia River from The Dalles to the first cabin,
where Kalama town now stands; to the pack on our
backs from the Columbia to the Sound; to the three
times passing the road to and fro to get the wife and
baby to tidewater—what a charm that word tidewater
had for me with a vision of the greatness of opportunities of the seaboard—and I may say it has never lost
its charm—of the great world opened up before me, and
so we were soon again housed in the little cabin with
its puncheon floor, "cat-and-clay" chimney, and clap-
board roof; its surroundings of scenery; of magnificent forests and of constantly moving life, the Indians
with their happy song and fishing parties.

All this and more, too, I wrote, every now and then
getting over to the Indian question. How could I help
it? We had been treated civilly, and I may say, kindly,
by them from the very outset, when we, almost alone,
were their white neighbors. I had been treated generously by some, and had always found them ready to
reciprocate in acts of kindness, and so we had come to
respect our untutored neighbors and to sympathize with
them in their troubles. Deep troubles came to them
when the treaty-making period arrived, and a little
later upon all of us, when war came, to break up all our

plans and amicable relations. As I began to write more about the Indians and their ways, a step further brought me to the consideration of our Territorial government and the government officials and their acts. It gradually dawned upon me this was a more important work than writing of humble individuals; that the history of our commonwealth was by far a more interesting theme, and more profitable to the generations to follow than recording of private achievements of the pioneer. It was but a step further until I realized that I was fairly launched upon the domain of history, and that I must need be more painstaking and more certain of my facts, and so then came a long rest for my pen and a long search of the records, of old musty letters, of no less old musty books, of forgetful minds of the pioneers left, and again I was carried away into the almost forgotten past.

An authoress once told me that she never named her book until after it was written. I could not then understand why, but I now do. While writing of pioneer life I could think of no other title than something like this: "Pioneer Life on Puget Sound Fifty Years Ago," a pretty long title, but that was what the writing treated of. But when I got on the Indian question and came to realize what a splendid true story was wrapped up in the darkness of impending oblivion; how the Indians had been wronged; how they had fought for their homes and won them; how the chief actors had been sacrificed, but the tribes had profited—I again became enthusiastic over my theme and over my ready-made heroes, and before I realized it, lo! a new name took possession of my mind and rang in it until there was born the title, "The Tragedy of Leschi."

When I come to think of it, that here were tribes that had never shed white men's blood until grim war came, and that then they refused to make war on their old neighbors, and that but one non-combatant settler had lost his life after the first day of frenzy of the Muckle-shoot band at the massacre of White River, that here were men we called savages, fighting for a cause, but threw themselves on the track of the military arm of the government and not against helpless settlers. I had myself been in their power and remained unharmed. I knew other of my neighbors also that had been exposed and remained unmolested; surely to tell the truth about such people is no more than justice and I said to myself, I will write it down and prove what I write by the records and the best obtainable witnesses alive, and having done so, will print it, two books in one, two titles, yet but one volume, "Pioneer Reminiscences of Puget Sound; The Tragedy of Leschi."

It is natural that in the stirring times of early days opinions would differ; that neighbors, and even members of families would look upon events from differing points of view, and so out of this maze I have tried to state exact facts and draw just conclusions. The chapter of this history begins with the creation of the Territory and ends with Governor Stevens' official life in the Territory in the period concerned. During that period, treaties were made with the Indians, the war with them was fought; massacres horrid to contemplate were perpetrated by the Indians and whites—by the Indians at the outbreak, and the whites later—murders were committed; martial law proclaimed, our courts invaded with armed men, judges dragged from the bench; our governor in turn brought before the courts, fined and reprieved by himself, and many other happenings unique in history are related, and so, when my labor was finished and my pen laid aside, my only regret was that the work had not been undertaken earlier in life when memory served more accurately, and my contemporaries were more numerous.

E. MEEKER.

Seattle, Dec. 29th, 1904.

MY SECOND FORE-WORD

"Why did you go to Puget Sound in that early day?" I have been asked a thousand times, I verily believe; so often, at least, that I feel prompted to write about it, although no very plausible reason may appear.

It is an American instinct to want to better one's condition; we may say that it is a worldwide instinct that pervades the human breast, but more particularly that of an American. The words or phrase, to "better his condition," may mean many things. It may mean he seeks a better climate; or seeks a better soil; or for better health; or a future better market. In a word, in so many ways that we become lost in the attempt to enumerate them.

"But" says one, "you had the whole of the Middle West to choose from fifty years ago, and why you should run over such a vast field and take such chances is an enigma to me." And so it is to many who participated in the great movement across the plains to this day.

The answer is not hard to find if one but seeks the moving motives that govern mankind. It is true that no such movement can be found in history where so great a number moved so great a distance as was witnessed in the immigration to the Pacific Coast in '52; and so we must need to look for exceptional causes governing this exceptional movement.

It was like an army moving out to battle and burning their bridges behind them. When the Missouri River was crossed, or at least when a short distance out, a return became impossible; the road was choked by teams all moving one way, or if not, left small parties returning at the mercy of the Indians, to be robbed, possibly murdered.

The motive prompting the movement had been gathering force for years. The great contrast in the early days, before cheap transportation came, between conditions on the Atlantic seaboard and the interior, set men to thinking about the great unoccupied territory within the reach of the Pacific—within reach of the world's market, within reach of the ocean's highway—and fired the imagination of the would-be immigrant. Here was the opportunity of a lifetime to get to the front and pick the choicest fruits of the earth. I say, and yet think, they were right, although many missed the mark. Another potent cause was the climate that was pictured in such glowing terms in contrast with the conditions existing in the Middle West. Then there came the incentive to better one's condition financially; get land; get gold; get choice locations. The argument was, there must be such opportunities in so large a country so sparsely settled.

Then another class, that had to take every third day off to shake with the ague, while the process was going on of turning the virgin soil of the Middle West, formed no inconsiderable number that counted this the moving cause that governed their actions—a search for health. Coupled with all this was the American desire for adventure, planted in the breasts of so many of the pioneers of the frontier, that some were willing to undertake the trip just for the fun of the thing; but they did not find it very funny before they got through. But let us now consider the start and what happened.

"Do you think it safe to prepare for the trip?" This question was asked in a rather hesitating manner, as though the speaker felt it was hardly proper at the time to make such an inquiry of the person addressed.

"Why, yes; I think so. Baby will be three weeks old to-morrow, and it will take three weeks to get ready. I think it will be all right, don't you?"

"Just like a woman," I said, "to answer one question by asking another; but I think that settles it, and we will go to Oregon this year."

This little talk took place in a small cabin near the Des Moines River, in Iowa, with a good deal more of like kind, between the little wife and young husband, the writer of this story, during the first week of April, 1852, and upon the conclusion to be reached depended whether we should become pioneers and go to Oregon or remain in the harsh Iowa climate and make our home on the prairies of the Middle West.

It is not the intention to write an autobiography of my life, though personal experiences will be drawn upon that are intimately interwoven with events in the further West for the fifty years following the incident just related. I could not do otherwise if I would, and write of the conditions of the pioneer life that followed.

So the preparations began in earnest for the great trip across the plains. Buck bought the outfit and I the team.

When as a boy I used to delight in breaking the calves to play work, and later the larger steers to sure work, little did I think the experience then gained would in after life stand me so well in hand to save me from danger and discomfort.

A few days sufficed to purchase four unbroken steers and four unbroken cows, and get the yokes fitted, with everything ready for the start during the last week of April, 1852.

"What are you going to do now?" asked Buck, as we halted for the first night's camp.

"Unyoke the cattle, of course, and turn them out to graze," I answered, and at the same time began preparing to do so.

"But you will never get them in the yoke again if you turn them loose here!" my friend excitedly replied.

While I contended it would not do to leave them in the yoke, Buck as firmly insisted that we must not turn them loose. At this juncture a stranger, camped near by, interrupted, and said he and his men would help us to yoke up in the morning; that his animals were gentle and that we would have no difficulty, and so the cattle were turned out on the range and we gave attention to the making of our first camp.

This stranger, the peacemaker, we soon came to know as one that would do to tie to, and for the next two months, and for a thousand miles, we traveled and camped near together, and thereafter never a word of contention passed between the three. Thomas McAuley —for that was his name—had, like William Buck and myself, fitted out light and with unbroken cattle, which proved to be a great boon to both of us, as we moved out on the long journey.

The trip across the plains has been so often written that it would seem the whole ground has been covered, though from start to finish it was pioneer life in dead earnest. Nevertheless, the after-experience would seem incomplete without some mention of how we got to the pioneer field of the farther West, and a little of the experience on the way.

"It will be necessary for your own safety to take yourself away from here, and that quite quick."

The individual addressed, who was no less a person than the sheriff of an Iowa county bordering on the Missouri River near Council Bluffs, concluded that discretion was the better part of valor, and at once obeyed the mandate of an orderly mob who had dug out of the sands an abandoned scow in which to cross the river, which an alleged owner concluded to take charge of as soon as in good running order. The crossing of the Missouri was the first real danger encountered. After waiting a week to get across with the ferry, and after seeing several lives sacrificed, our little crowd concluded to help themselves, with the result mentioned while preparing for a first trip.

The two sisters, Eliza and Margaret McAuley, with the little wife and baby, were set across the river on the first load and left to watch the outfit to prevent it falling into the hands of the pilfering Pawnee Indians. Then and there came near being the baptism of blood, figuratively, which they said seemed the only way to drive the thieves off. The show of guns in a most threatening attitude of the three women had the desired effect, though the guns were not loaded, and they were left unmolested.

It took every hand to man the boat, but we crossed without loss of life or property.

The number that crossed that river into the Indian country will never be known. We ascertained by the scribbling on rocks and other signs left that the army was nearly or quite five hundred miles long, and, no inconsiderable part of the way, three columns deep. The crowd was so great that at times all the wagons could not get into one track, especially during the morning hour, and so it often came about that there were parallel columns moving, usually in close proximity, with resultant strife for possession of the main beaten track. Moving columns of loose stock on either side of the road, of which there were driven great numbers at the start, added much to the discomfort and strife among the people.

I say at the start, because it was not long before the loss of stock was fearful to relate, and thinned their number, as likewise the teams, and caused many hundreds of wagons to be left standing by the roadside. With this loss of teams soon came the abandonment of all sorts of superfluous property, so that the road became lined with piles of all sorts of household goods, and later provisions, in large quantities.

The greater body of the immigrants formed themselves into large companies and elected captains. These combinations soon began to dissolve and reform, to dissolve again, until it seemed as though everybody was for himself, and I had liked to have said, "the devil for them all."

When, to add to the contentions going on, there came the epidemic of cholera, it appeared as though the people lost their reason and all sense of the responsibility resting upon them, like a panic-stricken army (as they were) fleeing from dangers they knew not how nor where —only to get away from where they were.

The result was a continued strife for mastery of the road, to see who could get ahead and who could travel farthest in a day, to try "to get out of this cholera."

But I must not tarry to tell too much about this, else we will never get across the plains with this story.

Suffice it to say that the loss of life and property was fearful to relate. In one camping place we counted fifty-odd fresh graves, none of which bore date of more than the previous week; and as for the carcasses of dead stock, certainly such could be counted by the thousands, for one might almost say literally we were never out of the sight or smell of them for a thousand miles on the trip.

Buck and McAuley were both older than myself, though both of them bachelors. They were cool, brave men. One of the sisters bordered on the old-maidish list, but never did a more courageous woman live, as after emergencies showed, though coupled with true ladylike character and modest demeanor.

The married man and the little wife were the youngest of the party (except the baby), and in all conscience were young enough indeed to assume such a responsibility; but we were there on the plains, the step had been taken and could not be retraced, and so with sobering surrounding circumstances and with the close circle of associates of great worth, disaster did not overtake us. And I will now say, in dismissing this part of the subject, that we did not throw away a pound of provisions or property of any kind, nor lose a hoof of stock.

There came a little touch of romance connected with the separation of Buck and myself at the big bend of Bear River. Buck was 28 years old, and according to commonly accepted belief a confirmed bachelor. He was in some respects an eccentric man, and as intense in his dislikes as he was in his friendships—so scrupulously neat and orderly that some of the thoughtless were ready to dub him as "old maidish," or bordering on the dude. Those who knew him well knew that there did not exist the least particle of either of these characteristics in his conduct.

One of the sisters met at our first camp and with whom we afterwards traveled so far, I could see attracted the attention of Buck in spite of himself, but the usual observer could not detect by his actions the least sign; but somehow or other the little wife and I came to feel we knew that Buck had lost his heart. He was passionately fond of children, and so uproriously so of our baby that casual neighbor campers would naturally think he was the father and husband, and not for a moment of the boyish-looking person in the company. Buck became the camp-man, one might say by natural selection. He was so handy, cleanly, untiring, never lagging until the last chore was done, the last tent secure, water provided, fuel secured for the morrow if to be had; in a word, he was not the man to leave anything undone that could be done for the convenience of the company—the McAuleys and ourselves.

At the very start he insisted that he wanted to go to California, but said he did not want to "keep bach" on the plains, and upon short acquaintance had agreed that he would go to Oregon with us (wife and me and baby) for the sake of company, and thence to California alone.

But as we approached the forks of the road the little wife nudged the young husband to whisper: "Don't you think we might let Buck go to California with the McAuleys?"

"Why do you ask that question; he hasn't said anything about it, has he?" asked the young husband.

"Oh, no, nor neither will he; but I know."

"Know what?"

"Well, I know he is—"

"Is what?" But the question remained unanswered, for the little wife knew that the young husband knew as well as she did what was "what."

Buck blushed scarlet to the very ears when I told him that we knew he would like to take the left-hand road that was then near ahead of us, and go to California with the McAuleys. And that was the only sign he gave, except, as one might say, an indescribable expression of the eyes for the moment, which, however, soon disappeared.

At the last camp we tarried together for many days, just turned loose for a big visit; but there were scarcely any dry eyes in the camp when good-byes were said to the baby as Buck and McAuley drove out on the California road.

We kept up our acquaintance until his death, which occurred a good many years ago. The last time I saw him was at his splendid home near San Filipe, California, a veritable fairy nook of fruit and flowers, showing the same orderly, artistic hand; but he was then a sure-enough bachelor over sixty years old, and he never married. He inquired about the baby, who was then married and had children of his own, and who is now a grandfather, but nothing was said about the episode of the plains; that is, as to that particular occurrence. Of course, we always lived the trip over again when we met.

Buck is the man that introduced the honey bee into Oregon and Washington, and I think California also. He sent me five swarms by steamer from San Francisco a few years after our trip, two of which I kept and sold the remainder for $125.00 for each swarm. It is a curious fact that before the advent of the American settlers no honey bees were found west of the Rocky Mountains. Some one attempted to bring a swarm by wagon across the plains, but Buck made two trips to the Atlantic seaboard via the Isthmus of Panama, and each trip brought a large number of swarms. He was a man that could accomplish such a feat if anyone in this wide world could. I loved Buck almost to the point of idòlatry, and I may say we formed a very small but select mutual admiration society that continued until his death. The last time I saw him away from home was at Puyallup some fifteen years ago. He had been robbed in Tacoma and came up for money to take him home. The humor of the incident was to see him hesitate to ask even this small favor, so independent in spirit was he, but he always took pleasure in bestowing a favor apparently on anyone, be he friend or stranger. He was one of nature's noblemen.

One morning while at breakfast, thirty years or more after the incidents first related, a letter was placed on the table and immediately opened, and read in part as follows:

"Ezra Meeker, my friend of ye Auld Lang Syne, Puyallup, Washington Territory:

"I have just read an item in a paper about an Ezra Meeker of Puyallup, Washington Territory, and have wondered if that is the Ezra Meeker I knew in my girlhood days. I suppose you will have looked at the signature to this letter to ascertain who your correspondent is, and are as yet none the wiser. (I had done that very thing and could not for

the life of me tell who the writer was.) Well, I thought
first to ask you how you are, is your wife living and are
you well, and how have you prospered (still a mystery),
and how is that baby, Dick?"

That let the whole secret out. It was one of the Mc-
Auley girls that was writing, and so the letter was read
aloud from beginning to end to the little wife who sat
opposite at the table.

The letter continued "that she was married and had
five children, two of whom had just graduated," and
much more of deep interest to the recipients of the letter, but not of particular interest to the general reader,
finishing with "an earnest hope we may some time meet
and become acquainted again."

"I will go and see her," the little wife said; and sure
enough, the visit was made, although it involved nearly
fifteen hundred miles of travel.

One of the sisters, the letter told us, was dead long
before, but nothing was said about Buck, or much of the
trip after we had separated at the big bend of Bear
River.

Of the meeting and greeting that followed little need
be said. Pen cannot describe the feelings of pioneers
upon meeting after a long separation, as time passes.
After a short interval of time there is a bond of union
that cannot be described, to be understood by those outside the class to which this peculiar experience belongs.

The incident illustrates how complete the isolation
of the pioneer who goes to a new country without post
roads (or, for that matter, roads of any kind), or post-
offices, or even towns, the names and locations of which
are all strange to the friends left behind and to the outside world of civilization.

Without question there were real hardships to be endured on that trip that were unavoidable. The dust at
times was intolerable, the water often bad, the heat op-
pressive, the road heavy and fatigue great; neverthe-

less, the greater part of these discomforts could be overcome or avoided, and were overcome by great numbers.

Three incidents have been so indelibly fixed in my mind that I feel prompted to first review them before attempting to follow the long train of events that ensued—the night stampede of the buffaloes, the crossing of the Snake River in our wagon beds, and the trip in a flatboat down the Columbia River from The Dalles to the Cascades.

It is difficult to realize that of those vast herds of buffalo we saw, none of their kind are left. Words can give no adequate idea as to number in sight from favorable points of view. As far as the eye could reach the animals would appear like the most tiny little specks in the distance, and finally in a further field show as a shaded tint on the landscape. There seemed to be no end to them. For hundreds of miles at times these herds were in sight, interspersed with the antelope, a lovely, graceful creature to behold, in great contrast to their companions afield, the ugly, ill-shapen buffaloes.

The incident of the stampede alluded to occurred one night several hundred miles out on our journey. On that particular evening the wagons had been placed in a semi-circle, with ropes connecting to make a complete inclosure. The usual guards sent with the stock when kept out on the range were asleep, save one sentinel. The first intimation of danger came when every hoof of stock within the enclosure sprang to their feet as if they had become possessed of an evil spirit. The resultant confusion and the roar of the approaching herd awoke every inmate in or under every wagon or tent to rally in undress to weak points of the enclosure. To hear that sound is never to forget it. Like the roar of the heaviest tornado, one could scarcely tell the direction from which it came, or the distance from which it emanated; neither the direction in which it was moving, and all we could do was to prepare for the onslaught,

which might or might not strike us, and await results.
Fortunately the great herd passed to one side of us,
though very near, so near we thought it was surely
upon us, though we escaped entirely unharmed and
without the loss of a single animal. Not so with many
of our camping neighbors, who lost heavily in stock
stampeded, and some of which they never recovered, and
detained their trains for days.

Snake River just below Salmon Falls is a comparatively placid stream, though quite too deep for fording,
and very wide. We knew if we crossed over we must
cross back in a hundred miles or so, and thus encounter
a double danger. But the temptation of good feed for a
season for our almost famished stock was too strong,
and we began the preparation for the crossing. The incident I can most distinctly remember of all is when I
reversed the usual order and ran my wagon into the
river over the wagon bed and gradually moved out into
deep water until the whole was afloat. The bed was so
deeply laden that the least ripple in the water would
slop over the sides, whilst I rowed the whole over to the
opposite side of the river. How it came it did not swamp
I can now scarcely realize, but I know only that I got
over safely and that very minute wished myself back
on the other side, for I knew not what was ahead of me
on the crossing further down the river.

We got all our little party over safely, and safely
back again, but we all took a long breath, a sigh of relief, when the last wagon bed was landed with the last
remnant of the outfit.

Not so fortunate were many of our neighboring fellow travelers, many of whom lost property, and some
their lives. Give me a wide berth from crossing Snake
River in a wagon bed, is my prayer.

' Strange as it may appear, yet it is true, that in the
face of all this danger, many were inclined to dispose
of their teams and start down that river in their wagon

beds—stark crazy, I should say—all of whom soon lost everything, and many their lives. Those who did escape came near starving before they reached the immigrant road. One boy, now a respected citizen of Tacoma, with a part of the family not drowned, was on the range for seven days without food other than roots and herbage, plucked as they traveled. Many never were heard of afterwards.

The third incident alluded to was the voyage down the Columbia River in a flatboat, from The Dalles to the Cascades, and is related in the chapter following, "Floating Down the River."

PIONEER REMINISCENCES

OF

PUGET SOUND

CHAPTER I.

Floating Down the River.

On a September day of 1852 an assemblage of persons could be seen encamped on the banks of the great Columbia, at The Dalles, now a city of no small pretensions, but then only a name for the peculiar configuration of country adjacent to and including the waters of the great river.

One would soon discover this assemblage was constantly changing. Every few hours stragglers came in from off the dusty road, begrimed with the sweat of the brow commingled with particles of dust driven through the air, sometimes by a gentle breeze and then again by a violent gale sweeping up the river through the mountain gap of the Cascade Range. A motley crowd these people were, almost cosmopolitan in nationality, yet all vestige of race peculiarities or race prejudices ground away in the mill of adversity and trials common to all alike in common danger. And yet, the dress and appearance of this assemblage were as varied as the human countenance and as unique as the great mountain scenery before them. Some were clad in scanty attire as soiled with the dust as their brows; others, while with better pretensions, lacked some portions of dress required in civilized life. Here a matronly dame with clean apparel would be without shoes, or there, perhaps, the husband without the hat or perhaps both shoes and hat absent; there the youngsters of all ages, making no pretensions to genteel clothing other than to cover their nakedness. An expert's ingenuity would be taxed to the utmost to discover either the texture or original color of the clothing of either juvenile or adult, so prevailing was the patch work and so inground the particles of dust and sand from off the plains.

Some of these people were buoyant and hopeful in the anticipation of meeting friends whom they knew were awaiting them at their journey's end, while others were downcast and despondent as their thoughts went back to their old homes left behind, and the struggle now so near ended, and forward to the (to them) unknown land ahead. Some had laid friends and relatives tenderly away in the shifting sands, who had fallen by the wayside, with the certain knowledge that with many the spot selected by them would not be the last resting place for the bones of the loved ones. The hunger of the wolf had been appeased by the abundance of food from the fallen cattle that lined the trail for a thousand miles or more, or from the weakened beasts of the immigrants that constantly submitted to capture by the relentless native animals.

The story of the trip across the plains in 1852 is both interesting and pathetic, but I have planned to write of life after the journey rather than much about the journey itself; of the trials that beset the people after their five months' struggle on the tented field of two thousand miles of marching was ended, where, like on the very battlefield, the dead lay in rows of fifties or more; where the trail became so lined with fallen animals, one could scarcely be out of sight or smell of carrion; where the sick had no respite from suffering, nor the well from fatigue. But this oft told story is a subject of itself, treated briefly to the end we may have space to tell what happened when the journey was ended.

The constant gathering on the bank of the Columbia and constant departures of the immigrants did not materially change the numbers encamped, nor the general appearance. The great trip had moulded this army of homeseekers into one homogeneous mass, a common brotherhood, that left a lasting impression upon the participants, and, although few are left now, not one but will greet an old comrade as a brother indeed, and in fact, with hearty and oftentimes tearful congratulations.

We camped but two days on the bank of the river. When I say we, let it be understood that I mean myself, my young wife, and the little baby boy, who was but seven weeks old when the start was made from near Eddyville, Iowa. Both were sick, the mother from gradual exhaustion during the trip incident to motherhood, and the little one in sympathy, doubtless drawn from the mother's breast.

Did you ever think of the wonderful mystery of the inner action of the mind, how some impressions once made seem to remain, while others gradually fade away, like the twilight of a summer sunset, until finally lost? And then how seemingly trivial incidents will be fastened upon one's memory while others of more importance we would recall if we could, but which have faded forever from our grasp? I can well believe all readers have had this experience, and so will be prepared to receive with leniency the confession of an elderly gentleman, (I will not say old), when he says that most of the incidents are forgotten and few remembered. I do not remember the embarking on the great scow for the float down the river to the Cascades, but vividly remember, as though it were but yes-

terday, incidents of the voyage. We all felt (I now
mean the immigrants who took passage) that now our
journey was ended. The cattle had been unyoked for the
last time. The wagons had been rolled to the last
bivouac; the embers of the last camp fire had died out;
the last word of gossip had been spoken, and now, we
were entering a new field with new present experience,
and with new expectancy for the morrow.

The scow or lighter upon which we took passage was
decked over, but without railing, a simple, smooth surface upon which to pile our belongings, which, in
the great majority of cases made but a very small
showing. I think there must have been a dozen
families, or more, of sixty or more persons, principally women and children, as the young men (and
some old ones, too) were struggling on the mountain
trail to get the teams through to the west side. The
whole deck surface of the scow was covered with the
remnants of the immigrants' outfits, which in turn were
covered by the owners, either sitting or reclining upon
their possessions, leaving but scant room to change position or move about in any way.

Did you ever, reader, have the experience when some
sorrow overtook you, or when some disappointment had
been experienced, or when deferred hopes had not been
realized, or sometimes even without these and from
some unknown, subtle cause, feel that depression of
spirits that for lack of a better name we call "the blues?"
When the world ahead looked dark; when hope seemed
extinguished and the future looked like a blank? Why
do I ask this question? I know you all to a greater or
less degree have had just this experience. Can you
wonder that after our craft had been turned loose upon
the waters of the great river, and begun floating lazily
down with the current, that such a feeling as that
described would seize us as with an iron grip? We
were like an army that had burned the bridges behind

them as they marched, and with scant knowledge of what lay in the track before them. Here we were, more than two thousand miles from home, separated by a trackless, uninhabited waste of country, impossible for us to retrace our steps. Go ahead we must, no matter what we were to encounter. Then, too, the system had been strung up for months, to duties that could not be avoided or delayed, until many were on the verge of collapse. Some were sick and all reduced in flesh from the urgent call for camp duty, and lack of variety of food. Such were the feelings of the motley crowd of sixty persons as we slowly neared that wonderful crevice through which the great river flows while passing the Cascade mountain range.

For myself, I can truly say, that the trip had not drawn on my vitality as I saw with so many. True, I had been worked down in flesh, having lost nearly twenty pounds on the trip, but what weight I had left was the bone and sinew of my system, that served me so well on this trip and has been my comfort in other walks of life at a later period. And so, if asked, did you experience hardship on the trip across the plains, I could not answer yes without a mental reservation that it might have been a great deal worse. I say the same as to after experience, for these subsequent fifty years or more of pioneer life, having been blessed with a good constitution, and being now able to say that in the fifty-three years of our married life, the wife has never seen me a day sick in bed. But this is a digression and so we must turn our attention to the trip on the scow, "floating down the river."

In our company, a party of three, a young married couple and an unmarried sister, lounged on their belongings, listlessly watching the ripples on the water, as did also others of the party. But little conversation was passing. Each seemed to be communing with himself or herself, but it was easy to see what were the

thoughts occupying the minds of all. The young husband, it was plain to be seen, would soon complete that
greater journey to the unknown beyond, a condition
that weighed so heavily upon the ladies of the party,
that they could ill conceal their solicitude and sorrow.
Finally, to cheer up the sick husband and brother, the
ladies began in sweet subdued voices to sing the old
familiar song of Home, Sweet Home, whereupon others
of the party joined in the chorus with increased volume
of sound. As the echo of the echo died away, at the
moment of gliding under the shadow of the high mountain, the second verse was begun, but was never finished.
If an electric shock had startled every individual of the
party, there could have been no more simultaneous effect
than when the second line of the second verse was
reached, when instead of song, sobs and outcries of grief
poured forth from all lips. It seemed as if there was a
tumult of despair mingled with prayer pouring forth
without restraint. The rugged boatmen rested upon
their oars in awe, and gave away in smypathy with the
scene before them, until it could be truly said no dry
eyes were left nor aching heart but was relieved. Like
the down pour of a summer shower that suddenly clears
the atmosphere to welcome the bright shining sun that
follows, so this sudden outburst of grief cleared away the
despondency to be replaced by an exalted exhilarating
feeling of buoyancy and hopefulness. The tears were
not dried till mirth took possession—a real hysterical
manifestation of the whole party, that ended all depression for the remainder of the trip.

But our party was not alone in these trials. It seems
to me as like the dream of seeing some immigrants floating on a submerged raft while on this trip. Perhaps, it
is a memory of a memory, or of a long lost story, the
substance remembered, but the source forgotten.

Recently a story was told me by one of the actors
in the drama, that came near a tragic ending. Robert

Parker, who still lives at Sumner, one of the party, has told me of their experience. John Whitacre, afterwards Governor of Oregon, was the head of the party of nine that constructed a raft at The Dalles out of dry poles hauled from the adjacent country. Their stock was then started out over the trail, their two wagons put upon the raft with their provisions, bedding, women, and children in the wagons, and the start was made to float down the river to the Cascades. They had gotten but a few miles until experience warned them. The waves swept over the raft so heavily that it was like a submerged foundation upon which their wagons stood. A landing a few miles out from The Dalles averted a total wreck, and afforded opportunity to strengthen the buoyancy of their raft by extra timber packed upon their backs for long distances. And how should they know when they would reach the falls? Will they be able to discover the falls and then have time to make a landing? Their fears finally got the better of them; a line was run ashore and instead of making a landing, they found themselves hard aground out of reach of land- except by wading a long distance, and yet many miles above the falls (Cascades). Finally, a scow was procured, in which they all reached the head of the Cascades in safety. The old pioneer spoke kindly of this whole party, one might say affectionately. One, a waif picked up on the plains, a tender girl of fifteen, father-less and motherless, and sick; a wanderer without relatives or acquaintances—all under the sands of the plains—recalled the trials of the trip vividly. But, he had cheerful news of her in after life, though impossible at the moment to recall her name. Such were some of the experiences of the finish of the long, wearisome trip of those who floated down the river on flatboat and raft.

CHAPTER II.

The Arrival.

About nine o'clock at night, with a bright moon shining, on October 1st, 1852, I carried my wife in my arms up the steep bank of the Willamette River, and three blocks away in the town of Portland to a colored man's lodging house.

"Why, sah, I didn't think yuse could do that, yuse don't look it," said my colored friend, as I deposited my charge in the nice, clean bed in a cozy, little room.

From April until October, we had been on the move in the tented field, with never a roof over our heads other than the wagon cover or tent, and for the last three months, no softer bed than either the ground or bottom of the wagon bed. We had found a little steamer to carry us from the Cascades to Portland, with most of the company that had floated down the river from The Dalles, in the great scow. At the landing we separated, and knew each other but slightly afterwards. The great country, Oregon, (then including Puget Sound) was large enough to swallow up a thousand such immigrations and yet individuals be lost to each other, but a sorrier mess it would be difficult to imagine than confronted us upon arrival. Some rain had fallen, and more soon followed. With the stumps and logs, mud and uneven places, it was no easy matter to find a resting place for the tented city so continually enlarging. People seemed to be dazed; did not know what to do; insufficient shelter to house all; work for all impossible: the country looked a veritable great field of forest and mountain. Discouragement and despair seized upon some, while others began to enlarge the circle of observation. A few had friends and acquaintances, which fact began soon to relieve the situation by the removals that followed the reunions, while suffering, both mental and physical, followed the arrival in the winter storm that ensued, yet soon the atmosphere of discontent disappeared, and general cheerfulness prevailed. A few laid down in their beds not to arise again; a few required time to recuperate their strength, but with the majority, a short time found them as active and hearty as if nothing had happened. For myself, I can truly say, I do not remember the experience as a personal hardship. I had been born well of healthy parents. I knew of my father working eighteen hours a day for three years in the Carlisle mill at Indianopolis, Indiana, for 75 cents a day, and as an experienced miller at that. If his iron will or physical perfection or something had enabled him to endure this ordeal and retain his strength, why could not I, thirty years younger, hew my way? I did not feel fatigued. True, I had been "worked down" in flesh, but more from lack of suitable food than from excessive exertion. Any way, I resolved to try.

My brother, Oliver, who had crossed the plains with me—a noble man and one destined, had he lived, to have made his mark—came ahead by the trail. He had spied out the land a little with unsatisfactory results, met me and pointed the way to our colored friend's abode. We divided our purse of $3.75, I retaining two dollars and he taking the remainder, and with earliest dawn of the 2nd found the trail leading down the river, searching for our mutual benefit for something to do.

Did you, reader, ever have the experience of a premonition that led you on to success? Some say this is simply chance; others say that it is a species of superstition, but whatever it is, probably most of us, some time in our lives, have had some sort of trials to set us to thinking.

As we passed up the Willamette, a few miles below Portland, on the evening of our arrival, a bark lay seem-

ingly right in our path as we steamed by. Standing
upon the lower deck of our little steamer, this vessel
looked to our inexperienced eyes as a veritable monster,
with masts reaching to the sky, and hull towering high
above our heads. Probably not one of that whole party
of frontiersmen had ever before seen a deep sea vessel.
Hence, small wonder, the novelty of this great monster,
as we all thought of the vessel, should excite our admiration and we might almost say, amazement. That was
what we came so far for, to where ships might go down
to the sea, and return laden with the riches of the
earth. The word passed that she was bound for Portland with a cargo of merchandise and to take a return
cargo of lumber. There, as we passed, flashed through
my mind, will be my opportunity for work tomorrow,
on that vessel.

Sure enough, when the morrow came, the staunch
bark Mary Melville lay quietly in front of the mill, and
so, not losing any time in early morning, my inquiry was
made "do you want any men on board this ship?"   A
gruff looking fellow eyed me all over as much as to say,
"not you," but answered, "yes, go below and get your
breakfast." I fairly stammered out, I must go and see
my wife first, and let her know where I am, whereupon
came back a growl "of course, that will be the last of
you; that's the way with these new comers, always hunting for work and never wanting it" (this aside to a companion, but in my hearing). I swallowed my indignation with the assurance that I would be back in five
minutes and so went post haste to the little sufferer to
impart the good news.

Put yourself in my place, you land lubber, who
never came under the domination of a brutal mate of a
sailing vessel fifty years ago. My ears fairly tingled
with hot anger at the harsh orders, but I stuck to the
work, smothering my rage at being berated while doing
my very best to please and to expedite the work. The

fact gradually dawned on me that the man was not angry, but had fallen in the way of talking as though he was, and that the sailors paid slight heed to what he said. Before night, however, the fellow seemed to let up on me, while increasing his tirade on the heads of their regular men. The second and third day wore off with blistered hands, but with never a word about wages or pay.

"Say, boss, I'se got to pay my rent, and wese always gets our pay in advance. I doesn't like to ask you, but can't you get the old boss to put up something on your work?" I could plainly see that it was a notice to pay or move. He was giving it to me in thinly veiled words. What should I do? Suppose the old skipper should take umbrage, and discharge me for asking for wages before the end of the week? But when I told him what I wanted the money for, the old man's eyes moistened, but without a word, he gave me more money than I had asked for, and that night the steward handed me a bottle of wine for the "missus," which I knew instinctively came from the old captain.

The baby's Sunday visit to the ship; the Sunday dinner in the cabin; the presents of delicacies that followed, even from the gruff mate, made me feel that under all this roughness, a tender spot of humanity lay, and that one must not judge by outward appearances too much—that even way out here, three thousand miles from home, the same sort of people lived as those I had left behind me.

"St. Helens, October 7th, 1852.
"Dear Brother: Come as soon as you can. Have rented a house, sixty boarders; this is going to be the place. Shall I send you money? O. P. M."

The mate importuned me to stay until the cargo was on board, which I did until the last stick of lumber was stowed, the last pig in the pen, and when the ship swung off bound on her outward voyage, I felt as though I had an interest in her, but, remembering the forty dollars in the aggregrate I had received, with most of it to jingle in my pockets, I certainly could claim no financial interest, but from that day on I never saw or heard the name of the bark Mary Melville without pricking my ears, (figuratively, of course) to hear more about her and the old captain and his gruff mate.

Sure enough, I found St. Helens to be the place. Here was to be the terminus of the steamship line from San Francisco. "Wasn't the company building this wharf?" They wouldn't set sixty men to work on the dock without they meant business. "Ships can't get up that creek" (meaning the Willamette), "the big city is going to be here." This was the talk that greeted my ears, after we had carried the wife, (this time in a chair) to our hotel. Yes, our hotel, and had deposited her and the baby in the best room the house afforded.

It was here I made acquaintance with Columbia Lancaster, afterwards elected as the first delegate to Congress from Washington. I have always felt that the published history of those days has not done the old man justice, and has been governed in part, at least, by factional bias. Lancaster believed that what was worth doing at all was worth doing well, and he lived it. He used to come across the Columbia with his small boat, rowed by his own hand, laden with vegetables grown by himself on his farm opposite St. Helens, in the fertile valley of Lewis River. I soon came to know that what Lancaster said of his produce was true to the letter; that if he told me he had good potatoes, he had, and that they were the same in the middle or bottom of the sack as at the top. And so with all his produce. We at once became his heaviest customer, and learned to trust him implicity. I considered him a typical pioneer, and his name never would have been used so contemptuously had it not been that he became a thorn in the side of men who made politics a trade for personal profit. Lancaster upset their well laid plans, carried off the honors of the democratic nomination, and was elected as our first delegate in Congress from the new Territory of Washington.

One January morning of 1853, the sixty men, (our boarders) did not go to work dock building as usual. Orders had come to suspend work. Nobody knew why, or for how long. We soon learned the why, as the steamship company had given up the fight against Portland, and would thenceforward run their steamers to that port. For how long, was speedily determined, for the dock was not finished and was allowed to fall into decay and disappear by the hand of time.

Our boarders scattered, and our occupation was gone, and our accumulation in great part rendered worthless to us by the change.

Meantime, snow had fallen to a great depth; the price of forage for cattle rose by leaps and bounds, and we found that we must part with half of our stock to save the remainder. It might be necessary to feed for a month, or for three months, but we could not tell, and so the last cow was given up that we might keep one yoke of oxen, so necessary for the work on a new place. Then the hunt for a claim began again. One day's struggle against the current of Lewis River, and a night standing in a snow and sleet storm around a camp fire of green wood, cooled our ardor a little, and two hours sufficed to take us back home next morning.

But claims we must have. That was what we had come to Oregon for; we were going to be farmers. Wife and I had made that bargain before we closed the other more important contract. We were, however, both of one mind as to both contracts. Early in January of 1853 the snow began disappearing rapidly, and the search became more earnest, until finally, about the 20th of

January, I drove my first stake for a claim, to include the site where the town, or city, of Kalama now stands, and here built our first cabin.

That cabin I can see in my mind as vividly as I could the first day after it was finished. It was the first home I ever owned. What a thrill of joy that name brought to us. Home. It was our home, and no one could say aye, yes, or no, as to what we should do. No more rough talk on ship board or at the table; no more restrictions if we wished to be a little closer together. The glow of the cheek had returned to the wife; the dimple to the baby. And such a baby. In the innocence of our souls we really and truly thought we had the smartest, cutest baby on earth. I wonder how many millions of young parents have since experienced that same feeling? I would not tear the veil from off their eyes if I could. Let them think so, for it will do them good—make them happy, even if, perchance, it should be an illusion—it's real to them. But I am admonished that I must close this writing now, and tell about the cabin, and the early garden, and the trip to Puget Sound in another chapter.

CHAPTER III.

The First Cabin.

What a charm the words our first cabin have to the pioneer. To many, it was the first home ever owned by them, while to many others, like myself, the first we ever had. We had been married nearly two years, yet this was really our first abiding place. All others had been merely way stations on the march westward from Indianapolis to this cabin. Built of small, straight logs, on a side hill, with the door in the end fronting the river, and with but little grading, for the rocky nature of the location would not admit of it. Three steps were required to reach the floor. The ribs projected in front a few feet to provide an open front porch, with a ground floor, not for ornament, but for storage for the dry wood and kindling so necessary for the comfort and convenience of the mistress of the house. The walls were but scant five feet, with not a very steep roof, and a large stone fire place and chimney—the latter but seven feet high—completed our first home.

The great river, nearly a mile and three quarters wide, seemed to tire from its ceaseless flow at least once a day as if taking a nooning spell, while the tides from the ocean, sixty miles away, contended for mastery, and sometimes succeeded in turning the current up stream. Immediately in front of our landing lay a small island of a few acres in extent, covered with heavy timber and drift-wood. This has long since disappeared and ships now pass over the spot with safety.

Scarcely had we become settled in our new home before there came a mighty flood that covered the waters

of the river with wrecks of property impossible to
enumerate. Our attention was immediately turned to
securing logs that came floating down the river in great
numbers. In a very short time we had a raft that was
worth quite a sum of money could we but get it to the
market. Encouraged by this find, we immediately turned our attention to some fine timber standing close to
the bank near by, and began hand logging to supplement
what we had already secured afloat. I have often wondered what we would have done had it not been for this
find, for in the course of seven weeks three of us marketed eight hundred dollars worth of logs that enabled us
to obtain flour, even if we did pay fifty dollars a barrel,
and potatoes at two dollars a bushel, and sometimes
more.

And yet, because of that hand logging work, Jane
came very near becoming a widow one morning before
breakfast, but did not know of it until long afterwards.
It occurred in this way. We did not then know how to
scaffold up above the tough, swelled butts of the large
trees, and this made it very difficult to chop them down.
So we burned them by boring two holes at an angle to
meet inside the inner bark, and by getting the fire
started, the heart of the tree would burn, leaving an
outer shell of bark. One morning, as usual, I was up
early, and after starting the fire in the stove and putting on the teakettle, I hastened to the burning timber
to start afresh the fires, if perchance, some had ceased
to burn. Nearing a clump of three giants, two hundred
and fifty feet tall, one began toppling over toward me.
In my confusion I ran across the path where it fell, and
while this had scarce reached the ground, a second started to fall almost parallel to the first, scarcely thirty feet
apart at the top, leaving me between the two with limbs
flying in a good many directions. If I had not become
entangled in some brush, I would have gotten under the
last falling tree. It was a marvelous escape, and would

almost lead one to think that there is such a thing as a charmed life.

The rafting of our precious accumulations down the Columbia River to Oak Point; the relentless current that carried us by where we had contracted our logs at six dollars a thousand; the following the raft to the larger waters, and finally, to Astoria, where we sold them for eight dollars, instead of six per thousand, thus, profiting by our misfortunes; the involuntary plunge off the raft into the river with my boots on; the three days and nights of ceaseless toil and watching would make a thrilling story if we had but the time to tell it. Our final success was complete, which takes off the keen edge of the excitement of the hour, and when finished, we unanimously voted we would have none of it more.

At Oak Point we found Alexander Abernethy, former Governor of Oregon, who had quite recently returned with his family from the "States," and had settled down in the lumber business. He had a mill running of a capacity of about 25,000 feet of lumber a day. It was a water power mill, and the place presented quite a smart business air for the room they had. But Oak Point did not grow to be much of a lumber or business center, and the water mill eventually gave way to steam, located elsewhere, better suited for the business.

The flour sack was nearly empty when we left home expecting to be absent but one night, and now we had been gone a week. There were no neighbors nearer than four miles and no roads—scarcely a trail—the only communication was by the river. What about the wife and baby alone in the cabin with the deep timber close by in the rear, and heavy jungle of brush in the front? Nothing about it. We found them all right upon our return, but like the log drivers with their experience, the little wife said she wanted no more of cabin life alone. And yet, like adventures and like experiences followed.

The February sun of 1853 shone almost like midsummer. The clearing grew almost as if by magic. We could not resist the temptation to begin planting, and before March was gone, the rows of peas, lettuce, and onions growing on the river bank could be seen from the cabin door, thirty rods away.

One day I noticed some three cornered bits of potatoes that had been cut out, not bigger than the end of my finger. These all ran to a point as though cut out from a pattern. The base, or outer skin, all contained an eye of the potato. The wife said these would grow and would help us out about seed when planting time came, and we could have the body of the potatoes to eat. That would have seemed a plausible scheme had we been able to plant at once, but by this time we had been forcibly reminded that there was another impending flood for June, incident to the melting of the snow on the mountains, a thousand miles away, as the channel ran. But the experiment would not cost much, so the potato eyes were carefully saved and spread out on shelves where they became so dry that they would rattle like dry onion sets when handled. Every steamer outward bound carried potatoes for the San Francisco market, until it became a question whether enough would be left for seed, so that three and even four cents per pound was asked and paid for sorry looking culls. We must have seed, and so, after experimenting with the dried eyes, planted in moist earth in a box kept warm in the cabin, we became convinced that the little lady of the household was right, so ate potatoes freely even at these famine prices. Sure enough, the flood came, the planting delayed until July, and yet a crop was raised that undug brought in nearly four hundred dollars, for we did not stay to harvest them, or in fact, cultivate them, leaving that to another who became interested in the venture.

In April, the word began to pass around that we were

to have a new Terrirtory to embrace the country north of
the Columbia River, with its capital on Puget Sound,
and here on the Columbia we would be way off to one side
and out of touch with the people who would shortly become a great, separate commonwealth. Besides, had we
not come all the way across the plains to get to the *Sea
Board,* and here we were simply on the bank of a river—
a great river to be sure, with its ship channel, but then,
that bar at the mouth, what about it? Then the June
freshet, what about that?

So, one bright morning in May, my brother Oliver
and myself made each of us a pack of forty pounds and
took the trail, bound for Puget Sound, camping where
night overtook us, and sleeping in the open air without
shelter or cover other than that afforded by some
friendly tree with drooping limbs. Our trail first led us
down near the right bank of the Columbia to the Cowlitz, thence up the latter river thirty miles or more, and
then across the country nearly sixty miles to Olympia,
and to the salt sea water of the Pacific sent inland a
hundred and fifty miles by the resistless tides, twice a
day for every day of the year.

Our expectations had been raised by the glowing accounts about Puget Sound, and so, when we could see in
the foreground but bare, dismal mud flats, and beyond
but a few miles of water with a channel scarce twice as
wide as the channel of the great river we had left, bounded on either side by high table, heavily timbered land,
a feeling of deep disappointment fell upon us, with the
wish that we were back at our cabin on the river.

Should we turn around and go back? No, that was
what we had not yet done since leaving our Indiana
home eighteen months before; but what was the use of
stopping here? We wanted a place to make a farm,
and we could not do it on such forbidding land as this.
Had not the little wife and I made a solemn bargain or
compact, before we were married that we were going to

be farmers? Here, I could see a dense forest stretched out before me quite interesting to the lumberman, and for aught I knew, channels for the ships, but I wanted to be neither a lumberman nor sailor, and so, my first camp on Puget Sound was not cheerful and my first night not passed in contentment.

Olympia at the time contained about 100 inhabitants. It could boast having three stores, a hotel, a livery stable, and saloon, with one weekly newspaper, then publishing its thirtieth number. A glance at the advertising columns of this paper, the "Columbian," (named for what was expected would be the name of the new Territory) did not disclose but few local advertisers, the two pages devoted to advertising being filled by announcements of business other than in Olympia. "Everybody knows everybody here," said a business man to me, "so what's the use of advertising?" And it was thus with those who had been in the place for a few weeks, and so it continued all over the pioneer settlements for years. To meet a man on the road or on the street without speaking was considered rude. It became the universal practice to greet even strangers as well as acquaintances, and to this day I doubt if there are many of the old settlers yet devoid of the impulse to pass the time of day with hearty greetings to whomsoever they may meet, be they acquaintances or strangers.

Edmund Sylvester in partnership with Levi L. Smith, located the claims where the town of Olympia is built, in 1848. Mr. Smith soon after died, leaving Sylvester as sole proprietor of the town, where I saw him, as it will appear, five years later. It is said that Colonel I. N. Ebey suggested the name Olympia, which was not given to the place until after Mr. Sylvester's flight to the gold mines of California and return in 1850.

But we could not stay here at Olympia. We had pushed on past some good locations on the Chehalis, and further south, without locating, and now, should we retrace our steps? Brother Oliver said no. My better judgment said no, though sorely pressed with that feeling of homesickness, or blues, or whatever we may call it. The resolve was quickly made that we would see more of this Puget Sound, that we were told presented nearly as many miles of shore line as we had traveled westward from the Missouri River to Portland, near sixteen hundred miles, and which we afterwards found to be true.

But how were we to go and see these, to us unexplored waters? I said I would not go in one of those things, the Indian canoe, that we would upset it before we were out half an hour. Brother Oliver pointed to the fact the Indians navigated the whole Sound in these canoes, and were safe, but I was inexorable and would not trust my carcass in a craft that would tip so easily as a Siwash canoe. When I came to know the Indians better, I ceased to use such a term, and afterwards when I saw the performances of these apparently frail craft, my admiration was greater in degree than my contempt had been.

Of the cruise that followed on Puget Sound, and in what manner of craft we made it, and of various incidents of the trip that occupied a month, I must defer telling now, and leave this part of the story for succeeding chapters.

CHAPTER IV.

Cruise on Puget Sound.

Put yourself in my place, reader, for a time—long enough to read this chapter. Think of yourself as young again, if elderly (I will not say old); play you have been old and now young again, until you find out about this trip on Puget Sound fifty and more years ago. Then think of Puget Sound in an inquiring mood, as though you knew nothing about it, only a little indefinite hearsay; enough to know there is such a name, but not what manner of place or how large or how small; whether it was one single channel, like a river, or numerous channels; whether it was a bay or a series of bays or whether it was a lake, but somehow connected with the sea, and then you will be in the mood these two young men were, when they descended the hill with their packs on their backs and entered the town of Olympia in May, 1853. Now, if you are in this inquiring mood, I will take you in my confidence and we will live the cruise over again of thirty-two days of adventures and observation on Puget Sound fifty years ago.

I was but a few months past twenty-three, while my brother Oliver could claim nearly two years seniority. We had always played together as boys, worked together as men, and lived together even after his marriage until the day of his death, now forty-five years ago, and so far as I can remember, never had a disagreement in our whole life.

So, when we cast off the line at Olympia, on or about the 28th day of May, 1853, we were assured of one thing and that was a concert of action, be there danger or only labor ahead. Neither of us had had much experience in boating, and none as to boat building, but when we decided to make the trip and discarded the idea of taking a canoe we set to work with a hearty good will to build us a skiff out of light lumber, then easily obtained at the Tumwater mill of Hays, Ward & Co., in business at that place.

I knew Ira Ward of the firm of Hays & Ward intimately for long years afterwards and I may say until the day of his death which recently occurred at the advanced age of 86 years, and can testify as to his worth as a citizen of the new commonwealth where he cast his lot and to his kindly nature with an unbounded hospitality to which so many of the early pioneers can testify.

We determined to have the skiff broad enough to not upset easily, and long enough to carry us and our light cargo of food and bedding. Like the trip across the plains we must provide our own transportation. We were told that the Sound was a solitude so far as transportation facilities, with here and there a vessel loading piles and square timber for the San Francisco market. Not a steamer was then plying on the Sound; not even a sailing craft that essayed to carry passengers. We did not really know whether we would go twenty miles or a hundred; whether we would find small waters or large; straight channels or intricate by-ways; in a word we knew but very little of what lay before us. If we had known a little more, we would not have encountered the risks we did. One thing we knew, we could endure sturdy labor without fatigue, and improvised camp without discomfort, for we were used to just such experiences. Poor innocent souls, we thought we could follow the shore line and thus avoid danger, and perhaps float with the tide, and thus minimize the labor, and yet keep our bearings.

George A. Barnes sold us the nails and oakum for

building the boat and charged us 25 cents per pound for the former, but he could not sell us any pitch as that was to be had for the taking. However, articles of merchandise were not high, though country produce sold for extreme prices.

Recently I have seen a "retail prices current of Puget Sound, Washington Territory, corrected weekly by Parker, Colter & Co.," in which, among many others, the following prices are quoted in the columns of the only paper in the Territory then published in Olympia, the "Columbian," as follows:

Pork, per lb	$ .20
Flour, per 100 lbs	10.00
Potatoes, per bushel	3.00
Butter, per lb	1.00
Onions, per bushel	4.00
Eggs, per dozen	1.00
Beets, per bushel	3.50
Sugar, per lb	.12½
Coffee, per lb	.18
Tea, per lb	75c and 1.00
Molasses, per gallon	50 and .75
Salmon, per lb	.10
Whisky, per gallon	1.00
Sawed lumber, fir, per M	20.00
Cedar, per M	30.00
Shingles,, per M	$4.25 to 5.00
Piles, per foot	5 to .08
Square timber, per foot	12 to .15

Thus it will be seen that what the farmer had to sell was high while much he must buy was comparatively cheap, even his whisky, then but a dollar a gallon, while his potatoes sold for $3.00 a bushel.

This Parker, of Parker, Colter & Co., is the same John G. Parker, Jr., of steamboat fame who yet lives in Olympia, now an old man, but never contented without his hand on the wheel in the pilot house, where I saw him but a few months ago on his new steamer the Caswell, successor to his first, the Traveler, of fifty years before.

Two or three other stores besides Barnes' and Parker's were then doing business in Olympia, the Kandall Company, with Joseph Cushman as agent; A. J. Moses, and I think the Bettman Brothers.

Rev. Benjamin F. Close, Methodist, held religious service in a small building near Barnes' store, but there was no church edifice for several years. Near by, the saloon element had found a foothold, but I made no note of them in my mind other than to remember they were there and running every day of the week including Sunday.

The townsite proprietor, Edmund Sylvester, kept the hotel of the town, the "Washington," at the corner of 2nd and Main Street, a locality now held to be too far down on the water front, but then the center of trade and traffic.

G. N. McConaha and J. W. Wiley dispensed the law and H. A. Goldsborough & Simmons (M. T. Simmons) looked out for the real estate and conveyances. Add to these a bakery, a livery stable, and a blacksmith shop and we have the town of Olympia in our mind again of possibly 100 people who then believed a great future lay in store for their embryo city "at the head of Puget Sound."

Three leading questions occupied the attention of all parties while we were in this little ambitious city, the new Territorial organization so soon to be inaugurated, the question of an overland railroad, and of an over mountain immigrant wagon road. The last was the absorbing topic of conversation, as it was a live enterprise dependent upon the efforts of the citizens for success. Meetings had been held in different parts of the district west of the Cascade Mountains and north of the Columbia River, and finally subscription lists were circulated, a cashier and superintendent appointed, with

the result, as stated elsewhere, of opening the way for
the first immigration over the Cascade Mountains via
the Natchess Pass, but the particulars of this work are
given in other chapters following.

As the tide drew off the placid waters of the bay at
Olympia with just a breath of air, our little craft
behaved splendidly as the slight ripples were jostled
against the bow under the pressure of the sail and
brought dreams of a pleasure trip, to make amends for
the tiresome pack across the country. Nothing can be
more enjoyable than favorable conditions in a boating
trip, the more especially to those who have long been in
the harness of severe labor, and for a season must enjoy enforced repose. And so we lazily floated with the
tide, sometimes taking a few strokes with the oars, and
at other times whistling for the wind, as the little town
of Olympia to the south, became dimmed by distance.

At this southern extremity of the Sound without the
accumulations of water to struggle for passage, as
through the channel to the north, the movement is
neither swift, nor disturbed with cross currents to agi-
tate the surface—more like the steady flow of a great
river.

But we were no sooner fairly out of sight of the little
village and out of the bay it was situated upon (Budd's
Inlet), than the query came up as to which way to go.
Was it this channel or that or yet another one we should
take? Let the tide decide; that will take us out toward
the ocean we urged. No, we are drifting into another
bay; that cannot be where we want to go; why, we
are drifting right back almost in the same direction from
which we came, but into another bay. We'll pull this
way to that point to the northeast. But there seems a
greater opening of waters to the northwest; yes, but
I do not see any way out there. Neither is there beyond
that point (Johnson's Point); and so we talked and
pulled and puzzled until finally it dawned upon us that

the tide had turned and we were being carried back to almost the spot from whence we came, into South bay.

"Now the very best thing we can do is to camp," said the senior of the party of two, to which the junior, your humble writer, readily assented, and so our first night's camp was scarcely twelve miles from where we had started in the morning.

What a nice camping place this. The ladies would say lovely, and why not? A beautiful pebbly beach that extended almost to the water's edge even at low tide with a nice grassy level spit; a back ground of evergreen giant fir timber; such clear cool water gushing out from the bank near by, so superlative in quality as to defy word to adequately describe; and such fuel for the camp fire, broken fir limbs with just enough pitch to make a cheerful blaze and yet body enough to last well. Why, we felt so happy that we were almost glad the journey had been interrupted. Oliver was the carpenter of the party, the tent builder, wood getter, and general roust-a-bout, to coin a word from camp parlance, while I, the junior, was the "chief cook and bottle washer," as the senior would jocularly put it.

At the point a little beyond where we landed we found next morning J. R. Johnson, M. D., with his cabin on the point under the pretentious name of "Johnson's Hospital," opened as he said for the benefit of the sick, but which, from what I saw in my later trips think his greatest business was in disposing of cheap whisky of which he contributed his share of the patronage.

An Indian encampment being near by, a party of them soon visited our camp and began making signs for trade. "*Mika tik-eh clams?*" came from out the mouth of one of the matrons of the party as if though half choked in the speaking, a cross between a spoken word and a smothered gutteral sound in the throat.

"What does she say, Oliver?" the junior said, turning for counsel to the superior wisdom of the elder brother.

"I'm blessed if I know what she says, but she evidently wants to sell some clams."

And so, after considerable dickering, and by signs and gestures and words oft repeated we were able to impart the information that we wanted a lesson in cookery; that we wanted her to show us how to cook them, and that we would buy some. This brought some merriment in the camp. The idea, that there lived a person that did not know how to cook clams. Without saying by your leave or any thing else the motherly looking native began tearing down our camp fire.

"Let her alone," said the senior, "and see what she's up to," noticing that the younger man was going to remonstrate against such an interference with his well laid plans for bread baking. And so the kitchen of the camp was surrendered to the native matron, who quietly covered the hot pebbles and sand where the fire had been, with a light layer of pebbles, upon which the clams were deposited and some fine twigs placed on top, upon which earth was deposited. "*K-l-o-s-h-e*," said the matron. "*Hy-as-kloshe*," said her seignior, who sat squatting watching the operation with evident pride upon the achievement of his dame.

"What did they say?" innocently inquired the junior brother.

"I know what they said, but I don't know what they meant," responded the elder one, "unless it was she had done a good job, which I think she has," and thus began and ended our first lesson in the Chinook jargon, and our first introduction to a clam bake.

What memories hover around these three words, "the clam bake." Did you ever, may I ask my readers, other than those of ye olden times, did you ever participate in the joys of a regular old-fashioned clam bake, with or without the corn, with or without the help of the deft native hand? If you never have, then go straighway, before you die, to the end that you may ever after have the memory of the first clam bake, even if it be but a memory, and likewise be the last.

Our first clam bake gave us great encouragement. We soon learned that these bivalves were to be found in almost unlimited quantity, and were widely distributed; that the harvest was ready twice a day, when the tide was out, and that we need have no fear of a famine even if cast away in some unfrequented place.

"*Yah-ka kloshe al-ta,*" said the dame, uncovering the steaming mass and placing them on a sliver found near by, "*de-late kloshe; kloshe muck-a-muck alt-ta,*" and so, without understanding what she said, but knowing well what she meant, we fell to in disposing of this, our first clam dinner.

Dividing with them the bread that had been baked, and some potatoes that had been boiled, the natives soon withdrew to their own camp, where, before retiring for the night, we repaid the visit.

To see the little fellows of the camp scud behind the mother when the strangers entered, and shyly peep out from their retreat, and the mother lovingly reassuring them with kind, affectionate caresses, and finally coaxing them out from under cover, revealed the character of the natives we had neither of us realized before. We had been in the Indian country for nearly a year, but with guns by our sides if not in our hands for nearly half the time, while on the plains, but we had not stopped to study the Indian character. We took it for granted that the Indians were our enemies and watched them suspiciously accordingly, but here seemed to be a disposition manifested to be neighborly and helpful. We took a lesson in Chinook, and by signs and words combined held conversation until a late hour, when, upon getting ready for taking leave, a slice of venison was handed us, sufficient for several meals. Upon offering to pay for it we were met with a shake of the head, and with the words, "*wake, wake, kul-tus-pot-latch,*" which we un-

derstood by their actions to mean they made us a present
of it.

This present from the Indian let in a flood of light
upon the Indian character. We had made them a
present first, it was true, but we did not expect any
return, except perhaps good will, and in fact, cannot
now say we particularly expected that, but were impelled to do our act of courtesy from the manner of their
treatment and from the evident desire to be on friendly
terms. From that time on during the trip, and I may
say, for all time since, I have found the Indians of
Puget Sound ready to reciprocate acts of kindness, and
hold in high esteem a favor granted if not accompanied
by acts apparently designed to simply gain an advantage.

We often forget the sharp eyes and ears of little children and let slip words that are quickly absorbed to
their hurt by affecting their conduct. While the Indian
is really not a suspicious person, nevertheless, he is quick
to detect and as quick to resent a real or supposed slight
as the little five year old who discovers his elders in
their fibs or deceit. Not that the Indian expects socially
to be received in your house or at your table, yet little
acts of kindness, if done without apparent design,
touch their better nature and are repaid more than a
hundred fold, for you thereafter have a friend and neighbor, and not an enemy or suspicious maligner.

All of this did not dawn on the young men at the time,
though their treatment of the Indians was in harmony
with friendly feelings which we found everywhere and
made a lasting impression.

Subsequent experience, of course, has confirmed these
first impressions with the wider field of observation in
after years, while employing large numbers of these
people in the hop fields of which I hope to write later.
And so now must end this chapter with the subject of
the "cruise" to be continued at another sitting.

CHAPTER V.

Cruise on Puget Sound—Continued.

"Keep to the right, as the law directs," is an old western adage that governs travelers on the road, but we kept to the right because we wanted to follow the shore, as we thought it safer, and besides, why not go that way as well as any other,—it was all new to us. So, on the second morning, as we rounded Johnson's Point and saw no channel opening in any direction; saw only water in the foreground and timber beyond, we concluded to skirt the coast line and see what the day would bring forth. This led us a southeasterly course and in part doubling back with that traveled the previous day, and past what became the historic grounds of the Medicine Creek Treaty council, or, rather leaving this two miles to our right as the Nisqually flats were encountered. Here we were crowded to a northerly course leaving the Nisqually House on the beach to the east without stopping for investigation.

According to Finlayson's journal, as I afterwards ascertained, this had been built twenty-three years before. At least, some house had been built on this spot at that time, (1829 or 1830) though the fort by that name one fourth mile back from the water was not constructed until the summer of 1833, just twenty years previous to our visit.

This fort mentioned must not be confounded with the Nisqually fort built some three years later (1836) a mile farther east and convenient to the waters of Segwal-itchew creek, which there runs near the surface of the surrounding country. All remains of the old fort have

long since vanished, but the nearly filled trenches where
the stockade timbers stood can yet be traced, showing
that a space 250 feet square had been enclosed. Another
visible sign was an apple tree yet alive near the spot,
grown from seed planted in 1833, but now, when I
visited the place in June, 1903, overshadowed by a lusty
fir that is sapping the life of the only living, though
mute, witness (except it may be the Indian, Steilacoom)
we have of those early days, when the first fort was built
by the intrepid employes of the Hudson Bay Company.

An interesting feature of the intervening space between the old and the newer fort is the dense growth
of fir timber averaging nearly two feet in diameter and
in some cases fully three, and over a hundred feet high
on what was prairie when the early fort builders began
work. The land upon which this timber is growing still
shows unmistakable signs of the furrow marks that can
be traced through the forest. Verily, this *is* a most wonderful country where forest product will grow, if properly protected, more rapidly than the hand of man will
destroy.

As the tide and wind favored us we did not stop, but
had not proceeded far before we came in sight of a fleet
of seven vessels lying at anchor in a large bay of several
miles in extent.

Upon the eastern slope of the shores of this bay lay the
two towns, Port Steilacoom, established January 23rd,
1851, by Captain Lafayette Balch and Steilacoom City,
upon an adjoining land claim taken by John B. Chapman, August 23rd, of same year and later held by his
son John M. Chapman. These two rival towns were
built, as far apart as possible on the frontage lands of
the claim owners (about one mile apart) and became
known locally as Upper and Lower Steilacoom, the latter
name being applied to Balch's town.

We found the stocks of goods carried by the merchants of these two towns exceeded those held by the

Olympia merchants, and that at Fort Nisqually, six miles distant, the merchandise carried by the Puget Sound Agricultural Company would probably equal that of all three of the towns combined, possibly, in the aggregate, over one hundred thousand dollars for the whole district under review.

Evidently a far larger trade centered on Steilacoom Bay and vicinity than at any other point we had seen and, as we found afterwards, than any other point on Puget Sound. Naturally we would here call a halt to examine the country and to make ourselves acquainted with the surroundings that made this early center of trade.

One mile and a half back from the shore and east of lower Steilacoom, we found what was by courtesy called Fort Steilacoom, but which was simply a camp of a company of United States soldiers, in wooden shells of houses and log cabins. This camp, or fort, had been established by Captain Bennett H. Hill with Company M, 1st Artillery, August 27th, 1849, following the attempted robbery of Fort Nisqually the previous May by Pat Kanim and his followers, the Snoqualmie Indians.

Dr. Tolmie, Chief Factor of the Puget Sound Agricultural Company at Fort Nisqually, quickly seized the opportunity to demand rent from the United States for the occupancy of the site of Fort Steilacoom of six hundred dollars a year, and actually received it for fifteen years and until the final award was made extinguishing the claims of his company. We found the plains alive with this company's stock (many thousand head) running at large and fattened upon the scant but nutritious grass growing upon the adjacent prairie and glade lands.

Balch and Webber were driving a thriving trade in their store at the little town of Steilacoom, besides their shipping trade of piles and square timber, shingles, lumber, cord wood, hides, furs, fish, and other odds and ends. Just across the street from their store stood the main hotel of the place with the unique history of being the only building erected on Puget Sound from lumber shipped from the eastern seaboard. Captain Balch brought the building with him from Maine, ready to set up. At the upper town Philip Keach was merchandising while Abner Martin kept a hotel. Intense rivalry ran between the two towns in the early days when we were at Steilacoom.

Thomas M. Chambers, father of the prominent members of the Olympia community of that name, had built a saw-mill on Steilacoom creek, two miles from the town and a grist mill where farmers oftentimes came with pebbles in their wheat to dull the burrs.

We are wont now to speak of this place as "poor old Steilacoom," with its tumbled-down houses, rotting sidewalks and decayed wharves, the last vestige of the latter of which has disappeared; but then everything was new, with an air of business bustle that made one feel here was a center of trade. The sight of those seven vessels lying in the offing made a profound impression upon our minds. We had never before seen so many ships at one place as were quietly lying at anchor in front of the embryo city. Curiously enough, here was the very identical vessel we had first seen on the Willamette River, the bark "Mary Melville," with her gruff mate and the big hearted master, Capt. Barston, with whom the reader has been made acquainted in a previous chapter. I took no special note of the names of these vessels other than this one, but from the columns of the Columbian I am able to glean the names of twenty-two vessels, brigs, barks, and schooners, then plying between Puget Sound and San Francisco, which are as follows:

Brig Cyclops, Perkins; Bark Delegate, ———; Brig Tarquina, ———; Bark John Adams, McKelmer; Brig G. W. Kendall, Gove; Brig Merchantman, Bolton;

Brig Kingsbury, Cook; Schooner Cynosure, Fowler; Brig George Emery, Diggs; Bark Mary Melville, Barston; Bark Brontes, Blinn; Bark Sarah Warren, Gove; Ship Persia, Brown; Brig I. C. Cabot, Dryden; Brig Jane, Willett; Ship Rowena, ————; Brig Willingsly, Gibbs; Brig Mary Dare, Mowatt; Brig John Davis, Pray; Bark Carib, Plummer; Brig Leonesa, Howard; and Schooner Franklin, Leary. There were probably more, but I do not recall them, but these were enough to keep every man busy that could swing an axe, drag a saw or handle that instrument of torture, the goad stick, and who was willing to work.

All this activity came from the shipment of piles, square timbers, cordwood, shingles, with small quantities of lumber—all that was obtainable, which was not very much, to the San Francisco market. The descent of timber on the roll-ways sounded like distant thunder, and could be heard almost all hours of the day, even where no camps were in sight, but lay hidden up some secluded bay or inlet. ·

We were sorely tempted to accept the flattering offer of $4.00 each per day for common labor in a timber camp, but soon concluded not to be swerved from the course we had outlined.

It was here, and I think at this time, I saw the Indian "Steilacoom" who still lives. I saw him recently at his camp in the Nisqually bottom, and judge he is bordering on ninety years. Steilacoom helped to build old Fort Nisqually in 1833, and was a married man at that time. People called him chief because he happened to bear the name adopted for the town and creek, but he was not a man of much force of character and not much of a chief. I think this is a remarkable case of longevity for an Indian. As a race, they are short lived. It was here, and during this visit, we began seeing Indians in considerable numbers. Off the mouth of the Nisqually and several places along the beach and floating on the

bay we saw several hundred in the aggregrate of all
ages and kind. There seemed to be a perfect abandon as
to care or thought for the future, or even as to the immediate present, literally floating with the tide. In those
days, the Indians seemed to work or play by spurts and
spells. Here and there that day a family might be seen
industriously pursuing some object, but as a class there
seemed to be but little life in them, and we concluded
they were the laziest set on earth. I afterwards materially modified that opinion, as I became better acquainted with their habits, for I have found just as industrious Indians, both men and women, and as reliable
workers, as among the whites though this class, it may
be said, is exceptional with the men. The women are
all industrious.

Shall we camp here and spy out the land, or shall we
go forward and see what lay before us? Here were the
ideals, that had enticed us so far from our old home,
where "ships went down into the sea," with the trade
of the whole world before us. We waxed eloquent,
catching inspiration from people of the town. After
a second sober thought we found we had nothing to
trade but labor, and we had not come this far to be
laborers for hire. We had come to look up a place to
make a farm and a farm we were going to have. We,
therefore set about searching for claims, and the more
we searched the less we liked the looks of things.

The gravelly plains near Steilacoom would not do;
neither the heavy fir timber lands skirting the waters of
the Sound, and we were nonplussed and almost ready to
condemn the country. Finally, on the fourth day after
a long, wearisome tramp, we cast off at high tide, and
in a dead calm, to continue our cruise. The senior soon
dropped into a comfortable afternoon nap, leaving me
in full command. As the sun shone nice and warm and
the tide was taking us rapidly in the direction we wanted

to go, why not join, even if we did lose the sight seeing for which the journey was made.

I was shortly after aroused by the senior exclaiming, "What is that?" and then answering half to himself and half to me, "Why, as I live, it's a deer swimming way out here in the bay." Answering, half asleep and half awake, that that could not be, the senior said: "Well, that's what it is." We gave chase and soon succeeded in getting a rope over its horns. We had by this time drifted into the Narrows, and soon found that we had something more important to look after than towing a deer among the tide-rips of the Sound, and turning him loose pulled for dear life for the shore, and found shelter in an eddy. A perpendicular bluff rose from the high water mark, leaving no place for a camp fire or bed. The tide seemed to roll in waves and with contending forces of currents, and counter currents, yet all moving in a general direction. It was our first introduction to a real genuine, live tide-rip, that seemed to harry the waters as if boiling in a veritable caldron, swelling up here and there in centers to whirl in dizzy velocity and at times break into a foam, and, where a light breeze prevailed, into spray. Then in some areas would seem the waters in solid volume would leap up in conical, or pointed shape—small waves broken into short sections, that would make it quite difficult for a flat bottom boat like our little skiff to float very long. We congratulated ourselves upon the escape, while belittling our careless imitation of the natives of floating with the tide. Just then some Indian canoes passed along moving with the tide. We expected to see them swamped as they encountered the troubled waters, but to our astonishment they passed right through without taking a drop of water. Then here came two well manned canoes creeping along shore against the tide. I have said well-manned, but in fact, half the paddles were wielded by women, and the post of honor, or that where most dexterity was required, was occupied by a woman. In shore, short eddies would favor the party, to be ended by a severe tug against the stiff current.

"*Me-si-ka-kwass kopa s'kookum chuck*," said the maiden in the bow of the first canoe, as it drew along side our boat, in which we were sitting.

Since our evening's experience at the clam bake camp, we had been industriously studying language, and pretty well mastered the chinook, and so we with but little difficulty understood her to ask if we were afraid of the rough waters, to which we responded, part in English and part in Chinook, that we were, and besides that it was impossible for us to proceed against the strong current.

"*Ne-si-ka mit-lite*," that is to say, she said they were going to camp with us and wait for the turn of the tide, and accordingly landed near by, and so we must wait for the remainder of this story in chapters to follow.

CHAPTER VI.

Cruise on Puget Sound—Continued.

By the time the tide had turned, night had come and we were in a quandary as to what to do; whether to camp in our boat, or to start out on unknown waters in the dark. Our Indian visitors began making preparations to proceed on their journey, and assured us it was all right ahead, and offered to show us the way to good camping grounds in a big bay where the current was not strong, and where we would find a great number of Indians in camp.

It did not occur to us to have any fear of the Indians. We did not at all depend on our prowess or personal courage, but felt that we were among friends. We had by this time come to know the general feeling existing between Indians and whites, and that there were no trouble, as a class, whatever there might be as to individuals. I do not want my reader to understand we thought we were doing an heroic act in following a strange party of Indians into unknown waters and into an unknown camp of the natives after dark, or that I think so now. There was no danger ahead of us other than that incident to the attempt of navigating such waters with so frail a boat, and one so unsuited in shape as well as build, for rough waters, and by persons so inexperienced on the water.

Sure enough, a short pull with a favorable current, brought us through the Narrows and into Commence-

ment Bay and in sight of numerous camp fires in the
distance. Our Indian friends lazily paddled along in
company, while we labored vigorously with our oars
as we were by this time in a mood to find a camp where
we could have a fire and prepare some food. I remember
that camp quite vividly, though cannot locate it exactly,
but know that it was on the water front within the
present limits of the City of Tacoma. A beautiful small
rivulet came down a ravine and spread out on the beach,
and I can remember the shore line was not precipitous
and that it was a splendid camping ground. The particular thing I do remember is our supper of fresh salmon. Of all the delicious fish known, give me the salmon
caught by trolling in early summer in the deep waters
of Puget Sound; so fat that the excess of oil must be
turned out of the pan while cooking. We had not then
learned the art of cooking on the spit, or at least, did not
practice it. We had scarcely gotten our camp fire under
way before a salmon was offered us, but I cannot recall
what we paid, but I know it was not a high price, else
we would not have purchased. At the time we did not
know but trolling in deep water for this king of fish was
the only way, but afterwards learned of the enormous
quantities taken by the seine direct from salt water.

Two gentlemen, Messrs. Swan and Riley, had established themselves on the bay, and later in the season
reported taking two thousand large fish at one haul with
their seine, three fourths of which were salmon. As I
have a fish story of my own to tell of our experience
later, I will dismiss the subject for the present.

We were now in the bay, since made famous in history
by that observing traveler, Theodore Winthrop, who
came from the north a few months later and saw that
great mountain, that "cloud compeller," reflected in the

TACOMA HARBOR, 1888.

placid waters of the Sound, "Tacoma"* as he wrote,
Rainier, as we saw it. A beautiful sight it was and
is, whatever the name, but to us it was whatever others
said it was, while Winthrop, of a poetic mind, was on
the alert for something new under the sun, if it be no
more than a name for a great mountain.*

Winthrop came in September, while we were in the
bay in June, thus ante-dating his trip by three months
or more. To Winthrop belongs the honor of originating
the name Tacoma from some word claimed to have been
spoken by the Indians as the name of the mountain.
As none of the pioneers ever heard the word until many
years afterwards, and not then until after the post-
humous publication of Winthrop's works ten years after
his visit, I incline to the opinion that Winthrop coined
the word out of his imaginative brain.

We again caught sight of the mountain the next day,
as we approached the tide flats off the mouth of the
Puyallup River. We viewed the mountain with awe
and admiration, but gave no special heed to it, more than
to many other new scenes engaging our attention. It
was land we wanted whereby we might stake a claim,
and not scenery to tickle our fancy. Yet, I doubt if there

---

*Winthrop, in his delightful book, "The Canoe and the Saddle," describing
his trip from Port Townsend to Nisqually, in September, 1853, says:

"We had rounded a point and opened Puyallop Bay, a breath of sheltered
calmness, when I, lifting sleepy eyelids for a dreamy stare about, was suddenly aware of a vast white shadow in the water. What cloud, piled mas-
sive on the horizon, could cast an image so sharp in outline, so full of vigorous detail of surface? No cloud, as my stare, no longer dreamy, presently
discovered—no cloud, but a cloud compeller. It was a giant mountain dome
of snow, swelling and seeming to fill the aerial spheres as its image displaced
the blue deeps of tranquil water. The smoky haze of an Oregon August hid
all the length of its lesser ridges, and left this mighty summit based upon
uplifting dimness. Only its splendid snows were visible, high in the un-
earthly regions of blue noonday sky. The shore line drew a cincture of pines
across its broad base, where it faded unreal into the mist. The same dark
girth separated the peak from its reflection, over which my canoe was now
pressing, and sending wavering swells to scatter the beautiful vision before it.

"Kingly and alone stood this majesty, without any visible consort, though
far to the north and to the south its brethren and sisters dominated their
realms, each in isolated sovereignty, rising from the pine-darkened sierra of
the Cascade Mountains—above the stern chasm where the Columbia, Achilles
of rivers, sweeps, short lived and jubilant, to the sea—above the lovely valley
of the Willamette and Ningua. Of all the peaks from California to Fraxier
River, this one was royalest. Mount Regnier, Christians have dubbed it in
stupid nomenclature, perpetuating the name of somebody or nobody. More
melodiously the Siwashes call it Tacoma—a generic term, also applied to all
snow peaks."

lives a man, or ever did, who has seen that great mountain, but has been inspired with higher thoughts, and we may say higher aspirations, or who has ever tired looking upon this grand pile, the father of five great rivers.

We floated into the mouth of the Puyallup River with a vague feeling as to its value, but did not proceed far until we were interrupted by a solid drift of monster trees and logs, extending from bank to bank up the river for a quarter of a mile or more. We were told by the Indians there were two other like obstructions a few miles farther up the river, and that the current was "*de-late-hyas-skoo-kum*," which interpreted means that the current was *very* strong. We found this to be literally true during the next two or three days we spent on the river.

We secured the services of an Indian and his canoe to help us up the river, and left our boat at the Indian's camp near the mouth.

The tug of two days to get six miles up the river, the unloading of our outfit three times to pack it over cutoff trails, and the dragging of our canoe around the drifts, is a story of constant toil with consequent discouragement, not ending until we camped on the bank of the river within the present limits of the little thriving city of Puyallup, founded afterwards by me on a homestead claim taken many years later. The little city now contains nearly four thousand inhabitants, and is destined to contain many thousand more in the lapse of time.

The Puyallup valley at that time was a solitude. No white settlers were found, though it was known two, who lived with Indian women, had staked claims and made some slight improvements—a man by the name of Hayward, near where the town of Sumner is now located, and William Benson, on the opposite side of the river, and a mile distant from the boundaries of Puyallup. An Indian trail led up the river from Commencement Bay, and one westward to the Nisqually plains, over which pack animals could pass, but as to wagon roads, there were none, and as to whether a feasible route for one could be found only time with much labor could determine.

When we retraced our steps, and on the evening of the third day landed again at the mouth of the river after a severe day's toil of packing around drifts and hauling the canoe overland past drifts, it was evident we were in no cheerful mood. Oliver did not sing as usual while preparing for camp, or rally with sallies of wit and humor as he was wont to do when in a happy mood. Neither did I have much to say, but fell to work mechanically preparing the much needed meal, which we ate in silence, and forthwith wrapped ourselves in our blankets for the night, but not for immediate slumber.

We had crossed the two great states of Illinois and Iowa, over hundreds of miles of unoccupied prairie land as rich as anything that "ever laid out of doors," on our way from Indiana to Oregon, in search of land on which to make a home, and here, at what we might say "at the end of our rope" had found the land, but under such adverse conditions that seemed almost too much to overcome. It was a discouraging outlook, even if there had been roads. Such timber! It seemed an appalling undertaking to clear it, the greater portion being covered with a heavy growth of balm and alder trees, and thick tangle of underbrush besides, and so, when we did fall to sleep that night, it was without visions of new found wealth.

And yet, later, I did tackle a quarter section of that heaviest timber land, and never let up until the last tree, log, stump, and root disappeared, though of course, not all of it by my own hands. Nevertheless, with a goodly part, I did say come, boys, and went into the thickest of the work.

But, of the time of which I am writing, there were more to consider than the mere clearing, which we estimated would take thirteen years of solid work for one man to clear a quarter section; the question of going where absolutely there were no neighbors, no roads, no help to open them, and in fact, without a knowledge as to whether a feasible route could be found, compelled us to decide against locating.

A small factor came in to be considered. Such swarms of mosquitoes we had never seen before. These we felt would make life a burden, forgetting that as the country became opened they would disappear. I may relate here a curious phenomenon brought to light by after experience. My donation claim was finally located on high table land, where no surface water could be found in summer for miles around, and there were swarms of mosquitoes, while on the Puyallup homestead taken later, six miles from the mouth of the river, and where water lay on the surface, in spots, the whole summer long, we seldom saw one of these pests there. I never could account for this, and have long since ceased to try; I only know it was so.

If we could have but known what was coming four months later, I doubt not, notwithstanding our discouragement, we would have remained and searched the valley diligently for the choicest locations. In October following, there came the first immigrants that ever crossed the Cascade Mountains, and located in a body nearly all of the whole valley, and before the year was ended had a rough wagon road out to the prairies and to Steilacoom, the county seat.

As I will give an account of the struggles and trials of these people later in this work, I will here dismiss the subject by saying that no pioneer who settled in the Puyallup valley, and stuck to it, failed finally to prosper and gain a competence.

We lingered at the mouth of the river in doubt as to what best to do. My thoughts went back to the wife and baby in the lonely cabin on the Columbia River, and then again to that bargain we had made before marriage that we were going to be farmers, and how could we be farmers if we did not have the land? Under the donation act we could hold three hundred and twenty acres, but we must live on it for four years, and so it behooved us to look out and secure our location before the act expired, which would occur the following year. So, with misgivings and doubts, we finally, on the fourth day, loaded our outfit into our skiff and floated out on the receding tide, whither, we did not know.

CHAPTER VII.

Cruise on Puget Sound—Continued.

As we drew off on the tide from the mouth of the Puyallup River, numerous parties of Indians were in sight, some trolling for salmon, with a lone Indian in the bow of his canoe, others with a pole with barbs on two sides fishing for smelt, and used in place of a paddle, while again, others with nets, all leisurely pursuing their calling, or more accurately speaking, seemed waiting for a fisherman's luck. Again, other parties were passing, singing a plaintive ditty in minor key with two or more voices, accompanied by heavy stroke of the paddle handle against the side of the canoe, as if to keep time. There were really some splendid female voices to be heard, as well as male, and though there were but slight variations in the sounds or words, they seemed never to tire in repeating, and, I must confess, we never tired listening. Then, at times, a break in the singing would be followed by a hearty laugh, or perhaps a salutation be given in a loud tone to some distant party, which would always bring a response, and with the resumption of the paddles, like the sailors on the block and fall, the song would be renewed, oftentimes to bring back a distant echo from a bold shore. These scenes were repeated time and again, as we encountered the natives in new fields that constantly opened up to our view.

We laid our course in the direction the tide drew us, directly to the north in a channel three miles in width, and discarded the plan of following the shore line, as we found so little variation in the quality of soil. By

YESLER'S FAMOUS COOK HOUSE, SEATTLE, 1853.

this time we began to see that opportunities for farms on the immediate shores of Puget Sound were few and far between—in fact, we had seen none. During the afternoon and after we had traveled, by estimate, near twenty miles, we saw ahead of us larger waters, where, by continuing our course, we would be in a bay of five or six miles in width, with no very certain prospect of a camping place. Just then we spied a cluster of cabins and houses on the point to the east, and made a landing at what proved to be Alki Point, the place then bearing the pretentious name of New York.

We were not any too soon in effecting our landing, as the tide had turned and a slight breeze had met it, the two together disturbing the water in a manner to make it uncomfortable for us in our flat bottomed boat.

Here we met the irrepressible C. C. Terry, proprietor of the new townsite, but keenly alive to the importance of adding to the population of his new town. But we were not hunting townsites, and of course lent a deaf ear to the arguments set forth in favor of the place.

Captain William Renton had built some sort of a sawmill here, that laid the foundation to his great fortune accumulated later at Port Blakely, a few miles to the west, to which point, he later removed. Terry afterwards gave up the contest, and removed to Seattle.

We soon pushed on over to the east where the steam from a saw-mill served as the guiding star, and landed at a point that cannot have been far removed from the western limit of the present Pioneer Place of Seattle, near where the totem pole now stands.

Here we found the never to be forgotten Yesler, not whittling his pine stick as in later years, but as a wide awake, business man, on the alert to drive a trade when an opportunity offered, or spin a yarn, if perchance time would admit. I cannot recall meeting Mr. Denny, though I made his acquaintance soon after at my own

cabin on McNeil's Island. In fact, we did not stay very
long in Seattle, not being very favorably impressed with
the place.   There was not much of a town, probably
twenty cabins in all, with a few newer frame houses.
The standing timber could scarcely have been farther
removed than to be out of reach of the mill, and of
course, scarcely the semblance of a street. The lagoon
presented an uninviting appearance and scent, where the
process of filling with slabs and saw dust had already
begun.   The mill, though, infused activity in its immediate vicinity, and was really the life of the place.

As we were not looking for a millsite or a townsite,
we pushed on north the next day. We had gone but
a few miles until a favorable breeze sprang up, bringing
with it visions of a happy time sailing, but with the
long stretch of open waters back of us of ten miles, or
more, and of several miles in width, and with no visible
shelter ahead of us, or lessening of width of waters, we
soon felt the breeze was not so welcome after all. We
became doubtful as to the safety of sailing, and were by
this time aware of the difficulty of rowing a small, flat
bottom boat in rough waters with one oar sometimes in
the water and the other in the air, to be suddenly reversed. While the wind was in our favor, yet the boat
became almost unmanageable with the oars. The sail
once down was not so easy to get up again, with the boat
tipping first one way and then another, as she fell off
in the trough of the waves. But finally, the sail was set
again, and we scudded before the wind at a rapid
rate, not feeling sure of our bearings, or what was going
to happen. The bay looked to us as if it might be five
miles or more wide, and in fact, with the lowering
weather, we could not determine the extent. The east
shore lay off to our right a half a mile or so distant,
where we could see the miniature waves break on the
beach, and at times, catch the sound as they rolled up on
the gravel banks. We soon realized our danger, but

"I HAVE A FISH STORY OF MY OWN TO TELL."

feared to attempt a landing in the surf. Evidently the
wind was increasing, the clouds were coming down lower
and rain began to fall. There was but one thing to do.
We must make a landing, and so the sail was hastily
taken down again, and the junior of the party took to
the oars, while the senior sat in the stern with paddle
in hand to keep the boat steady on her course, and help
a little as opportunity offered. But fortune favored us
in luckily finding a smooth pebbly beach, and while we
got a good drenching in landing, and the boat partially
filled before we could haul her up out of reach of the
surf, yet we lost nothing outright, and suffered but
slight loss by damage from water. We were glad enough
to go ashore and thankful that the mishap was no worse.
Luckily our matches were dry and a half hour or so sufficed to build a rousing camp fire, haul our boat above
high tide, and utilize it as a wind break and roof turned
bottom up at an angle of forty-five degrees. Just how
long we were compelled to remain in this camp, I cannot
recall, but certainly two days, and I think three, but we
did not explore the adjacent land much, as the rain kept
us close in camp. And it was a dismal camp, although
we had plenty to eat and could keep dry and warm. We
here practiced the lesson taught us the evening of our
first camp, by the native matron, and had plenty of clams
to supplement our other provisions during the whole
period, and by the time we broke up camp, concluded we
were expert clam-bakers. But all such incidents must
have an end, and so the time came when we broke camp
and pulled for the head of Whidby's Island, a few miles
off to the northwest.

And now, I have a fish story to tell. I have always
been shy of telling it, lest some smart one should up
and say I was just telling a yarn and drawing on my
imagination, but "honor bright," I am not. But to be
sure of credence, I will print the following telegram

recently received, which, as it is printed in a newspaper, must be true.

Nanaimo, B. C., Friday, Jan. 29.—Another tremendous destruction of herring occurred on the shores of Protection Island a day or two ago in exactly the same way as took place near Departure Bay about three weeks ago, and to-day the entire atmosphere of the city carries the nauseous smell of thousands upon thousands of tons of decaying fish which threatens an epidemic of sickness.

The dead fish now cover the shores of Protection Island continuously for three miles to a depth ranging all the way from fifteen inches to three feet. The air is black with sea gulls. So thick have the fish been at times that were a fishing boat caught in the channel while a shoal of herring was passing, the rush of fish would literally lift the boat out of the water.

We had not proceeded far before we heard a dull sound like that often heard from the tide-rips where the current meets and disturbs the waters as like in a boiling caldron. But as we approached the disturbance, we found it was different from anything we had seen or heard before. As we rested on our oars, we could see that the disturbance was moving up toward us, and that it extended as far as we could see in the direction we were going. The sound had increased and became as like the roar of a heavy rainfall, or hailstorm in water, and we became aware that it was a vast school of fish moving south while millions were seemingly dancing on the surface of the water and leaping in the air. We could sensibly feel them striking against the boat in such vast numbers as to fairly move it as we lay at ease. The leap in the air was so high as to suggest tipping the boat to catch some as they fell back, and sure enough, here and there one would leap into the boat. We soon discovered some Indians following the school, who quickly loaded their canoes by using the barbed pole as a paddle and throwing the impaled fish into their canoes in surprising numbers. We soon obtained all we wanted by an improvised net.

We were headed for Whidby's Island, where, it was reported, rich prairie land could be found. The bay here at the head of the island was six or seven miles wide and there was no way by which we could keep near shore. Remembering the experience of a few days before, in waters not so large as here, the younger of the two confided his fears to his older companion, and that it was unwise to loiter and fish, howsoever novel and interesting, and so began pulling vigorously at the oars to find himself greatly embarassed by the mass of fish moving in the water. So far as we could see there was no end to the school ahead of us, the water, as far as the eye could reach, presenting the appearance shown with a heavy fall of hail. It did seem at times, as if the air was literally filled with fish, but we finally got rid of the moving mass, and reached the island shore in safety, only to become again weather bound in an uninhabited district of country that showed no signs of the handiwork of civilized man.

CHAPTER VIII.

Cruise on Puget Sound—Continued.

This camp did not prove so dreary as the last one, though more exposed to the swell of the big waters to the north, and sweep of the wind. To the north we had a view of thirty miles or more, where the horizon and water blend, leaving one in doubt whether land was in sight or not, though as we afterwards ascertained, our vision could reach the famous San Juan Island, later the bone of contention between our government and Great Britain. Port Townsend lay some ten miles northerly from our camp, but was shut out from view by an intervening headland. Marrowstone Point lay about midway between the two, but we did not know the exact location of the town, or for that matter, of our own. We knew, like the lost hunters, where *we* were, but the trouble was, we "didn't know where any place else was;" not lost ourselves, but the world was lost from us. In front of us, the channel of Admiralty Inlet, here, but about four miles wide, stretched out to the north into a fathomless sea of waters that for aught we knew, opened into the wide ocean. Three ships passed us while at this camp, one, coming as it would seem from out of space, a mere speck, to a full fledged, deep sea vessel, with all sails set, scudding before the wind and passing up the channel past us on the way to the anchorage of the seven vessels, the other two gracefully beating their way out against the stiff breeze to the open waters beyond. What prettier sight can one see than a full rigged vessel with all sails spread, either beating or sailing before the wind? Our enthusiam, at the sight, knew no bounds; we felt like cheering, clapping our hands, or adopting any other method of manifesting our pleasure. We had, as a matter of prudence, canvassed the question of returning from this camp as soon as released from this stress of weather, to the bay of the anchored ships in the more southern waters, but the sight of these ships, and the sight of this expanse of waters, coupled with perhaps a spirit of adventure, prompted us to quietly bide our time and to go farther, when released.

When I look back upon that decision, and in fact, upon this whole incident of my life, I stand amazed to think of the rashness of our actions and of the danger encountered from which we escaped. Not but two men with proper appliances, and with ripe experience, might with perfect security, make just such a trip, but we were possessed of neither and ran the great risks accordingly.

It was a calm, beautiful day when we reached Port Townsend, after a three hours run from our camp on the island. As we rounded Marrowstone Point, near four miles distant, the new village came into view. A feeling of surprise came over us from the supposed magnitude of the new town. Distance lends enchantment, the old adage says, but in this case the nearer we approached the embryo city, the greater our admiration. The beautiful, pebbly beach in front, the clear, level spot adjoining, with the beautiful open and comparatively level plateau in the background, and with two or three vessels at anchor in the foreground, there seemed nothing lacking to complete the picture of a perfect city site. The contrast was so great between the ill-smelling lagoon of Seattle or the dismal extensive tide flats of Olympia, that our spirits rose almost to a feeling of exultation, as the nose of our little craft grounded gently on the beach. Poor, innocent souls, we could not see beyond to discover that cities are not built upon pleasure grounds, and that there are causes beyond the ken of

man to fathom the future destiny of the embryo towns
of a new commonwealth.

We found here the enthusiastic Plummer, the plod-
ding Pettygrove and the industrious, enterprising Hast-
ings, jointly intent upon building up a town, "the greatest shipping port on the coast," as they were nearest
possible to the sea, while our Olympia friends had used
exactly the opposite arguments favoring their locality,
as "we are the farthest possible inland, where ships can
come." Small wonder that land-lubbers as we were
should become confused.

Another confusing element that pressed upon our
minds, was the vastness of the waters explored, and that
we now came to know were yet left unexplored. Then
Puget Sound was looked upon as anchorage ground from
the Straits on the north to Budd's Inlet on the south, forgetting, or rather not knowing, of the extreme depth
of waters in many places. Then that wonderful stretch
of shore line of sixteen hundred miles, with its forty or
more islands of from a few acres in extent to thirty miles
of length, with the aggregate area of waters of several
hundred square miles, exclusive of the Straits of Fuca
and Gulf of Georgia. All these marvels gradually
dawned upon our minds as we looked and counselled,
forgetting for the time the imminent risks we were taking.

Upon closer examination of the little town, we found
our first impression from the distance illusory. Many
shacks and camps, at first mistaken for the white men's
houses, were found to be occupied by the natives, a
drunken, rascally rabble, spending their gains from
the sale of fish and oil, in a debauch that would last as
long as their money was in hand.

This seemed to be a more stalwart race of Indians,
stronger and more athletic, though strictly of the class
known as fish Indians, but better developed than those
to the south, from the buffeting received in the larger

waters of the Straits, and even out in the open sea in their fishing excursions with canoes, manned by thirty or more men.

The next incident of the trip that I can remember, is when we were pulling for dear life to make a landing in front of Colonel Ebey's cabin, on Whidby's Island, opposite Port Townsend. We were carried by the rapid current quite a way past the landing, in spite of our utmost efforts. It would be a serious thing to be unable to land, as we were now in the open waters, with a fifteen mile stretch of the Straits of Fuca before us. I can remember a warm greeting at the hands of Ebey, the first time I had ever seen him. He had a droll stoppage in his speech that at first acquaintance would incline one to mirth, but after a few moments conversation, such a feeling would disappear. Of all the men we had met on the whole trip, Colonel Ebey made the most lasting impression. Somehow, what he did say came with such evident sincerity and sympathy, and with such an unaffected manner, that we were drawn close to him at once. It was while living in these same cabins where we visited him, that four years later the northern Indians, from British Columbia, came and murdered him and carried off his head as a trophy of their savage warfare.

We spent two or three days in exploring the island, only to find all the prairie land occupied, but I will not undertake from memory to name the settlers we found there. From after acquaintance, and from published reports, I came to know all of them, but do not now recall a single individual adult alive who was there then; a striking illustration of having outlived the most of my generation.

Somehow, our minds went back to the seven ships we had seen at anchor in front of Steilacoom; to the sound of the timber camps; to the bustle and stir of the

little, new village; to the greater activities that we saw
there than anywhere else on the waters of the Sound,
and likewise my thoughts would go beyond to the little
cabin on the Columbia River, and the little wife domi-
ciled there, and the other little personage, and so when
we bade Colonel Ebey good bye, it was the signal to
make our way as speedily as possible to the waters of the
seven ships.

Three days sufficed to land us back in the coveted bay
with no greater mishap than getting off our course into
the mouth of Hood's Canal, and being lost another half
day, but luckily going on the right course, the while.

But, lo and behold, the ships were gone. Not a sailing craft of any kind was in sight of the little town,
but the building activity continued. The memory of
those ships, however, remained and determined our
minds as to the important question where the trade
center was to be, and that we would look farther for the
coveted spot upon which to make a home.

I look back with amazement at the rash undertaking
of that trip, so illy provided, and inexperienced, as we
were, and wonder that we escaped with no more serious
mishap than we had. We were not justified in taking
these chances, or at least I was not, with the two dependents left in the cabin on the bank of the Columbia
River, but we did not realize the danger until we were
in it, and hence did not share in the suspense, and uneasiness of that one left behind. Upon the whole, it was
a most enjoyable trip, and one, barring the risk and
physical inability to play my part, I could with great
enjoyment encounter the same adventure of which I have
only related a mere outline. Did you ever, reader, take
a drive, we will say in a hired outfit, with a paid coach-
man, and then take the lines in your own hands by way
of contrast? If so, then you will realize the thrill of
enjoyment where you pull your own oars, sail your own

craft, cook your own dinner, and lie in your own bed of boughs, and go when and where you will with that keen relish incident to the independence and uncertainties of such a trip. It was a wild, reckless act, but we came out stronger than ever in the faith of the great future in store for the north country, where we finally made our home and where I have lived ever since, now over fifty years.

CHAPTER IX.

From Columbia River to Puget Sound.

"Can I get home to-night?" I asked myself, while the sun was yet high one afternoon of the last week of June (1853).

I was well up river, on the left bank of the Cowlitz. I could not tell how far, for there were no mile stones, or way places to break the monotony of the crooked, half obstructed trail leading down stream. I knew that at the best it would be a race with the sun, for there were many miles between me and the cabin, but the days were long, and the twilight longer, and I would camp that much nearer home if I made haste. My pack had been discarded on the Sound; I did not even have either coat or blanket. The heavy, woolen shirt, often worn outside the pants, will be well remembered by my old time pioneer readers. Added to this, the well worn slouch hat, and worn shoes, both of which gave ample ventilation, completed my dress; socks, I had none, neither suspenders; the improvised belt taking their place, and so I was dressed suitable for the race, and was eager for the trial.

I had parted with my brother at Olympia, where he had come to set me that far on my journey; he to return to the claims we had taken, and I to make my way across country for the wife and baby, to remove them to our new home. I did not particularly mind the camping so much if necessary, but did not fancy the idea of lying out so near home, if I could by extra exertion reach the cabin that night. I did not have the friendly ox to snug up to for warmth, as in so many bivouacs, while on the plains, but I had matches, and there were many mossy places for a bed and friendly shelter of the drooping cedars. We never thought of "catching cold," by lying on the ground or on cedar boughs, or from getting a good drenching. Somehow it did seem I was free from all care of bodily ailment, and could endure continued exertion for long hours without the least inconvenience. The readers of this generation doubtless will be ready to pour out their sympathy for the hardships of the lone trail, and lone camp, and the supperless bed of boughs, but they may as well reserve this for others of the pioneers whose systems were less able to bear the unusual strain of the new conditions. But the camp had to be made; the cabin could not be reached, for the trail could not be followed at night, nor the Kalama Creek crossed; so, slackening my pace at nightfall to gradually cool my system, I finally made my camp and slept as sound as if on a bed of down, with the consolation that the night was short and that I could see to travel by 3 o'clock, and it did not make so very much difference, after all.

I can truly say that of all those years of camp and cabin life, I do not look upon them as years of hardship. To be sure, our food was plain as well as dress, our hours of labor long and labor frequently severe, and that the pioneers appeared rough and uncouth, yet underlying all this, there ran a vein of good cheer, of hopefulness, of the intense interest always engendered with strife to overcome difficulties where one is the employer as well as the employed. We never watched for the sun to go down, or for the seven o'clock whistle, or for the boss to quicken our steps, for the days were always too short, and interest in our work always unabated.

The cabin could not be seen for a long distance on the trail, but I thought I caught sight of a curl of smoke and then immediately knew I did, and that settled it that all was well in the cabin. But when a little nearer, a little lady in almost bloomer dress was espied milking a cow, and a frisking, fat calf in the pen was seen, then I knew, and all solicitude vanished. The little lady never finished milking that cow, nor did she ever milk others when the husband was at home, though she knew how well enough, and never felt above such work if a necessity arose, but we parceled out duties on a different basis, with each to their suited parts. The bloom on the cheek of the little wife, the baby in the cabin as fat as the calf, told the story of good health and plenitude of food, and brought good cheer with the welcome home. The dried potato eyes had just been planted, although it was then the first week of July, following the receding waters of the June freshet up the Columbia, and were sprouting vigorously. I may say, in passing, there came a crop from these of nearly four hundred bushels at harvest time.

It did seem there were so many things to talk about that one could scarcely tell where to begin or when to stop. Why, at Olympia, eggs were a dollar a dozen. I saw them selling at that. That butter you have there on the shelf would bring a dollar a pound as fast as you could weigh it out; I saw stuff they called butter sell for that; then potatoes were selling for $3.00 a bushel and onions at $4.00. Everything the farmer raises sells high. "Who buys?" "Oh, almost everbody has to buy; there's the ships and the timber camps, and the hotels, and the—

"Where do they get the money?"

"Why, everybody seems to have money. Some take it there with them. Then men working in the timber camps get $4.00 a day and their board. I saw one place where they paid $4.00 a cord for wood to ship to San Francisco, and one can sell all the shingles he can make at $4.00 a thousand, and I was offered 5 cents a foot for piles. If we had Buck and Dandy over there we could make twenty dollars a day putting in piles."

"Where could you get the piles?"

"Off the government land, of course. All help themselves to all they want. Then there are the fish, and the clams, and the oysters, and—"

"But, what about the land for a claim?"

That question was a stumper. The little wife never lost sight of that bargain made before we were married, that we were going to be farmers; and here now I found myself praising a country I could not say much for its agricultural qualities, but other things quite foreign to that interest.

But if we could sell produce higher, might we not well lower our standard of an ideal farm? The claim I had taken was described with a tinge of disappointment, falling so far below in quality of what we had hoped to acquire, and still adhering to the resolution to be farmers, we began the preparations for removal to the Sound.

The wife, baby, bedding, ox yoke, and log chain, were sent up the Cowlitz in a canoe, while Buck and Dandy and I renewed our acquaintance by taking to the trail where we had our parting bivouac. We had camped together many a night on the plains, and slept together literally, not figuratively. I used to crowd up close under Buck's back while napping on watch, for the double purpose of warmth and signal—warmth while at rest, signal if the ox moved. On this occasion I was illy prepared for a cool night camp, having neither blanket, nor coat, as I had expected to reach "Hard-Bread's" Hotel, where the people in the canoe would stop over night. But I could not make it and so again laid on the trail to renew the journey bright and early the next morning.

Hard Bread's is an odd name for a hotel, you will say; so it is, but the name grew out of the fact that Gardner, the old widower that kept "bachelor's" hall at the mouth of Toutle River (opposite Pumphrey's place, on the left bank of the Cowlitz), fed his cus-

tomers on hard tack three times a day, if perchance
any one was unfortunate enough to be compelled to take
three meals at his place.

I found the little wife had not fared any better than
I had on the trail, and in fact, not so well, for the floor
of the cabin was a good deal harder than the sand spit
where I had passed the night, with plenty of pure, fresh
air, while she, in a closed cabin, in the same room with
many others, could neither boast of fresh air, nor freedom from creeping things that make life miserable.
With her shoes for a pillow, a shawl for covering, small
wonder the report came "I did not sleep a wink, last
night."

Judge Olney and wife were passengers in the same
canoe and guests at the same house with the wife, as
also Frank Clark, who afterwards played a prominent
part at the bar, and in the political affairs of Pierce
County in particular, and incidentally of the whole Territory.

We soon arrived at the Cowlitz landing, and at the
end of the canoe journey, so, striking the tent that had
served us so well on the plains, and with a cheerful camp
fire blazing for cooking, speedily forgot the experience
of the trail, the cramped passage in the canoe, the hard
bread, dirt and all, while enjoying the savory meal, the
like of which only the expert hands of the ladies of the
plains could prepare.

But now we had fifty miles of land to travel before
us, and over *such* a road! Words cannot describe that
road, and so I will not try. One must have traveled it
to fully comprehend what it meant. However, we had
one consolation, and that was it would be worse in
winter than at that time. We had no wagon. Our
wagon had been left at the Dalles, and we never saw
nor heard of it again. Our cows were gone—given for
provender to save the lives of the oxen during the deep
December snow, and so when we took account of stock,

we had Buck and Dandy, the baby, and a tent, an ox yoke and chain, enough clothing and bedding to keep us comfortable, with but very little food and no money—that had all been expended on the canoe passage.

Shall we pack the oxen and walk, and carry baby, or shall we build a sled and drag our things over to the Sound, or shall I make an effort to get a wagon? This latter proposition was the most attractive, and so next morning, driving Buck and Dandy before me, leaving the wife and baby to take care of the camp, the search for a wagon began.

That great hearted, old pioneer, John R. Jackson, did not hesitate a moment, stranger as I was, to say "Yes, you can have two if you need them." Jackson had settled eight years before, ten miles out from the landing, and had an abundance around him, and like all those earlier pioneers, took a pride in helping others who came later. Retracing the road, night found me again in camp, and all hands happy, but Jackson would not listen to allowing us to proceed the next day any farther than his premises, where he would entertain us in his comfortable cabin, and send us on our way the morning following, rejoicing in plenty.

Without special incident or accident, we in due time arrived at the foot of the falls of the Deschutes (Tumwater), and on the shore of Puget Sound. Here camp must be established again; the little wife and baby left while I drove the wagon over the tedious road to Jackson's and then returned with the oxen to tide water.

The reader may well imagine my feelings, when, upon my return, my tent, wife, baby, and all were gone. We knew before I started on my return trip that smallpox was raging among the Indians, and that a camp where this disease was prevalent was in sight less than a quarter of a mile away. The present day reader must remember that dread disease had terrors then that, since universal vaccination, it does not now possess. Could it be possible my folks had been taken sick and had been removed? The question, however, was soon solved. I had scarcely gotten out of sight upon my trip before one of those royal pioneer matrons came to the camp and pleaded and insisted and finally almost frightened the little wife to go and share her house with her which was near by, and be out of danger from the smallpox.

And that was the way we traveled from the Columbia River to Puget Sound.

God bless those earlier pioneers; they were all good to us, sometimes to the point of embarassment by their generous hospitality.

I cannot dismiss this subject without reverting to one such, in particular, who gave his whole crop during this winter of which I have just written, to start immigrants on the road to prosperity, and in some instances, to prevent suffering.

In consequence of the large immigration and increased demand, prices of provisions had run sky high, and out of reach of some of the recent immigrants with large families. George Bush had squatted on a claim seven miles south of Olympia, in 1845, and had an abundance of farm produce, but would not sell a pound of anything to a speculator; but to immigrants, for seed or for immediate, pressing wants, to all alike, without money and without price—"return it when you can,"— he would say, and so divided up his whole crop, then worth thousands of dollars. And yet this man's oath could not at that time be taken; neither could he sue in the courts or acquire title to the land upon which he lived, or any land. He had negro blood in his veins, and under the law of this great country, then, was a proscribed outcast. Conditions do change as time passes. The wrong was so flagrant in this particular case that a special act of Congress enabled this old, big-hearted pioneer of 1845 to hold his claim, and his descendents are living on it yet.

CHAPTER X.

The Second Cabin.

What I am now about to write may provoke a smile, but I can only say, reader, put yourself in my place. That there should be a feeling akin to affection between a man and an ox will seem past comprehension to many. The time had come that Buck and Dandy and I must part for good and all. I could not transport them to our island home, neither provide for them. These patient, dumb brutes had been my close companions for the long, weary months on the plains, and had never failed me; they would do my bidding to the letter. I often said Buck understood English better than some people I had seen in my life time. I had done what not one in a hundred did; that was, to start on that trip with an unbroken ox and cow team. I had selected these four-year-old steers for their intelligent eyes as well as for their trim build, and had made no mistake. We had bivouacked together; actually slept together, lunched together. They knew me as far as they could see, and seemed delighted to obey my word, and I did regret to feel constrained to part with them. I knew they had assured my safe transit on the weary journey, if not even to the point of having saved my life. I could pack them, ride them, drive them by the word and receive their salutations, and why should I be ashamed to part with feelings of more than regret.

But I had scant time to spend on sentiment. The brother did not expect my return so soon. The island claim, (and cabin, as I thought) must be reached; the little skiff obtained in which to transport the wife and baby, not yet feeling willing to trust them in a canoe.

So, without further ado, a small canoe was chartered, and my first experience to "paddle my own canoe" materialized. It seemed this same place where we had our first clam bake was the sticking point again. The tide turned, night overtook me, and I could go no farther. Two men were in a cabin, the Doctor Johnson, heretofore mentioned and a man by the name of Hathaway, both drunk and drinking, with a jug handy by, far from empty. Both were men that seemed to me to be well educated, and, if sober, refined. They quoted from Burns, sang songs and ditties, laughed and danced until late in the night, when they became exhausted and fell asleep. They would not listen to my suggestion that I would camp and sleep outside the cabin, and I could not sleep inside, so the night passed off without rest or sleep until the tide turned, and I was glad enough to slip away, leaving them in their stupor.

A few miles vigorous paddling brought me to McNeil Island, opposite the town of Steilacoom, where I expected to find our second cabin, my brother and the boat. No cabin, no brother, no boat, were to be seen. A raft of cabin logs floating in the lagoon near by, where the United States penitentiary now stands, was all the signs to be seen, other than what was there when I left the place for my return trip to the Columbia River. I was sorely puzzled as to what to do. My brother was to have had the cabin ready by the time I returned. He not only had not done that, but had taken the boat, and left no sign as to where it or he could be found. Not knowing what else to do I mechanically paddled over to the town, where, sure enough, the boat was anchored, but nobody knew where the man had gone. I finally found where the provisions had been left, and, after an earnest parley, succeeded in getting possession. I took my canoe in tow and soon made my way back to where the little folks were, and speedily transferred the whole outfit to the spot that was to be our island home; set up our tent, and felt at home once more.

The village, three miles away, across the bay, had grown during my absence and in the distance looked like a city in fact as well as in name. The mountain looked bigger and taller than ever. Even the songs of the Indians sounded better, and the canoes seemed more graceful, and the paddles wielded more expertly. Everything looked cheerful, even to the spouting clams on the beach, and the crow's antics of breaking clams by rising in the air and dropping them on the boulders. So many new things to show the folks that I for a time almost forgot we were about out of provisions and money, and did not know what had happened to the brother. Thoughts of these suddenly coming upon us, our spirits fell, and for a time we could hardly say we were perfectly happy.

"I believe that canoe is coming straight here," said the little wife, the next morning, about nine o'clock. All else is dropped, and a watch set upon the strange craft, moving slowly, apparently in the long distance, but more rapidly as it approached, and there sat the brother. Having returned to the village and finding that the boat and provisions had been taken, and seeing smoke in the bight, he knew what had happened, and, following his own good impulse, we were soon together again, and supremely happy. He had received a tempting offer to help load a ship, and had just completed his contract, and was able to exhibit a "slug" * of money and more besides that looked precious in our eyes.

The building of the cabin with its stone fire-place, cat-and-clay chimney, its lumber floor, real window with glass in it, together with the high post bedstead out of tapering cedar saplings, the table fastened to the wall,

---

*A "slug" was fifty dollars value in gold, minted by private parties, in octagon form, and passed current the same as if it had borne the government's stamp. "Slugs" were worth as much melted as in the coined form. My ideas about the gold standard were formed at that time, and I may say my mind never changed on this subject.

with rustic chairs, seemed but like a play spell. No eight hour a day work there—eighteen would be nearer the mark—we never tired.

There came a letter: "Boys, if Oliver will come back to cross with us, we will go to Oregon next year," this signed by the father, then fifty years old. The letter was nearly three months old when we received it. What should we say and what should we do? Would Davenport pay for the Columbia River claims and the prospective potato crop in the fall—could he? We will say yes, Oliver will be with you next Spring. We must go to the timber camp to earn the money to pay expenses of the trip and not depend altogether on the Columbia River asset.

"What shall we do with the things?" said the little wife.

"Lock them up in the cabin," said the elder brother.

"And you go and stay with Dofflemire," said the young husband.

"Not I," said the little wife, "I'm going along to cook," and thus it was that all our well laid plans were suddenly changed, our clearing land deferred, the chicken house, the inmates of which were to make us rich, was not to be built, the pigs were not brought to fatten on the clams, and many other pet schemes dropped that we might accomplish this one object, that Oliver might go back to Iowa to "bring the father out" across the plains.

We struck rapid, heavy, but awkward strokes in the timber camp established on the bluff overlooking the falls at Tumwater, while the little wife supplied the huckleberry pudding for dinner, plenty of the lightest, whitest bread, vegetables, meat, and fish served in style good enough for kings; such appetites! No coaxing required to eat a hearty meal; such sound sleep; such satisfaction! Talk about your hardships. We would have none of it. It was a pleasure as we counted the

"WE STRUCK RAPID, HEAVY, BUT AWKWARD STROKES."

eleven dollars a day that the Tullis brothers paid us for cutting logs, at one dollar and seventy cents a thousand, which we earned every day, and Sundays, too, seventy-seven dollars a week. Yes, we were going to make it. "Make what?" the reader will say. Why succeed in getting enough money together to pay the passage of the elder brother to Iowa. And what a trip. Over to the Columbia River, out from there by steamer to San Francisco, then to the Isthmus, then New York after which by rail as far west as there was a railroad and then walk to Eddyville, Iowa, from where the start was again to be made.

Again the younger brother was left without money and but a scant supply of provisions, and winter had come on. The elder brother was speeding on his way, and could not be heard from frequently. How our little family succeeded in getting enough together to eat is not an interesting topic for the general reader. Suffice to say, we always secured abundance, even if at times the variety was restricted.

It was soon after Oliver's departure that I first made the acquaintance of Dr. Tolmie. It was upon the occasion when our new baby was born, now the mother of eight grown up children, and several times a grandmother, Mrs. Ella Templeton of Halsey, Oregon.

Of course, Dr. Tolmie did not practice medicine. He had the cares of the great foreign corporation, the Puget Sound Agricultural Company, on his shoulders. He was harassed by the settlers, who chafed because a foreign corporation had fenced up quite large tracts of grazing and some farming lands, and had thousands of sheep and cattle on the range. Constant friction was the result. The cattle were wild; therefore, some settler would kill one every now and then, and make the remainder still wilder, and again, therefore, the more the reason that others might be killed. The Doctor was a patient, tactful man, with an impulse to always do one a good turn for the sake of doing it. Consequently, when asked to attend, he did so without hesitation, though the request came from a perfect stranger and compliance was to his great inconvenience, yet without fee and without expectation of ever meeting the parties again. This first acquaintance ripened into friendship life long, that became closer as he neared his end. But recently, fifty years after this event, I have had the pleasure of a visit from two of his daughters, and I may say there has been scarcely a year in all this time but some token of friendship has passed. He was a noble man, with noble impulses. He died on his farm near Victoria many years ago.

Soon after this, I made my first acquaintance with Arthur A. Denny. It came about this way. He and two other gentlemen were returning from the first Territorial Legislature, then just adjourned. Wind and tide compelled them to suspend their journey from Olympia to Seattle, and to stay over night with us in the little cabin. This was early in May, 1854. Mr. Denny remarked in the morning that he thought there was a good foundation under my cabin floor, as he did not find any spring to the bed. He and his companion laid on the floor, but I remember we did not go to bed very early. All during the session we had heard a great deal about removing the capital of the Territory from Olympia to Steilacoom. The legislature had adjourned and no action had been taken, and, in fact, no bill for the purpose was introduced. Mr. Denny said that before the recess a clear majority of both houses were in favor of removal to Steilacoom, but for the mistake of Lafayette Balch, member of the council from Pierce County, the removal would have been accomplished. Balch, so Denny told me, felt so sure of his game that he did not press to a vote before the recess.

At that, the first session of the Legislature, the mania was for Territorial roads; everybody wanted a Territorial road. One, projected from Seattle to Bellingham Bay, did not meet with approval by Balch. Stroking his long beard as he was wont to do almost mechanically, he "thought they had gone far enough in establishing roads for one session." It was impolitic in the highest degree for Balch to offend the northern members in this way, as also unnecessary, as usually these roads remained on paper only, and cost nothing. However, he lost his majority in the council, and so the project died, to the very great disappointment of the people of Steilacoom and surrounding country.

CHAPTER XL.

Trip Through the Natchess Pass.

The latter part of August, 1854, James K. Hurd, of Olympia, sent me word that he had been out on the immigrant trail and heard that some of my relations on the road were belated and short of provisions. He advised that I should go to their assistance, and particularly if I wanted to be sure they should come direct to Puget Sound over the Cascade Mountains, and not go down the Columbia River into Oregon. How it could be, with the experience of my brother Oliver to guide them, that my people should be in the condition described, was past my comprehension. However, I accepted the statement as true and particularly felt the importance of their having certain knowledge as to prevailing conditions of an over-mountain trip through the Natchess Pass. But how could I go and leave wife and two babies on our island home? The summer had been spent clearing land and planting crops, and my finances were very low. To remove my family would cost money, besides the abandonment of the season's work to almost certain destruction. The wife said at once, and without a moment's hesitation, to go, and she and Mrs. Darrow, who was with us as nurse and companion friend, would stay "right where we are until you get back," with a confidence in which I did not share. The trip at best was hazardous to an extent, even when undertaken well prepared and with company. So far as I could see, I might have to go on foot and pack my food and blanket on my back, and I knew that I would have to go alone. I knew some work had

been done on the road during the summer, but was
unable to get definite information as to whether any
camps were yet left in the mountains, and did not have
that abiding faith in my ability to get back that rested
in the breast of the little, courageous wife, but I dared
not impart my forebodings to harass and intensify her
fears and disturb her peace of mind while absent. The
immigration the previous year, as related elsewhere,
ihad encountered formidable difficulties in the mountains, narrowly escaping the loss of everything if not
facing actual starvation. Reports were current that
the government appropriation for a military road had
been expended, and that the road was passable for teams,
but a like report had been freely circulated the previous
year, with results almost disastrous to those attempting
to come through. I could not help feeling that possibly
the same conditions yet existed. The only way to determine the question was to go and see for myself; meet
my father's party and pilot them through the pass.

It was on the third day of September of 1854 that I
left home. I had been planting turnips for two days,
and made a memorandum of the date, and by that fix
the date of my departure. Of that turnip crop I shall
have more to say later, as it had a cheering effect upon
the incoming immigrants.

At Steilacoom there was a character then understood
by few, and I may say by not many even to the end, in
whom somehow, I had implicit confidence. Dr. J. B.
Webber, afterwards of the firm of Balch & Webber, of
Steilacoom, the largest shipping and mercantile firm on
the Sound, was a very eccentric man. Between him and
myself, there would seem to be a gulf that could not be
closed. Our habits of life were as diametrically opposite as possible for two men to be. He was always drinking; never sober, neither ever drunk. I would never
touch a drop while the doctor would certainly drink a
dozen times a day, just a little at a time, but seemingly

tippling all the time. Then, he openly kept an Indian woman in defiance of the sentiment of all the families of the community. He was addicted to other vices which I will not here relate. It was with this man that I entrusted the safe keeping of my little family. I knew my wife had such an aversion to this class that I did not even tell her with whom I would arrange to look out for her welfare; but suggested another to whom she might apply in case of need. I knew Dr. Webber for long years afterwards, and until the day of his horrible death with delirium tremens, and never had my faith shaken as to the innate goodness of the man. Why these contrary traits of character should be, I cannot say, but so it was. His word was as good as his bond, and his impulses were all directly opposite to his personal habits. Twice a week an Indian woman visited the cabin on the island, always with some little presents and making inquiries about the babies and whether there was anything needed, with the parting *"alki nika keel-apie"* (by and by I will return); and she did, every few days during my absence.

When I spoke to Webber about what I wanted, he seemed pleased to be able to do a kind act, and, to reassure me, got out his field glass and turned it on the cabin across the water, three miles distant. Looking through it intently for a moment and handing the glass to me, said, "I can see everything going on over there, and you need have no uneasiness about your folks while gone," and I did not.

With a fifty pound flour sack filled with hard bread, or navy biscuit, a small piece of dried venison, a couple of pounds of cheese, a tin cup and half of a three point blanket, all made into a pack of less than forty pounds, I climbed the hill at Steilacoom and took the road leading to Puyallup, and spent the night with Jonathan Mc-Carty, near where the town of Sumner now is.

McCarty said "you can't get across the streams on foot; I will let you have a pony. He is small, but sure-footed, and hardy, and will in any event carry you across the rivers." McCarty also said: "Tell your folks this is the greatest grass country on earth; why, I am sure I harvested five tons of timothy to the acre this year." Upon my expressing a doubt, he said he knew he was correct by the measurement of the mow in the barn and the land. In after years, I came to know he was correct, though at the time, I could not help but believe he was mistaken.

The next day found me on the road with my blanket under the saddle, my sack of hard bread strapped on behind the saddle, and myself mounted to ride on level stretches of the road, or across streams, of which, as will appear later, I had full forty crossings to make, but had only one ahead of me the first day. That one, though, as the Englishman would say, was a "nasty" one, across White River at Porter's place.

White River on the upper reaches is a roaring torrent only at all fordable in low water and in but few places. The rush of waters can be heard for a mile or more from the high bluff overlooking the narrow valley, or rather canyon, and presented a formidable barrier for a lone traveler. The river bed is full of boulders worn rounded and smooth and slippery, from the size of a man's head to very much larger, thus making footing for animals uncertain. After my first crossing, I dreaded those to come, which I knew were ahead of me, more than all else of the trip, for a mistep of the pony meant fatal results in all probability. The little fellow, though, seemed to be equal to the occasion. If the footing became too uncertain, he would stop stock still, and pound the water with one foot and finally reach out carefully until he could find secure footing, and then move up a step or two. The water of the river is so charged with the sediment from the glaciers above, that the bottom

could not be seen—only felt—hence the absolute necessity of feeling one's way. It is wonderful, the sagacity or instinct or intelligence, or whatever we may call
it, manifested by the horse. I immediately learned that
my pony could be trusted on the fords better than myself, thereafter I held only a supporting, but not a guiding rein, and he carried me safely over the forty crossings on my way out, and my brother as many on the
return trip.

Allen Porter then lived near the first crossing, on the
farther side, and as this was the last settler I would see
and the last place I could get feed for my pony, other
than grass or browse, I put up for the night under his
roof. He said I was going on a "Tom fool's errand," for
my folks could take care of themselves, and tried to
dissuade me from proceeding on my journey. But I
would not be turned back, and the following morning
cut loose from the settlements and, figuratively speaking, plunged into the deep forest of the mountains.

The road (if it could be properly called a road), lay
in the narrow valley of White River, or on the mountains adjacent, in some places (as at Mud Mountain),
reaching an altitude of more than a thousand feet above
the river bed. Some places the forest was so dense
that one could scarcely see to read at mid-day, while
in other places large burns gave an opening for day-
light.

During the forenoon of this first day, while in one of
those deepest of deep forests, where, if the sky was clear,
and one could catch a spot you could see out overhead,
one might see the stars as from a deep well, my pony
stopped short, raised his head with his ears pricked up,
indicating something unusual was at hand. Just then,
I caught an indistinct sight of a movement ahead, and
thought I heard voices, while the pony made an effort
to turn and flee in the opposite direction. Soon there
appeared three women and eight children on foot, com-

ing down the road in blissful ignorance of the presence of any one but themselves in the forest.

"Why, stranger! Where on earth did you come from? Where are you going to, and what are you here for?" was asked by the foremost woman of the party, in such quick succession as to utterly preclude any answer, as she discovered me standing on the road holding my uneasy pony. Mutual explanations soon followed. I soon learned their teams had become exhausted, and that all the wagons but one had been left, and this one was on the road a few miles behind them; that they were entirely out of provisions and had had nothing to eat for twenty hours, except what natural food they had gathered, which was not much. They eagerly inquired the distance to food, which I thought they might possibly reach that night, but in any event the next morning early. Meanwhile I had opened my sack of hard bread and gave each a cracker, in the eating of which the sound resembled pigs cracking dry, hard corn.

Of those eleven persons, I only know of but one now alive, although, of course, the children soon outgrew my knowledge of them, but they never forgot me.

Mrs. Anne Fawcet, the spokesman of the party, I knew well in after years, and although now eighty years old (she will pardon me for telling her age), is living in good circumstances a mile out from the town of Auburn, nearly twenty miles south of Seattle, and but a couple of miles from the scene of the dreadful massacre related elsewhere, and also where the gallant Lieutenant Slaughter lost his life.

Mrs. Fawcet can scarcely be called a typical pioneer woman, yet there were many approaching her ways. She was of too independent a character to be molded into that class; too self-reliant to be altogether like her neighbor housewives; and yet was possessed of those sturdy virtues so common with the pioneer—industry and frugality, coupled with unbounded hospitality. The other ladies of the party, Mrs. Herpsberger and Mrs. Hall, I never knew afterwards, and have no knowledge as to their fate, other than that they arrived safely in the settlements.

But we neither of us had time to parley or visit, and so the ladies with their children, barefoot and ragged, bareheaded and unkempt, started down the mountain intent on reaching food, while I started up the road wondering whether or not this scene was to be often repeated as I advanced on my journey. A dozen biscuits of hard bread is usually a very small matter, but with me it might mean a great deal. How far would I have to go? When could I find out? What would be the plight of my people when found? Or would I find them at all? Might they not pass by and be on the way down the Columbia River before I could reach the main immigrant trail? These and kindred questions weighed heavily on my mind as I slowly and gradually ascended the mountain.

Some new work on the road gave evidence that men had recently been there, but the work was so slight one could easily believe immigrants might have done it as they passed. Fifteen thousand dollars had been appropriated by Congress for a military road, which report said would be expended in improving the way cut by the immigrants and citizens through the Natchess Pass during the summer of 1853. I saw some of the work, but do not remember seeing any of the men, as I stuck close to the old trail, and so my first camp was made alone, west of the summit and without special incident. I had reached an altitude where the night chill was keenly felt, and, with my light blanket, missed the friendly contact of the back of the faithful ox that had served me so well on the plains. My pony had nothing but browse for supper, and was restless. Nevertheless I slept soundly and was up early, refreshed and ready to resume the journey.

CHAPTER XII.

Trip Through the Natchess Pass—Continued.

It is strange how the mind will vividly retain the memory of some incidents of no particular importance while the recollection of other passing events so completely fades away. I knew I had to cross that ugly stream, White River, five times during the first day's travel, but cannot recall but one crossing, where my pony nearly lost his balance, and came down on his knees with his nose in the water for the moment, but to recover and bravely carry me out safely.

The lone camp well up on the mountain had chilled me, but the prospect before me and that I had left behind brought a depressed feeling most difficult to describe. I had passed through long stretches of forest so tall and so dense that it seemed incredible that such did exist anywhere on earth. And then, the road; such a road, if it could be called a road. Curiously enough, the heavier the standing timber, the easier it had been to slip through with wagons, there being but little undecayed or down timber. In the ancient of days, however, great giants had been uprooted lifting considerable earth with the upturned roots, that, as time went on and the roots decayed, formed mounds two, three, or four feet high, leaving a corresponding hollow in which one would plunge, the whole being covered by a dense, short, evergreen growth, completely hiding from view the unevenness of the ground. Over these hillocks and hollows the immigrants had rolled their wagon wheels, and over the large roots of the fir, often as big as one's body and nearly all of them on top of the ground. I will not undertake to say how many of these giant trees were to be found to the acre, but they were so numerous and so large that in many places it was difficult to find a passage way between them, and then only by a tortuous route winding in various directions. When the timber burns were encountered the situation was worse. Often the remains of timber would be piled in such confusion that sometimes wagons could pass under logs that rested on others; then again, others were encountered half buried, while still others would rest a foot or so from the ground, these, let the reader remember, oftentimes were five feet or more in diameter, with trunks from two to three hundred feet in length. All sorts of devices had been resorted to in order to overcome these obstructions. In many cases, where not too large, cuts had been taken out, while in other places, the larger timber had been bridged up to by piling smaller logs, rotten chunks, brush, or earth, so the wheels of the wagon could be rolled up over the body of the tree. Usually three notches would be cut on the top of the log, two for the wheels and one for the reach or coupling pole to pass through.

In such places, the oxen would be taken to the opposite side, a chain or rope run to the end of the tongue, a man to drive, one or two to guide the tongue, others to help at the wheels, and so with infinite labor and great care the wagons would gradually be worked down the mountain in the direction of the settlements. Small wonder that the immigrants of the previous year should report they had to cut their way through the timber, while the citizen road workers had reported that the road was opened, and small wonder that the prospect of the road should have as chilling effect on my mind as the chill mountain air had had on my body.

But, the more difficulties encountered, the more determined I became, at all hazards, to push through, for the more the necessity to acquaint myself with the obstacles to be encountered and to be with my friends to encourage and help them. Before me lay the great range or pass, five thousand feet above sea level, and the rugged mountain climb to get to the summit, and the summit prairies where my pony could have a feast of grass. It was on this summit hill the immigration of the previous year had encountered such grave difficulties. At the risk of in part repeating, I am tempted to quote some of my own words to a select party of friends, the teachers of the county in which I have lived so long, prepared for that special occasion.

"About twenty miles north of the great mountain of the Cascade range is a picturesque, small scope of open country known as Summit Prairie, in the Natchess Pass, some seventy miles southeasterly from this city (Tacoma). In this prairie, fifty years ago this coming autumn, a camp of immigrants was to be seen. * * * Go back they could not; either they must go ahead or starve in the mountains. A short way out from the camp a steep mountain declivity lay square across their track. As one of the ladies of the party said, when she first saw it: 'Why, Lawsee Massee! We have come to the jumping off place at last!' This lady felt, as many others of the party felt, like they had come to the end of the world (to them), and the exclamation was not for the stage effect, but one of fervent prayer for deliverance.

"Stout hearts in the party were not to be deterred from making the effort to go ahead. Go around this hill they could not; go down it with logs trailed to the wagons, as they had done before, they could not, as the hill was so steep the logs would go end over end and be a danger instead of a help. So the rope they had was run down the hill and found to be too short to reach the bottom. One of the leaders of the party (I knew him well) turned to his men and said, 'Kill a steer;' and they killed a steer, cut his hide into strips and spliced it to the rope. It was found yet to be too short to reach to the bottom. The order went out: 'Kill two more steers!' And two more steers were killed, their hides cut into strips and spliced to the rope, which then reached the bottom of the hill; and by the aid of that rope and strips of the hides of those three steers, twenty-nine wagons were lowered down the mountain side to the bottom of the steep hill.

"Now, my friends, there is no fiction about this story,—it is a true story, and some of the actors are yet alive, and some of them live in this county. Nor were their trials ended when they got their wagons down to the bottom of that hill.

"Does it now seem possible for mortal man to do this? And yet this is only a plain statement of an incident of pioneer life without giving any names and dates, that can yet be verified by living witnesses; but these witnesses are not for here long.

"James Biles, who afterwards settled near Olympia, was the man who ordered the steers killed to procure the hides to lengthen out the rope. Geo. H. Himes, of Portland, who is still living, was one of the party; so was Stephen Judson, of Steilacoom; also Nelson Sargeant, of Grand Mound, now a very old man.

"The feat of bringing that train of twenty-nine wagons in with the loss of only one is the greatest of anything I ever knew or heard of in the way of pioneer travel.

"With snail-like movements, the cattle and men becoming weaker and weaker, progress was made each day until finally it seemed as if the oxen could do no more, and it became necessary to send them forward on the trail ten miles, where it was known plenty of grass could be had. Meantime the work on the road continued until the third day, when the last particle of food was gone. The teams were brought back, the trip over the whole ten miles made, and Connell's Prairie reached at dark.

"The struggle over that ten miles, where to a certain extent each party became so intent on their particular surroundings as to forget all else, left the women and children to take care of themselves while the husbands tugged at the wagons. I now have in mind to relate the experience of one of these mothers with a ten-year-old boy, one child of four years and another of eight months.

"Part of the time these people traveled on the old trail and part on the newly-cut road, and by some means fell behind the wagons, which forded that turbulent, dangerous stream, White River, before they reached the bank, and were out of sight, not knowing but the women and children were ahead.

"I wish every little boy of ten years of age of this great State, or, for that matter, twenty years old or more, could read and profit by what I am now going to relate, especially if that little or big boy at times thinks he is having a hard time because he is asked to help his mother or father at odd times, or perchance to put in a good solid day's work on Saturday, instead of spending it as a holiday; or if he has a cow to milk or wood to split, or anything that is work, to make him bewail his fate for having such a hard time in life. I think the reading of the experience of this little ten-year-old boy with his mother and the two smaller children would encourage him to feel more cheerful and more content with his lot.

"As I have said, the wagons had passed on, and there these four people were on the right bank of the river while their whole company was on the opposite bank and had left them there alone.

"A large fallen tree reached across the river, but the top on the further side lay so close to the water that a constant trembling and swaying made the trip dangerous.

"None of them had eaten anything since the previous day, and but a scant supply then; but the boy resolutely shouldered the four-year-old and safely deposited him on the other side. Then came next the little tot, the baby, to be carried in arms across. Next came the mother.

" 'I can't go!' she exclaimed; 'it makes me so dizzy.'

" 'Put one hand over your eyes, mother, and take hold of me with the other,' said the boy; and so they began to move out sideways on the log, a half step at a time.

" 'Hold steady, mother; we are nearly over.'

" 'Oh, I am gone!' was the only response, as she lost her balance and fell into the river, but happily so near the farther bank that the little boy was able to catch a bush with one hand that hung over the bank, while holding on to his mother with the other, and so she was saved.

"It was then nearly dark, and without any knowledge of how far it was to camp, the little party started on the road, only tarrying long enough on the bank of the river for the mother to wring the water out of her skirts, the boy carrying the baby while the four-year-old walked beside his mother. After nearly two miles of travel and ascending a very steep hill, it being now dark, the glimmer of camp lights came in view; but the mother could see nothing, for she fell senseless, utterly prostrated.

"I have been up and down that hill a number of times, and do not wonder the poor woman fell senseless after the effort to reach the top. The great wonder is that she should have been able to go as far as she did. The incident illustrates how the will power can nerve one up to extraordinary achievements, but when the object is attained and the danger is past, then the power is measureably lost, as in this case, when the good woman came to know they were safe. The boy hurried his two little brothers into camp, calling for help to rescue his mother. The appeal was promptly responded to, the woman being carried into camp and tenderly cared for until she revived.

"Being asked if he did not want something to eat, the boy said 'he had forgot all about it,' and further, 'he didn't see anything to eat, anyway;' whereupon some one with a stick began to uncover some roasted potatoes, which he has decided was the best meal he has ever eaten, even to this day.

"This is a plain recital of actual occurrences, without exaggeration, obtained from the parties themselves and corroborated by numerous living witnesses.

"There were 128 people in that train, and through the indefatigable efforts of Mr. Geo. H. Himes, of Portland, Oregon, who was one of the party, and in fact the ten-year-old boy referred to, I am able to give the names in part.

"I have been thus particular in telling this story to illustrate what trials were encountered and overcome by the pioneers of that day, to the end that the later generations may pause in their hasty condemnation of their present surroundings and opportunities and to ask themselves whether in all candor they do not feel they are blessed beyond the generation that has gone before them, the hardy pioneers of this country.

This book could easily be filled by the recital of such heroic acts, varying only in detail and perhaps in tragic results; yet would only show in fact the ready, resourceful tact of the pioneers of those days.

I want to repeat here again that I do not look upon that generation of men and women as superior to the present generation, except in this: The pioneers had lost a large number of physically weak on the trip, thus applying the great law of the survival of the fittest; and further, that the great number were pioneers in the true sense of the word—frontiersmen for generations before —hence were by training and habits eminently fitted to meet the emergencies of the trip and conditions to follow.

One of the incidents of this trip should be related to perpetuate the memory of heroic actions of the times, that of the famous ride across these mountains and to Olympia, of Mrs. Catherine Frazier, one of this party, on an ox.

Three days after arrival, Mrs. Frazier gave birth to the third white child born in Pierce County, Washington Frazier, named after the great territory that had been chosen for the home of the parents and descendants.

The first report, that the "mother and son were doing well," can again and again be repeated, as both * are yet alive, the mother now past seventy-three and the son fifty, and both yet residing at South Bay, near Olympia, where the parents settled soon after arrival.

The curious part of such incidents is the perfect unconsciousness of the parties, of having done anything

---

*Since these lines were penned Mrs. Frasier has joined the majority of that generation in the life beyond.

that would be handed down to posterity as exhibiting any spirit of fortitude or of having performed any heroic act. The young bride could not walk, neither could she be taken into the wagons, and she *could* ride an ox, and so without ceremony, mounted her steed and fell into the procession without attracting especial attention or passing remark. Doubtless the lady, at the time, would have shrunk from any undue notice, because of her mount, and would have preferred a more appropriate entry into the future capitol of the future State, but it is now quite probable that she looks upon the act with a feeling akin to pride, and in any event, not with feelings of mortification or false pride that possibly, at the time, might have lurked within her breast.

The birth of children was not an infrequent incident on the plains, the almost universal report following, "doing as well as could be expected," the trip being resumed with but very short interruption, the little ones being soon exhibited with the usual motherly pride.

CHAPTER XIII.

Trip Through the Natchess Pass—Continued.

Readers of previous chapters will remember the lonely camp mentioned and the steep mountain ahead of it to reach the summit.

What with the sweat incident to the day's travel, the chill air of an October night in the mountains, with but half of a three-point blanket as covering and the ground for a mattress, small wonder my muscles were a little stiffened when I arose and prepared for the ascent to the summit. Bobby had, as I have said, been restless during the night, and, when the roll of blankets and the hard bread was securely strapped on behind, suddenly turned his face homeward, evidently not relishing the fare of browse for supper. He seemingly had concluded he had had enough of the trip, and started to go home, trotting off gaily down the mountain. I could do nothing else but follow him, as the narrow cut of the road and impenetrable obstructions on either side utterly precluded my getting past to head off his rascally maneuvers. Finally, finding a nip of grass by the roadside, the gait was slackened so that after several futile attempts I managed to get a firm hold of his tail, after which we went down the mountain together much more rapidly than we had come up the evening before. Bobby forgot to use his heels, else he might for a longer time been master of the situation. The fact was, he did not want to hurt me, but was determined to break up the partnership, and, so far as he was concerned, go no further into the mountains where he could not get a supper. By dint of persuasion and main strength of muscle the contest was finally settled in my favor, and I secured the rein. Did I chastise him? Not a bit. I did not blame him. We were partners, but it was a one-sided partnership, as he had no interest in the enterprise other

than to get enough to eat as we went along, and when
that failed, rebelled.

It is wonderful, the sagacity of the horse or ox. They
know more than we usually think they do. Let one be
associated (yes, that's the word, associated), with them
for a season alone. Their characteristics come to the
front and become apparent without study. Did I talk
to my friend, Bobby? Indeed, I did. There were but
few other animate things to talk to. Perhaps one might
see a small bird flit across the vision or a chipmunk, or
hear the whirr of the sudden flight of the grouse, but all
else was solitude, deep and impressive. The dense forest through which I was passing did not supply conditions for bird or animal life in profusion.

"You are a naughty lad, Bobby," I said, as I turned
his head eastward to retrace the mile or so of the truant's
run.

We were soon past our camping ground of the night
before, and on our way up the mountain. Bobby would
not be led, or if he was, would hold back, till finally
making a rush up the steep ascent, would be on my heels
or toes before I could get out of the way. "Go ahead,
Bobby," I would say, and suiting action to words seize
the tail with a firm grasp and follow. When he moved
rapidly, by holding on, I was helped up the mountain.
When he slackened his pace, then came the resting spell.
The engineering instinct of the horse tells him how to
reduce grades by angles. So Bobby led me up the mountain in zig-zag courses, I following always, with the
firm grasp of the tail that meant we would not part
company, and we did not. I felt that it was a mean trick
to compel the poor brute to pull me up the mountain
by his tail, supperless, breakfastless, and discontented.
It appeared to me it was just cause to sever our friendship, which by this time seemed cemented closely, but
then I thought of the attempted abandonment he had
been guilty of, and that perhaps he should submit to
some indignities at my hand in consequence.

By noon we had surmounted all obstacles, and stood upon the summit prairie—one of them, for there are several—where Bobby feasted to his heart's content, while I—well, it was the same old story, hard tack and cheese, with a small allotment of dried venison.

To the south apparently but a few miles distant, the old mountain, Rainier of old, Tacoma by Winthrop, loomed up into the clouds full ten thousand feet higher than where I stood, a grand scene to behold, worthy of all the effort expended to attain this view point. But I was not attuned to view with ecstasy the grandeur of what lay before me, but rather to scan the horizon to ascertain if I could, what the morrow might bring forth. The mountain to the pioneer has served as a huge barometer to foretell the weather. "How is the mountain this morning?" the farmer asks in harvest time. "Has the mountain got his night cap on?" the housewife inquires before her wash is hung on the line. The Indian would watch the mountain with intent to determine whether he might expect *"snass"* (rain), or *"kull snass"* (hail), or *"t'kope snass"* (snow), and seldom failed in his conclusions, and so I scanned the mountain top that day partially hid in the clouds, with forebodings verified at night fall, as will be related later.

The next camp was in the Natchess Canyon. I had lingered on the summit prairie to give the pony a chance to fill up on the luxuriant but rather washy grass, there found in great abundance. For myself, I had had plenty of water, but had been stinted in hard bread, remembering my experience of the day before, with the famishing women and children. I began to realize more and more, the seriousness of my undertaking, particularly so, because I could hear no tidings. A light snow storm came on just before nightfall, which, with the high mountains on either side of the river, spread approaching darkness rapidly. I was loth to camp; somehow I just wanted to go on, and doubtless would have traveled all

night if I could have safely found my way. The canyon
was but a few hundred yards wide, with the tortuous
river first striking one bluff and then the other, neces-
sitating- numerous crossings; the intervening space
being glade land of large pine growth with but light
undergrowth and few fallen trees. The whole surface
was covered with coarse sand, in which rounded boulders
were imbedded so thick in places as to cause the trail
to be very indistinct, particularly in open spots, where
the snow had fallen unobstructed. Finally, I saw that
I must camp, and after crossing the river, came out in
an opening where the bear tracks were so thick that
one could readily believe the spot to be a veritable play
ground for all the animals round about.

I found two good sized trunks of trees that had fallen;
one obliquely across the other, and, with my pony tethered as a sentinel and my fire as an advance post, I
slept soundly, but nearly supperless. The black bears
on the west slope of the mountain I knew were timid
and not dangerous, but I did not know so much about
the mountain species, and can but confess that I felt
lonesome, though placing great reliance upon my fire,
which I kept burning all night

Early next morning found Bobby and me on the trail,
a little chilled with the cold mountain air and very willing to travel. In a hundred yards or so, we came upon
a ford of ice cold water to cross, and others following
in such quick succession, that I realized that we were
soon to leave the canyon. I had been told that at the
32nd crossing I would leave the canyon and ascend a
high mountain, and then travel through pine glades,
and that I must then be careful and not lose the trail.
I had not kept strict account of the crossings like one
of the men I had met, who cut a notch in his goad stick
at every crossing, but I knew instinctively we were
nearly out, and so I halted to eat what I supposed would
be the only meal of the day, not dreaming what lay in

store for me at nightfall. It would be uninteresting to the general reader to relate the details of that day's travel, and in fact I cannot recall much about it, except going up the steep mountain; so steep that Bobby again practiced his engineering instincts and I mine, with my selfish hand having a firm hold of the tail of my now patient comrade.

From the top of the mountain grade I looked back in wonderment about how the immigrants had taken their wagons down; I found out by experience afterwards.

Toward nightfall I heard a welcome sound of the tinkling of a bell, and soon saw the smoke of camp fires, and finally the village of tents and grime covered wagons. How I tugged at Bobby's halter to make him go faster, and then mounted him with not much better results, can better be imagined than told.

Could it be the camp I was searching for? It was about the number of wagons and tents that I had expected to meet. No. I was doomed to disappointment, yet rejoiced to find some one to camp with and talk to other than the pony.

It is not easy to describe the cordial greeting accorded me by those tired and almost discouraged immigrants. If we had been near and dear relatives, the rejoicing could not have been mutually greater. They had been toiling for nearly five months on the road across the plains, and now there loomed up before them this great mountain range to cross. Could they do it? If we cannot get over with our wagons, can we get the women and children through in safety? I was able to lift a load of doubt and fear from off their jaded minds. Before I knew what was happening, I caught the fragrance of boiling coffee and of fresh meat cooking. It seemed the good matrons knew without telling that I was hungry (I doubtless looked it), and had set to work to prepare me a meal, a sumptuous meal at that, taking into account the whetted appetite incident to a diet of hard bread straight, and not much of that either, for two days.

We had met on the hither bank of the Yakima River, where the old trail crosses that river near where the flourishing city of North Yakima now is. These were the people, a part of them, that are mentioned elsewhere in the chapter on the White River massacre. Harvey H. Jones, wife and three children, and George E. King, wife and one child. One of the little boys of the camp is the same person—John I. King—who has written the graphic account of the tragedy that follows, in which his mother and step father and their neighbors lost their lives—that horrible massacre on White River a year later, and the other, George E. King, (but no relation) the little five-year-old who was taken and held captive for nearly four months, and then safely delivered over by the Indians to the military authorities at Fort Steilacoom. I never think of those people but with feelings of sadness; of their struggle, doubtless the supreme effort of their lives, to go to their death. I pointed out to them where to go to get good claims, and they lost no time, but went straight to the locality recommended and immediately to work, preparing shelter for the winter.

"Are you going out on those plains alone?" asked Mrs. Jones, anxiously. When informed that I would have the pony with me, a faint, sad smile spread over her countenance as she said, "Well, I don't think it is safe." Mr. Jones explained that what his wife referred to was the danger from the ravenous wolves that infested the open country, and from which they had lost weakened stock from their bold forages, "right close to the camp," he said, and advised me not to camp near the watering places, but up on the high ridge. I followed his advice with the result as we shall see of missing my road and losing considerable time, and causing me not a little trouble and anxiety.

CHAPTER XIV.

Trip Through the Natchess Pass—Continued.

The start for the high table desert lands bordering the Yakima valley cut me loose from all communication, for no more immigrants were met until I reached the main traveled route beyond the Columbia River. I speak of the "desert lands" adjacent to the Yakima from the standpoint of that day. We all thought these lands were worthless, as well as the valley, not dreaming of the untold wealth the touch of water would bring out. The road lay through a forbidding sage plain, or rather an undulating country, seemingly of shifting sands and dead grass of comparatively scant growth. As the sun rose the heat became intolerable. The dust brought vivid memories of the trip across the plains in places. The heated air trembling in the balance brought the question of whether or not something was the matter with my eyes or brain; whether this was an optical illusion, or real, became a debatable question in my mind. Strive against it with all my might, my eyes would rest on the farther horizon to catch the glimpse of the expected train, till they fairly ached. Added to this, an intolerable thirst seized upon me, and compelled leaving the road and descending into the valley for water. Here I found as fat cattle as ever came to a butcher's stall, fed on this self same dead grass, cured without rain. These cattle belonged to the Indians, but there were no Indians in sight. The incident, though, set me to thinking about the possibilities of a country that could produce such fat cattle from the native grasses. I must not linger off the trail, and take chances of missing the expected train, and so another stretch of travel, of thirst, and suffering came until during the afternoon, I found water

on the trail, and tethered my pony for his much needed
dinner, and opened my sack of hard bread to count the
contents, with the conclusion that my store was half
gone, and so lay down in the shade of a small tree or
bush near the spring to take an afternoon nap. Rousing up before sun down, refreshed, we (pony and I),
took the trail in a much better mood than before the
nooning. When night came, I could not find it in my
heart to camp. The cool of the evening invigorated the
pony, and we pushed on. Without having intended to
travel in the night, I had, so to speak, drifted into it
and finding the road could be followed, though but
dimly seen, kept on the way until a late hour, when I
unsaddled and hobbled the pony. The saddle blanket
was brought into use, and I was soon off in dream land,
and forgot all about the dust, the train or the morrow.

Morning brought a puzzling sense of helplessness that
for the time, seemed overpowering. I had slept late, and
awoke to find the pony had wandered far off on the hill
side, in fact, so far, it required close scanning to discover him. To make matters worse, his hobbles had
became loosened, giving him free use of all his feet, and
in no mood to take the trail again. Coaxing was of no
avail, driving would do no good, so embracing an opportunity to seize his tail again, we went around about
over the plain and through the sage brush in a rapid
gait, which finally lessened and I again became master
of him. For the life of me I could not be sure as to the
direction of the trail, but happened to take the right
course. When the trail was found, the question came
as to the whereabouts of the saddle. It so happened
that I took the wrong direction and had to retrace my
steps. The sun was high when we started on our journey.

A few hundred yards travel brought feelings of uneasiness, as it was evident that we were not on the
regular trail. Not knowing but this was some cut off,

so continued until the Columbia River bluff was reached, and the great river was in sight, half a mile distant, and several hundred feet of lower level. Taking a trail down the bluff that seemed more promising than the wagon tracks, I began to search for the road at the foot of the bluff to find the tracks scattered, and any resemblance of a road gone; in a word, I was lost. I never knew how those wagon tracks came to be there, but I know that I lost more than a half day's precious time, and again was thrown in a doubting mood as to whether I had missed the long sought for train.

The next incident I remember vividly, was my attempt to cross the Columbia just below the mouth of Snake River. I had seen but very few Indians on the whole trip, and in fact, the camp I found there on the bank of the great river was the first I distinctly remember. I could not induce them to cross me over. From some cause they seemed surly and unfriendly. The treatment was so in contrast to what I had received from the Indians on the Sound, that I could not help wondering what it meant. No one, to my knowledge, lost his life by the hands of the Indians that season, but the next summer all, or nearly all, were ruthlessly murdered that ventured into that country unprotected.

That night I camped late, opposite Wallula (old Fort Walla Walla), in a sand storm of great fury. I tethered my pony this time, rolled myself up in the blanket, only to find myself fairly buried in the drifting sand in the morning. It required a great effort to creep out of the blanket, and greater work to relieve the blanket from the accumulated sand. By this time the wind had laid and comparative calm prevailed, and then came the effort to make myself heard across the wide river to the people of the fort. It did seem as though I would fail. Traveling up and down the river bank for half a mile, or so, in the hopes of catching a favorable breeze to carry my voice to the fort, yet, all to no avail. I sat upon the bank hopelessly discouraged, not knowing what to do. I think I must have been two hours halloaing at the top of my voice until hoarse from the violent effort. Finally, while sitting there, cogitating as to what to do, I spied a blue smoke arising from the cabin, and soon after a man appeared who immediately responded to my renewed efforts to attract attention. The trouble had been they were all asleep, while I was in the early morning expending my breath.

Shirley Ensign, of Olympia, had established a ferry across the Columbia River, and had yet lingered to set over belated immigrants, if any came. Mr. Ensign came over and gave me glad tidings. He had been out on the trail fifty miles or more, and had met my people, whom he thought were camped some thirty miles away, and thought that they would reach the ferry on the following day. But I would not wait, and, procuring a fresh horse, I started out in a cheerful mood, determined to reach camp that night if my utmost exertions would accomplish it. Sundown came and no signs of camp; dusk drew on, and still no signs; finally, I spied some cattle grazing on the upland, and soon came upon the camp in a ravine that had shut them out from view. Rejoicing and outbursts of grief followed. I inquired for my mother the first thing. She was not there; had been buried in the sands of the Platte Valley, months before; also a younger brother lay buried near Independence rock. The scene that followed is of too sacred memory to write about, and we will draw the veil of privacy over it.

Of that party, all are under the sod save two—Mrs. Lulu Packard, now of Portland, Oregon, and Mrs. Amanda C. Spinning, then the wife of the elder brother so often heretofore mentioned.

With fifty odd head of stock, seven wagons, and seventeen people, the trip was made to the Sound without serious mishap or loss. We were twenty-two days on

the road, and thought this was good time to make, all
things considered. Provisions were abundant, the
health of the party good, and stock in fair condition.
I unhesitatingly advised the over-mountain trip; meanwhile cautioning them to expect some snow, a goodly
amount of hard labor, and plenty of vexation. How
long will it take? Three weeks. Why, we thought we
were about through. Well, you came to stay with us,
did you? But what about the little wife and the two
babies on the island home? Father said some one must
go and look after them. So, the elder brother was detailed to go to the island folks, whilst I was impressed
into service to take his place with the immigrants. It
would hardly be interesting to the general reader to
give a detailed account, even if I remembered it well,
which I do not. So intent did we all devote our energies
to the one object, to get safely over the mountains, that
all else was forgotten. It was a period of severe toil
and anxious care, but not more so than to others that
had gone before us, and what others had done we felt
we could do, but there was no eight-hour-a-day labor,
nor any drones; all were workers. I had prepared the
minds of the new-comers for the worst, not forgetting
the steep hills, the notched logs, and rough, stony fords,
by telling the whole story. But do you really think we
can get through? said father. Yes, I know we can, if
every man will put his shoulder to the wheel. This latter
expression was a phrase in use to indicate doing one's
duty without flinching, but in this case, it had a more
literal meaning, for we were compelled often to take
hold of the wheels to boost the wagons over logs, and
ease them down on the opposite side, as likewise, on the
steep mountain side. We divided our force into groups;
one to each wagon to drive, four as wheelmen as we
called them, and father with the women folks on foot,
or on horseback, with the stock.

God bless the women folks of the plains; the immigrant women, I mean. A nobler, braver, more uncomplaining people were never known. I have often thought that some one ought to write a just tribute to their valor and patience; a book of their heroic deeds. I know this word valor, is supposed to apply to men and not to women, but I know that the immigrant women earned the right to have the word, and all it implies, applied to them. Such a trip with all its trials is almost worth the price to bring out these latent virtues of the so called weaker sex. Strive, however, as best we could, we were unable to make the trip in the alloted time, and willing hands came out with the brother to put *their* shoulders to the wheels, and to bring the glad tidings that all was well on the island home, and to release the younger brother and the father from further duty, when almost through to the settlements.

Do you say this was enduring great hardships? That depends upon the point of view. As to this return trip, for myself, I can truly say that it was not. I enjoyed the strife to overcome all difficulties, and so did the greater number of the company. They felt that it was a duty and enjoyed doing their duty. Many of them, it is true, were weakened by the long trip across the plains, but with the better food obtainable, and the goal so near at hand, there was a positive pleasure to pass over the miles, one by one, and become assured that final success was only a matter of a very short time.

One day, we encountered a new fallen tree, as one of the men said, a whopper, cocked up on its own upturned roots, four feet from the ground. Go around it, we could not; to cut it out seemed an endless task with our dulled, flimsy saw. Dig down, boys, said the father, and in short order every available shovel was out of the wagons and into willing hands, with others standing by to take their turn. In a short time the way was open fully four feet deep, and oxen and wagons passed through under the obstruction.

CHAPTER XV.

Trip Through the Natchess Pass—Continued.

People now traversing what is popularly known as Nisqually Plains, that is, the stretch of open prairie, interpersed with clumps of timber, sparkling lakes, and glade lands, from the heavy timber bordering the Puyallup to a like border of the Nisqually, will hardly realize that once upon a time these bare gravelly prairies supplied a rich grass of exceeding fattening quality of sufficient quantity to support many thousand head of stock, and not only support but fatten them ready for the butcher's stall. Nearly half a million acres of this land lie between the two rivers, from two to four hundred feet above tide level and beds of the rivers mentioned, undulating and in benches, an ideal park of shade and open land of rivulets and lakes, of natural roads and natural scenery of splendor.

So, when our little train emerged from the forests skirting the Puyallup Valley, and came out on the open at Montgomery's, afterwards Camp Montgomery, of Indian war times, twelve miles southeasterly of Fort Steilacoom, the experience was almost as if one had come into a noonday sun from a dungeon prison, so marked was the contrast. Hundreds of cattle, sheep and horses were quietly grazing, scattered over the landscape, as far as one could see, fat and content. It is not to be wondered that the spirits of the tired party should rise as they saw this scene of content before them, and thought they could become participants with those who had come before them, and that for the moment rest was theirs if that was what they might choose,

Fort Nisqually was about ten miles south-westerly from our camp at Montgomery's, built, as mentioned elsewhere, by the Hudson Bay Company, in 1833.

In 1840-41, this company's holdings at Nisqually and Cowlitz were transfered to the Puget Sound Agricultural Company. This latter company was organized in London at the instance of Dr. Wilham F. Tolmie, who visited that city to conduct the negotiations in person with the directors of the Hudson Bay Company. He returned clothed with the power to conduct the affairs of the new company, but under the direction of the Hudson Bay Company, and with the restriction not to enter into or interfere with the fur trade; he later became the active agent of both companies at Nisqually.

It was principally the stock of this company that we saw from our camp and near by points. At that time, the Agricultural Company had several farms on these plains, considerable pasture land enclosed, and fourteen thousand head of stock running at large; sheep, cattle, and horses.

The United States government actually paid rent to this foreign company for many years for the site where Fort Steilacoom was located for account of the shadowy title of the company under the treaty of 1846.

During this lapse of time, from 1833 to the time our camp was established, many of the company's servants time had expired and in almost every case, such had taken to themselves Indian wives and had squatted on the choice locations for grazing or small farming. Montgomery himself, near whose premises we were camping, was one of these. A few miles to the south of this place, ran the small creek "Muck," on the surface for several miles to empty into the Nisqually. Along this little creek, others of these discharged servants had settled, and all taken Indian wives. These were the settlers that were afterwards denounced by Governor Stevens, and finally arrested for alleged treason, as is fully set

out in other chapters.   Each of these had abundance
of stock and farm produce, and was living in affluence
and comfort.   One of these, reputed to be the rightful
owner of thirteen cows, one summer raised thirty-three
calves, the handy lasso rope having been brought into
play among the company's herds in secluded places;
yet, as the rule, these people were honorable, upright
men, though as a class, not of high intelligence, or of
sober habits.

Added to this class just mentioned, was another; the
discharged United States soldiers.   The men then comprising the United States army were far below in moral
worth and character than now.   Many of these men
had also taken Indian wives and settled where they had
chosen to select.   Added to these were a goodly number
of the previous years' immigrants.   By this recital the
reader will be apprised of the motley mess our little
party were destined to settle among, unless they should
choose to go to other parts of the Territory.   I did not
myself fully realize the complications to be met until
later years.

All this while, as we have said, settlers were crowd-
ing into the district, taking up donation claims until
that act expired by limitation in 1854, and afterwards
by squatter's rights, which to all appearances, seemed
as good as any.   My own donation claim afterwards was
involved in this controversy, in common with many
others.   Although our proofs of settlement were made
and all requirements of the law complied with, nevertheless, our patents were held up and our title questioned
for twenty years, and so, after having made the trip
across the plains, because Uncle Sam had promised to
give us all a farm, and after having made the required
improvements and resided on the land for the four years,
then to be crowded off without title did seem a little
rough on the pioneers.

I have before me one of the notices served upon the

settlers by the company's agent which tells the whole
story.* The then thriving town of Steilacoom was involved, as likewise part of the lands set apart for the
Indian Reservation, and it did seem as though it would
be hard to get a more thorough mix-up as to titles of the
land, than these knotty questions presented.

All this while, as was natural there should be, there
was constant friction between some settler and the company, and had it not been for the superior tact of such
a man as Dr. Tolmie in charge of the company's affairs,
there would have been serious trouble.

As it was, there finally came a show of arms when the
company undertook to survey the boundary line to in-
close the land claimed, although the acreage was much
less than claimed on paper. But the settlers, (or some
of them), rebelled, and six of them went armed to the
party of surveyors at work and finally stopped them.
An old-time friend, John McLeod, was one of the party
(mob, the company called it), but the records do not
show whether he read his chapter in the Bible that day,
or whether instead, he took a double portion of whiskey
to relieve his conscience.

It is doubtful whether the old man thought he was
doing wrong or thought anything about it, except that
he had a belief that somehow or other a survey might
make against him getting a title to his own claim.

ORIGINAL WARNING TO THOMAS HADLEY.

We hereby certify that a correct copy of the within notice was presented
to T. Hadley by Mr. Wm. Greig this 6th day of April, 1857.   . .

WILLIAM GREIG.
ALFRED McNEILL.
AMBROSE SKINNER.

Nisqually, W. T., 12th March, 1857.

To Mr. Thomas Hadley.—Sir: I hereby warn you that, in cultivating land
and making other improvements on your present location in or near the Tal-
entire precinct, Pierce County, Washington Territory, you are trespassing on
the lands confirmed to the Puget's Sound Agricultural Company by the
Boundary Treaty, ratified in July. 1846, between Great Britain and the
United States of America. Very Respectfully

Your Obed't Servt.,

W. F. TOLMIE.

Agent Puget's Sound Agricultural Company.

I had similar experience at a later date with the
Indians near the Muckleshute Reservation, as elsewhere
related, while attempting to extend the sub-divisional
lines of the township near where the reserve was located.
I could not convince the Indians that the survey meant
no harm to them.

The case was different in the first instance, as in fact,
neither party was acting within the limits of their legal
rights, and for the time being, the strongest and most
belligerent prevailed, but only to be circumvented at a
little later date by a secret completion of the work, sufficient to platting the whole.

All this while the little party was halting. The father
said the island home would not do, and as he had come
two thousand miles to live neighbors, I must give up
my claim and take another near theirs, and so, aband-
oning over a year's hard work, I acted upon his request
with the result told elsewhere, of fleeing from our new
chosen home, as we supposed, to save our lives, upon the
outbreak of the Indian War in less than a year from
the time of the camp mentioned.

One can readily see that these surroundings did not
promise that compact, staid settlement of energetic, wide
awake pioneers we so coveted, nevertheless, the promise
of money returns was good, and that served to allay any
discontent that would otherwise arise. I remember the
third year we began selling eighteen months' old steers
at fifty dollars each, off the range that had never been
fed a morsel. Our butter sold for fifty cents a pound,
and at times, seventy-five cents, and many other things
at like prices. No wonder all hands soon became contented; did not have time to be otherwise.

It came about though, that we were in considerable
part a community within ourselves, yet, there were
many excellent people in the widely scattered settlements. The conditions to some extent encouraged lawlessness, and within the class already mentioned, a good

deal of drunkenness and what one might well designate as loose morals, incident to the surroundings. A case in point:

A true, though one might say a humorous, story is told on Doctor Tolmie, or one of his men, of visiting a settler where they knew one of their beeves had been slaughtered and appropriated. To get direct evidence he put himself in the way of an invitation to dinner, where, sure enough, the fresh, fat beef was smoking on the table. The good old pioneer (I knew him well), asked a good, old-fashioned Methodist blessing over the meat, giving thanks for the bountiful supply of the many good things of the world vouchsafed to him and his neighbors, and thereupon in true pioneer hospitality, cut a generous sized piece of the roast for his guest, the real owner of the meat.

This incident occurred just as here related, and although the facts are as stated, yet we must not be too ready to scoff at our religious friend and condemn him without a hearing. To me, it would have been just as direct thieving as any act could have been, and yet, to our sanctified friend I think it was not, and upon which thereby hangs a tale.

Many of the settlers looked upon the company as interlopers, pure and simple, without any rights they were bound to respect. There had been large numbers of cattle and sheep run on the range and had eaten the feed down, which they thought was robbing them of their right of eminent domain for the land they claimed the government had promised to give them.

The cattle become very wild, in great part on account of the settlers' actions, but the curious part was they afterwards justified themselves from the fact that they were wild, and so it happened there came very near being claim of common property of the company's stock, with not a few of the settlers.

One lawless act is almost sure to breed another, and

there was no exception to the rule in this strange community, and many is the settler that can remember the disappearance of stock which could be accounted for in but one way—gone with the company's herd. In a few years, though, all this disappeared. The incoming immigrants from across the plains were a sturdy set as a class, and soon frowned down such a loose code of morals.

For a moment let us turn to the little camp on the edge of the prairie, of seven wagons and three tents. There came a time it must be broken up. No more camp fires, with the fragrant coffee morning and evening; no more smoking the pipe together over jests, or serious talk; no more tucks in the dresses of the ladies, compelled first by the exigencies of daily travel and now to be parted with under the inexorable law of custom or fashion; no more lumps of butter at night, churned during the day by the movement of wagon and the can containing the morning's milk. We must hie us off to prepare shelter from the coming storms of winter; to the care of the stock; the preparations for planting; to the beginning of a new life of independence.

CHAPTER XVI.

Trip Through the Natchess Pass—Concluded.

It almost goes without saying, that before the final break up of the camp and separation of the parties there must be some sort of a celebration of the event, a sort of house warming or surprise party—something must be done out of the usual course of events. So, what better could these people do than to visit the island * home they had heard so much about, and see for themselves some of the wonder land described.

My cabin stood on the south side of the bight or lagoon within stone throw of where the United States penitentiary now stands and only a few feet above high tide level. The lagoon widens and deepens from the entrance and curves to the south with gentle slope on either side, the whole forming a miniature sheltered valley of light, timbered, fertile land. On the higher levels of the receding shore, great quantities of the sallal and high bush huckleberries grew in profusion, interspersed with what for lack of a better name we called Sweet Bay, the perfumes from the leaves of which permeated the atmosphere for long distances. In the near by front a long flat or sandy beach extended far out from the high tide line where the clams spouted in countless numbers, and crows played their antics of breaking the shell by dropping to the stony beach the helpless bivalve they had stealthily clutched and taken to flight with them.

Off to the eastward and three miles distant the town of Steilacoom, or rather the two towns, loomed up like

---

*McNeil Island, twelve miles westerly as the crow flies from Tacoma.

quite a city, on the ascending slope of the shore, to' make us feel after all we were not so far off from civilization, particularly at the time as two or more deep sea vessels, (ships we called them) were in port discharging merchandise. South-easterly, the grand mountain, before mentioned, rose so near three miles high above the tide level that that was the height spoken by all and as being fifty miles distant.

Nisqually House, on the arm of the bay known as Nisqually Reach, five miles distant, could be seen in clear weather, while the Hudson Bay Fort of that name was hidden from view by intervening timber, two miles easterly from the beach.

The Medicine Creek council grounds, afterwards made famous by the treaty council held a few months later than the date of which I am writing, lay across the Nisqually tide flats, south from Nisqually House, near three miles distant, but the view of this was cut off by an intervening island (Anderson), of several sections in extent, and of varying elevations to a maximum of near four hundred feet.

Fortunately one of those "spells" of weather had settled over the whole country, a veritable Indian Summer, though now bordering on the usually stormy month of November, a little hazy, just enough to lend enchantment to the landscape, and warm enough to add pleasurable experience to the trip the little party was to make. Add to these surroundings, the smooth glassy waters of the bay, interspersed here and there by streaks and spots of troubled water to vary the outlook, small wonder that enthusiasm ran high as the half-rested immigrants neared the cabin in their boat and canoe, chartered for the trip, piloted and paddled by the Indians and supplemented by the awkward stroke of the landlubber's oar.

"What in the world are we going to do with all these people?" I said to the little wife, half apologetically, partly quizzical and yet with a tinge of earnestness illy concealed.

"Oh, never mind, we will get along all right some way; I'll venture father has brought a tent." And sure enough, the party had brought the three tents that had served them so well for so long a time, on the long journey, and much of their bedding also.

Father had been over to the cabin before, and taken the measurement.

"Eighteen feet square," he said, "that's a pretty, good size, but I don't see why you boys didn't build it higher; it's scant seven feet."

Yes, the walls were but seven feet high. When building, the logs ran out, the sky was threatening and we had a race with the storm to get a roof over our heads.

"But that's a good fireplace," he continued; "there must be pretty good clay here to hold these round stones so firmly. And that's as good a cat-and-clay chimney as I had in Ohio, only mine was taller, but I don't see that it would draw any better than this." This one was just nine feet high, but I said there was plenty of room to build it higher.

The floor was rough lumber, or had been when laid, but the stiff scrub brush of twigs and strong arms of house cleaners had worn off the rough till when cleaned it presented a quite creditable appearance. And the walls! "Why, you have a good library on these walls; all the reading matter right side up too; the Tribune is a great paper, indeed; you must have sent for it right away when you got here," and so I had, and continued steadily for eighteen years, and thereby hangs a tale, which, though a digression I will tell before writing more about our visitors.

Eighteen years after my arrival from across the plains in October, 1852, I made my first trip to the "States," to our old home and to New York. I had to go through the mud to the Columbia River, then out over the dreaded bar to the Pacific Ocean, and to San Francisco, then on a seven days' journey over the Central, Union Pacific and connecting lines and sit bolt upright all the way—no sleeper cars then, no diners either, that I remember seeing. I remember I started from Olympia on this trip the first week in December. Mr. ——— Woodard of Olympia suggested that we gather all the varieties of flowers obtainable in the open air and that I press them in the leaves of my pamphlets (presently to be mentioned), and in that way to dry and press them, so I might exhibit the product of our wonderful mild climate up to the month of December. We succeeded in getting fifty-two varieties then in bloom in the open air, and all were well dried and preserved when I arrived at my original starting place, Eddyville, Iowa. Here, loving friends, Mrs. Elizabeth Male, (Aunt Lib, we call her now) and a little sprightly youngster, Miss Molly Male, the well-known teacher in Tacoma, artistically arranged my treasures on tinted paper ready for exhibition upon my arrival in New York.

I had written an eighty page pamphlet (long since out of print), descriptive of Washington Territory, and my friend E. T. Gunn, of the Olympia Transcript, printed them—five thousand copies—most of which I took with me. The late Beriah Brown gave me a letter of introduction to his old-time friend, Horace Greeley, to whom I presented it and was kindly received and commended to chairman Ely of the New York Farmer's Club, and by him given an opportunity to exhibit my flowers, speak to the club about our country and tell them about our climate. This little talk was widely circulated through the proceedings of the club printed in a number of the great papers, among them the Tribune.

This coming to the notice of Jay Cooke, of Northern Pacific fame, with his six power presses just started at

Philadelphia to advertise the Northern Pacific route,
I was called to his presence and closely questioned,
and finally complimented by the remark that he "did not
think they could afford to have any opposition in the
field of advertising," took up my whole edition and sent
them on their way to his various financial agencies.

In the chapter, "The Morning School," the sequel to
this story will be given, and so now we must return to
the party at the island home.

Our visitors were all soon at home with their tents up,
their blankets out airing, the camp fires lit and with an
abandon truly refreshing turned out like children from
school to have a good time. The garden, of course, was
drawn upon and "such delicious vegetables I never
saw before," fell from a dozen lips, during the stay.
That turnip patch was planted in September. "Why,
that beats anything I *ever* saw," father said, and as
insignificent an incident as it may seem, had a decided
effect upon the minds of the party. "Why, here they are
growing in November. At home (Iowa) they would
by this time be frozen as solid as a brick." "Why, these
are the finest flavored potatoes I *ever* saw," said another.
The little wife had a row of sweet peas growing near
by the cabin that shed fragrance to the innermost corner and to the tents, and supplied bouquets for the tables, and plenty of small talk comparing them with
those "in the States."

And so the little garden, the sweet peas, and other
flowers wild and cultivated, brought contentment among
those who at first had had a feeling of despondency and
disappointment.

Didn't we have clam bakes? I should say! And didn't
the women folks come in loaded with berries? And,
what whoppers of huckleberry puddings, and huckleberry pies and all sorts of good things that ingenuity of
the housewives could conjure up.

I had frequently seen deer trotting on the beach and told my visitors so, but somehow they could not so readily find them—had been too noisy, but soon a fat buck was bagged, and the cup of joy was full, the feast was on.

My visitors could not understand, and neither could I, how it came that a nearby island (Anderson) of a few sections in extent, could contain a lake of clear, fresh water several hundred feet above tide level, and that this lake should have neither inlet nor outlet. It was on the margin of this lake that the first deer was killed and nearby where the elder brother had staked his claim.

Mowich Man, an Indian whom I have known for many years, and, by the way, one of those interfering with the survey of Muckleshute, as related elsewhere, was then one of our neighbors, or at least, frequently passed our cabin with his canoe and people. He was a great hunter, a crack shot, and an all round Indian of good parts, by the standard applicable to his race. Many is the saddle of venison that this man has brought me in the lapse of years. He was not a man of any particular force of character, but his steadfast friendship has always impressed me as to the worth, from our own standpoint, of this race to which he belonged. While our friends were with us visiting, my Indian friend came along and as usual brought a nice ham of venison to the camp, and at my suggestion, went with the younger men of the visitors to where their first exploit of hunting bore fruit. Our young men came back with loud praise on their lips for the Indian hunter. There was nothing specially noteworthy in the incident only as illustrating what, to a great extent, was going on all over the settled portion of the Territory leading up to a better understanding between the two races. I can safely say that none of the pioneers was without what might be designated as a favorite Indian, that is, an Indian who was particular to gain the good will of his

chosen friend, and 'in most cases would assume, or custom would bring about, the adoption of the white man's
name and the Indian would ever afterwards be known
by his new name.   Mowich Man, however, like Leschi,
as we shall see later, while friendly to the whites was
possessed of a more independent spirit.   Some of Mowich Man's people were fine singers, and in fact his
camp, or his canoe if traveling, was always the center
for song and merriment, but it is a curious fact one
seldom can get the Indian music by asking for it, but
rather must wait for its spontaneous outburst.   But
Indian songs in those days came out from nearly every
nook and corner and seemed to pervade the whole country, so much that we often and often could hear the songs ·
and accompanying stroke of the paddle long before our
eyes would rest on the floating canoes.

Will the reader in his mind dwell on the hardships of
the pioneers, or will he rather look upon the brighter
side, that the so called hardships were simply the drill
that developed the manhood and womanhood, to make
better men and better women, because they had faced
a duty they could not shirk, and were thereby profited?
Neither did the pioneers as a class want to shirk a
duty and those of the later generation who have poured
out their sympathy for the hardships of the poor pioneers may as well save some of it for the present generation, the drones of the community that see no pleasure
in the stern duties of life.   But I must have done with
these reflections to resume my story, now nearly ended,
of the visitors at the island home and of the long trip.

Never did kings or queens enjoy their palaces more,
nor millionaires their princely residences, than the
humble immigrant party did the cabin and tents in
their free and luxurious life.   Queens might have their
jewels, but did we not have ours? Did we not have our
two babies, "the nicest, smartest, cutest in all the
world?" Did we not have a profusion of fresh air to

inhale at every breath, and appetites that made every morsel of food of exquisite flavor?

But we were all far away from what all yet thought of as home, and admonished that winter was coming on and that after a short season of recreation and rest we must separate, each to his task, and which we did, and the great trip was ended. The actors separated; and now, as I write, almost all have gone on that greater journey, in which the three of us left are so soon to join.

CHAPTER XVII.

The First Immigrants Through the Natchess Pass, 1853.

While the breaking of the barrier of the great mountain range for the immigrants to Puget Sound through the Natchess Pass was not in a baptism of blood, certainly it was under the stress of great suffering and anxiety, as shown by the graphic letter following, of that indefatigable worker and painstaking searcher after historic facts, Geo. H. Himes, now of Portland, Oregon, the real father of that great institution, the Oregon State Historical Society.

Having, as the reader will see by the reading of other chapters of this work, had some keen personal experiences through this gap of the mountains, it is but natural the incidents will come nearer home to me than to the general reader, particularly as I know the sincerity of purpose of the writer and the utter absence of any spirit of exaggeration. Although some errors have crept into Mr. Himes' letter, where he has drawn from other sources, yet this in nowise detracts from the value of his statement, but shows how very difficult it is to ascertain exact facts so long after the events.

The letter follows:

"Portland, Oregon, Jan. 23, 1905.
"My Dear Meeker:

"Some time early in August, 1853, Nelson Sargent, from Puget Sound, met our party in Grand Ronde valley, saying to his father, Asher Sargent, mother, two sisters and two brothers, and such others as he could make an impression on, 'You want to go to Puget Sound. That is a better country than the Willamette valley. All the good land is taken

EDWARD JAY ALLEN, 1853.   NELSON SARGENT, 1849.   BREAKING THE BARRIER
THROUGH THE NATCHESS PASS.

up there; but in the Sound region you can have the pick
of the best. The settlers on Puget Sound have cut a road
through Natchess Pass, and you can go direct from the Columbia through the Cascade Mountains, and thus avoid the
wearisome trip through the mountains over the Barlow
route to Portland, and then down the Columbia to Cowlitz
River, and then over a miserable road to Puget Sound.'

"A word about the Sargents. Asher Sargent and his son
Nelson left Indiana in 1849 for California. The next year
they drifted northward to the northern part of Oregon—
Puget Sound. Some time late in 1850 Nelson and a number
of others were shipwrecked on Queen Charlotte Island, and
remained among the savages for several months. The
father, not hearing from the son, supposed he was lost, and
in 1851 returned to Indiana. Being rescued in time, Nelson
wrote home that he was safe; so in the spring of 1853 the
Sargents, Longmire, Van Ogle, and possibly some others
from Indiana, started for Oregon. Somewhere on the Platte
the Biles (two families), Bakers (two families), Downeys,
Kincaids, my father's family (Tyrus Himes), John Dodge
and family—John Dodge did the stone work on the original
Territorial university building at Seattle; Tyrus Himes was
the first boot and shoemaker north of the Columbia River;
James Biles was the first tanner, and a lady, Mrs. Frazier,
was the first milliner and dressmaker—all met and jour-
neyed westward peaceably together, all bound for Willamette valley. The effect of Nelson Sargent's presence and
portrayal of the magnificent future of Puget Sound, caused
most members of this company of 140 or more persons—or
the leaders thereof, James Biles being the most conspicu-
ous—to follow his (Sargent's) leadership. At length the
Umatilla camp ground was reached, which was situated
about three miles below the present city of Pendleton.
From that point the company headed for old Fort Walla
Walla (Wallula of to-day), on the Columbia River. It was
understood that there would be no difficulty in crossing,
but no boat was found. Hence a flatboat was made by
whipsawing lumber out of driftwood. Then we went up
the Yakima River, crossing it eight times. Then to the
Natchess River, through the sage brush, frequently as high

as a covered wagon, which had to be cut down before we could pass through it. On Sept. 15th we reached the mountains and found that there was no road, nothing but an Indian trail to follow. Indeed, there was no road whatever after leaving the Columbia, and nothing but a trail from the Umatilla to the Columbia; but being an open country, we had no particular difficulty in making headway. But I remember all hands felt quite serious the night we camped in the edge of the timber—the first of any consequence that we had seen—on the night of the 15th of September. Sargent said he knew the settlers had started to make a road, and could not understand why it was not completed; and since his parents, brothers and sisters were in the company, most of us believed that he did not intend to deceive. However, there was no course to pursue but to go forward. So we pushed on as best we could, following the bed of the stream part of the time, first on one bank and then on the other. Every little ways we would reach a point too difficult to pass; then we would go to the high ground and cut our way through the timber, frequently not making more than two or three miles a day. Altogether, the Natchess was crossed sixty-eight times. On this journey there was a stretch of fifty miles without a blade of grass—the sole subsistence of cattle and horses being browse from young maple and alder trees, which was not very filling, to say the least. In making the road every person from ten years old up lent a hand, and there is where your humble servant had his first lessons in trail-making, barefooted to boot, but not much, if any, worse off than many others. It was certainly a strenuous time for the women, and many were the forebodings indulged in as to the probability of getting safely through. One woman, 'Aunt Pop,' as she was called—one of the Woolery women—would break down and shed tears now and then; but in the midst of her weeping she would rally and by some quaint remark or funny story would cause everybody in her vicinity to forget their troubles.

"In due time the summit of the Cascades was reached. Here there was a small prairie—really, it was an old burn that had not grown up to timber of any size. Now it was October, about the 8th of the month, and bitter cold to the youth with bare feet and fringed pants extending half way down from knees to feet. My father and the teams had left camp and gone across the little burn, where most of the company was assembled, apparently debating about the next movement to make. And no wonder; for as we came across we saw the cause of the delay. For a sheer thirty feet or more there was an almost perpendicular bluff, and the only way to go forward was by that way, as was demonstrated by an examination all about the vicinity. Heavy timber at all other points precluded the possibility of getting on by any other route. So the longest rope in the company was stretched down the cliff, leaving just enough to be used twice around a small tree which stood on the brink of the precipice; but it was found to be altogether too short. Then James Biles said: 'Kill one of the poorest of my steers and make his hide into a rope and attach it to the one you have.' Three animals were slaughtered before a rope could be secured long enough to let the wagons down to a point where they would stand up. There one yoke of oxen was hitched to a wagon, and by locking all wheels and hitching on small logs with projecting limbs, it was taken down to a stream then known as 'Greenwater.' It took the best part of two days to make this descent. There were thirty-six wagons belonging to the company, but two of them, with a small quantity of provisions, were wrecked on this hill. The wagons could have been dispensed with without much loss. Not so the provisions, scanty as they were, as the company came to be in sore straits for food before the White River prairie was reached, probably South Prairie* of to-day, where food supplies were first obtained, consisting of potatoes without salt for the first meal. Another trying experience was the ascent of Mud Mountain in a drenching rain, with the strength of a dozen yoke of oxen attached to one wagon, with scarcely anything in it save camp equipment, and taxing the strength of the teams to the utmost. But all trials came to an end when the company reached a point six miles from Steilacoom, about October 17th, and got some good, fat beef

*It was Connell's Prairie. The route had been viewed at the outset through South Prairie, but afterwards it was discovered that a road had previously been opened to White River through Connell's Prairie, and the latter route was adopted and the old road cleared by Allen's party.

and plenty of potatoes, and even flour, mainly through the kindness of Dr. W. F. Tolmie. The change from salmon skins was gratifying.

"And now a word about the wagon road. That had been cut through to Greenwater. There, it seems, according to a statement made to me a number of years ago by James Longmire, and confirmed by W. O. Bush, one of the workers, an Indian from the east side of the mountains, met the road workers, who inquired of him whether there was any 'Boston men' coming through. He replied, "Wake"—no. Further inquiry satisfied the road builders that the Indian was truthful, hence they at once returned to the settlements, only to be greatly astonished two weeks later to find a weary, bedraggled, forlorn, hungry and footsore company of people of both sexes, from the babe in arms—my sister was perhaps the youngest, eleven months old, when we ceased traveling—to the man of 55 years, but all rejoicing to think that after trials indescribable they had at last reached the 'Promised Land.'

"Mrs. James Longmire says that soon after descending the big hill from the summit, perhaps early the next day, as she was a few hundred yards in advance of the teams, leading her little girl, three years and two months old. and carrying her baby boy, then fifteen months old, that she remembers meeting a man coming towards the immigrants leading a pack animal, who said to her: "Good God almighty, woman, where did you come from? Is there any more? Why, you can never get through this way. You will have to turn back. There is not a blade of grass for fifty miles."

"She replied: 'We can't go back; we've got to go forward.'

"Soon he ascended the hill by a long detour and gave supplies to the immigrants. Mrs. Longmire says she remembers hearing this man called 'Andy,' and is of the opinion that it was Andy Burge.

"When the immigrant party got to a point supposed to be about six miles from Steilacoom, or possibly near the cabin of John Lackey, it camped. Vegetables were given them by Lackey, and also by a man named Mahon. Dr. Tolmie gave a beeve. When that was sent to the camp the Doctor gave

it in charge of Mrs. Mary Ann Woolery—'Aunt Pop'—
and instructed her to keep it intact until the two oldest men
in the company came in, and that they were to divide it
evenly. Soon a man came with a knife and said he was going to have some meat. Mrs. Woolery said: 'No, sir.'
He replied: 'I am hungry, and I am going to have some of
it.' In response she said: 'So are the rest of us hungry;
but that man said I was not to allow anyone to touch it until the two oldest men came into camp, and they would divide it evenly.' He said: 'I can't wait for that.' She said:
'You will have to.' He then said: 'By what authority?'
'There is my authority,' holding up her fist—she weighed
a hundred pounds then—and she said: 'You touch that
meat and Ill take that oxbow to you,' grabbing hold of one.
The man then subsided. Soon the two oldest men came
into camp. The meat was divided according to Dr. Tolmie's directions, and, with the vegetables that had been
given, by the settlers, all hands had an old-fashioned boiled
supper—the first for many a day."

I know from experience just what such a supper meant
to that camp and how it tasted. God bless that company. I came to know nearly all of them personally,
and a bigger hearted set never lived. They earned the
right to be called Pioneers in the true sense of the word,
but a large percentage have gone on to pleasant paths,
where the remainder of us are soon to be joined in enduring fellowship.

"In the list following are the names of the Natchess Pass
immigrants of 1853. The names followed by other names
in parentheses are those of young ladies who subsequently
married men bearing the names within the parentheses:

"James Biles,* Mrs. Nancy M. Biles,* Geo. W. Biles, James
D. Biles,* Kate Biles (Sargent), Susan B. Biles (Drew),
Clark Biles,* Margaret Biles,* Ephemia Biles (Knapp), Rev.
Chas. Byles,* Mrs. Sarah W. Byles,* David F. Byles,* Mary
Jane Hill (Byles), Rebecca E. Byles (Goodell),* Chas. N.
Byles,* Sarah I. Byles (Ward), John W. Woodward,* Bar-

*Dead.

tholomew C. Baker,* Mrs. Fanny Baker,* James E. Baker,*
John W. Baker, Leander H. Baker, Elijah Baker,* Mrs.
Olive Baker,* Joseph N. Baker, Wm. LeRoy Baker, Martha
Brooks (Young),* Newton West, William R. Downey,*
Mrs. W. R. Downey,* Christopher C. Downey,* Geo. W.
Downey,* James H. Downey,* William A. Downey,* R. M.
Downey, John M. Downey, Louise Downey (Guess),* Jane
Downey (Clark)*, Susan Downey (Latham),* Laura B.
Downey (Bartlett), Mason F. Guess,* Wilson Guess,* Aus-
tin E. Young, Henry C. Finch,* Varine Davis,* James
Aiken, John Aiken, Glenn Aiken, Wesley Clinton, J. Wilson
Hampton, John Bowers, William M. Kincaid,* Mrs. W. M.
Kincaid,* Susannah Kincaid (Thompson), Joseph C. Kin-
caid, Laura Kincaid (Meade),* James Kincaid, John Kin-
caid,* James Gant, Mrs. James Gant, Harris Gant, Mrs.
Harris Gant. All the of the foregoing were from Kentucky.
Isaac Woolery,* Mrs. Isaac Woolery, Robert Lemuel Wool-
ery, James Henderson Woolery, Sarah Jane Woolery
(Ward) (born on Little Sunday), Abraham Woolery,* Mrs.
Abraham Woolery (Aunt Pop), Jacob Francis Woolery,*
Daniel Henry Woolery, Agnes Woolery (Lamon), Erastus
A. Light,* Mrs. E. A. Light,* Henry Light, George Melville,*
Mrs. George Melville,* Kate Melville (Thompson),* Robert
Melville,* Isaac H. Wright,* Mrs. I. H. Wright,* Benjamin
Franklin Wright,* Mrs. B. F. Wright, James Wright, Eliza
Wright (Bell), Rebecca Wright (Moore), William Wright,
Byrd Wright,* Grandfather — Wright, Grandmother —
Wright, Jas. Bell, Annis Wright (Downey). The foregoing
were from Missouri. Tyrus Himes,* Mrs. Tyrus Himes,*
George H. Himes, Helen L. Himes (Ruddell), Judson W.
Himes, Lestina Z. Himes (Eaton),* Joel Risdon,* Henry
Risdon, Chas. R. Fitch,* Frederick Burnett,* James Long-
mire,* Mrs. James Longmire, Elcaine Longmire, David
Longmire, John A. Longmire, Tillathi Longmire (Kandle),
Asher Sargent,* Mrs. A. Sargent,* E. Nelson Sargent, Wil-
son Sargent,* F. M. Sargent,* Matilda Sargent (Saylor),*
Rebecca Sargent (Kellet), Van Ogle, John Lane, Mrs. John
Lane, Joseph Day, Elizabeth Whitesel (Lane), Wm.
Whitesel, Mrs. Wm. Whitesel, William Henry Whitesel.

*Dead.

Nancy Whitesel (Leach), Clark N. Greenman, Daniel E. Lane,* Mrs. D. E. Lane,* Edward Lane, William Lane, Timothy Lane, Albert Lane, Margaret Whitesel, Alexander Whitesel, Cal Whitesel. The foregoing were from Indiana. Widow Gordon, Mary Frances Gordon, or McCullough, Mrs. Mary Ann McCullough Porter, —— McCullough, —— Frazier,* Mrs. Elizabeth Frazier,* Peter Judson,* Mrs. Peter Judson,* Stephen Judson, John Paul Judson, Gertrude Shoren Judson (Delin), John Neisan.* The foregoing were from Illinois. In addition to the above were William H. Mitchell and John Stewart,* from states unknown."

This makes a total of 148 of the immigrants who completed the road—that is, all but Melville. He refused to assist in making the road and kept about a half day behind, notwithstanding James Biles asked him to lend a hand.

Accompanying the party of road workers was Quiemuth, a half-brother of Leschi, who acted as guide and led the horse upon which were packed the blankets and provisions of Parker and Allen.

---

*Dead.

CHAPTER XVIII.

Building of the Natchess Pass Road.

We have seen with what trevail the first immigrants passed through the Natchess Pass. We will now tell about that other struggle to construct any kind of a road at all, and so we must need go back a little in our story.

While I had been struggling to get the little wife and baby over from the Columbia River to the Sound, and a roof over their heads, the sturdy pioneers of this latter region set resolutely to work building a wagon road through this pass, to enable the immigration of 1853, and later years, to come direct to Puget Sound.

For unknown ages the Indians had traveled a well-worn but crooked and difficult trail through this pass, followed by the Hudson Bay people later in their intercourse with the over-mountain tribes, but it remained for the resolute pioneers of 1853 to open a wagon road over the formidable Cascade Range of mountains to connect the two sections of the new Territory, otherwise so completely separated from each other.

Congress had appropriated twenty thousand dollars for the construction of a military road from Fort Steilacoom to Wallula on the Columbia River, but it was patent to all the appropriation could not be made available in time for the incoming immigration known to be on the way.

This knowledge impelled the settlers to make extraordinary efforts to open the road, as related in this and succeeding chapters.

Meetings had been held at various points to forward the scheme and popular subscription lists circulated for prosecuting this laudable enterprise. It was a great undertaking for the scattered pioneers, particularly where so many were newcomers with scant provision yet made for food or shelter for the coming winter.

But everyone felt this all important enterprise must be attended to, to the end that they might divert a part of the expected immigration which would otherwise go down the Columbia or through passes south of that river, and thence into Oregon, and be lost to the new but yet unorganized Territory of Washington.

And yet in the face of all the sacrifices endured and the universal public spirit manifested, there are men who would belittle the efforts of the citizens of that day and malign their memories by accusing them of stirring up discontent among the Indians. "A lot of white men who were living with Indian women, and who were interested in seeing that the country remained common pasture as long as possible." A more outrageous libel was never penned against the living or dead. In this case but few of the actors are left, but there are records, now fifty years old that it is a pleasure to perpetuate for the purpose of setting this matter aright, and also of correcting some errors that have crept into the treacherous memories of the living, and likewise to pay a tribute to the dead. Later in life I knew nearly all these sixty-nine men, subscribers to this fund, and so far as I know now all are dead but eight, and I know the underlying motive that prompted this strenuous action; they wanted to see the country settled up with the sturdy stock of the overland immigrants.

The same remark applies to the intrepid road workers, some of whom it will be seen camped on the trail for the whole summer, and labored without money and without price to the end.

It is difficult to abridge the long quotation following, illustrating so vividly as it does the rough and ready

pioneer life of Winthrop saw and so sparklingly described. Such tributes ought to be perpetuated, and I willingly give up space for it from his work, "The Canoe and
Saddle," which will well repay the reader for careful
persual. Winthrop gives this account as he saw the
road-workers the last week of August, 1853, in that famous trip from Nisqually to The Dalles. Belated and a
little after nightfall, he suddenly emerged from the surrounding darkness where, quoting his words:

"A score of men were grouped about a fire. Several had
sprung up, alert at our approach. Others reposed untrou-
bled. Others tended viands odoriferous and frizzing. Others stirred the flame. Around the forest rose, black as
Erebus, and the men moved in the glare against the gloom
like pitmen in the blackest coal mines.

"I must not dally on the brink, half hid in the obscure
thicket, lest the alert ones below should suspect an ambush
and point toward me open-mouthed rifles from their stack
near at hand. I was enough out of the woods to halloo, as
I did heartily. Klale sprang forward at shout and spur.
Antipodes obeyed a comprehensible hint from the whip of
Loolowcan. We dashed down into the crimson pathway,
and across among the astonished road makers—astonished
at the sudden alighting down from Nowhere of a pair of
cavaliers, Pasaiook and Siawsh. What meant this incursion
of a strange couple? I became at once the center of a
red-flannel-shirted circle. The recumbents stood on end.
The cooks let their frying pans bubble over, while, in response to looks of expectation, I hung out my handbill and
told the society my brief and simple tale. I was not running away from any fact in my history. A harmless person, asking no favors, with plenty of pork and spongy biscuit in his bags—only going home across the continent, if
may be, and glad, gentlemen pioneers, of this unexpected
pleasure.

"My quality thus announced, the boss of the road makers,
without any dissenting voice, offered me the freedom of
their fireside. He called for the fattest pork, that I might
be entertained right republicanly. Every cook proclaimed

supper ready. I followed my representative host to the windward side of the greenwood pyre, lest smoke wafting toward my eyes should compel me to disfigure the banquet with lachrymose countenance.

"Fronting the coals, and basking in their embrowning beams, were certain diminutive targets, well known to me as defensive armor against darts of cruel hunger—cakes of unleavened bread, light flapjacks in the vernacular, confected of flour and the saline juices of fire-ripened pork, and kneaded well with drops of the living stream. Baked then in frying pan, they stood now, each nodding forward and resting its edge upon a planted twig, toasting crustily till crunching time should come. And now to every man his target! Let supper assail us! No dastards with trencher are we.

"In such a platonic republic as this a man found his place according to his powers. The cooks were no base scullions; they were brothers, whom conscious ability, sustained by universal suffrage, had endowed with the frying pan. Each man's target of flapjacks served him for platter and edible table. Coffee, also, for beverage, the fraternal cooks set before us in infrangible tin pots—coffee ripened in its red husk by Brazilian suns thousands of leagues away, that we, in cool Northern forests, might feel the restorative power of its concentrated sunshine, feeding vitality with fresh fuel.

"But for my gramniverous steeds, gallopers all day long, unflinching steeplechase, what had nature done here in the way of provender? Alas! little or naught. This camp of plenty for me was a starvation camp for them.

"My hosts were a stalwart gang. I had truly divined them from their cleavings on the hooihut (road). It was but play for any one of these to whittle down a cedar five feet in diameter. In the morning this compact knot of comrades would explode into a mitraille of men wielding keen axes, and down would go the dumb, stolid files of the forest. Their talk was as muscular as their arms. When these laughed, as only men fresh and hearty and in the open air can laugh, the world became mainly grotesque; it seemed at once a comic thing to live—a subject for chuckling, that we were bipeds with noses—a thing to roar at; that we had all met there from the wide world to hobnob by a frolicsome fire with tin pots of coffee, and partake of crisped bacon and toasted doughboys in ridiculous abundance. Easy laughter infected the atmosphere. Echoes ceased to be pensive and became jocose. A rattling humor pervaded the feast, and Green River* rippled with noise of fantastic jollity. Civilization and its dilettante diners-out sneer when Clodpole at Dive's table doubles his soup, knifes his fish, tilts his plate into his lap, puts muscle into the crushing of his meringue, and tosses off the warm beaker in his finger bowl. Camps by Tacoma sneer not at all, but candidly roar at parallel accidents. Gawkey makes a cushion of his flapjack. Butterfingers drops his red-hot rasher into his bosom, or lets slip his mug of coffee into his boot drying by the fire—a boot henceforth saccharine. A mule, slipping his halter, steps forward unnoticed, puts his nose in the circle and brays resonant. These are the jocular boons of life, and at these the woodsmen guffaw with lusty good-nature. Coarse and rude the jokes may be, but not nasty, like the innuendoes of pseudo-refined cockneys. If the woodsmen are guilty of uncleanly wit, it differs from the uncleanly wit of cities as the mud of a road differs from the sticky slime of slums.

'It is a stout sensation to meet masculine, muscular men at the brave point of a penetrating Boston hooihut—men who are mates—men to whom technical culture means naught—men to whom myself am naught, unless I can saddle, lasso, cook, sing and chop; unless I am a man of nerve and pluck, and a brother in generosity and heartiness. It is restoration to play at cudgels of jocoseness with a circle of friendly roughs, not one of whom ever heard the word bore—with pioneers who must think and act and wrench their living from the closed hand of nature.

"* * * While fantastic flashes were leaping up and illuminating the black circuit of forest, every man made his bed, laid his blankets in starry bivouac and slept like a mummy. The camp became vocal with snores; nasal with

---

*This should read Green Water. This camp was far up in 'the mountains and the stream referred to came from the main range and not from the glaciers of the great mountain, and hence was a sparkling, dancing rivulet of clearest water. Green River is forty miles or more farther down the mountain.

snores of various calibre was the forest. Some in triumphant tones announced that dreams of conflict and victory
were theirs; some sighed in dulcet strains that told of
lovers' dreams; some strew shrill whistles through cavern-
ous straits; some wheezed grotesquely and gasped pit-
eously; and from some who lay supine, snoring up at the
fretted roof of forest, sound gushed in spasms, leaked in
snorts, bubbled in puffs, as steam gushes, leaks and bubbles
from yawning valves in degraded steamboats. They died
away into the music of my dreams; a few moments seemed
to pass, and it was day.

"*   *   * If horses were breakfastless, not so were their
masters. The road makers had insisted that I should be
their guest, partaking not only of the fire, air, earth and
water of their bivouac, but an honorable share at their
feast. Hardly had the snoring ceased when the frying of
the fryers began. In the pearly-gray mist of dawn, purple
shirts were seen busy about the kindling pile; in the golden
haze of sunrise cooks brandished pans over fierce coals raked
from the red-hot jaws of flame that champed their breakfast of fir logs. Rashers, doughboys, not without molasses,
and coffee—a bill of fare identical with last night's—were
our morning meal. *   *   *

"And so adieu, gentlemen pioneers, and thanks for your
frank, manly hospitality! Adieu, 'Boston tilicum,' far better types of robust Americanism than some of those selected
as its representatives by Boston of the Orient, where is
too much worship of what is, and not too much uplifting of
hopeful looks of what ought to be.

"As I started, the woodsmen gave me a salute. Down, to
echo my shout of farewell, went a fir of fifty years' standing.. It cracked sharp, like the report of a howitzer, and
crashed downward, filling the woods with shattered branches. Under cover of this first shot, I dashed at the woods.
I could ride more boldly forward into savageness, knowing
that the front ranks of my nation were following close behind."

The men who were in that camp of road workers were
E. J. Allen, A. J. Burge, Thomas Dixon, Ephraim Allen,
Jas. Henry Allen, George Githers, John Walker, John

H. Mills, R. S. More, R. Foreman, Ed. Crofts, Jas. Boise, Robert Patterson, Edward Miller, Edward Wallace, Lewis Wallace, Jas. R. Smith, John Burrow, and Jas. Mix.

The names of the workers on the east slope of the mountains are as follows: Whitfield Kirtley, Edwin Marsh, Nelson Sargent, Paul Ruddell, Edward Miller, J. W. Fonts, John L. Perkins, Isaac M. Brown, James Alverson, Nathaniel G. Stewart, William Carpenter, and Mr. Clyne.

The Pioneer and Democrat published at Olympia, in its issue of September 30th, 1854, contains the following self-explanatory letter and account that will revive the memory of many almost forgotten names and set at rest this calmuny cast upon the fame of deserving men.

"Friend Wiley: Enclosed I send you for publication the statement of the cash account of the Puget Sound emigrant road, which has been delayed until this time, partly on account of a portion of the business being unsettled, and partly because you could not, during the session of the last legislature, find room in your columns for its insertion. As you have now kindly offered, and as it is due the citizens of the Territory that they should receive a statement of the disposition of the money entrusted to me, I send it to you, and in so doing close up my connection with the Cascade road, and would respectfully express my gratitude to the citizens for the confidence they have reposed in me, and congratulate them upon the successful completion of the road.

JAMES K. HURD.

RECEIPTS.

By subscription of		John M. Swan	$	10.00
"	"	" S. W. Percival		5.00
"	"	" Jos. Cushman		5.00
"	"	" Milas Galliher		5.00
"	"	" C. Eaton		5.00
"	"	" Chips Ethridge		5.00
"	"	" Wm. Berry		5.00
"	"	" J. C. Patton		5.00
"	"	" T. F. McElroy		5.00
"	"	" James Taylor		5.00
"	"	" George Gallagher		5.00
"	"	" J. Blanchard		5.00
"	"	" Weed & Hurd		100.00
"	"	" Kendall Co.		50.00
"	"	" G. A. Barnes		50.00
"	"	" Parker, Colter & Co		30.00
"	"	" Brand & Bettman		25.00
"	"	" J. & C. E. Williams		25.00
"	"	" Waterman & Goldman		25.00
"	"	" Lightner, Rosenthal & Co		10.00
"	"	" A. J. Moses		10.00
"	"	" Wm. W. Plumb		10.00
"	"	" Isaac Wood & Son		15.00
"	"	" D. J. Chambers		20.00
"	"	" John Chambers		5.00
"	"	" McLain Chambers		10.00
"	"	" J. H. Conner		5.00
"	"	" H. G. Parsons		5.00
"	"	" Thomas J. Chambers		20.00
"	"	" Puget Sound Agricultural Co		100.00
"	"	" Wells, McAllister & Co		30.00
"	"	" Henry Murray		25.00
"	"	" L. A. Smith		25.00
"	"	" Chas. Wren		25.00
"	"	" James E. Williamson		10.00
"	"	" H. C. Mosely		5.00
"	"	" J. M. Bachelder		5.00
"	"	" Lemuel Bills		25.00

By subscription of W. Boatman 15.00
"   "   " W. M. Sherwood 5.00
"   "   " James Barron 5.00
"   "   " S. W. Woodruff 5.00
"   "   " R. S. More 5.00
"   "   " John D. Press 5.00
"   "   " Samuel McCaw 5.00
"   "   " Philip Keach 10.00
"   "   " Abner Martin 20.00
"   "   " George Brail 10.00
"   "   ' T. W. Glasgow 10.00
"   "   " McGomery 10.00
"   "   " Thos. Tallentire 10.00
"   "   " Garwin Hamilton 5.00
"   "   " John McLeod 25.00
"   "   " Richard Philander 5.00
"   "   " W. Gregg 5.00
"   "   " David Pattee 20.00
"   "   " Thomas Chambers 50.00
"   "   " W. A. Slaughter 10.00
"   "   " W. Hardin 15.00
"   "   " L. Balch 50.00
"   "   " W. W. Miller 10.00
"   "   " J. B. Webber 25.00
"   "   " J. W. Goodell 10.00
"   "   " —— Kline 10.00
"   "   " A. Benton Moses 5.00
"   "   " —— Parsons 5.00
"   "   " H. Hill 5.00
By amount received for horse 35.00
By amount received for horse (Woods)............ 35.00
By subscription of Nelson Barnes 30.00

                                              $1,220.00
Amount note from Lemuel Bills 25.00

Whole amount received as per subscription paper....$1,195.00

This list of subscribers to the road fund will revive
memories of almost forgotten names of old-time friends

and neightbors, and also will serve to show the interest
taken by all classes. It must not for a moment be taken
this comprises the whole list of contributors to this enterprise, for it is not half of it, as the labor subscription
far exceeded the cash receipts represented by this published statement. Unfortunately, we are unable to obtain a complete list of those who gave their time far beyond what they originally had agreed upon, but were
not paid for their labor.

The *Columbian,* published under date of July 30th,
1853, says:

"Captain Lafayette Balch, the enterprising proprietor of
Steilacoom, has contributed one hundred dollars in money
towards the road to Walla Walla. To each and every man
who started from that neighborhood to work on the road,
Captain Balch gives a lot in the town of Steilacoom. He
is security to the United States Government for a number
of mules, pack saddles, and other articles needed by the men.
He furnished the outfit for the company who started from
that place with Mr. E. J. Allen, at just what the articles cost
in San Francisco."

Mr. Hurd's expenditure is set out in his published
report, but none of it is for labor, except for Indian hire,
a small sum. We know there were thirty men at work
at one time, and that at least twelve of them spent most
of the summer on the work and that at least fifty
laborers in all donated their time, and that the value
of the labor was far in excess of the cash outlay.

By scanning the list the "Old Timer" will readily
see the cash subscribers and road workers were by no
means confined to Olympia, and that many of the old
settlers of Pierce County are represented, and even the
foreign corporation, the Puget Sound Agricultural Company, came down with a heavy subscription. Everybody was in favor of the road. Such can also pick out
the names of those "white men who were living with

Indian women" among the liberal subscribers to the fund for opening the road.

Nor were the Indians lacking in interest in the enterprise. A. J. Baldwin, then and for many years afterwards a citizen of Olympia, and whom it may be said was known as a truthful man, in a recent interview, said:

"We all put our shoulders to the wheel to make the thing go. I helped to pack out grub to the working party myself. It seemed to be difficult to get the stuff out; entirely more so than to get it contributed. I was short of pack animals one trip, and got twelve horses from Leschi, and I believe Leschi went himself also."*

" 'Do you remember how much you paid Leschi for his horses?'

" 'Why, nothing. He said if the whites were working without pay and were giving provisions, it was as little as he could do to let his horses go and help. He said if I was giving my time and use of horses then he would do the same, and if I received pay then he wanted the same pay I got. Neither of us received anything.' "

These were the Indians, as the reader will see by perusal of later chapters, who were actually driven from their farms into the war camp, leaving the plow and unfinished furrow in the field and stock running at large, to be confiscated by the volunteers.

And such were the road workers in the Natchess Pass in the fall of 1853, and such were the pioneers of that day. Fortunate it is we have the testimony of such a gifed and unbiased writer as Winthrop to delineate the character of the sturdy men who gave their strenuous efforts and substance that their chosen commonwealth might prosper.

---

*Baldwin is mistaken. Queimuth, Leschi's brother, went as guide and packer, but Leschi doubtless supplied the horses.

CHAPTER XIX.

Building the Natchess Pass Road—Concluded.

Allen's party left Steilacoom for this work July 30th, (1853), and was still at work on the 26th of September, when he wrote: "We will be through this week, having completed the western portion of the road." With twenty men in sixty days and over sixty miles to cut, he could not be expected to build much of a road.

The other party, under Kirtley, left Olympia, thirteen strong, July 19th, and was back again August 20th, and so could not have done very effective work on the east slope, as it would take at least a third of the time to make the trip out and back from their field of labor.

With the view of trying to settle the disputed points, I wrote to my old time friend, A. J. Burge, one of the Allen party, to get information from first hands, and have this characteristic reply:

"Wenass, December 8th, 1904.

"Friend Meeker.—Sir: Your letter dated Nov. 26, 1904, at hand. Sir, I am quite sick. I will try to sit up long enough to scratch an answer to your questions. Kirtley's men fell out among themselves. I well remember Jack Perkins had a black eye. Kirtley, as I understood, was to go (to) Wenass creek, thence cut a wagon road from Wenass to the Natchess River, thence up the Natchess River until they met Allen's party. It is my opinion they did commence at Wenass. There were three notches cut in many of the large trees (logs). I can find some of these trees yet where these notches show. Allen did not know Kirtley and his party had abandoned the enterprise until Ehformer told him. He expressed much surprise and re-

gret. I packed the provisions for Allen's party. The last
trip I made I found Allen and his party six or eight miles
down the Natchess River. I was sent back to the summit
of the mountain to search for a pack mule and a pack horse.
These two animals were used by the working party to move
their camp outfit, and their provisions. When they returned
they told me that they cut the road down to where Kirtley's
party left off. Of my own knowledge I can safely say Allen's party cut the road from John Montgomery's* to some
six or maybe eight miles down the Natchess River, and it
was four days after that before they came to the summit on
their return.

"It is possible Kirtley's party slighted their work to the
extent that made it necessary for the immigrants to take
their axes in hand. I consider Kirtley a dead failure at anything. Kirtley's party came home more than a month before
we came in. If Van Ogle is not insane he ought to remember.

"Allen's party cut the road out from six to eight miles
down the Natchess River to John Montgomery's. The valley
on the Natchess River is too narrow for any mistake to
occur.

"The first men that came through came with James and
his brother, Charles Biles, Sargent, Downey, James Longmire, Van Ogle, two Atkins, Lane, a brother-in-law of Sargent, Kincaid, two Woolery's, Lane of Puyallup, E. A.
Light, John Eagan (Reagan), Charley Fitch. Meeker, I
am quite sick; when I get well I will write more detailed
account; it is as much as I can do to sit up.

"Yours in haste, as ever,

"A. J. BURGE."

This man I have known for over fifty years, and it
touched me to think at the age bordering on eighty, he
should get up out of a sick bed to comply with my request. He has written the truth, and some of the information we could get in no other way.

---

*Nisqually Plains.

It seems that some people live a charmed life. Burge was shot by a would-be assassin a few miles out from Steilacoom over forty years ago, the bullet going through his neck, just missing the jugular vein.

While it is a complete digression, nevertheless, just as interesting here as elsewhere, so I will tell the story of this shooting to further illustrate conditions of early settlement on the Nisqually plains. The man with the thirteen cows and thirty calves mentioned elsewhere, lived near Burge. The most desperate character I ever knew, Charles McDaniel, also was a near neighbor, but a friend of Andy, as we used to call Burge. Both lost stock that could be traced directly to their neighbor, Wren, the man with the extra calves, but it was no use to prosecute him as a jury could not be procured that would convict. I had myself tried it in our court with the direct evidence of the branded hide taken from him, but a bribed juryman refused to convict. For a few years and for this district and with the class previously described as occupying the country adjacent to Steilacoom, there seemed to be no redress through our courts. Finally Burge and McDaniel waylaid their neighbor a few miles out from Steilacoom, tied him to a tree, and whipped him most unmercifully. I have never yet given my approval to mob law and never will, believing that it is better to suffer awhile, bide one's time until laws can be enforced, rather than to join in actions that will breed contempt for law and lead to anarchy. But, if ever there was a justifiable case of men taking the law in their own hands, this was one of them, and is introduced here to illustrate a condition of affairs that had grown up which seemed well nigh intolerable. After the whipping Wren was warned to leave the country, which he could not well do, tied to a tree as he was until third parties discovered and released him, but which he speedily did, although the wealthiest man in the county. No prosecutions followed, but in the lapse of time a colored man appeared at Steilacoom and spent much time hunting herds on the prairies, until one day Burge was going home from Steilacoom in his wagon, when this centre shot was fired with the result as related. The colored man disappeared as mysteriously as he came, but everyone believed he had been hired to assassinate Burge and McDaniel, and as afterwards proven was the case.

But the trouble was not ended here. The lawless neighbor had gone, but not lawlessness. The old story that lawlessness begets lawlessness was again proven. McDaniel and others concluded that as Wren was gone, they could prey upon his land holdings, which for twenty-five years in Pierce County was no more than squatter's rights, in consequence of that intolerable claim of the Puget Sound Agricultural Company, mentioned elsewhere. At this, most of the community rebelled and warned McDaniel, but to no purpose, until finally he was shot down on the streets of Steilacoom, or rather a vacant lot in a public place, and lay for hours in his death struggles uncared for, and his pal murdered in the wagon that was carrying him to a scaffold. The two had been waylaid, but had escaped, only to meet their fate in a more public manner. Burge narrowly escaped a like fate at the hands of the mob, because of his near neighborship with McDaniel and of his participation with him in the first instance that had led up to the final catastrophe. But Burge was an honorable man, though rough in manner, yet just in his dealings, while McDaniel was a gambler and a blackleg of the very worst, imaginable type. The Indian war had brought to the front many vicious characters, and the actions of some officials in high places had encouraged lawlessness, so, as a community, the near by country round and about Steilacoom was scourged almost beyond belief.

And yet there were genuine pioneer settlements in

not very far off regions of this storm center of lawlessness, where the law was as cheerfully obeyed as in any
old and well settled community, where crime was scarcely known, and where family ties were held as sacred as
any place on earth, and where finally the influence
spread over the whole land and the whole community
leavened.

By these incidents related it will be seen that pioneers
were neither all saints nor all sinners, but like with older
communities had their trials other than the supposed
discomforts incident to pioneer life.

The reader may not have noticed that Burge in his
letter mentions that there are still trees (he means
logs), yet to be seen with the three notches cut in them,
where the immigrant road had been cut. I had forgotten the third notch, but it all comes back to me now
that he has mentioned it. These logs that we bridged
up to and cut the notches in for the wheels in most
cases had to have the third notch in the center to save
the coupling pole or reach from catching on the log,
especially where the bridging did not extend out far
from the log to be crossed. Oftentimes the wagon would
be unloaded, the wagon box taken off, the wagon un-
coupled and taken over the obstruction or down or up
it, as the case might be, to be loaded again beyond.

It will be noticed by Mr. Himes' letter that their party
came all the way up the canyon and crossed the Natchess
River 68 times while I crossed it but thirty odd times.
At or near the 32d crossing, the road workers took to
the table land and abandoned the lower stretch of the
canyon, and through that portion the train which Mr.
Himes refers to was compelled to cut their own road for
a long stretch. But that part reported cut was certainly a hard road to travel, and we had to work more
or less all the way down the mountain; as Colonel E.
J. Allen, who is yet alive, quaintly put it in a recent
letter: "Assuredly the road was not sand papered." I

should say not. I think the Colonel was not much of a teamster and had never handled the goad stick over the road or elsewhere, as I did, else he would be more sympathetic in responses to outcries against the "execrable shadow of a road."

Nelson Sargent mentioned by Mr. Himes still lives and is a respected, truthful citizen, but he certainly did take great risks in leading that first train of immigrants into that trap of an uncut road up the Natchess River. The whole party narrowly escaped starvation in the mountains and Sargent a greater risk of his neck at the hands of indignant immigrants while in the mountains, if we may believe the reports that came out at the time from the rescued train. However, I never believed that Sargent intended to deceive, but was oversanguine and was himself deceived, and that Kirtley's failure to continue in the field was the cause of the suffering that followed.

Allen sent 300 pound of flour to Wenas and a courier came out to Olympia, whereupon "Old Mike Simmons," Bush, Jones, and others, forthwith started with half a ton of flour, onions, potatoes, etc., and met them beyond the outskirts of the settlement. All that was necessary those days for a person to get help was to let it become known that some one was in distress and there would always be willing hands without delay; in fact, conditions almost approached the socialistic order of common property as to food, by the voluntary actions of the great, big hearted early settlers, as shown in other instances related, as well as in this. God bless those early settlers, the real pioneers of that day.

The Indian Leschi, who we have seen contributed to the work, utilized the road to make his escape with seventy of his people, after his disastrous defeat at the hands of the volunteers and United States troops in March, 1856, to cross the summit on the snow, so that after all, in a way, he received a benefit from his liberality in times of peace.

Two years after the opening the road, the Hudson Bay Company sent a train of three hundred horses loaded with furs, from the interior country to Fort Nisqually, with a return of merchandise through the same pass, but never repeated the experiment.

CHAPTER XX.

The Mud Wagon Road.

Writing of the Natchess Pass immigrant road reminds me of another that everybody said was "a bad road," and most people, that "it is the worst road I ever saw in all my life." I refer to the old road from Monticello, on the Cowlitz River, near the Columbia River, to Olympia.

Monticello was more a name than a town, being the farm house and outbuildings of Uncle Darb Huntington, as we all called him, with a blacksmith shop, store, two or three families and a stable. Here the passengers were dumped from the little steamers from Portland and other Columbia River points, and here, in the earliest days, the hapless traveler either struck the trail (afterwards supplanted by the road), or would tuck himself with others into a canoe, like sardines in a box, where an all-day journey was his fate, unmoved and immovable except as an integral part of the frail craft that carried him to "Hard Breads" tavern for the night. We have taken a peep into Hard Bread's hostelry in a previous chapter, and of the trail and canoe passage, but that was before the days of the road now under notice. At first, travelers to the Sound ascended the Cowlitz to the landing farther up the river than where the mud-wagon road left the Cowlitz, and from the landing were sent on their way by saddle train or over the make-shift of a road cut by the Simmons-Bush party in 1845, over which they dragged their effects on sleds to the head of the Sound, or, to be specific, to the mouth of the Deschutes River, afterwards and now known as Tumwater.

I have no history of the construction of the later road

all the way up the right bank of the Cowlitz to the mouth of the Toutle River (Hard-Breads'), and thence deflecting northerly to the Chehalis, where the old and new routes were joined, and soon emerged into the gravelly prairies, where there were natural road beds everywhere. The facts are, this road, like Topsy, "just growed," and so gradually became a highway one could scarcely say when the trail ceased to be simply a trail and the road actually could be called a road. First, only saddle trains could pass. On the back of a stiff jointed, hard trotting, slow walking, contrary mule, I was initiated into the secret depths of the mud holes of this trail. And such mud holes! It became a standing joke after the road was opened that a team would stall with an empty wagon going down hill, and I came very near having just such an experience once, within what is now the city limits of the thriving city of Chehalis.

After the saddle train came the mud wagons in which passengers were conveyed (or invited to walk over bad places, or preferred to walk), over either the roughest corduroy or deepest mud, the one bruising the muscles the other straining the nerves in the anticipation of being dumped into the bottomless pit of mud.

In 1853, Henry Winsor ran canoes up the Cowlitz River to what was known as Cowlitz Landing, where Fred A. Clark kept a hotel, and also horses for a saddle train to Olympia. Clark afterwards became my neighbor in the Puyallup Valley, and Winsor lived for many years in Olympia, and now lives near Shelton, Mason County, in this state, at the ripe age of nearly eighty years.

Following the change of route Winsor transferred his interests from the water route to the land, and extended his field to the Sound, and finally, as related, became a resident of Olympia.

This reminds me of Winsor's marriage to Miss Huntington, daughter of "Uncle Darb," under circumstances so peculiar that I am again tempted to digress and tell about the wedding. Because of the prominence of the parties, and peculiar circumstances attending it, the wedding had been the talk of the day from one end of the land to the other.

The illustration on the opposite page shows these pioneer, fifty years after, what a friend terms "their romantic and unique wedding" at Rainier, June 2d, 1853.

Reluctantly Mrs. Winsor has supplied the facts that led to the marriage without courtship, and to a life of pleasant paths of honorable citizenship.

"At that time any one wishing the service of a minister," she writes, "had to send to Portland. Rev. C. H. Kingsley had been down to Rainier to marry a couple just two weeks before. Mr. Winsor was one of the guests, and also one at the marriage of Mr. Fox and Miss Dray, and as everyone was joking him unmercifully about losing Miss Dray, he was wearing crape on his hat, but did not act like he was mourning much. Quite a crowd went from Monticello. There was lots of fun. There were Miss Burbee and Mr. Smith (married later), Mr. Winsor and Miss Chapman, Charles Holman (afterwards Captain Holman on Columbia River boats for many years), and myself and others.

"I was young and thoughtless—anything for fun. Girls were scarce in those days and took many privileges. Two or three young men were there and they were teasing me, and I suppose I was a little saucy. As we were at supper Mr. Winsor said to Mr. Kingsley: 'You better marry a lot of them this time so you won't have to come so often.' He said, 'Here is Mr. Smith and Miss Burbee, Mr. Holman and Miss Huntington, and so on.' The first said they were not ready. Mr. H. said he would have to wait till he asked her father. Mr. Winsor then turned to me and asked if I was ready. I asked him if he ever knew a girl that was not ready to marry, if she had a chance, and so one thing led to another, and finally Mr. Kingsley proposed that, as we seemed the only ones ready, we had better be married, and

MR. AND MRS. HENRY WINSOR

Mr. Winsor then said he guessed we would have to wait till he could see my father, and I then supposed that ended it, but every now and then something else would come up, and they finally dared us to sit down in the chairs that the couple had just occupied (the supper was before the ceremony there), and we did so. Then they dared us to stand up. Some of them told the minister to say the ceremony in fun. He said: 'If I say the ceremony it will be no fun.' We did not know he said that. There did not have to be a license then. We still stood. Then the minister came forward. We thought he would say a long ceremony, as he did before, and Mr. Winsor thought if I didn't back out he would, but I think he meant to punish us for our frivolity, and said a very short ceremony and pronounced us man and wife before we had time to think. It was such a shock that Mr. Winsor could not speak when he realized what we had done. I was so much younger and full of Old Nick that I did not realize it as soon as he did. I went home to my father's house and stayed about two weeks. Mr. Winsor was visiting me there. He said as we neither of us cared for another that if I was willing and wished it, as we had been so foolish, we would try what life had in store for us together. We celebrated our fiftieth anniversary last June."

This frank letter was written upon the author's earnest solicitation to "get at the truth of the matter," and the lady wrote privately because there had been so much misrepresentation published, she complied with the request. The aged couple still live in Mason County not far from Olympia.

I have already told of my trip from the Columbia River to the Sound by the trail and wagon road. Subsequently the trial of a mule back ride, to be followed later in the mud wagon, and after that the stage coach, all of these modes of travel it had fallen my lot to test. When the rail road came in 1873, it was my good fortune to make the trip in the first car that ran out from Tacoma carrying passengers, of which there were five of us, including General John W. Sprague, the superintendent of the road.

CHAPTER XXI.

The Fraser River Stampede.

On the 21st day of March, 1858, the Schooner Wild Pigeon arrived at Steilacoom, and brought the news that the Indians had discovered gold on Fraser River; had traded several pounds of the precious metal with the Hudson Bay Company, and that three hundred people had left Victoria and vicinity for the new eldorado. And further, the report ran the mines were exceedingly rich.

The next day there came further reports from the north, that the Bellingham Bay Company's coal mines had been compelled to suspend work, as all their operatives but three had started for the mines, that many of the logging camps had shut down, and all the mills were running on short time from the same cause.

The wave of excitement that ran through the little town upon the receipt of this news was repeated in every town and hamlet of the whole Pacific Coast, and continued around the world, sending thither adventurous spirits from all civilized countries of the earth.

But when the word came the next week that one hundred and ten pounds of gold had actually been received in Victoria, and that hundreds of men were outfitting, the virulence of the gold fever knew no bounds, and everybody, women folks and all, wanted to go, and would have started pell-mell had there not been that restraining influence of the second sober thought of people who had just gone through the mill of adversity. My family was still in the block house we had built during the war in the town of Steilacoom. Our cattle were peacefully grazing on the plains a few miles distant, but there remained a spirit of unrest that one could not fail to observe. There had been no Indian depredations for two years west of the Cascade Mountains, but some atrocious murders had been committed by a few renegade white men, besides the murder of Leschi under the forms of law that had but recently taken place. The Indians just over the mountains were in a threatening mood, and in fact soon again broke out into open warfare and inflicted heavy punishment on Steptoe's command, and came very near annihilating that whole detachment.

The close of the Indian war of 1855-6 had engendered a reckless spirit among what may be called the unsettled class that to many of the more sober minded was looked upon as more dangerous than the Indians among us. In the wake of the United States army paymaster came a vile set of gamblers and blacklegs that preyed upon the soldiers, officers and men alike, who became a menace to the peace of the community, and, like a veritable bedlam turned loose, often made night hideous with their carousals. The reader need not feel this is an overdrawn picture for it is not. We must remember the common soldiers of the United States army fifty years ago were very different from our army of the present time. At least such was the case with the forces stationed at Fort Steilacoom at the time of which I am writing.

One illustration. Having drifted into a small business conducted in our block house at Steilacoom, in an unguarded moment I let a half dozen of the blue-coats (as the soldiers were then universally called), have a few articles on credit. These men told their comrades, who came soliciting credit but were refused, when some drunken members of the party swore they would come strong enough to take the goods anyway, and actually did come at night thirty strong, and having been refused admission, began breaking down the door. A shot through the door that scattered splinters among the assembled crowd served as a warning that caused them to desist, and no damage was done, but the incident serves to illustrate the conditions prevailing at the time the gold discovery was reported. Pierce County contributed its contingent of gold seekers, some of the desperados and some of the best citizens. One Charles McDaniel, who killed his man while gone returned to plague us; another, one of our merchants, Samuel Mc-Caw, bundled up a few goods, made a flying trip up Fraser River, came back with fifty ounces of gold dust and with the news the mines were all that had been reported, and more too, which of course added fuel to the burning flame of the all-prevalent gold fever. We all then believed a new era had dawned upon us, similar to that of ten years before in California that changed the world's history. High hopes were built, most of them to end in disappointment. Not but there were extensive mines, and that they were rich, and that they were easily worked, but, how to get there was the puzzling question. The early voyagers had slipped up the Fraser before the freshets that came from the melting snows to swell the torrents of that river. Those going later either failed altogether and gave up the unequal contest, or lost an average of one canoe or boat out of three in the persistent attempt. How many lives were lost, never will be known.

"Beginning at a stump in the bank of said creek (Squalecum), about 20 feet above the bridge near the mouth of said creek; thence running due west 240 feet; thence due south 60 feet; thence due east 240 feet; thence due north 60 feet to the place of beginning." Such is the description of a tract of land as recorded on the book of records of deeds for the county of Whatcom, bearing date of June 25th, 1858. On that date I was in Whatcom, and saw the sights and acted my part as one of the wild men of the north country, received

a deed for the land as described from Edward Eldridge,
who then resided on his claim adjoining the town of
Whatcom, and where he continued until his death.   No
public surveys had up to that time been made, and so,
to describe a lot I was purchasing of Mr. Eldridge, what
more durable monument could we select than a big
stump of one of those giants of the monster forests
fronting on Bellingham Bay.

Going back a little in my story to the receipt of the
news of the discovery on the Fraser and Thompson
Rivers, each succeeding installment of news that came
to Steilacoom more than confirmed the original report.
Contingents began to arrive in Steilacoom from Oregon,
from California, and finally from "the States," as all
of our country east of the Rocky Mountains was designated by pioneers.   Steamers great and small began
to appear with more or less cargo and passenger lists,
which we heard were as nothing compared to what was
going on less than a hundred miles to the north of us.
These people landing in Whatcom in such great numbers
must be fed, we agreed, and if the multitude would not
come to us to drink the milk of our dairies and eat
the butter, what better could we do than to take our
cows to the multitude where we were told people did
not hesitate to pay a dollar a gallon for milk and any
price one might ask for fresh butter.

But, how to get even to Whatcom was the "rub."   All
space on the steamers was taken from week to week
for freight and passengers, and no room left for cattle.
In fact, the movement of provisions was so great that
at one time we were almost threatened with a veritable
famine, so close had the stock of food been shipped.
Finally, our cattle, mostly cows, were loaded in an open
scow and taken in tow along side of the steamer (Sea
Bird, I think it was), where all went smoothly enough
until we arrived off the head of Whidby Island, where
a chopped sea from a light wind began slopping over

into the scow and evidently would sink us despite our utmost efforts at bailing. When the captain would slow down the speed of his steamer all was well, but the moment greater power was applied, over the gunwales would come the water. The dialogue that ensued between myself and the Captain was more emphatic than elegant and perhaps would not look well in print, but he dare not either let go of us or run us under without incurring the risk of heavy damages and probable loss of life. But I stood by my guns (figuratively), and would not consent to be landed, and so about the 20th of June, tired and sleepy, we were set adrift in Bellingham Bay, and landed near the big stump described as the starting point for the land purchased later.

But our cows must have feed, must be milked, and the milk marketed, and so there was no rest nor sleep for us for another thirty-six hours. In fact, there was but little sleep for anybody on that beach at the time. Several ocean steamers had just dumped three thousand people on the beach, and the scramble still continued to find a place to build a house or stretch a tent, or even to spread a blanket, for there were great numbers already on hand landed by previous steamers. The staking of lots on the tide flats at night, when the tide was out, seemed to be a staple industry. Driving of piles or planting of posts as permanent as possible often preceded and accompanied by high words between contestants came to be a commonplace occurrence. The belief among these people seemed to be that if they could get stakes or posts to stand on end, and a six-inch strip nailed to them to encompass a given spot of the flats, that they would thereby become the owner, and so the merry war went on until the bubble bursted.

A few days after my arrival four steamers came with an aggregate of over two thousand passengers, many of whom, however, did not leave the steamer and took passage either to their port of departure San Francisco,

Victoria, or points on the Sound. The ebb tide had set in, and although many steamers came later and landed passengers, their return lists soon became large and the population began to diminish.

Taking my little dory that we had with us on the scow, I rowed out to the largest steamer lying at anchor surrounded by small boats so numerous that in common parlance the number was measured by the acre, "an acre of boats." Whether or not an acre of space was covered by these crafts striving to reach the steamer I will not pretend to say, but can say that I certainly could not get within a hundred feet of the steamer. All sorts of craft filled the intervening space, from the smallest Indian canoe to large barges, the owners of each either striving to secure a customer from a hapless passenger, or, having secured one, of transferring his belongings to the craft.

There were but a few women in this crowd, but ashore, quite too many, a large majority of whom (those on the ground will remember), were too much like their arch representative, "Old Mother Damnable," well and truly named. But I draw the veil.

"Where's DeLacy?" became a by-word after weeks of earnest inquiry of the uninitiated as to what was transpiring out at the front, where supposed work was going on to construct a trail leading through the Cascade Mountains to the mouth of Thompson River, that emptied into the Fraser one hundred and fifty miles easterly from Whatcom. If a trail could be constructed through the mountains from Whatcom, then the town would at once bloom into a city, and the fortunes of townsite proprietors would be made, and all might go to the mines whose spirit moved them. It all looked very feasible on paper, but several obstacles not taken into account by the impatient crowd defeated all their hopes. A fund had been raised by subscription at the inception of the excitement to send out parties to search for a pass, and W. W. DeLacy, an engineer of considerable note, started out early in the season, and so far as I know never came back to Whatcom.

Directly this party was sent out to search for a pass through the mountains another party was set to work to follow and cut the trail. All seemingly went well for awhile, and until there came no word to the public from DeLacy. The trail workers were yet at work, but did not know what was ahead of them. DeLacy had to them become a sort of myth. The fact was he had failed to find a pass, and when he arrived at a point that he thought was the summit, he had yet fifty miles or more of the worst of the mountains ahead of him. Meanwhile, the trail out from Whatcom for forty or fifty miles became well worn by men and animals going and returning. I saw sixty men with heavy packs on their backs start out in one company, everyone of whom had to come back after floundering in the mountains for weeks. So long as there could be kept up a hope that the trail would be cut through, just so long a complete collapse of the townsite boom might be averted, and so DeLacy was kept in the mountains searching for a pass which was never found.

About the time I landed in Whatcom, H. L. Yesler and Arthur A. Denny headed a party to go through the Snoqualmie Pass, but they did not reach the open country. W. H. Pearson, the intrepid scout, who won such laurels with Governor Stevens in his famous ride from the Blackfeet country, conducted a party of eighty-two persons, sixty-seven of whom packed their bedding and food on their backs, through the Snoqualmie Pass to the Wenatchee, where they were met by the Indians in such numbers and threatening mood that nearly all beat a hasty retreat.

Simultaneous with the movement through the Snoqualmie Pass, like action was set on foot to utilize the Natchess Pass, and large numbers must have gotten

through as on August 7th the report was published
that fourteen hundred miners were at work on the Natchess and Wenatchee. This report we known to be untrue, although it is possible that that many prospectors
were on those rivers, and we know also some gold was
taken out, and more for many years afterwards. But the
mines on these rivers did not prove to be rich nor extensive.

At the same time efforts were made to reach the mines
by crossing the mountains further south. The people
of Oregon were sure the best way was to go up the
Columbia River to The Dalles, and thence north through
the open country, and more than a thousand men were
congregated at The Dalles at one time preparing to make
the trip northward.

All this while the authorities of British Columbia
were not asleep, but fully awake to their own interests.
Soon Governor Dougless put a quietus upon parties
going direct from Puget Sound ports into the Fraser
River, and several outfits of merchandise were confiscated, among which was one of McCaw and Rogers from
Steilacoom. Another effectual barrier was the prohibition from entering the country without a miner's license,
which could be obtained only at Victoria. In this way
the Whatcom game was blocked, with or without a trail,
and the population disappeared nearly as rapidly and
more mysteriously than it had come, and the houses that
had been built were left tenantless, the stakes that had
been set were left to be swept away by the tides or to
decay, and Whatcom for a time became only a memory
to its once great population.

It is doubtful if a stampede of such dimensions ever
occurred where the suffering was so great, the prizes so
few and the loss of life, proportionately greater than that
to the Fraser in 1858. Probably not one in ten that
made the effort reached the mines, and of those who
did the usual percentage of blanks was drawn incident

to such stampedes. And yet, the mines were immensely rich, and many millions of dollars of gold value came from the find in the lapse of years, and is still coming, though now nearly fifty years has passed.

While the losses to the people of the Puget Sound country were great, nevertheless, good came out of the great stampede in the large accession of population that stayed after the return tide was over. Many had become stranded and could not leave the country, but went to work wth a will, of whom not a few are still honored citizens of the State that has been carved out of the Territory of that day.

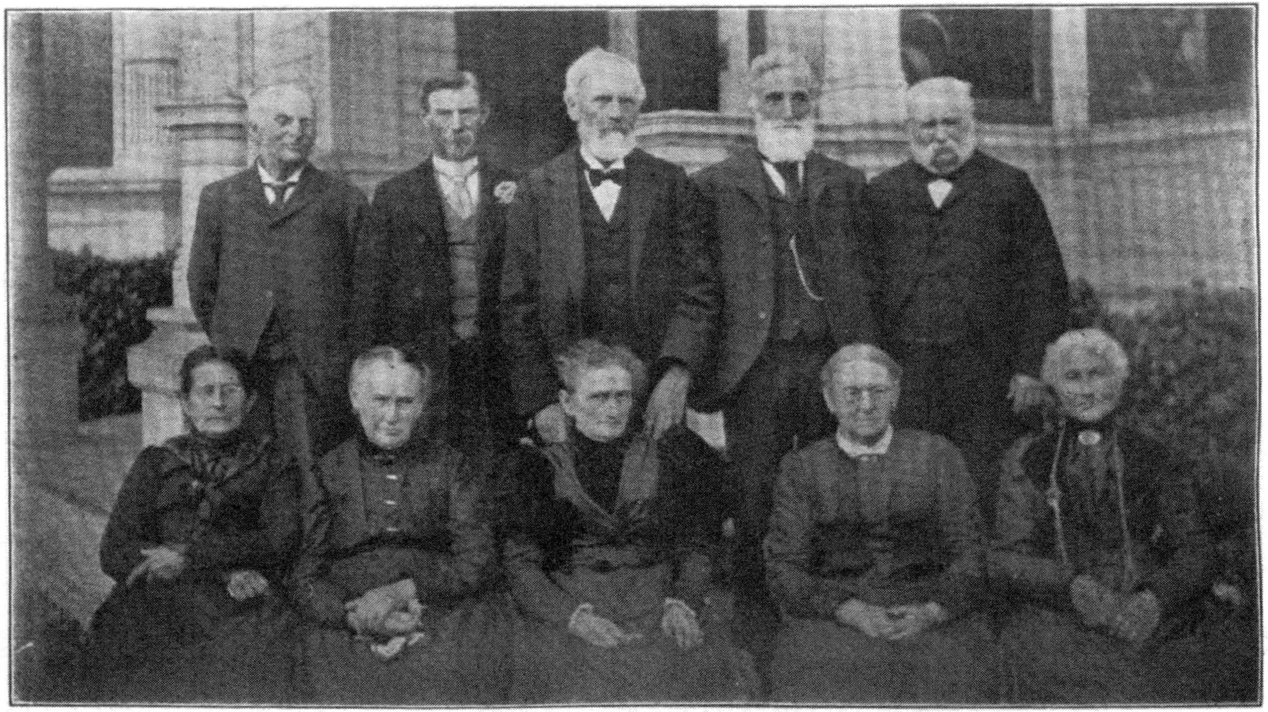

AN OLD SETTLERS' MEETING

CHAPTER XXII.

An Old Settlers' Meeting.

The fact that the generation that participated in the Indian war in this State (then Territory) will soon pass, an attempt was made to hold a reunion of all the adults who were in Pierce County at the outbreak of the Indian war in 1855, who are still living in the county.

Naturally, the incidents of the war coming under personal observation formed a never-ending topic of conversation. Mrs. Boatman related the incident of her boy "Johnny" (John Boatman, who now lives in Puyallup), two years and a half old, who was carried off by the Indians, as she firmly believes, but was found under an oak tree the following day. The whole garrison at Steilacoom turned out, together with a great many citizens, and scoured the prairie all night. Colonel Casey, the commandant, threatened vengeance against the Indians if the child was not returned. The theory was that the Indians had taken him for a ransom of their own people held by the whites.

A romantic incident was recalled of Kate Melville, the lady deputy sheriff. Her father was the first sheriff of Pierce County, and during his term of office was imprisoned for contempt of court. Kate was a beautiful girl, in ideal health, and a superb equestrian, but withal was a modest, retiring woman. When her father was incarcerated she was aroused to action and accepted the appointment of deputy sheriff with a resolute spirit, determined to take the responsibility of enforcing the law.

"Yes, I saw Kate coming down from the garrison one

day with some prisoners with a pistol strapped to her person," said Willis Boatman, "but I do not remember what her father was imprisoned for."

Scarcely one present but rememberd the incident "that seemed like a dream almost," in the lapse of forty-five years.

I remember seeing Kate on horseback, while acting as deputy sheriff during those troublous times, and had often thought to write up this romantic incident of stern real pioneer life, but space will not permit it here, further than to say that the responsibilities of the office were undertaken from a sense of duty and under intense loyalty to her father. Both now lie peacefully under the sod in the county in which their lot was cast.

"We moved out to my father's place about two months after the outbreak of the war," said George Dougherty. "The Indians sent us word not to be afraid—that they would not harm us. I had lived among the Indians from childhood, and in fact had learned to talk the Indian language before I could speak my mother tongue. At that time I believe there were twenty Indians to where there is one now. Most of the Indians were friendly. Had it been otherwise they could have wiped out the white settlement completely, in spite of the military and volunteers."

"Yes, and not left a grease spot of them," said Mr. Rogers. "But the fact is, the Indians did not want to fight the whites, but were dissatisfied with their treatment by the government. They wanted their land back, and got it, too, after they whipped the whites, which they did this side of the mountains. If it had not been that a majority of the Indians were in favor of peace with the whites, they could have held this country for a number of years. In fact, there were fifty or sixty Indians who fought on the side of the whites. There were a lot of whites who intended to stay out on their ranches, as they had perfect confidence in the Indians. The result of the war was that the Indians got all that they contended for. The good bottom land had been taken away from the Indians and they had been given the woods. This was done to open up the bottom lands for settlement. Notwithstanding this, many of the Indians were not hostile enough to go to war. The Indians east of the mountains initiated the war when they came over here and insisted that these Indians drive out the whites. In the meantime the Indians were given their lands back again. The Indians killed as many whites as the whites killed Indians. They had been living at peace with the whites and would have continued to do so had it not been for the Indians east of the mountains. I think that a mean advantage of the Indians was taken at that treaty."

"I think there were as many whites killed this side of the mountains as Indians," said Mr. Dougherty, resuming; "and there would have been no war had the Indians been properly treated. I remember Leschi and his band passed down through the prairie near my father's house, but did not stop to disturb us, but moved on to Muckleshoot and Green River."

"Yes, I remember considerable about the early condition of the Indian and their supply of food, for many and many is the time that I have enjoyed their hospitality and partaken of the various forms of what may be termed their land food as distinguished from fish. This was varied and abundant. I have seen trainloads of dried camas and sunflower roots carried by their ponies, and sometimes by the squaws on their backs. The Indians called the sunflower roots 'kalse.' It has now become almost extinct, except in small fields where it is protected. Kalse is a small root, about the size of an ordinary carrot, and has a yellow flower resembling the sunflower. The Indians would dig it with a crooked staff of ironwood stick, by twisting the stick among the roots and using it as a lever to pull up the roots. After getting a sufficient quantity of this sunflower root to-

gether the tops of the roots would be nipped off, then the
bark would be beaten off and a baking place arranged
in a hollow in the ground, with sallal berry twigs, leaves
and hemlock boughs. The roots would be piled up rounding, and covered over with the sallal and other material,
and the whole covered with earth. A fire would be made
over the ground and the roasting would occupy three or
four days, depending upon the size of the pile. After the
end of three or four days the remaining coals and hot
ashes would be removed from the top of the pile, and
there would be exposed the steaming sunflower roots.
The roots are very delicious in taste, though I cannot
compare it to anything now in use. They also made a
liquor from its roots by soaking, which was very exhilarating and strengthening. I have often partaken of
this food when a child. There was another food gathered from the prairie, which the Indians called 'lacamas'
or 'camas.' It is a small root, about the size of the end
of your thumb, and has a stalk that shows itself early in
the spring. It comes up as two leaves folded together,
and as it progresses in growth it spreads. From this appears a stem on the top of which is a blue flower. It is
very nutritious. It was generally prepared in large
quantities and could be kept until the following year. I
have always thought that it would be a great addition to
our garden products, and would be beneficial to us as a
health diet generally. The Indians who used it were
generally very healthy. There is another article of food
that I know the Indian name for, but not the white
man's. The Indian name is 'squelebs.' It grows in low,
marshy places and in creeks that run cold, clear water.
It has the appearance of the wild parsnip, and probably
is a species of it. It grows in joints. It is very delicious
to the taste in its season and is eaten raw. It is the finest
nervine that I ever used. Then comes 'kinnikinneck'
berries, or the Indian tobacco. The Indians will take
'kinnikinnick' leaves, roast them until brown, and then

mix half and half with tobacco, when it makes very fine smoking, and the odor is fragrant and very acceptable. It has an influence over the smoker like opium or ether. Some Indians that I have seen using it would keel over in a trance. It is very highly prized by them. The berries that grow and ripen on the 'kinnikinnick' when ripe are used as food by the Indians by mixing them with dried salmon eggs, and have the property of strengthening to an abnormal degree. They also used the young sprouts of the wild raspberry and salmon berry, which were very useful in cooling the system and very acceptable to the palate. There was another food product that the Indians called 'charlaque.' It throws out a broad, dark green leaf on one side of the stem, and on the end of the stem there is a bell-shaped flower of a brownish cast on the outside, and on the inside the color is orange, mottled with brown specks. It produces a flat root about the size of an ordinary walnut and is good either raw or roasted. It grows in shady places and near oak bushes. The root is white. There is also a species of the dandelion which has a very delicate-tasting root, which was eaten either raw or roasted. It is something similar to the wild parsnip, and the root is also white. When the root is broken it exudes a milk which is an excellent cure for warts. Another food plant was the 'wapato.' It grows in swampy places and sends its roots into the water. It grows luxuriantly in such places, and the tubers of the 'wapata' were highly prized by the Indians and could be eaten either raw or cooked. It had a delicate and pungent taste that was very acceptable to the palate. By this you will see that the Indians had a variety of food, when one takes into consideration the wild fruits, fish and game in which the country abounded."

Peter Smith* said: "We were crossing the plains in 1852 when Spotted Tail with about thirty warriors, fresh from the Crow war, rode up to our camp early one

*Died recently.

morning. I was cooking breakfast for our party, and I
tell you I was pretty well scared, but I thought to offer
them something to eat and after several attempts made
them understand what I wanted, and finally gave them
all a breakfast of bread and sugar and coffee. When
they first came they sat on their horses with feathers in
their hair, and said nothing to me and nothing to each
other, and I really thought my time had come. After
they had eaten their breakfast they went on up the
Platte River toward Fort Laramie. After we had traveled about three hundred miles we camped in the vicinity
of a large Indian force under the control of Spotted
Tail. I was with a group of men that had gathered
when I felt a tug at my coat tail. I looked around
quickly but saw no one, so I went on speaking to the
man that I had been talking to. Pretty soon I felt another tug, and looking around saw an Indian, whom I
recognized as the leader of the band that had eaten
breakfast at our camp a few days before. The Indian
told me that his name was Spotted Tail, and that he
wanted me to come to his camp a few miles away. I
told him I would go. Although the others in the party
tried to dissuade me from the undertaking, I went. The
chief treated me with great kindness and hospitality.
He was a tall, athletic Indian, and his daughters were
very pretty, having regular features and black hair. I
returned to the train well pleased with my visit. Forty
years after, while at the World's Fair, I met a young
man who had some office at Fort Laramie, which post
Spotted Tail often visited. He told me that Spotted
Tail often inquired about me, said that he had never
been so well treated by a white man in his life, and expressed a desire to have me come and see him. I was
very sorry that I never went through the reservation
where Spotted Tail lived to stop off and see him."

"The Indians have massacred all the white settlers
on White River and are coming down on us here in Puy-

allup," was passed from house to house on that fateful
October day of 1855. Mrs. Woolery and Mrs. Boatman
were the only survivors present at the reunion who witnessed the scenes that followed. Some had wagons;
some had none. Strive as best they could, they only got
across the river the first day. Two canoes were lashed
together and the wagons ferried across, after being first
taken apart. The trip out the next day was made on
foot, the women carrying the young children on their
backs. Then came the volunteer company a week later
to rescue the provisions, stock, clothing and other property that had been abandoned. This party consisted of
the settlers-of the valley, with a few others—nineteen in
all. The author was one of the "others," not having yet
settled in the valley. As we went in by the "lower" road
the column of United States troops and volunteers abandoned the field and withdrew by the "upper" road, leaving our little band in utter ignorance of our danger for
four days, when we crossed the trail of the retreating
column, which we afterwards learned had halted at
Montgomery's, at the edge of the prairie. Our women
folks were disturbed at our long stay, and the troops
were under orders to advance to our rescue, when lo!
and behold! at nightfall on the sixth day we returned,
loaded with property and provisions, in most cases being
all the possessions of the owners who formed a part of
the company, and there was great joy in camp. Not an
Indian had been seen nor a shot fired, except to empty
our guns to make sure that they would "go," as some of
the men quaintly expressed it.

After looking back over the vista of years, none of the
party could say that life had been a failure; there was
the lady bordering close on eighty years; the gentleman
eighty-four and past (Peter Smith), with the "kids" of
the party past the sixty-eighth mark, yet one would
scarcely ever meet a more cheerful and merry party than
this of the reunion of the old settlers of 1855.

CHAPTER XXIII.

A Chapter on Names.

In the latter part of the seventeenth century that intrepid English traveler, Jonathan Carver, wrote these immortal words:

"From the intelligence I gained from the Naudowessie Indians, among whom I arrived on the 7th of December (1776), and whose language I perfectly acquired during a residence of five months, and also from the accounts I afterwards obtained from the Assinipoils, who speak the same tongue, being a revolted band of the Naudowessies; and from the Killistinoes, neighbours of the Assinipoils, who speak the Chipeway language and inhabit the heads of the River Bourbon; I say from these natives, together with my own observations, I have learned that the four most capital rivers on the continent of North America, viz.: the St. Lawrence, the Mississippi, the River Bourbon and the Oregon, or the River of the West (as I hinted in my introduction), have their sources in the same neighbourhood. The waters of the three former are within thirty miles of each other; the latter, however, is rather further west."

All students of history acknowledge this is the first mention of the word Oregon in English literature. The narrative quoted was inspired by his observations on the upper Mississippi, and particularly upon the event of reaching his farthest point, sixty miles above the Falls of St. Anthony, November 17th, 1776. This was the farthest up the Mississippi that the white man had ever penetrated, "So that we are obliged solely to the Indians for all the intelligence we are able to give relative to the more northern parts," and yet this man, seemingly with prophetic sight, discovered the great river of the West, attempted to name it, and coined a word for the purpose. While Carver missed his mark and did not succeed in affixing the new-born name to the great river he saw in his vision, yet the word became immortal through the mighty empire for which it afterwards stood. Carver made no explanation as to where the word Oregon came from, but wrote as though it was well known like the other rivers mentioned. Probably for all time the origin of this name will be a mystery.

We have a like curious phenomenon in the case of Winthrop first writing the word Tacoma, in September, 1853. None of the old settlers had heard that name, either through the Indians or otherwise, until after the publication of Winthrop's work ten years later, "The Canoe and The Saddle," when it became common knowledge and was locally applied in Olympia as early as 1866, said to have been suggested by Edward Giddings of that place.

However, as Winthrop distinctly claimed to have obtained the word from the Indians, the fact was accepted by the reading public, and the Indians soon took their cue from their white neighbors.

It is an interesting coincident that almost within a stone's throw of where Winthrop coined the name that we find it applied to the locality that has grown to be the great city of Tacoma.

On the 26th of October, 1868, John W. Ackerson located a mill site on Commencement Bay, within the present limits of the City of Tacoma, and applied the name to his mill. He said he had gotten it from Chief Spot of the Puyallup tribe, who claimed it was the Indian name for the mountain, Rainier.

The word or name Seattle was unknown when the founders of this city first began to canvass the question of selecting a site for the town, and some time elapsed before a name was coined out of the word Se-alth.

Se-alth, or Seattle, as he was afterwards known, was reported to be the chief of six tribes or bands, but at best his control was like most all the chiefs on the Sound, but shadowy.

Arthur Denny says that we (meaning himself, Boren and Bell), canvassed the question as to a name and agreed to call the place Seattle, after the old chief (Se-alth), but we have no definite information as to when the change in the old chief's name took place. Sealth was quite disturbed to have his name trifled with and appropriated by the whites, and was quite willing to levy a tribute by persuasion upon the good people of the embryo city.

I have another historic name to write about, Puyallup, that we know is of Indian origin—as old as the memory of the white man runs. But such a name! I consider it no honor to the man who named the town (now city) of Puyallup. I accept the odium attached to inflicting that name on suffering succeeding generations by first platting a few blocks of land into village lots and recording them under the name Puyallup. I have been ashamed of the act ever since. The first time I went East after the town was named and said to a friend in New York that our town was named Puyallup he seemed startled.

"Named WHAT?"

"Puyallup," I said, emphasizing the word.

"That's a jaw breaker," came the response. "How do you spell it?"

"P-u-y-a-l-l-u-p," I said.

"Let me see—how did you say you pronounced it?"

Pouting out my lips like a veritable Siwash, and emphasizing every letter and syllable so as to bring out the *Peww* for Puy, and the strong emphasis on the *al,* and cracking my lips together to cut off the *lup,* I finally drilled my friend so he could pronounce the word, yet fell short of the elegance of the scientific pronunciation.

Then when I crossed the Atlantic and across the old London bridge to the Borough, and there encountered the factors of the hop trade on that historic ground, the haunts of Dickens in his day; and when we were bid to be seated to partake of the viands of an elegant dinner; and when I saw the troubled look of my friend, whose lot it was to introduce me to the assembled hop merchants, and knew what was weighing on his mind, my sympathy went out to him but remained helpless to aid him.

"I say—I say—let me introduce to you my American friend—my American friend from—my American friend from—from—from—"

And when, with an imploring look he visibly appealed to me for help, and finally blurted out:

"I say, Meeker, I cawn't remember that blarsted name—what is it?"

And when the explosion of mirth came with:

"All the same, he's a jolly good fellow—a jolly good fellow."

I say, when all this had happened, and much more besides, I could yet feel resigned to my fate.

Then when at Dawson I could hear the shrill whistle from the would-be wag, and hear:

"He's all the way from Puy-*al*-lup," I could yet remain in composure.

Then when, at night at the theaters, the jesters would say:

"Whar was it, stranger, you said you was from?"

"PUY-AL-LUP!"

"Oh, you did?" followed by roars of laughter all over the house. All this I could hear with seeming equanimity.

But when letters began to come addressed "Pewlupe," "Polly-pup," "Pull-all-up," "Pewl-a-loop," and finally

"Pay-all-up," then my cup of sorrow was full and I was ready to put on sackcloth and ashes.

The name for the town, however, came about in this way: In the early days we had a postoffice, Franklin. Sometimes it was on one side of the river, and then again on the other; sometimes way to one side of the settlement and then again to the other. It was not much trouble those days to move a postoffice. One could almost carry the whole outfit in one's coat pocket.

We were all tired of the name Franklin, for there were so many Franklins that our mail was continually being sent astray. We agreed there never would be but one Puyallup; and in that we were unquestionably right, for surely there will never be another.

Nevertheless, people would come and settle with us. Where the big stumps and trees stood and occupied the ground, we now have brick blocks and solid streets. Where the cabins stood, now quite pretentious residences have arisen. The old log-cabin school house has given way to three large houses, where now near eight hundred scholars are in attendance, instead of but eleven, as at first. And still the people came and built a hundred houses last year, each contributing their mite to perpetuating the name Puyallup. Puyallup has been my home for forty years, and it is but natural I should love the place, even if I cannot revere the name.

OLDEST BELL TOWER ON AMERICAN CONTINENT, TACOMA, WASH.
GIANT FIR, 500 YEARS OLD.

CHAPTER XXIV.

Pioneer Religious Experiences and Incidents.

If we were to confine the word religion to its strict construction as to meaning, we would cut off the pioneer actions under this heading to a great extent; but, if we will think of the definition as applied to morality, the duties of man to man, to character building—then the field is rich. Many of the pioneers, necessarily cut loose from church organizations, were not eager to enter again into their old affiliations, though their conduct showed a truly religious spirit. There were many who were outside the fold before they left their homes, and such, as a class, remained as they were; but many showed a sincere purpose to do right according to the light that was in them, and who shall say that if the spirit that prompted them was their duty to man, that such were not as truly religious as if the higher spiritual motives moved them?

We had, though, many earnest workers, whose zeal never abated, who felt it a duty to save souls, and who preached to others incessantly, in season and out of season, and whose work, be it said, exercised a good influence over the minds of the people.

One instance I have in mind—Father Weston, who came at irregular intervals to Puyallup, whose energy would make amends for his lack of eloquence, and whose example would add weight to his precepts. He was a good old man. Almost everyone would go to hear him, although it was in everybody's mouth that he could not preach. He would make up in noise and fervency what he lacked in logic and eloquence. Positively, one could often hear him across a ten-acre lot when he would preach in a grove, and would pound his improvised pulpit with as much vigor as he would his weld on his anvil week days.

One time the old man came to the valley, made his headquarters near where the town of Sumner now is, induced other ministers to join him, and entered on a crusade, a protracted union meeting, with the old-time mourners' bench, amen corner and shouting members. When the second Sunday came the crowd was so great that the windows were taken out of the little school house, and more than half the people sat or reclined on the ground, or wagons drawn near by, to listen to the noisy scene inside the house.

A peculiar couple, whom I knew well, had attended from a distance, the husband, a frail, little old man, intensely and fervently religious, while the wife, who was a specimen of strong womanhood, had never been able to see her way clear to join the church. Aunt Ann (she is still living), either from excitement or to please the husband, went to the mourners' bench and made some profession that led Uncle John, the husband, to believe the wife had at last got religion. Upon their return home the good lady soon began wavering, despite the urgent appeals from the husband, and finally blurted out:

"Well, John, I don't believe there is such a place as hell, anyhow."

This was too much for the husband, who, in a fit of sheer desperation, said:

"Well, well, Ann, you wait and you'll see." And the good lady, now past eighty, is waiting yet, but the good little husband has long since gone to spy out the land.

I have known this lady now for fifty years, and although she has never made a profession of religion or joined a church, yet there has been none more ready to help a neighbor or to minister to the sick, or open the door of genuine hospitality than this same uncouth, rough-spoken pioneer woman.

I recall one couple, man and wife, who came among us of the true and faithful, to preach and practice the Baptist Christian religion. I purposely add "Christian," for if ever in these later years two people embodied the true Christ-like spirit, Mr. and Mrs. Wickser did—lived their religion and made their professions manifest by their works.

Mrs. Wickser was a very tall lady of ordinary appearance as to features, while the husband was short and actually deformed. The disparity in their heights was so great that as they stood or walked side by side he could have gone beneath her outstretched arm. Added to this peculiar appearance, like a woman and a boy of ten years parading as man and wife, the features of the little man riveted one's attention. With a low forehead, flattened nose, and swarthy complexion, one could not determine whether he was white or part red and black, Chinaman or what not; as Dr. Weed said to me in a whisper when he first caught sight of his features: "What, is that the missing link?" In truth, the Doctor was so surprised that he was only half in jest, not at the time knowing the "creature," as he said, was the Baptist minister of the place.

But, as time went on, the strangeness of his features wore off, and the beauty of his character began to shine more and more, until there were none more respected and loved than this couple, by those who had come to know them.

A small factory had been established not far from the school house, where we had our Christmas tree. Some of the men from the factory took it into their heads to play what they called a joke on Mr. and Mrs. W. by placing on the tree a large bundle purporting to be a present, but which they innocently opened and found to contain a direct insult.

The little man, it could be seen, was deeply mortified,
yet made no sign of resentment, although it soon became
known who the parties were, but treated them with such
forbearance and kindness that they became so ashamed
of themselves as to inspire better conduct, and so that
night the most substantial contribution of the season
was quietly deposited at the good missionary's door,
and ever after that all alike treated them with the greatest respect.

, I have known this couple to walk through storm as
well as sunshine, on roads or on trails, for miles around,
visiting the pioneers as regularly as the week came,
ministering to the wants of the sick, if perchance
there were such, cheering the discouraged or lending a
helping hand where needed, veritable Good Samaritans
as they were, a credit to our race by the exhibition of
the spirit within them.

Take the case of George Bush, the negro, who refused
to sell his crop to speculators for cash, yet distributed
it freely to the immigrants who had come later, without
money and without price. Also Sidney Ford, another
early rugged settler, although neither of them church
members. Who will dare say theirs were not religious
acts?

In response to a letter, the following characteristic
reply from one of the McAuley sisters will be read with
interest, as showing "the other sort" of pioneer religious
experience, and following this, the brother's response
about the "mining camp brand." She writes:

"And now as to your question in a former letter, in regard
to religious experiences of pioneers. Tom had written me
just before your letter came, asking if I had heard from
friend Meeker and wife. I told him of your letter and asked
him if he ever heard of such a thing as religious experience
among pioneers. I enclose his answer, which is characteristic of him. The first church service I attended in California was in a saloon, and the congregation, comprising
nearly all the inhabitants of the place, was attentive and

orderly. I think the religion of the pioneers was carried in their hearts, and bore its fruit in honesty and charity rather than in outward forms and ceremonies. I remember an instance on the plains. Your brother, O. P., had a deck of cards in his vest pocket. Sister Margaret smiled and said: 'Your pocket betrays you.' 'Do you think it a betrayal?' said he. 'If I thought it was wrong I would not use them.' Here is Brother Tom's letter:

" 'Why, of course, I have seen as well as heard of pioneer religious experiences. But I expect the California mining camp brand differed some from the Washington brand for agricultural use, because the mining camp was liable to lose at short notice all its inhabitants on discovery of new diggings.'

"So, of course, large church buildings for exclusive church purposes were out of the question as impossible. And the only public buildings available were the saloons and gambling halls, whose doors, like the gates of perdition, were always open, day and night alike, to all, saint or sinner, who chose to enter, and having entered, had his rights as well as his duties well understood, and if need be, promptly enforced."

John McLeod used to almost invariably get gloriously drunk whenever he came to Steilacoom, which was quite often, and generally would take a gallon keg home with him full of the vile stuff. And yet this man was a regular reader of his Bible, and, I am told by those who knew his habits best, read his chapter as regularly as he drank his gill of whisky, or perhaps more regularly, as the keg would at times become dry, while his Bible never failed him. I have his old, well-thumbed Gaelic Bible, with its title page of 1828, which he brought with him to this country in 1833, and used until his failing sight compelled the use of another of coarser print.

I am loth to close this (to me) interesting chapter, but my volume is full and overflowing and I am admonished not to pursue the subject further. A full volume might be written and yet not exhaust this interesting subject.

CHAPTER XXV.

Wild Animals.

I will write this chapter for the youngsters, and the elderly wise-heads who wear specs may turn over the leaves without reading it, if they choose.

Wild animals in early days were very much more plentiful than now, particularly deer and black bear. The black bear troubled us a good deal and would come near the houses and kill our pigs; but it did not take many years to thin them out. They were very cowardly and would run away from us in the thick brush, except when the young cubs were with them, and then we had to be more careful.

There was one animal, the cougar, we felt might be dangerous, but I never saw but one in the woods. Before I tell you about it I will relate an adventure one of my own little girls had with one of these creatures near by our own home in the Puyallup valley.

I have written elsewhere about our little log cabin school house, but have not told how our children got to it. From our house to the school house the trail led through very heavy timber and *very* heavy underbrush —so dense that most all the way one could not see, in the summer time when the leaves were on, as far as across the kitchen of the house.

One day little Carrie, now an elderly lady (I won't say how old), now living in Seattle, started to go to school, but soon came running back out of breath.

"Mamma! Mamma! I saw a great big cat sharpening his claws on a great big tree, just like pussy does," she said as soon as she could catch her breath. Sure enough, upon examination, there were the marks as high up on the tree as I could reach. It must have been a big one to reach up the tree that far. But the incident soon dropped out of mind and the children went to school on the trail just the same as if nothing had happened.

The way I happened to see the cougar was this: Lew. McMillan bought one hundred and sixty-one cattle and drove them from Oregon to what we then used to call Upper White River, but it was the present site of Auburn. He had to swim his cattle over all the rivers, and his horses, too, and then at the last day's drive brought them on the divide between Stuck River and the Sound. The cattle were all very tame when he took them into the White River valley, for they were tired and hungry. At that time White River valley was covered with brush and timber, except here and there a small prairie. The upper part of the valley was grown up with tall, coarse rushes that remained green all winter, and so he didn't have to feed his cattle, but they got nice and fat long before spring. We bought them and agreed to take twenty head at a time. By this time the cattle were nearly as wild as deer. So Lew. built a very strong corral on the bank of the river, near where Auburn is now, and then made a brush fence from one corner down river way, which made it a sort of a lane, with the fence on one side and the river on the other, and gradually widened out as he got further from the corral.

I used to go over from Steilacoom and stay all night so we could make a drive into the corral early, but this time I was belated and had to camp on the road, so that we did not get an early start for the next day's drive. The cattle seemed unruly that day, and when we let them out of the corral up river way, they scattered and we couldn't do anything with them. The upshot of the matter was that I had to go home without any cattle.

We had worked with the cattle so long that it was very late before I got started and had to go on foot. At that time the valley above Auburn near the Stuck River crossing was filled with a dense forest of monster fir and cedar trees, and a good deal of underbrush besides. That forest was so dense in places that it was difficult to see the road, even on a bright, sunshiny day, while on a cloudy day it seemed almost like night, though I could see well enough to keep on the crooked trail all right.

Well, just before I got to Stuck River crossing I came to a turn in the trail where it crossed the top of a big fir that had been turned up by the roots and had fallen nearly parallel with the trail. The big roots held the butt of the tree up from the ground, and I think the tree was four feet in diameter a hundred feet from the butt, and the whole body, from root to top, was eighty-four steps long, or about two hundred and fifty feet. I have seen longer trees than that, though, and bigger ones, but there were a great many like this one standing all around about me.

I didn't stop to step it then, but you may be sure I took some pretty long strides about that time. Just as I stepped over the fallen tree near the top I saw something move on the big body near the roots, and sure enough the thing was coming right toward me. In an instant I realized what it was. It was a tremendous, great big cougar. He was very pretty, but did not look very nice to me. I had just had a letter from a man living near the Chehalis telling me of three lank, lean cougars coming into his clearing where he was at work, and when he started to go to his cabin to get his gun the brutes started to follow him, and he only just escaped into his house, with barely time to slam the door shut. He wrote that his dogs had gotten them on the run by the time he was ready with his gun, and he finally killed all three of them. He found they were literally starving and had, he thought, recently robbed an Indian grave, or rather an Indian canoe that hung in the trees with their dead in it. That is the way the Indians used to dispose of their dead, but I haven't time to tell about that now. This man found bits of cloth, some hair, and a piece of bone in the stomach of one of them, so he felt sure he was right in his surmise, and I think he was, too. I sent this man's letter to the paper, the Olympia *Transcript,* and it was printed at the time, but I have forgotten his name.

Well, I didn't know what to do. I had no gun with me, and I knew perfectly well there was no use to run. I knew, too, that I could not do as Mr. Stocking did, grapple with it and kick it to death. This one confronting me was a monstrous big one—at least it looked so to me. I expect it looked bigger than it really was. Was I scared, did you say? Did you ever have creepers run up your back and right to the roots of your hair, and nearly to the top of your head? Yes, I'll warrant you have, though a good many fellows won't acknowledge it and say it's only cowards that feel that way. Maybe; but, anyway, I don't want to meet wild cougars in the timber.

Mr. Stocking, whom I spoke about, lived about ten miles from Olympia at Glasgow's place. He was walking on the prairie and had a stout young dog with him, and came suddenly upon a cougar lying in a corner of the fence. His dog tackled the brute at once, but was no match for him, and would soon have been killed if Stocking had not interfered. Mr. Stocking gathered on to a big club and struck the cougar one heavy blow over the back, but the stick broke and the cougar left the dog and attacked his master. And so it was a life and death struggle. Mr. Stocking was a very powerful man. It was said that he was double-jointed. He was full six feet high and heavy in proportion. He was a typical pioneer in health, strength and power of endurance. He said he felt as though his time had come, but there was

one chance in a thousand and he was going to take that
chance. As soon as the cougar let go of the dog to tackle
Stocking, the cur sneaked off to let his master fight it
out alone. He had had enough fight for one day. As
the cougar raised on his hind legs Stocking luckily
grasped him by the throat and began kicking him in the
stomach. Stocking said he thought if he could get one
good kick in the region of the heart he felt that he
might settle him. I guess, boys, no football player ever
kicked as hard as Stocking did that day. The difference
was that he was literally kicking for dear life, while the
player kicks only for fun. All this happened in less time
than it takes me to tell it. Meanwhile the cougar was
not idle, but was clawing away at Stocking's arms and
shoulders, and once he hit him a clip on the nose. The
dog finally returned to the strife and between the two
they laid Mr. Cougar low and took off his skin the next
day. Mr. Stocking took it to Olympia, where it was
used for a base purpose. It was stuffed and put into a
saloon and kept there a long time to attract people into
the saloon.

Did my cougar hurt me, did you say? I hadn't any
cougar and hadn't lost one, and if I had been hurt I
wouldn't have been here to tell you this story. The fun
of it was that the cougar hadn't yet seen me, but just as
soon as he did he scampered off like the Old Harry himself was after him, and I strode off down the trail like
old Belzebub was after me.

Now, youngsters, before you go to bed, just bear in
mind there is no danger here now from wild animals,
and there was not much then, for in all the time I have
been here, now over fifty years, I have known of but two
persons killed by them.

And now I will tell you one more true story and then
quit for this time. Aunt Abbie Sumner one evening
heard Gus Johnson hallooing at the top of his voice, a
little way out from the house. Her father said Gus was

just driving up the cows, but Aunt Abbie said she never
knew him to make such a noise as that before, and went
out within speaking distance and where she could see
him at times pounding vigorously on a tree for awhile
and then turn and strike out toward the brush and yell
so loud she said she believed he could be heard for more
than a mile away. She soon saw something moving in
the brush. It was a bear. Gus had suddenly come upon
a bear and her cubs and run one of the cubs up a tree.
He pounded on the tree to keep it there, but had to turn
at times to fight the bear away from him. As soon as he
could find time to speak he told her to go to the house
and bring the gun, which she did, and that woman went
right up to the tree and handed Gus the gun while the
bear was near by. Gus made a bad shot the first time
and wounded the bear, but the next time killed her. But
lo, and behold! he hadn't any more bullets and the cub
was still up the tree. So away went Aunt Abbie two
miles to a neighbor to get lead to mold some bullets.
But by this time it was dark, and Gus stayed all night at
the butt of the tree and kept a fire burning, and next
morning killed the cub. So he got the hides of both of
them. This occurred about three miles east of Bucoda,
and both of the parties are living in sight of the spot
where the adventure took place.

CHAPTER XXVI.

The Morning School.

And now I will write another chapter for the youngsters, the boys and girls, and the old folks may skip it if they wish; but I am going to relate true stories.

Soon after the Indian war we moved to our donation claim. We had but three neighbors, the nearest nearly two miles away, and two of them kept bachelor's hall and were of no account for schools. Of course, we could not see any of our neighbors' houses, and could reach but one by a road and the others by a trail. Under such conditions we could not have a public school. I can best tell about our morning school by relating an incident that happened a few months after it was started.

One day one of our farther-off neighbors, who lived over four miles away, came to visit us. Naturally, the children flocked around him to hear his stories in Scotch brogue, and began to ply questions, to which he soon responded by asking other questions, one of which was when they expected to go to school.

"Why, we have school now," responded a chorus of voices. "We have school every day."

"And, pray, who is your teacher, and where is your school house?" came the prompt inquiry.

"Father teaches us at home every morning before breakfast. He hears the lessons then, but mother helps us, too."

Peter Smith, the neighbor (and one of the group in the old settlers' meeting), never tires telling the story, and maybe has added a little as memory fails, for he is eighty-four years old now.*

"Your father told me awhile ago that you had your breakfast at six o'clock. What time do you get up?"

"Why, father sets the clock for half-past four, and that gives us an hour while mother gets breakfast, you know."

You boys and girls who read this chapter may have a feeling almost akin to pity for those poor pioneer children who had to get up so early, but you may as well dismiss such thoughts from your minds, for they were happy and cheerful and healthy, worked some during the day, besides studying their lessons, but they went to bed earlier than some boys and girls do these days.

It was not long until we moved to the Puyallup valley, where there were more neighbors—two families to the square mile, but not one of them in sight, because the timber and underbrush was so thick we could scarcely see two rods from the edge of our clearing. Now we could have a real school; but first I will tell about the school house.

Some of the neighbors took their axes to cut the logs, some their oxen to haul them, others their saws and frows to make the clapboards for the roof, while again others, more handy with tools, made the benches out of split logs, or, as we called them, puncheons. With a good many willing hands, the house soon received the finishing touches. The side walls were scarcely high enough for the door, and one was cut in the end and a door hung on wooden hinges that squeaked a good deal when the door was opened or shut; but the children did not mind that. The roof answered well for the ceiling overhead, and a log cut out on each side made two long,

*Smith has just died as this work is going through the press. He was one of our most respected pioneers, possessed of sterling qualities of manhood. Like Father Kincaid, he was without enemies.

narrow windows for light. The larger children sat with their faces to the walls, with long shelves in front of them, while the smaller tots sat on low benches near the middle of the room. When the weather would permit the teacher left the door open to admit more light, but had no need for more fresh air as the roof was quite open and the cracks between the logs let in plenty. You can see the face of one of the teachers on the opposite page who is now over eighty years of age.

Sometimes we had a lady teacher, and then her salary was smaller, as she boarded around. That meant some discomfort part of the time, where the surroundings were not pleasant.

Some of those scholars are dead, some have wandered to parts unknown, while those that are left are nearly all married and are grandfathers or grandmothers, but all living remember the old log school house with affection. This is a true picture, as I recollect, of the early school days in the Puyallup valley, when, as the unknown poet has said:

> "And children did a half day's work
> Before they went to school."

Not quite so hard as that, but very near it, as we were always up early and the children did a lot of work before and after school time.

When Carrie was afterwards sent to Portland to the high school she took her place in the class just the same as if she had been taught in a grand brick school house. "Where there is a will there is a way."

You must not conclude that we had no recreation and that we were a sorrowful set devoid of enjoyment, for there never was a happier lot of people than these same hard-working pioneers and their families. I will now

THE OLD SCHOOLMASTER

tell you something about their home life, their amusements as well as their labor.

Before the clearings were large we sometimes got pinched for both food and clothing, though I will not say we suffered much for either, though I know of some families at times who lived on potatoes "straight." Usually fish could be had in abundance, and considerable game—some bear and plenty of deer. The clothing gave us the most trouble, as but little money came to us for the small quantity of produce we had to spare. I remember one winter we were at our wits' end for shoes. We just could not get money to buy shoes enough to go around, but managed to get leather to make each member of the family one pair. We killed a pig to get bristles for the wax-ends, cut the pegs from a green alder log and seasoned them in the oven, and made the lasts out of the same timber. Those shoes were clumsy, to be sure, but they kept our feet dry and warm, and we felt thankful for the comforts vouchsafed to us and sorry for some neighbors' children, who had to go barefooted even in quite cold weather.

Music was our greatest pleasure and we never tired of it. "Uncle John," as everyone called him, the old teacher, never tired teaching the children music, and so it soon came about they could read their music as readily as they could their school books. No Christmas ever went by without a Christmas tree, in which the whole neighborhood joined, or a Fourth of July passed without a celebration. We made the presents for the tree if we could not buy them, and supplied the musicians, reader and orator for the celebration. Everybody had something to do and a voice in saying what should be done, and that very fact made all happy .

We had sixteen miles to go to our market town, Steilacoom, over the roughest kind of a road. Nobody had horse teams at the start, and so we had to go with ox teams. We could not make the trip out and back in one day, and did not have money to pay hotel bills, and so we would drive out part of the way and camp and the next morning drive into town very early, do our trading, and, if possible, reach home the same day. If not able to do this, we camped again on the road; but if the night was not too dark would reach home in the night. And oh! what an appetite we would have, and how cheery the fire would be, and how welcome the reception in the cabin home.

One of the "youngsters," fifty years old to-morrow, after reading "The Morning School," writes:

"Yes, father, your story of the morning school is just as it was. I can see in my minds's eye yet us children reciting and standing up in a row to spell, and Auntie and mother getting breakfast, and can remember the little bed room; of rising early and of reading 'Uncle Tom's Cabin' as a dessert to the work."

Near where the old log cabin school house stood our high school building now stands, large enough to accommodate four hundred pupils. In the district where we could count nineteen children of school age, with eleven in attendance, now we have one thousand and seven boys and girls of school age, three large school houses and seventeen teachers.

The trees and stumps are all gone and brick buildings and other good houses occupy much of the land, and as many people now live in that school district as lived both east and west of the mountains when the Territory was created in March, 1853. Instead of ox teams, and some at that with sleds, the people have buggies and carriages, or they can travel on any of the eighteen passenger trains that pass daily through Puyallup, or on street cars to Tacoma, and also on some of the twenty to twenty-four freight trains, some of which are a third of a mile long. Such are some of the changes wrought in fifty years since pioneer life began in the Puyallup valley.

Now, just try your hand on this song that follows, one that our dear old teacher has sung so often for us, in company with one of those scholars of the old log cabin, Mrs. Frances Bean, now of Tacoma, who has kindly supplied the words and music:

FIFTY YEARS AGO

How wondrous are the changes Since fifty years a - go, When

girls wore woolen dresses   And boys wore pants of tow;   And

shoes were made of cowhide   And socks of homespun wool;   And

children did a half-day's work   Be - fore they went to school.

CHORUS.—Some fif - ty years a - go;   Some   fif - ty years a-

go; The men and the boys And the girls and the toys; The

work and the play, And the night and the day, The

world and its ways Are all turned around Since fif - ty years a - go.

VERSE 2D.

The girls took music lessons
  Upon the spinning wheel,
And practiced late and early
  On spindle swift and reel.
The boy would ride the horse to mill,
  A dozen miles or so,
And hurry off before 'twas day
  Some fifty years ago.   —CHO.

VERSE 3D.

The people rode to meeting
  In sleds instead of sleighs,
And wagons rode as easy
  As buggies nowadays;
And oxen answered well for teams,
  Though now they'd be too slow;
For people lived not half so fast
  Some fifty years ago.   —CHO.

VERSE 4TH.

Ah! well do I remember
  That Wilson's patent stove,
That father bought and paid for
  In cloth our girls had wove:
And how the people wondered
  When we got the thing to go,
And said 'twould burst and kill us all,
  Some fifty years ago.   —CHO.

LESCHI

CHAPTER XXVII.

Characteristics of Leschi.

The life, achievements and fate of Leschi are so intimately connected with those of the pioneers that the history and life struggles of the one cannot well be written without that of the other.

Seven years of the life of Isaac I. Stevens, first Governor of the Territory of Washington, are almost synonymous with those of Leschi for the like period. Both were representatives of their respective races, and their names became household words in the early days of the new Territory of Washington.

Leschi was living a quiet life fifty years ago on the Nisqually plains, not far from the head waters of Puget Sound, and only a private member of the tribe of Indians known as the Nisquallies. This was an obscure, small tribe or band of Indians, not particularly distinguished from other numerous bands inhabiting the region west of the Cascade Mountains north of the Columbia River.

The reader who has taken the pains to read the introductory chapter of Pioneer Reminiscences, under this cover, will there find the reason stated that it was an afterthought to write The Tragedy of Leschi—a growth out of the attempt to write a few reminiscences of pioneer life of fifty years ago in Washington Territory; that it was impossible to write of the white race inhabiting the region around about the headwaters of Puget Sound of that period without reference to the Indians, who constituted a large majority of the population, and whose everyday life was so intimately connected that the one could not be written without the other. The title has not been selected as a catchword to attract attention, but as expressing a fact in real life —of telling in a phrase of a real historic character that made a profound impression upon our early history in the Territory—a fact that could not be ignored and write a history of those early times.

This writing is intended as a history, and no fiction will find place in the pages to follow, and yet the story will read like fiction; as though impossible to be true, and that some of it must come from the brain of the writer or his contemporaries.

To give the reader an insight into the character of Leschi, I will introduce the testimony of a few of my contemporaries of that period—men of known character for truth and high standing in the community in which they lived, and prominent in the affairs of the commonwealth in which they cast their lot.

Lieutenant A. V. Kautz (afterwards General in the Union army) wrote of Leschi and published immediately after the close of the war of 1855-6:

"Being required to abandon their herds and cattle and go to Olympia, a conditional prisoner of the acting Governor, Leschi hesitated and delayed, and when Eaton's Rangers were sent to bring him in he fled with his brother (Quiemuth) to the enemy. His course during the war seems to be characterized by greater intelligence and humanity than that of any of the other chiefs. He protested against killing women and children, and against pillaging and plundering the settlements. On several occasions during the war he had individual white men in his power, and his influence saved them from being killed by Kanasket." [The author, E. M., was one.]

Speaking of what followed after the first outbreak, and of the resumption of active operations on the part of the regulars and volunteers in February, 1856, Lieutenant Kautz writes:

"The Indians at this time were considerably disaffected among each other. The winter had given them time to reflect. They would willingly have made peace if they could have done so with safety to themselves. The winter passed without any act of hostility. No forays were made, no descent on the settlements, nothing of that hostile character which might be expected from such a foe took place during the winter; but frequent overtures of peace. At the suggestion of Leschi a white child* (one of their prisoners) was sent in by way of an overture.

"That Leschi was the cause of this moderate policy is proved by his visit to the reservation, meeting on his way a number of white men whose lives he spared by his interposing his influence against that of Kanasket. He returned without committing any acts of hostilities, except to take off as many friendly Indians as he could induce to follow him to the hostile camp. His course in these matters created enemies for him in his own camp, and disaffection arose.

"But Leschi's name seems to have become unaccountably familiar in the mouths of the people, and obtained a notoriety beyond that of any other Indian in the war."

This testimonial from Lieutenant Kautz is particularly valuable, coming as it does from a man who fought in the war against the Indians, and was himself wounded, and who had exceptional opportunities to obtain exact facts.

Owen Bush, a respected citizen of this State, who still resides near Olympia, and has lived on the same place for nearly sixty years, said to the author a few months ago:

"Leschi was as good a friend as we ever had. He was dignified in his intercourse and proud of his country, and, I may say, proud of himself. He had a benevolent countenance that unmistakably stamped him as a good man. Leschi told me before going to the war that the Indians would not hurt any of the settlers, and advised us to stay

*Lieutenant Kautz was the officer at Fort Stellacoom who received the child and sent the little fellow, a boy of five years, to the author for care.

on our farms, which we did. I never was afraid to go wherever I wanted to during the war and did as I wished, and
was never molested. I could talk the Indian languages, but
Stevens did not seem to want anyone to interpret in their
own tongue, and had that done in Chinook. Of course, it
was utterly impossible to explain the treaties to them in
Chinook. Stevens wanted me to go into the war, but I
wouldn't do it. I knew it was his bad management that
brought on the war, and I wouldn't raise a gun against
those people who had always been so kind to us when we
were so weak and needy. The Indians could have killed us
all at any time during the eight years we were here before
Governor Stevens came, but instead of molesting us in any
way they helped us all they could."

As the old, resolute pioneer talked his lips trembled
and eyes moistened from the thought of the ill-treatment
of his old-time friends.

Colonel B. F. Shaw, who fought all through the war
and to the finish at Grand Ronde, said in a recent interview:

"Leschi was the greatest Indian orator on the coast. I
never considered him so great a warrior, but he was the
greatest orator I ever heard. He could sway his people by
his tongue better than he could by his sword. However, if
Leschi had been provided with provisions and ammunition,
with a few more men like himself, he would have put up a
stiff fight for us in the dense forests and thickets west of the
mountains."

And he did, as it was.

Colonel Granville O. Haller says:

"Leschi, like many citizens during the struggle for seces-
sion, appealed to his instincts—his attachment to his tribe
—his desire at the same time to conform to the requirements of the whites, which to many of his people were repulsive and incompatible. When Colonel George Wright,
commanding the Department of the Columbia, displayed

such an overwhelming force in the Klickitat country that it convinced the hostile Indians of the hopelessness of pursuing the war to a successful issue, and when they asked the terms of peace, Colonel Wright directed them to go to their former homes, be peaceful, and they would be protected by the soldiers, Leschi, though shrewd and daring in war, adopted Colonel Wright's directions, dropped hostilities, laid aside his rifle and repaired to Puget Sound, his home. He was entitled to protection from the officers and soldiers. But on the testimony of a perjured man, whose testimony was demonstrated by a survey of the route claimed by the deponent to be a falsehood, he was found guilty by the jury—not of the offense alleged against him, for it was physically an impossibility for Leschi to be at the two points indicated in the time alleged; hence he was a martyr to the vengeance of the unforgiving white men."

Old Wahoolit (Yelm Jim), one of Leschi's warriors, after a close-mouthed silence of forty years, finally, in 1896, unbosemed himself and gave out a long interview, which was printed at the time. The following extract from his talk, referring to the character of Leschi, will show in what esteem the great chief was held by his followers:

"Kul-la-wa-wutt, my wife's father, was chief of the Puyallups, and Leschi, whose mother was a Klickitat and his father a Nisqually, became chief of the Nisquallies. Leschi was tall, heavy built, and strong. He lived on the big prairie near Fort Nisqually, and was very rich. He had many horses scattered over the prairies, and had Indian boys to ride after them. He had much money in gold and hiaqua shells, and a big, good heart. He gave much to old sick men and women, and was kind to all people. Whenever there was a potlatch Leschi gave more than anybody. He was a dead shot and a great hunter. He would lead parties to the chase far into the mountains, where they would kill all the big game they could carry out. He often went by himself and returned with the skins of bear and elk. One day when he was alone in the mountains he saw some yellow dust in a little creek. Gathering it together

he enclosed it in a piece of buckskin. It was gold. He said
nothing about the circumstance until years after. He was
close mouthed, but was wise and could speak several Indian
languages. All the best Indians, King George men and
Boston men liked Leschi. He was a good man.'

In describing him in battle, he said:

"Leschi had incurred more danger than any of his warriors. He often exposed himself and was senseless as a
soldier in taking risks. But they could not get his head.
He was too agile and strong, and killed whenever he shot.
His ear was sharp and his eye keen. As the bad whites
were not content to have peace, but said they would hang
all the chief Indians,* a number of us sought safety in the
woods on the Nisqually. Sluggia, Leschi's nephew, was
among the hiding Indians. He was a bad man and had
quarreled with Leschi because the chief would not allow
him to kill women and children during the war. But he had
made friends again with his uncle."

Forty-seven years ago Dr. William F. Tolmie wrote:

"In 1843 the Puget Sound Agricultural Company's flocks
and herds, already numbering several thousand head, had
overspread the prairies lying between the Puyallup and
Nisqually Rivers, and, as feeding off the pastures interfered with the root-digging operations of the natives, discontent and ill-feeling occasionally arose on this account.
Another and more frequent cause of actual disturbance was
the poisoning of Indian hunting dogs by wolf-baits, or their
being shot by the shepherds when in the act of worrying
sheep. In July, 1843, when I came to reside at Nisqually,
an Indian was in irons in one of the bastions on suspicion
of having wounded a Sandwich Islands shepherd, with
whom a few days before he had had a squabble about killing
a dog. Leschi and Quiemuth I found had aided the whites
in capturing the Indian, and they were then, particularly
the one known as McLean's friend, or "Shikles," and the

---

*Wa-hoo-lit had been under sentence of death for killing William White
near Olympia, but had at the last moment been reprieved.

other as the friend of Taylor, these being the names of the two white men who lived on the prairies, superintending the management of the sheep. From the early days the brothers were noted for their readiness to assist the whites on all occasions, and with the first American settlers they, I think, obtained a similar reputation. In the fall of 1855 I pointed out Leschi to Governor Mason as an Indian of superior shrewdness, who, if properly managed, might be made very useful in quieting the Indian panic and preserving peace. With this in view I suggested himself and brother as the fittest Indians to accompany Governor Mason on his visits to the natives of White and Green Rivers —which they did, acting as interpreters and guides. On his return, in order to have the power of closely observing his movements, I gave Leschi employment as horseguard on the plains, where he would have been duly under the notice of white men, and whence, it is my opinion, he would not have stirred for the winter had he been left unmolested. By these steps, and by subsequently inquiring of Mr. Rabbeson whether he knew Leschi, as detailed in the evidence taken at the trials, I contributed to give the unfortunate man a notoriety he would not have had, and which since operated much to his prejudice. On this account, and in remembrance of important services by him rendered in early days to myself and others, I have done my best to save Leschi from his impending fate; and the inward monitor does not reproach me for any step taken in the matter."

In his paper filed with the State Historical Society, quoted elsewhere, Judge James Wickersham wrote:

"Leschi was, Colonel Benj. F. Shaw says, nearly six feet tall, and weighed about one hundred and seventy-five pounds. He was a true flathead, and had large brain room. He was an eloquent man, of strong force of character, and of great energy. He was born and lived on the Nisqually River. He had a winter home built strongly and permanently out of split cedar, and here he passed the long winter months, hunting and fishing, and frequently visiting the Hudson Bay people at Fort Nisqually. In the spring he moved out along the meadows skirting Muck creek (Yll-

Whaltz), his people hunting, fishing, racing horses, digging camas, and he leading a truly patriarchal life, free from care or burdens. His people were free and happy. They owned herds of horses, and frequently on their meadows might be seen the riding horses of their friends and relatives from Yakima, Klickitat or the Muckelshoot, while around their summer mat houses they sat and talked of hunting, trapping, or even of Indian myths and religions. Of this type of independent, free and strong men was the class opposed to the treaty of Medicine Creek."

But this is enough for the present to show who this man Leschi was, and is sufficient to illustrate a character worthy of a place in history did we but take into account his native worth as the "simple man," as he was; but he was more than this, as will be shown as this story progresses—a sacrifice to a principle, a martyr to a cause, and a savior of his people, for to his efforts mainly was due the granting of a place where his tribe might live and prosper, while he languished in prison and was finally led to the scaffold and judicially murdered.

CHAPTER XXVIII.

The Outbreak.

On the morning of October 28, 1855, three families were attacked, near the mouth of Green River, sixteen miles south of Seattle, by the Indians inhabiting the upper reaches of White and Green Rivers. Nine persons were killed, their cabins plundered and burned, as likewise were shortly afterwards nearly all remaining the whole length and breadth of the White River and Duwamish valleys.

Before giving the details of this crime, I will invite the reader to go with me a little way into the earlier history of the American settlements, and of the Indians inhabiting the country, and try to discover, if we can, the cause that led up to this tragedy. Although nearly fifty years have now elapsed since that October night, the memory of the scenes following in quick succession is yet vivid in my mind, stunned as we were by the action of our neighbors, the Indians, who had been before only kind to us, but whom now, for the moment, we could only look upon as our enemies ready to destroy us. We had lived together in peace and harmony, and as a rule were helpful to each other in neighborly friendship. We had worked together in the fields, and our flocks had run together on the commons. We had often joined together in the chase and in our sports, and now all was changed from a condition of peace to that of a war which, it appeared to us, was one of extermination.

Following the Hudson Bay Company's occupation of the country in 1833, came the Simmons-Bush party in 1845, who settled near where the City of Olympia has

since been built, the vanguard of the American settlers
north of the Columbia River. One of these, James Mc-
Allister, with his family, settled in the Nisqually bottom a year later, and was soon followed by others. More
came each year, and finally a large number in 1853, yet
no discontent was manifested by the Indians.

The Indians, as a class, from the earliest settlements
down to the time of making the treaties in 1854-5,
evinced not only a willingness that the white men should
come and enjoy the land with them, but were pleased to
have them do so. Here and there a murder had been
committed by vicious individuals of tribes, but no con-
certed action hostile to the peaceable occupation of
the country by the white race, until after the Medicine
Creek treaty council was held, December 26, 1854, unless we take the actions of the Snoqualmie Indians under that rascally chief, Pat Kanim, in attacking Fort
Nisqually, and the threat against the settlers on Whidby Island, as evincing such hostility.

There had not even been any organized bands for robbery among these Indians, except by the more northern
tribes, the Snohomish and Snoqualmies, who during the
war following the treaty professed friendship and took
part in the war against their own race, and I may say
that at no time more than one-tenth of the Indians west
of the Cascade Mountains were at war.*

At the outset it is proper to say that I refer to the
tribes west of the Cascade Mountains, and more partic-

---

*According to the crude census of the Indians taken at the time the
treaties were made, there were no more than 6,000 in all of the Puget Sound
basin. The superintendent during the war reported he was feeding 4,000 on
the reservation, after the war broke out, and we know of some that were not
fed and yet remained friendly. At the close of the war 600 were reported as
giving in their submission, men, women and children, so it is a safe estimate
to say that no more than ten per cent. of the Indians went on the warpath,
or about two hundred warriors.
    I am not unmindful of the fact that Governor Stevens in April, 1857,
reported that there were 9,712 west of the Cascade Mountains, being all out
of proportion to the number reported in the crude census taken at the time
of making the treaties. In his last report to the department Stevens set
down the number coming under the Medicine Creek treaty as 1,200, while his
previous report of the census taken at the time was 900. At best, all enumeration of Indians in considerable part is but guess work.

ularly those inhabiting the region covered by the Medicine Creek treaty, and in part the territory and inhabitants of the next succeeding, the Point Elliott council, in all including the country covering both sides of the Sound and lying south of Seattle to the Chehalis.

As evidence of this friendly spirit, we have the testimony of many that Leschi met the small immigration of 1845 part way between the Columbia River and the Sound with horses loaded with food and presents for the "white squaws," of whom he and his tribe had seen so few.* One of these new incoming settlers, James McAllister, who had selected a location in the Nisqually bottom where the Nisqually tribe in part lived, took a donation claim of a mile square of the choicest land, covering a long stretch of the Medicine Creek, that gave the name to the first treaty made, the first negotiated with the Indians north of the Columbia River.

The McAllisters were upright, honest and industrious people, and treated their Indian neighbors justly, and were in turn respected by them and were kindly helped in times of need during the earlier period of their settlement among them. From a personal experience among this class of Indians, at a little later date, I can readily believe the story told by the McAllisters of the numerous acts of kindness shown them by the Nisqually tribe, and particularly Leschi, who, as we shall see by abundant testimony, had a character for liberality and benevolence far beyond the average of his race, and in fact, considering his means, of the white race.

The channels of the creeks that flowed through the McAllister claim furnished a common meeting ground for the Indians of the Sound (the "fish" Indians) and those of the plains (the "horse"), or those Indians who lived principally by the chase, and where came a gradual blending of the two, including the extremes of pov-

*Only the two missionaries near Fort Nisqually, Mrs. John P. Richmond and Miss Chloe Clark, who arrived in 1840.

erty and ignorance and of better thrift and greater intelligence.

The Nisqually tribe embodied both classes, the former predominating and spreading their language, habits and customs far and wide on Puget Sound, the first even in one isolated settlement on the upper reaches of the Snohomish River. The Nisqually tongue was the most widely spoken language covering the Sound region, and to that fact may be attributed the importance of the tribe as compared to their number.

The tribal relation engendered hospitality; so, also, did a life of leisure, and particularly so where the bond of union is not governed by a strong will, the tribe separated into small bands, and a central authority was absent, or at best but shadowy, or entirely nominal. This hospitable habit extended to strangers as well as to kinfolk, and to the pioneer as well as Indians, but where not reciprocated the Indians at once became distant and distrustful and mercenary. The tribal government of the Nisquallies, whatever in time gone by it may have been, had ceased many years before the advent of the American immigration and was never revived* until the Medicine Creek treaty solidified the more active and intelligent members of the tribe, to war against a common danger—the danger of being deprived of their homes.

Before the treaty Leschi was but a common citizen of the Nisqually tribe, yet one of influence and universally liked. He had, as if by common consent, become what might be termed a judge or arbitrator, who held court without law and whose judgment was without appeal,

*Up to 1849 "Laghlet" was the legitimate and acknowledged chief of the Nisquallies, and his eldest son, "Wyamock" (The Man Who Fights) was his lawful successor, but he was such a wild, ill-behaved young man that the people would have nought to do with him, and the tribe went without a chief until the Medicine Creek treaty occurred, when Governor Stevens appointed Quiemuth chief. I never heard of Leschi having another brother besides Quiemuth. He had a sister. Stahl was his brother-in-law.—Edward Huggins' private letter.

but he was over and above all a citizen of wealth and sobriety, and one whose word commanded respect.

But little is known of the father of Leschi, farther than that he was an humble citizen of the tribe, married a Yakima from the east side of the great range of mountains, who brought with her not only wealth in horses, but an active mind and healthy body, and bore him the two sons and one daughter, all famous in local history.

With the Indians none of the sons bear the name of the father, as with the white race. The usages of the tribe allowed each child to select his own name, unless perchance some incident of birth or of the life should suggest one, which was often the case. This custom, as will readily be seen, precluded the possibility of building up a large family name. The name Leschi, adopted by the young man, has no special significance, but is a purely arbitrary invention of a word to suit the fancy. None of that name ever preceded him, though a numerous following has succeeded, by individuals adopting the name for the honor supposed to come from the name of the great citizen, whom the exigencies of war made chief.

A large portion of the tribe used to go out on the near-by Sound, both for pleasure and for food, often camping where night or adverse winds overtook them. There they met wandering families of other bands, who, like themselves, were in quest of adventure.

Fifty years ago one could scarcely go upon any nook or corner of this vast inland sea, Puget Sound, without hearing the measured stroke of the paddle upon the canoes, struck in time with the plaintive song in minor key of merry voices of maiden and gallant or spouse. In the quiet summer evenings these voices could be heard for miles around about, while their light canoes would be propelled through the water with astonishing rapidity.

The song of the Indian, like that of the sailor, seemed to be a part of the life afloat, as it was seldom heard ashore. The temporary camps were made from light mats of their own manufacture, and were quickly put in place, and as speedily repacked when the camp was struck. I am safely within the bounds of truth to say that I have certainly seen and heard thirty of these canoeing parties at a time within a radius of five miles of the Nisqually during the years of 1853-4-5, while residing near these people. Their food was scattered all over the beach, always accessible when the tides were out, if shell fish was wanted, or, if fish, whenever there was calm water.

On these expeditions these people seemed to have no care; it was a season of indolent outing, where all thought of the future was cast aside. Often a temporary landing would be made to gather the wild fruits found in great abundance in places, and quite often a deer or smaller game would be bagged.

At these times schools of small fish would rise to the surface and with their splashing disturb the water like a heavy hail storm. Then the Indians would take a pole with numerous barbs on either side and use it as with the stroke of a paddle and soon load their canoes to their hearts' content. There seemed to be no end to fresh fields for this enjoyment. The distant reader can scarcely realize the extent of these waters, but can gather a faint idea when considering there are sixteen hundred miles of shore line in all the bays and channels comprising the whole. Small wonder, with such surroundings, we should find a people without high aspirations or high intelligence, or that would care much for the soil or for the treaties of governments, so long as they might float and fish and sing and gamble unmolested. But there came disturbing elements, as we shall see later.

Issuing from this camping ground on the banks of the

Medicine Creek, there came a better development of manhood that turned their faces eastward toward the plains and mountains.

Bordering on the Nisqually River, and some three hundred feet above the level of the river, the Nisqually plains of gravelly soil extended either way, north and south, that afforded a rich bunch grass, the fattening qualities of which was almost equal to the cereals grown by our farmers. These plains were studded with clumps of evergreen, as also margins of heavy timber, both to the east toward the mountains and to the west bordering the Sound. Numerous lakes of varying sizes dotted the surface with living spring water, thus affording an ideal spot for game or domestic stock. It was in this region that Leschi had chosen his home and where he pastured his stock.

That portion of his tribe inhabiting the uplands made frequent incursions into the foothills of the Cascade Mountains that extended within a dozen miles of their chosen place of abode, where the larger game was found —the elk, bear and deer—in great abundance. Their journeys were frequently extended beyond the summit to the great plains, now known as the Inland Empire, and then inhabited by a numerous, hardy and more warlike race.

With this latter race there came frequent intermarriages that grafted the stock of the eastern tribes on to that of the western, and brought with it that community of interest that served the tribe so well in the stress of war following the treaties.

We never hear much of the family on the waters of the Sound, and I doubt if Leschi often left his favorite haunts of the chase for the lower levels of the salt sea waters. We hear of him frequently to the south, sometimes on the eastern slopes of the mountains, but I do not recall an instance of his being on the Sound until his visit near Steilacoom during the war, with thirty-two of his followers, where he boldly confronted the troops sent over to capture him and his party, which they failed to do.

The chief factor of the Puget Sound Agricultural Company, Dr. Wm. F. Tolmie, exercised great and beneficent influence over the tribes adjacent to their work. No doubt his efforts tended to elevate the tribes coming within the sphere of the company's influence. This particularly applied to the nearby horse Indians of the up-river portion of the Nisqually, as they had great need of just such help as this afforded. To this influence may well be attributed in part the development of Leschi's character, as the Doctor laid great store by him. Leschi never entered into the service of the company, but there soon grew a community of interest helpful to both. Tolmie trusted Leschi implicitly, and in fact the whole up-river band, but Leschi was particularly helpful to him because of his superior intelligence.

Although a digression, I am tempted to relate an incident of later years illustrating some characteristics of these people, how strong their affection and how steadfast their friendship.

Sixteen years after the Doctor removed to Victoria he made his first visit to his old friends and came to my house, where a great congregation of the natives were picking hops. We went together to a field where 140 were at work. As soon as he was discovered a shout of joy went up; all hands quit their work and surrounded the doctor, shaking hands and exhibiting great manifestations of pleasure. An elderly woman shed tears of joy, whereupon some youngsters began to laugh. Turning upon them she said: "I don't care; he was all the same to me as my father," and wept freely.

The Doctor called my attention to the fact that all of the Leschi relatives were there, which he attributed to the known fact of my friendship for the chief during his lifetime.

In a spirit of fun one day I gave an Indian mother a dollar upon the report made that her child had been born on my place during the hop harvest. Ever after that each mother employed that gave birth during the hop harvest claimed this head money, which was cheerfully paid. That morning while the Doctor and I made the rounds of the hop fields, an Indian woman at work with her box nearly full pointed significantly to a narrow board leaning against a hop pole, with an infant securely strapped to it, whereupon without either of us saying a word I handed her a dollar, and would have thought no more of the incident had not the action brought inquiry from Tolmie. We found upon investigation that the child had been born Saturday night, and yet in thirty-six hours the mother was at work in the field.

CHAPTER XXIX.

The Primitive Peoples.

I love to live over the experiences of early pioneer life and could I but feel my readers would enjoy the tales and folk lore of that period as well as I do myself, I would be tempted to cast the history writing aside and continue in the freer field of reminiscences, but I am admonished a duty of recording history lies before me of more importance than of walking in the green fields of old time experiences.

However, I am tempted to invite my readers to a further study of the life and experiences of these primitive peoples, the Indian and early pioneers, to gain an insight into their lives, what impulses governed their actions and what influences surrounded them before taking up the inquiry of the causes of the war that followed the peaceful period already noted.

We are wont to look upon the native race as indolent, filthy and worthless. And so they are, many of them. But, of tribes that will go into the hop fields and earn thirty thousand dollars in a month, as the Indians did with me, we cannot say they are wholly indolent; and that they are filthy, so they are many individuals, but I can recall numerous cases of tidy houseworkers to help our pioneer women, and neatly dressed men and women with their holiday attire. And that they are worthless. So there are many of them; perhaps a majority, and yet I can recall hundreds of cases whose word was good, who kept a contract if he made one and paid a debt if he incurred one. I have had this class contract for clearing land, and I must say they stuck to their work and com-

INDIAN GAMBLING SCENE

pleted their contracts as loyally as the average of the white men in the same line.

Edward Huggins, who has had so large an experience in employing Indian labor while in charge of the Puget Sound Agricultural Company's affairs, writes:

"After the outbreak of the Indian war in 1855, the exigencies of the company's business caused me to take charge of the live stock and farming part of the business, and in the fall of 1855 I moved to Muck Station, with a party of fifteen or twenty men—Englishmen, Canadians and Kanakas. I remained at that station until 1859. After the conclusion of the war (end of 1856), I continued to reside at Muck and had several Indians employed along with English and Canadian laborers, thus affording me a good opportunity of learning the comparative merits of each class, and I do not hesitate to say that I found the Indian laborer much superior as a workman to the English and Canadian workman. The Indians made capital plowmen and cared for their horses much better than did the others; and, to cut the matter short, I would sooner have my Indian laborers than the white men I had with me during my five years of service as farm overseer at Muck. I had a few Indians who were good rough carpenters, and firstrate axmen. I had three Indians who were, as farm workers in general, incomparably superior to any white men the company had employed."

Naturally, there would be some turbulence in such a large congregation of Indian laborers as came into the hop fields in the hey-day of that industry. There came an army of gamblers, thieves, confidence men, peddlers and idlers of both races who caused much trouble. Sometimes we would have a little jar with the laborers, but seldom, and quickly settled, and then here and there with individuals, but almost always adjusted in good humor. Sometimes with a boisterous drunken Indian we would make a law unto ourselves and confine him, but can scarcely remember a case of resistance, but when there was, there would be ten willing hands to help to one that would object.

Our Indian neighbors did not steal from us; the women might pilfer a few potatoes from the hill, or a few apples from the tree (and so might some of the white brethren if the truth must be told), but for taking articles of considerable value, never once did the settlers suffer by their hands. The cabins remained unlocked night and day, the tools of the farmer left in open sheds or in the fields; the stock allowed to range at will, and yet no losses occurred. Many Indians camped near the settlers' cabins, and worked for their white neighbors in the fields or in the clearings, and in many cases were reliable, industrious, good laborers.

This writing now is from the book of experience, and a very large experience at that, in later years when in the hop fields I have, not infrequently, employed from seven hundred to nearly a thousand of men, women and children of this race at a time during the harvest season. We need not attribute this spirit of good will and apparent honesty inherent to this race to account for their actions. We know full well the abject ignorance that prevades these tribes. We know that only in a dim way have they the power to discriminate in the abstract as to right or wrong, but they can readily see what is to their material advantage and are not slow to appreciate a just treatment, and to freely render in kind that which is meted to them.

As a class they are without ambition; without mental capacity to embrace a real civilized life and without keen perception to quickly grasp the new problems incident to higher culture. For generations their measure of right to a great extent had been that of might; and hence we need not wonder that their promptings to honest actions were those of interest. The pioneers with but rare exceptions treated their Indian neighbors justly, and we may say generously, and were met by the Indians with a like spirit, and so it came about that there was a real community of interest and good feeling between them and their Indian neighbors.

Some details of particular instances as illustrating the conditions related will be interesting and useful in showing the final cause that led up to the catastrophe of war, so ruinous to all.

I will take the case of Sky-uck (Jim Meeker, as he was afterwards universally known till the day of his death). Sky-uck came to us while young. He worked diligently and gained our confidence. There was not a lazy bone in his body. He would work just as hard and just as diligently when alone as when under my eye. He took a pride in doing his work well and in learning the ways of the whites. When he married, his wife became useful in the field or laundry, house cleaning, or whatever might be required. While not as intelligent as many others of her class nor as good natured, yet one could see she was improving in her habits of life and learning many useful ways that were helpful in all her after life. Old Sal, as we later called her, remained grateful to the last for the schooling she received from the little wife presiding over the pioneer home.

I will take another instance; that of Sarah Kitsap. She was in fact an intelligent woman—full blooded Indian—kept her clothing tidy and always appeared well in company. This woman received her lessons in household work from one of our neighbors. In time, no white lady in the whole neighborhood could put out more spotless linen on the line than this Indian woman, nor more smoothly iron and starch the same. Another case of one of the same tribe we used to know by the simple name, Jane, or as Tom's Jane, following the "Boston" name of her husband. Jane was always in pleasant mood, always happy in her work and proud of her white friend, Mrs. D. M. Ross, whom she served so well and from whom she received so many valuable lessons, helpful to both. Nor were the husbands lacking in their appreciation of the benefits accruing from their contact with civilized people. They constantly strove to imitate their white neighbors and to profit by the lessons received from them. These incidents related were not of much importance considered separately from the larger community, but they illustrate what was happening all over the Territory where the pioneers and native race had come into intimate neighborly relationship. What Jane and Sarah Kitsap or Old Sal were learning, others of various shades of worth were learning all over the land—a great industrial school where pupils and preceptors were alike interested and alike benefited.

The reader must not conclude that it is intended to convey the impression that these cases recited and similar instances referred to, by any means comprised a majority of the native race. As a matter of fact, they did not, but were numerous enough to make the situation hopeful for eventually elevating the greater portion of them. There were many worthless persons too indolent, too ignorant and too degraded to be reached by precept or example. Such in particular belonged to the class elsewhere described as the fish Indians, whose condition seemed hopeless, and yet, even out of this class there came individuals who would receive benefits from the contact with the superior race. The leaven was at work that would have gradually elevated the natives far above their original position if it had been left to work out to its logical sequence. But this was not to be. A power three thousand miles away, working under a mistaken idea, that essayed to control and govern the Indians in our midst, applying rules that were inapplicable and unjust, became paramount in the dealings with these people. These rules had grown from the experience of the nation with other native races of entirely different habits and motives and under entirely different surroundings. With the Indian of the Atlantic sea-board and thence westerly to and beyond the Rocky Mountains there had been either constant warfare or an armed truce. Treaty after treaty had been made, only to be broken by both parties. The gathering white clouds of settlers from the east continually crowded upon the warlike tribes, and steadily doubled them back upon the advancing frontier. The government had adopted, first possibly from necessity and afterwards from force of precedent, the fiction of Indian Nationalities, of independent governing powers within the territory of the United States, as unsound in principle as it was unjust and fatal to both races. It required the experience of a century to bring about the final overthrow of the treaty theory of dealing with the Indians; of dealing with them as organized and independent communities; of treating with them in one breath as tribes and in the next as dependents (which they were); of acknowledging their ownership of the soil on the one hand while grasping it firmly by the other; of making professions of peace, when under prevailing conditions there could be no peace and finally professing the desire to have them adopt the habits of civilized life while driving them into conditions to make such a life impossible. This writing is not intended as a wholesale denunciation of our government for its dealings with the Indian race. A government that has expended over five hundred million dollars on its civil list in an attempt to better the condition of less than three hundred thousand people is not a government to condemn without stint. The conditions confronting the government were abnormal and of necessity in a way experimental. Grave blunders were made—blunders, not of the heart, but from a supposed necessity to keep peace, yet none the less fatal to the welfare of the frontiersman as to the native race. This fatal policy has now all been changed by a four line proviso in a thirty page appropriation bill, approved March 3rd,

1871, as follows: "Provided, That hereafter no Indian nation or tribe within the territory of the United States shall be acknowledged or recognized as an independent nation, tribe, or power with whom the United States may contract by treaty." *

Had this proviso been the law of the land twenty years before, there would have been no Indian war west of the Cascade Mountains. I speak with great confidence from the fact that where treaties were not made, as with the Chehalis band or tribe, and others, no war ensued. It is true, a large majority of the Indians who entered into treaty stipulations remained friendly, and that not necessarily because a treaty is made that war must ensue, but this does not alter the fact that the making of the Medicine Creek and Point Elliot treaties was the sole cause of the war that followed, that caused the horrible massacre mentioned, that drove the pioneers from their homes, the Indians into either hiding, the war camp or the worse and more demoralizing, dependent pauper making camps to be fed by the government. *

Nevertheless, while these facts are true, that the policy pursued by the government contained the germ that caused the war, this does not exonerate the instrument that carried that policy into effect. While the policy, to put it temperately, was vicious, yet a mild and just application would have as certainly averted as that the contrary action did cause the war. This treatment will be reviewed later in the consideration of the treaties made or alleged to have been made within a month that could not have properly been considered and executed within a year or more.

---

*United States statistics at large, Vol. 16, page 566.
*During the winter of 1855-6 the Government fed over four thousand Indians—two-thirds of the whole Indian population.

ISAAC I. STEVENS

CHAPTER XXX.

Medicine Creek Treaty.

However much we may condemn the treaty making policy of the Government (the people of the United States), and point out the fiction underlying the system, we must not close our eyes to the formidable difficulties confronting the "Fathers" while struggling for independence with as unrelenting and heartless foe as ever waged war on a supposed weaker party. From the discovery of the continent down to the revolutionary period, all civilized governments had entered into treaties with the natives, while at the same time they refused to acknowledge their independence. Each European government based its claim to any particular part of the continent by right obtained from discovery, which right was held to apply only as against other civilized nations and not as against the native peoples. All conceded to the natives the right of occupancy, but not of title to the soil. The Indian might occupy, but could not sell to other than the Government claiming a particular portion of the continent. And this right of occupancy soon was properly construed to a reasonable occupancy, holding that the rights of civilized people were equal to those of the savage or natives, although the native races were the first occupants. The trouble came from abuse of power by the stronger party; from the failure to do equity under a righteous rule; a rule which said you must make room for a people that will utilize this fair country, exploit its mines and ascertain its possibilities for contributing to the sustenance of mankind.

Speaking of civilized nations Chief Justice Marshall says, "When the conquest is complete and the conquered inhabitants can be blended with the conquerors, or safely governed as a distinct people, public opinion, which not even the conqueror can disregard, imposes these restraints (that the conquered shall not be wantonly oppressed) upon him; and he cannot neglect them without injury to his fame, and hazard to his power."

"But the tribes of Indians inhabiting this country were fierce savages, whose occupation was war, and whose subsistence was drawn chiefly from the forest. To leave them in possession of their country, was to leave the country a wilderness; to govern them as a distinct people was impossible, because they were as brave and as high spirited as they were fierce, and ready to repel by arms every attempt on their independence." Hence, we must treat them as a dependent people, else abandon this great continent capable of sustaining hundreds of millions of people to a race of three hundred thousand to roam over at will. This last suggestion, to leave the country in the hands of the native races, is simply an unthinkable proposition that no civilized man will entertain.

But when the American Confederacy appeared on the stage, the statesmen of that day were confronted with a problem that could only be solved by an acknowledgment of existing conditions. The Government of England had Indian allies in the field against the struggling patriots. Could they shut their eyes to an existing power confronting them, the power of great tribes of Indians upon their borders? They did the only thing possible to do; that was to enter into a treaty with an existing power. So we find the first treaty with the Indians made dates Sept. 17, 1778, which is not a treaty for land nor a treaty for peace, but a treaty for war; of offence and defence against a common foe, with the "Delaware Nation" on the one part and the "United States of North America" on the other part, "articles of agreement and confederation," and thus was the treaty system with the Indians born. It was then no fiction, whatever may be said of aftertime negotiation. We know these early treaties were broken and new conditions prevailed until it did seem there was nothing but fiction; the one party, the Indians, in the words of Gen. Otis, being "neither citizens nor aliens; neither subjects nor rulers; neither slaves nor freemen." We might say, a people without a country; without a flag; without a history. Did space permit, this interesting topic would be pursued further, but we must forbear with this remark that the subject is introduced here simply to illustrate that Indian treaties in all cases and under all circumstances were not fiction, but in many instances very real.

But the conditions calling out the first treaties with various tribes were ever changing, and called for new rules of action. As I have said these early treaties were broken—perhaps were made to be broken—and doubtless first the one party and then the other were to blame, but when, in the lapse of time, the Indians could not or would not observe the conditions of a treaty, and when events which no human power could control pressed upon the Government, there came a time the question must be met and things called by their right names, and the only wonder is that it should have taken so long, so near a century, to finally bring the nation to acknowledge the change.

The making of treaties with the Indians of this part of the United States was sheer fiction. The so-called tribes could scarcely be called tribes at all. Their organization where they had any, was loose and broken up into families acknowledging no authority, except family ties, and so these tribal relations were constantly changing according to the whims of the individual or supposed benefits to accrue from a change. There was not even an unwritten law governing the tribe; no authorized chief or head men that had any but the most unstable authority, or that even made a pretense of having, and to be able to treat with them as a tribe at all (except in a few cases), such chiefs were appointed by the Superintendent of Indian Affairs on the part of the United States. Of course the whole proceeding was a farce.

We will now take under consideration the Medicine Creek and Point Elliot treaties, the real cause of the war west of the Cascade Mountains. The fiction of the nine tribes to deal with, in the Medicine Creek Council, can readily be seen when the facts are stated. There were less than nine hundred Indians, nearly eight hundred of whom belonged to the Nisqually and Puyallup tribes, leaving but a hundred to comprise the remaining seven so called tribes, probably fifteen to the tribe.

George Gibbs, who was present as surveyor, took a census either at that time or a few weeks before, and could find but 893 all told. Governor Stevens, who was also Superintendent of Indian Affairs for the new Territory, assumed all the authority for the Government in making the treaty. He appointed chiefs with whom to treat, in several cases, if not in all.

He did not possess either the time or knowledge to deal with this question intelligently; neither the temperament, habits, or training. If one wants a house built he does not send for a watchmaker, or if he wants a case tried in Court, for a clergyman. Gov. Stevens had his special training in a special walk of life, war— and in his special department of that profession he was proficient, but sorry is the day for the Indians, and settlers as well, and we may also say, for Governor Stevens himself, when he was turned loose here with a free hand as Superintendent of Indian Affairs.

After a long absence from the Territory, at Washington City, adjusting the affairs of the overland trip of the previous year, the Governor returned in time to find a Legislature on his hands. Sending them a hasty message, he then began preparation to make treaties

"OLD MIKE SIMMONS," 1845. WITH FIRST PERMANENT AMERICAN SETTLER

with the Indians, nearly two years after his appointment as Governor. He had previously made a flying
trip on the Sound but had embraced no opportunity to
make a study of the situation, and in fact had had no
time. His trip had afforded him about the measure of
information that a ride on a railroad car will a traveler
of the country traversed, and so equipped he began the
preparation for making treaties with all the Indians
on the Sound, and west of the Cascade Mountains, and
undertook to do in a month what could not have been
properly done under years of patient labor after obtaining painstaking information; in a word, he undertook
an impossible task.

The first move was to block out a form of treaty in
his office at Olympia with the aid of M. T. Simmons,
who had previously been appointed as agent. The form
soon developed into the substance, as he was informed
the Indians would sign anything presented to them,*
and so, when the Medicine Creek treaty was ready in
the office it was presented to the Indians without change
of any kind, including reservations and all without consultation with the Indians.

After writing the treaty and sending men ahead to
notify the Indians and clear a spot for holding the council, the Governor and suite embarked aboard a schooner
at Olympia, and soon reached the treaty ground, some
twenty miles distant by sail and twelve as the crow flies.

The ground selected for holding the council is a small
wooded knoll on the right bank of the She-nah-nam
Creek (known locally as the McAllister Creek), about
one mile above the mouth, where the waters of the creek
fall into and mingle with the tides of Puget Sound.

The Squa-quid (Medicine Creek), falls into the She-
nah-nam nearly a mile above the treaty grounds, and is
lost in the former, which is very much the larger. Hereafter these creeks will be referred to as the McAllister

*See Colonel Shaw's statement to Wickersham in following chapter.

and Medicine Creeks respectively, for convenience, and their Indian names dropped, as has been done locally by the settlers.

As has been said, the McAllister Creek is very much the larger of the two. It is a creek of absolutely pure spring water, less than four miles in length, venting an astonishing volume from such a small area. At the head is a deep pool or spring, the delight of sportsmen for all the country round about, where the finest of trout rise to the fly of such size and flavor as to make one shy of telling the true story, lest he be accused of exaggeration, if not of downright lying. The Medicine Creek sends out an insignificant volume of water, which is slightly covered from the vegetable growth obstructing its flow, hence its name. Both creeks flow through the alluvial soil of the Nisqually bottom, ten feet below the level of the valley surface, the current in the lower stretches of each obstructed, and in fact, reversed by the incoming tides from Puget Sound twice a day. Into these creeks the happy Indians in times gone by used to float their canoes in countless number, laden with the shell fish and other products of the salt inland Sound. As I recently drove down the right bank of the McAllister Creek to the treaty ground not an Indian was to be seen, not a canoe; but the grinding wheels of our wagon uncovered great beds of shells, the remains of the feasts of the primitive race in by-gone days.

When the treaty making party started from Olympia bringing presents and food for the Indians and with a small army of attaches of near twenty persons, it was expected an easy victory would be gained, as the Governor had been told, as before mentioned, the Indians would sign anything presented to them. The party, however, were doomed to meet with disappointment. The first day was passed in anxious solicitude as to what the morrow would bring forth. From Indian testimony we know that the Governor was nervous and uneasy

all day, walking back and forth with his head down
and hands behind his back, as the fact dawned upon him
that he could not have everything his own way without
a struggle. All of the Indians had not arrived, although
it is recorded over six hundred were present, men, women
and children, though we have no certain intelligence
that any material accessions to their number were made
during the continuance of the council. The Indians
from the up-river districts came with their horses as
usual, and in considerable force. That class of the tribe,
or so called nine tribes, though not numerous, were on
the alert to know what was going to happen. They had
heard all sorts of rumors, even that the Government
contemplated shipping all the Indians out of the country
to the land of perpetual darkness (Alaska). This idea
became real when it was discovered the intention was to
huddle the whole tribe on a small tract of land convenient to salt water, where they could not possibly live or
keep their horses or even have a potato patch, or so much
as a place to be out of reach of the forest and tides.
Plausibility of this story became fixed in the Indian
mind when an attempt was made to explain in jargon,
the right was reserved to remove the Indians at the will
of the Government to some unknown point.

In a recent interview Colonel B. F. Shaw (who was
at the time a young man and acted as interpreter on this
occasion, and who, I may say, is yet of vigorous mind),
said, the intention, as he understood it, was to make the
reservation allotted temporary, and remove all the Indians in the whole Sound country to one large reservation
further north. Be that as it may, it is certain no progress could be made with the Indians the first day of the
council.

Every effort was made by the assembled attaches to
create diversion from the serious work in hand during
the evening of the first day by story telling and other
means to create good humor in the minds of the Indians,

but with slight success. The second day developed a very stubborn opposition, and resulted in the spectacular action of Leschi, as related elsewhere, when he tore up his commission as sub-chief before the Governor's eyes, and left the council grounds.

With Leschi out of the way, and with the accession of the Olympia Indians headed by John Hiton, referred to elsewhere, and with the assent of the Squoxons, upon whose land one of the reservations was to be located, together with the urgent solicitation of at least a part of the Governor's suit, some progress was made on the second day to induce the reluctant Indians to subscribe, but only such, as has been said, that would sign anything presented to them, gave their assent. On the third day the presents were distributed, but these did not, as expected, create a favorable impression and in fact, the opposite, when it became known how small the value allotted to each person, two yards of calico here, a yard or two of ribbon there, and of like value all around.

And so ended the first treaty council held by the new Superintendent in the new Territory, that wrought ruin not only to the Indians, yet likewise to many of the pioneers and to Governor Stevens himself, for in its injustice inflicted upon the natives came the war that followed within a year, and the season of so many years of strife among the citizens long after the Indians had been pacified by the tardy justice of larger and suitable reservations.

I would have the reader remember this writing refers to the Indians coming wholly under the Medicine Creek treaty, and a part (the Muckleshoot and neighboring bands), under that of Point Elliot.

The partisans of Governor Stevens at a later date claimed that the Governor was not so responsible for the harsh treatment meted out to the Indians as was the department at Washington in prescribing iron-clad rules to govern his action. It is not of record, and I doubt if Governor Stevens ever made such a claim, though it became patent that under the stress of political exigencies he remained silent and let such a claim go undisputed. The following letter of original instruction from the Department of the Interior under date of August 30th, 1854, is well worth perusal by the student of history as not only embodying the instructions to Governor Stevens, yet likewise outlining the general policy of the Government in dealing with the Indian question fifty years ago. This, it will be seen, is very different from that prevailing now, where treaty making with the Indians is forbidden by law, where tribal relations are being rapidly broken up and the individuals brought directly under the control of the law without the intervening fiction of a treaty.

The following are the instructions referred to:

"Department of the Interior, Office Indian Affairs, August 30, 1854.

"His Excy.: Isaac I. Stevens, Governor, &c., of Washington Territory, Present.

"Sir: * * * In concluding articles of agreement and convention with the Indian tribes in Washington Territory, you will endeavor to unite the numerous bands and fragments of tribes into tribes and provide for the concentration of one or more of such tribes upon the reservations which may be set apart for their future homes.

"The formation of distinct relations with each of the forty or fifty separate bands of Indians in Washington Territory would not be as likely to promote the best interests of the white settlers or of the Indians as if the latter could be concentrated on a limited number of reservations, or on contiguous reservations, in a limited number of districts of country, apart from the settlement of the whites.

"Unless some such arrangement can probably be effected you will at present conclude treaties with such tribes or bands only as are located immediately adjacent to the settlements of the whites, and between whom and our citizens animosities prevail, or disturbances of the peace are reasonably apprehended, and in entering upon the execution of the duty, with which you are hereby charged, you will turn your attention first to even tribes and bands.

"It is desirable also that the stipulations to be fulfilled annually on the part of the United States be few in number, and that the Department retain the authority to apply the funds to a variety of objects, such as the circumstances of the Indians at the time of payment may require.

"This suggestion you will regard particularly, if you are unable to effect the combination of all the bands into six or eight tribes, or to arrange half a dozen treaties, or less, so that every one of the tribes shall be a party to them.

"It is not deemed necessary to give you specific instructions as to the details of the treaties. I, however, enclose to you herewith copies of the treaties recently concluded by Superintendent Palmer at Table Rock and Cow Creek, Oregon Territory, with the Rogue River and Cow Creek Indians, and also printed copies of treaties lately concluded at this city with the Omaha and Ottoe and Missouri Indians.

"Those negotiated by Superintendent Palmer are regarded as exhibiting provisions proper on the part of the Government and advantageous to the Indians, and will afford you valuable suggestions. Those with the Omahas and Ottoes and Missouris will indicate the policy of the Government in regard to the ultimate civilization of the Indian tribes; the graduation of the annuity payments secured to them; the encouragement of schools and missions among them; the exclusion of ardent spirits from their settlements, the security to be given against the application of their annuity funds for payment of debts and claims, the terms on which roads and railroads may be constructed through their reservations, and the authority proper to reserve to the President of determining the manner in which annuities of Indians shall be applied for their benefit.

"I would here remark that the amounts secured to tribes in Nebraska will not be a criterion for you, in regard to the amount of the annual or other payments to be made to tribes in Washington under stipulations of the proposed treaties, inasmuch as the former held lands which had become valuable by reason of their proximity to the State of

Iowa, whilst the latter have claims of title based on occupancy alone, and that occupancy of a nature not fixed and well defined as to boundaries, and the lands which they claim are far removed from the portions of the country which have long been settled and highly improved and cultivated.

"I would also refer you to the late annual report of this office, and the last annual report of the Secretary of the Interior, from which you will perceive that it is regarded by the Department as the best policy to avoid, as far as it can be judiciously done, the payment of Indian annuities in money, and to substitute implements of agriculture, stock, goods, and articles necessary to the comfort and civilization of the tribes.

"You will bear in mind the distance that separates you from the Capital, and the time which must elapse from the negotiation of treaties until you hear of the action of the President and Senate upon them, and you will hence caution the Indians against expecting the first payments of annuities too soon after the conclusion of negotiations.

"You will at your earliest convenience furnish to this office a skeleton map of Washington Territory, showing the location of the different tribes and bands, and the boundaries of the regions respectively claimed by each, and as treaties are concluded from time to time, in your reports accompanying them, furnish a description of the reservation provided for the occupation of the Indians, with such precision that it may be marked on the map here.

"With these general views you will nevertheless exercise a sound discretion, where the circumstances are such as to require a departure from them; and you will take care in all treaties made to leave no question open, out of which difficulties may hereafter arise, or by means of which the treasury of the United States may be approached.

"It is expected that a due regard to economy will govern all your acts, and that you will promptly report progress in the execution of the trust now confided in you.

"Very respectfully, your obt. servant,

"CHARLES E. MIX.
"Acting Commissioner."

CHAPTER XXXI.

Medicine Creek Council Reviewed.

The statement that Leschi did not assent to the treaty, although his name appears third on the list as having signed it, will no doubt at first thought be received with incredulity by the general reader. I can only say that I believe it is true, and the facts will be given supporting this belief.

It is not necessary to attack the credibility of the witnesses to Leschi's signature while saying he did not sign, although certified to by them. All know how careless we are in such matters. Besides the question of carelessness comes the fact that perhaps not more than two or three of the witnesses knew Leschi by sight, or for that matter, any of the Indians. * Then the further fact that the council extended over a period of three days, and that the utmost confusion prevailed, with a babel of unknown tongues in several languages, to constantly distract attention. As to the particular parties having the treaty in their possession for signature, little can be said in extenuation.

We have one well authenticated case where the name of a noted chief was affixed to a treaty by another chief at the instance of Governor Stevens himself.

We have no less authority than Hazard Stevens, son of the Governor, for the following account of how the

---

*To show the utter disregard as to the fitness of things, we have only to note the name of Hazard Stevens, then a boy of twelve years, to the treaty as one of the witnesses. Recently interviewing George Leschi and interrogating him as to whether his uncle (Leschi) had signed the treaty, he said: "Oh, I don't know; I was a boy then about the size of Governor Stevens' tenas-man (Hazard Stevens), and we were having a good time eating black strap and playing jewsharps while the men were talking. We didn't know what they were talking about."

signature to the Walla Walla treaty of one great chief, Looking Glass, was obtained without his consent, and in fact, by means no less than forgery to be committed by another chief of another tribe, Kam-i-ah-kan:

"Looking Glass, just returned from the Blackfeet country, hearing that the Nez Perces were at a great council, and concluding a treaty without his presence (I quote Hazard Stevens' own words)* pushed on with a few chosen braves, crossed the Bitter Root Mountains, where for some distance the snow was shoulder deep on their horses, and, having ridden three hundred miles in seven days, at the age of seventy, reached the council ground while Governor Stevens was urging Kam-i-ah-kan to give his assent to the treaty, for the Governor, hearing the arrival of Looking Glass announced, seized the occasion to call upon the Yakima chief to sign the treaty in the name of Looking Glass, there being great friendship between the two. Scarcely had he concluded when Looking Glass, surrounded by his knot of warriors, with scalps tossing above them, rode up, excited and agitated, received his friends coldly, and finally broke forth into a most angry philippic against his tribe and the treaty:

"My people, what have you done, While I was gone you have sold my country. I have come home, and there is not left me a place on which to pitch my lodge. Go home to your lodges. I will talk to you." And the council was immediately adjourned.

If the Governor could obtain the signature to the treaty of one chief, as here related, in one instance, we are justified in believing that he would do so in another case when met with obstinate opposition, especially where we have overwhelming testimony, even if the witnesses are Indians. We have the testimony of Leschi himself that he did not sign the treaty, and the testimony of numerous Indians present, who have uniformly, for forty-five years, declared that he did not sign it; of Dr. William F. Tolmie as to Leschi's opposition to the

*Life of Isaac I. Stevens, by his son, Hazard Stevens, Vol. 2, page 54.

treaty, shown in his letter to Governor McMullin; of Lieutenant A. V. Kautz, who wrote in February, 1858:

Kanasket was at the council (Medicine Creek) and was cognizant of the miserable piece of fir timber that was given to the Nisquallies. He saw how Leschi was spurned when he spoke up and protested. They told him to go away. "You are half Klickitat; you have nothing to say; the treaty is made."

Senator L. F. Thompson, who at the time lived within two miles of the council grounds when the treaty was made, wrote:

"After the treaty was over the Indians came to me and said that Leschi would not sign the treaty for the Nisquallies and Puyallups. They were the Indians Leschi represented. But M. T. Simmons told Leschi that if he did not sign it he would sign it for him. From what the Indians told me at the time and from what the whites told me, I am positive that Leschi never signed the treaty."

And finally, of the disappearance of the records of the council from the files of the Government at Washington, after the partisans of Governor Stevens had published garbled extracts from the proceedings but suppressed all reference to Leschi or to the speech he made, which we know was a matter of record.

I have recently interviewed John Hiton, an Indian, one of the five survivors of the signers, who steadfastly refused to go into the war. He says Leschi did not sign; that he stood up before the Governor and said that if he "could not get his home, he would fight, and that the Governor then told him it was fight, for the treaty paper would not be changed." Continuing, Hiton said, "Leschi then took the paper out of his pocket that the Governor had given him to be sub-chief, and tore it up before the Governor's eyes, stamped on the pieces, and left the treaty ground, and never came back to it again."

Hiton still lives on his own farm near Tenino, where his father lived before him, and is looked upon as a truthful man by all his neighbors amongst whom he has lived so long.

Subsequent to the penning of these lines and before the manuscript had been handed to the printer, I received the following interesting letter:

Olympia, Wash., Dec. 21, 1903.

Hon. Ezra Meeker, Seattle.—Dear Sir: In the Indian war of 1855-6 a family named King on White River, or thereabouts, was massacred. One boy was saved through the efforts of an Indian* (Friendly) now living near here. The boy was adopted by a family named Gunn, and now lives in Connecticut. The Indian has property worth quite a little money and he wants to will it to this boy. Mr. Billings says he thinks you can give me the address of him or his people. Please do so, as it means a modest fortune to the beneficiary. Yours,

PHIL SKILLMAN.

Fortunately, I was able to give the desired information through John King, the only survivor of the massacre, but who is not of kin though of same name and at the time of the massacre lived on an adjoining claim. I happen to know all the parties, and also to know the property, which does mean a nice "modest fortune to the beneficiary" and feel extremely gratified to be able to record this generous impulse of my old friend Hiton, whom I have known so long and whom I have always known as a truthful upright citizen.

Hiton has always been friendly to the whites and steadily refused to go into the war but he feels deeply the injustice done his race, yet he condemned the acts of the Indians in murdering those poor, innocent people, and now, at the age of seventy, wants to make amends

---

*Hiton is the Indian referred to. He has valuable land property, both at Tenino and on the Puyallup reservation, the latter worth several thousand dollars.

for the wrongful acts of his race. I had heard that
Hiton was unfriendly towards Leschi, but I found this
was a mistake; that his sympathies were with Leschi,
but his judgment was that it was useless to make war
as they were certain to be overcome in the end.

I introduce this incident here to show the character
of the man and to ask the reader candidly, whether the
utterances of such a man are not worthy of credence
even if he is an Indian.

Hiton, though shrewd enough to obtain an allotment
on the Puyallup Reservation, never made that his real
home, but obtained title to land twelve miles out from
Olympia, where he has always lived and where his father
lived before him.

I have visited Hiton twice in the preparation of this
work and when he and his wife both told me that Leschi
did not sign the treaty, but left the council grounds in
a rage, I believed as I have said that they have told
me the truth, and I believe so yet.

Tyee Dick, another signer of the treaty, recently told
me that Leschi did not sign the treaty, and that Leschi
told the Indians, "If you sign that paper, I will go away,
but I will come back and get what I want."

"What did he mean by that, Dick?" I asked.

"O, he meant he would fight until he got his home."

I have quite recently interviewed Dick for three hours
at one time, and tested his memory by asking about
things I knew, and found his answers almost invariably
correct.

Dick signed the treaty and then went in to the war
"like a fool for signing," he said.

"Then why did you sign, Dick?" I asked.

"Oh, John Hiton made a speech. This was the second
day. Hiton he said we sign treaty, and then we take
farms all the same as white man" and then all the whites
and the Governor took off their hats and cheered, and

then the Olympia Indians began to sign, and the Squax-ons they signed and I held back, but Simmons come and patted me on the back and told me "that's a good fellow, Dick, you go and sign, and I will see you are treated right and well taken care of, and I knew Simmons and thought him good man and signed."

"Did you understand what the treaty was?"

"No, I don't think any of the Indians did understand. Why would they agree to give up all the good land, and that was what we found afterwards the treaty read."

Hiton said, "The reservation was no good; all stones; all big timber; up on bluff; nobody live there; nobody live there now."

"Then why did you sign it?" I asked.

"Why, what's the use for Indians to fight whites? Whites get big guns; lots ammunition; kill off all soldiers, more come; better sign and get something some other way."

Old Pa-al-la hearing that I was on the treaty grounds searching for information, came to volunteer his testimony. This man went to the war with his three sons and was very bitter against the Governor.

Said he: "S'pose no Governor Stevens, no war. Les-chi tear up the paper; I saw him do it, and then I knew he would fight," and much more in the same strain, but I forbear to record it. To my mind the fact is abundantly proven that the Indians strenuously objected to having all their land taken from them save a small area of heavily timbered upland, totally unfit for cultivation; that the Governor stubbornly refused to give way an inch, but insisted that they must submit to his will, and that not only did Leschi not sign the treaty, but many others whose names are attached as signers did not sign, or give their assent.

The question will naturally arise in the reader's mind, why was this done? It cannot be true! What object could Governor Stevens have in view to make him do such a thing? That it was preposterous to make such a statement, for it carries its own refutation by its improbability, and in fact, was impossible for men occupying such a position under our Government to do so.

I have racked my brain on this question a good many years, and confess that such thoughts would crowd upon me, and then I would awake to the cold fact that it was so; that it was written in Articles of the Medicine Creek Treaty; that the land described I knew was as I have said, totally unfit for occupancy or cultivation, and so would come back to the question, Why was it so? Then why was the quantity so restricted? Why less than four thousand acres allotted for nine hundred Indians of nine tribes? We know this is so, for it is so written in the treaty and signed, Isaac I. Stevens, Governor & Superintendent; ratified by the great United States Senate as attested by Asbury Dickens, Secretary, and finally, by no less august signature than that of Franklin Pierce, President of the United States, and attested by W. L. Marcy, Secretary of State.

So we must accept the fact as proven that out of the millions of acres of this broad domain, only these tracts, aggregating less than four thousand acres of the poorest land that could be found, were allotted to the original occupants of the district described.

This chapter having been submitted to Thos. W. Prosch, of Seattle, for criticism, that gentleman, without the knowledge of the author, wrote to General Hazard Stevens with reference to the foregoing extraordinary statement with reference to Looking Glass and received the following reply and explanation, which is cheerfully here printed as follows:

Olympia, July 29th, 1903.

Thomas W. Prosch, Esq.—Dear Sir: I am astonished at your misconception of the sentence in the account of the Walla Walla council that you quote, viz.: "The Governor, hearing the arrival of Looking Glass announced, seized the occasion to call upon the Yakima chief to sign the treaty in the name of Looking Glass, there being great friendship between the two," etc. The meaning I wished to express is that the Governor called upon Kamiakan in the name of Looking Glass to sign the treaty for himself, Kamiakan. It seems to me the sentence is quite plain to this effect, although it would have been better had the clauses been transferred. To charge Governor Stevens with attempting such a fraud, and one so impossible to carry out with those intelligent and proud Indians, is simply preposterous.

My account is drawn almost wholly from the official* journal, which is very full. Colonel Kipp's account is excellent, too. I am interested in what you say about the manuscript. I doubt if anything that I or any one could say would satisfy a writer who could seize upon the sentence you quote to support so outrageous a charge. If it is not a secret I would like to know who the writer is. As for any agitations, etc., I have no fears. Governor Stevens' record and character are proof against such imputations. Whatever else may be charged, no instance of double dealing or indirection can be found in his entire career.

Should I publish another edition of the life I will certainly make this sentence clear by changing the clauses. I am exceedingly obliged to you for calling my attention to it.

Very truly yours,

HAZARD STEVENS.

Whatever may be the true version of the incident at the Walla Walla Council, the facts as to whether Leschi signed the Medicine Creek Treaty remain unchanged. We have a right to weigh testimony by the rules of probabilities as well as by that of the respectability of witnesses. On the one side we have the signature of Leschi affixed to the treaty with the words, "his mark," while on the other we have the testimony of all the Indians that he did not in any way assent to

---

*The italics are the autnor's. The reader's attention is called to the fact that this "official journal" is not now to be found on file at Washington, although the journals of all the other treaties are there.

the treaty, but on the contrary, that he vehemently opposed the treaty and finally left the council grounds,
after tearing up his commission as sub-chief, in the
presence of the Governor. This, it may be said, is assuming to accept as true, Indian evidence instead of the
white man's testimony. Let us then look at the probability of the case. All agree, both Americans and
Indians, that Leschi was a man of more than ordinary
intelligence. He was wealthy beyond any of his tribe.
He had his farm and substantial improvements, as
shown by Wiley's letter quoted elsewhere, on the upper
reach of the Nisqually River. He was a hunter, and
lived by the chase and the products of his herds that
pastured on the prairies of the Nisqually plains. He
had numerous bands of horses at that very time, so
numerous that when he finally started from home he
could not take all of them with him, and fifteen head
fell into the hands of the volunteers and were turned
over to the Government. His wife, who is still living,
told me recently, they had a "whole field full of horses"
at the outbreak of the war, but they lost all of them.
I judge from the manner she described them there were
at least fifty head.

Is it at all probable that as shrewd a business man
as Leschi had proved himself to be, would sign away
his home, and agree to give up everything, and in company with four or five hundred Indians go upon a reservation of two section (1280 acres), * of heavy timbered
land bordering on the salt water, where the soil was
stertile, the timber so dense he could not even build a
house without great labor of clearing off the tall giant
trees likely to crush it, and finally where no pasturage
existed on the reservation or even anywhere near it
where he could keep his herds? This to me seems in
the words of Hazard Stevens, "simply preposterous."

*The treaty called for 1280 acres for the Nisqually reservation, but when
the final selection was made 1204 acres only were reserved, but none of it was
ever occupied by the Indians.

Such a grave charge as this should not be lightly made. Hearing that a record of the speeches made had been kept and forwarded with the treaty, I made an attempt to get a certified copy of the proceedings. The following letter is self explanatory:

Refer in reply to the following land: 45202—1903.

Department of the Interior, Office of Indian Affairs.

Washington, August 1, 1903.

E. Meeker, Esq., Puyallup, Wash.—Sir: You request in your letter of July 14, 1903, to be furnished with a copy of the proceedings of the Medicine Creek treaty, December, 1854, negotiated by Governor Isaac Stevens with the Nisqually and other tribes.

In reply you are advised that the proceedings of the treaty (council) to which you refer appear to have been mislaid or lost. Search has heretofore been made for them, but the office has been unable to find them. It is suggested that you read, for a full history of this subject, the life of Governor Stevens, by his son, Hazard. The best account of the Medicine Creek treaty known to this office is given in the book referred to. It appears that you are seeking historical information and knowledge concerning the councils held and the proceedings reported concerning the negotiation of the said treaty. If so, the perusal of the Life of Governor Stevens by his son is respectfully recommended.*

Very respectfully,

A. C. TOUNER.

Commissioner, Act.

Turning to the book cited, I find the following:

The Indians had some discussion and Governor Stevens then put the question: "Are you ready? If so, I will sign

---

*Subsequently, through the courtesy of Senator Foster of this State, a diligent search for the missing document was made in the sacred archives of the Senate, as it had been suggested the last proceeding had been forwarded with the treaty to the Senate and not returnd, but with no better result. An attorney has been employed with directions to spare no time or expense until the lost document is found, if in existence, but the word comes back, "We can find no trace of them anywhere." And so it is to be feared they have been destroyed or carried away.

it." There were no objections, and the treaty was then signed by Governor I. I. Stevens and the chiefs, delegates and head men on the part of the Indians, and duly witnessed by the secretary, special agent, and seventeen citizens present.

But not a word is said about what sort of a "discussion" the Indians had. Upon what they said an ominous silence prevails, in view of the fact that the son of the Governor had access to these very papers during the preparation of his work. I have been equally unfortunate from Colonel B. F. Shaw, the interpreter of the Medicine Creek Council. Three courteous letters of inquiry remain unanswered, and hence we must look elsewhere for his testimony.

In a paper read before the Washington State Historical Society, October 9th, 1893, by Hon. James Wickersham, now United States Judge for Alaska, signed by that gentleman before filing in the archives of that society under the caption of "The Indian Side of the Puget Sound War," that gentleman after quoting numerous authorities tending to prove that Leschi did not sign the Medicine Creek Treaty, says:

Let us pass, however, for the sake of the argument, that they (the Indians) did sign the treaty. Did they understand it? Did it contain the contract agreed upon? Were they over-persuaded by their guardian? Were they deceived and mistaken. If so, it is not their contract and should be set aside as being obtained through fraud and intimidation. Let us continue our evidence on these points and call the interpreter at the Medicine Creek treaty, Col. B. F. Shaw, of Clark County, now a member of the State Senate. On the 11th of March, 1893, Col. Shaw made a statement in writing which I have in my possession touching these matters, and from it I make the following suggestive quotations. He said: "Leschi and Quiemuth did sign the treaty, The fault was in the treaty. They said: 'Can you get the Indians to sign this treaty?' I answered: 'Yes, I can get the Indians to sign their death warrant.' Their idea was that in a few years the Indians would die out and the reservations would be large enough. My opinion is that the treaties were humbugs—premature, and that the Indians did not understand them*, although we endeavored to do it; they did not realize it. When they got home they were dissatisfied. Two or three days after the treaty was made I rode over to Nisqually and met Leschi and Stahi, and they were very much dissatisfied and they complained very much. I told them that if anything was wrong it would be fixed by the Government. They were very much excited and accused me of deceiving them. I denied it and told them that I had told them just what the Governor had said. They tried to get a new treaty. They asked me to report their dissatisfaction to the Governor. I told the Governor, but the treaty was sent to Washington. The Governor promised to get them other reservations. The trouble seemed to die out slowly until after the Walla Walla treaty; then there was dissatisfaction. Over-persuasion and persistency brought about the Walla Walla treaty. The Governor was a persistent man. It did not seem to dawn upon Leschi what the treaty was, what it meant. He was called a tyee, etc., and flattered."

"Now, this is the evidence of the interpreter, the mind through which the contracting parties made this treaty— the contract. The treaty or contract was prepared and given to the interpreter. "Can you get the Indians to sign this treaty?" "Yes. I can get the Indians to sign their death warrant." In this question and answer you have the whole injustice of the Medicine Creek treaty laid bare. It was a contract obtained through over-persuasion and deceit; through promises not in the record; by imposition upon minds unaccustomed to written contracts; a contract obtained from the weak by the strong; from the ward by the guardian; from the child by the parent, and wholly without consideration—unfair, unjust, ungenerous and illegal. Any American court of justice would set such a contract aside as fraudulent and void because of the imposition upon the weak by the strong, and for failure of agreement of minds and considerations."

---

*How could they, when the Chinook jargon, containing only 300 words, was used as the medium to interpret the treaty?

CHAPTER XXXII.

Cause of Governor Stevens' Failure.

The Governor and his suit in due time proceeded to other points down the Sound (North), where notice had been sent for other tribes to assemble, and with headlong speed, concluded three other treaties with the numerous bands to the north of the Medicine Creek district, aggregating in all about six thousand persons, and in but little over a month's time from the start, reported as having extinguished the Indian title for the whole district west of the Cascade Mountains, except with the Chehalis and Quillehute tribes.

Of course, this break neck speed utterly precluded the possibility of any knowledge of the tribes or their wants, suitableness of their reservations or consultation with their head men.

After concluding these treaties with the Indians to the North and making an abortive attempt to treat with the Chehalis tribes, the Governor suddenly transferred his operations to points east of the Cascade Mountains, and was seen no more for over a year, and not for two months after the war had broken out with the tribes under the Medicine Creek Treaty.

The nine tribes of the Medicine Creek District being left to themselves, many of them immediately became restless and discontented as the more stupid members were made aware of what the so called treaty meant. So pronounced was the discontent, that in three days' time B. F. Shaw, who had acted as interpreter, was sent among them to quiet their fears, as before mentioned, and by some means succeeded in part, but could

do nothing with Leschi.   Leschi went to his home on
the upper Nisqually River, and stayed there very closely
until spring.   As soon as spring opened he left home
and was gone for over three months.   Scarcely any one
knew what had become of him, and it did seem for
a while as though there had been unnecessary alarm
at the prospects of an Indian war following the signing
of the treaties.   Notwithstanding this apparent dead
calm in the west side district, unrest had followed in
the wake of the Governor's work in making treaties east
of the mountains, and finally before he got through, the
country both east and west of the mountains was ablaze
with grim war.

Meanwhile Leschi had returned home where he remained until the 23d of October.   Five days after that
time, the terrible massacre on White River, near where
the town of Auburn now stands, occurred.   He was
doubtless in the near vicinity when McAllister and Connell were killed, which was on the 27th.   The account of
this occurrence as well as that of the massacre will be
found elsewhere, and is mentioned here as fixing the
date of the actual outbreak of hostilities west of the
Cascade Mountains, on the part of the Indians, as both
these events preceded the killing of Moses, for which
Leschi was tried and finally after two trials and a third
sentence, was executed, more than two years after the
event and after the new reservations were given, won in
great part by his valor.

The acts of hostilities east of the mountains began
early in the summer of 1855, culminating with the murder of Agent Bolon on the 23d day of September, 1855.

At the time hostilities began here (October 27th),
by the killing of McAllister, followed on the 28th by the
massacre of innocent settlers, men, women and children, nine in all, in one day and in one place, Governor
Stevens, then more than a thousand miles from his cap-

ital, turned his face westward from the Blackfeet Council on the upper reaches of the Missouri River and
started for home. He had held three councils; marched
nearly two thousand miles, treated with twenty thousand
Indians, and felt that his work was about done. Instead of that he was doomed· to bitter disappointment
to find that it had hardly begun, and that he had to
run the gauntlet of hostile Indians with many of whom
he had lately treated.

It would be an interesting subject to investigate these
mid-continent treaties made in such haste, affecting
so many people and covering so wide extent of country,
but justice cannot be done without more painstaking investigation than time and opportunity will permit within the plan of this work. It is to be hoped some one
will take up this work soon before all living witnesses
are gone, and make a record of the tragedies following
so soon after the events mentioned.

We know most of these treaties were urged upon a
reluctant people in great haste; that time was not given
to properly mature plans to consult the wishes and
quiet the jealousies of the Indians; that bands whose
interests ran upon different lines were grouped upon
reservations not of their choosing, and that the Governor
at the Walla Walla Council employed reprehensible
means to obtain signatures.

This incident came very near costing Governor
Stevens his life and that of the whole party with him,
and had it not been for General Palmer's tact, the council then and there would have broken up in a row. I
have noticed this particularly because of the bearing
it certainly had upon the outbreak of the war east of
the mountains, which in turn directly concerned us to
the west of the same range as furnishing a plausible
reason in the minds of the chiefs on both sides of the
mountains, that they were not bound by the terms of

treaties·obtained by such methods, and other means, while not so reprehensible, yet just as impolitic.

As I have indicated elsewhere, there were hours if not days in which the Governor was not responsible for his acts, and to such influences we must attribute the actions here related, for we knew Governor Stevens to be too shrewd a man if in his right mind not to realize that in the end a transaction of this kind would redound. against him.

In my recent visit to the Medicine Creek Treaty ground, an old time acquaintance and friend, the sub-Chief Steilacoom, accompanied the party and showed us the exact spot where Leschi stood, and where the Governor stood and walked to and fro, and told the words and acted the part of each with vivid reality.

I first met Steilacoom in the summer of 1853, at the then most important town of all on Puget Sound, that bore and still bears his name. He was then in the prime of life and was considered an important personage of the community in which he lived. In our last meeting referred to, I questioned Steilacoom closely, and found that he was a married man when the Hudson Bay people first landed at Nisqually in 1830, and conclude he is certainly at this time (Jan. 1905), over ninety years old. Upon this occasion the hospitable Mrs. Hartman placed a feast before the antiquated Chief and myself in which she joined, where, over the cups (of tea), we three lived our old time lives over again. It was indeed pathetic to see the old Chief shed tears of anger at the thought of his fallen condition, which he attributed solely to the treaty.

Although a little out of its regular order, I will here relate what Steilacoom said, and how he acted while on this visit. Going to a clump of stately firs on the treaty ground that had evidently been silent witnesses of the scenes enacted under their shade fifty years before,

the old man stopped at a point near the bank of the
creek and said (I will render his words in English,
though of course he only spoke Chinook), "Leschi stood
just about here, and Governor Stevens over there (going
to a point about ten feet distant from the first pointed
out.) The other men and Indians all around. Leschi
said we want some of the bottom land so our people
can learn to farm, and some of the prairie where we can
pasture our horses, and we want some land along this
creek so our people may come in from the Sound and
camp and go to the prairies for our horses." Evidently
Leschi must have made quite a lengthy speech, judging
from our friend's actions and gestures and loud voice,
as he became quite excited and gesticulated violently.

Then he would walk over to where he had said Governor Stevens stood. "Governor Stevens said; No, you
can have that land over there," pointing to the high
timber land beyond the creek. "Leschi said we won't
take that land." Governor Stevens said, "You must—
then Leschi said that we will fight, and tore up the
paper."

The paper Leschi tore up, we know from other sources,
was the appointment as Sub-Chief made by Governor
Stevens and not the treaty as Steilacoom thought. His
relation of the incident only corroborated the testimony
of three living witnesses of the fact that Leschi did tear
up a paper in a rage, before the Governor, left the treaty
ground, and did not sign the treaty.

The critical student of history should study this treaty
to realize how one-sided it is and how completely the
interests of the Indians were ignored. One vital question to the Indians of the more advanced mind was their
homes, their place of abode. Curiously enough, the
Indians had been led to believe the Government wished
them to adopt the habits and customs of the whites of
a settled place of abode; to till the soil, to send their

children to school, in a word, make a start on the road to civilized life, and yet not one acre of arable land was allowed them in their reservations, which in area aggregated only six sections (3840 acres), for nine tribes, nearly nine hundred persons in all. Now why this was done is a question often and often asked and never as yet satisfactorily answered. The two tribes of Puyallups and Nisquallies comprising nearly all of the whole number—about four hundred of each—and each alloted but 1280 acres of high bluff, heavily timbered land, the one tract near the mouth of the Nisqually, the other a part of the present site of the City of Tacoma including the high table land of that city, but not an acre of the bottom land in either case, where the Indians were living at the time of making the treaty. No intelligent man in his right mind would have insisted on making such a one sided bargain as the Medicine Creek Treaty and those who have attempted to justify that act do themselves a great wrong in undertaking to falsify history.

In September, 1854, Governor Stevens submitted a report to the Indian Bureau in which he said:

"Although my attention has been earnestly directed to measures which should be adopted for ameliorating the condition of the Indians in Washington Territory, I do not propose here to enlarge upon the subject. As the duty will devolve upon myself to negotiate treaties with the Indians of the Territory, it would be obviously improper to commit myself to views which might need modification when deliberate consultation shall take place with the Indians in council. The great end to be looked to is the gradual civilization of the Indians, and their ultimate incorporation with the people of the Territory. It is obviously necessary that a few reservations of good lands should be large enough to give to each Indian a homestead and land sufficient to pasture their animals, of which land they should have the exclusive occupation. The location and extent of the reservations should be adapted to the peculiar wants and habits of the different tribes. Farms should be attached to each reservation, under the charge of a farmer competent to fully instruct the Indians in agriculture and the use of tools. * * * In conclusion, I would express the hope that the administration of Indian affairs in this new and interesting field may illustrate not so much the power as the beneficence and paternal care of the Government."

These words, outlining the broad principles of justice in dealing with Indians, show the general impulse of the Governor while acting dispassionately and without excitement and are worthy of commendation and if this policy had been adhered to would have been an imperishable monument to his fame that would have brightened as memories faded. But they were not. In three months' time the first treaty was made, and instead of allowing the Indians a homestead, they were accorded but *four acres* each under the terms of the Medicine Creek Treaty; instead of reservations of good land, they were given poor land covered with heavy timber; instead of "land sufficient to pasture their horses," they were given none such; in fact, nothing was done in accordance with this beneficent policy outlined by the Governor, prompted while in his sober senses, doubtless from sincerity of purpose to treat the Indians justly.

The reason why this awful blunder was made is not hard to find if we will but search a little and tell what we know. Governor Stevens was intoxicated and unfit for transacting business while making these treaties.

George Gibbs, who was present at the Medicine Creek and Point Elliot Treaty Councils, wrote May 30th, 1857, and his letter was published in the Washington Republican over his signature, June 5, 1857, as follows:

We have a right to resent public officers exhibiting themselves drunk. When he appears intoxicated on important public occasions, as Governor Stevens did at Fort Colville, at the treaties here on the Sound, at the Blackfeet Council, and more lately at that with the Nez Perces, thus bringing his official station in contempt with the Indians, destroying his influence over them and endangering the peace of the Territory; when he comes forward to make public addresses in the condition that he did at Vancouver and Portland (and he might have added Steilacoom, where the author saw him in the condition described), it is perfectly proper that he should be met by exposure. These things are a part of his "conduct and official acts," for which he ought to be held responsible to the Department at Washington. That I said no more than what was true when I stated that in his fits of intoxication he knew no bounds to his language and his actions, almost every one who has had official connection with him is aware. His vulgar and indecent abuse of his prisoners at Olympia justified the statement, and he furnished new proof of it when swaggering in the barrooms of Portland, he swore that, by G—d, he would crush every one who had opposed his martial law.

Mrs. Burrows stated that on returning from the funeral of her husband, Governor Stevens took a seat at the head of the table on the small steamer, and that he was so much intoxicated that he spat upon the food before him, and was in consequence removed from the table.*

It is a melancholy truth told in these letters. The incidents were well known by the citizens of the Territory and caused great concern, and which at a later period, came near causing the shedding of blood in the court house at Steilacoom on two separate occasions.

This disease (for the use of intoxicants becomes a disease as impossible to resist as a malignant fever), had taken such a deep hold on the Governor as to become utterly irresistible, and caused him to commit acts he otherwise would not have done.

As a historian I would have let this subject sink into oblivion, had it not been the cause to change the whole

---

*See letter Columbia Lancaster in Washington Republican, July 3d, 1857.

current of events, and is introduced here from necessity to account for the many strange incidents that occurred during Stevens' administration. Either we must give the true cause, or write Stevens down as a *very* bad and dishonest man. I do not think he was either, although he was possessed of weakness of character other than this noted, that reflected upon his actions though not upon his integrity, which carried him into excesses no less reprehensible, but which were as impossible for him to resist.

He would take no counsel, nor brook opposition to his will. He believed in himself, and he was willing to take all responsibility. He would not shrink from the severest strain of labor nor tolerate idleness in others. He was scrupulously honest in the handling of public money, though it must be said his appointments of others to fill the numerous offices in many cases were made to build up a personal following rather than for fitness, a weakness clinging to our public men too often to this day. Coupled with these inherent defects came the further misfortune, he was possessed of small measure of patience, a characteristic so essential in dealing with Indians. His education had been under military discipline of strict submission to those in command and his habits of obedience had been formed under the experience of war. With these defects of character and training, it is easy to see that his dealings with the Indians were from the first doomed to failure.

The situation was further complicated because of the numerous duties undertaken by the Governor—so numerous as to utterly preclude the possibility of giving attention to all assigned him. We are lost in amazement at the action of the Government in intrusting such vast powers and responsibilities in the hands of one man. He had charge of the Northern Pacific Railroad Exploration, a duty requiring his whole energies for two years with near two hundred and fifty men under his control the summer following his appointment as Governor. To this was added the responsibility of organizing the new Territory for which he had been appointed Governor. He was also delegated to fill the very important position of Superintendent of Indian Affairs for all the Indians in the Territory, and to jointly with another commissioner, conduct the Blackfeet Council and to make treaties with those tribes inhabiting the district east of the Rocky Mountains more than a thousand miles from his capital and without the reach of the National capital as well.

The Superintendency of Indian Affairs for the Territory alone should have had the undivided attention of not less than two resident superintendents, instead of the divided care of one, who was for the first year absent in Washington in adjusting his work of the great railroad exploration, and the following year when the war broke out a thousand miles from his capital with hostile camps in his path.

I have been thus particular in portraying the character and describing the difficulties to the end the reader may look upon the failure of Stevens with a knowledge of the obstacles that confronted him. Hereafter these difficulties will be elaborated while at the same time many acts of his administration condemned in no unmeasured terms, but it is the wish of the author that the reader will bear in mind that it is the acts, not the man that will be condemned, according to the man the credit of doing the best he knew how under the handicap of unfitness for his position and multiplied care that developed upon him.

Before dismissing this subject it is but just to pay a tribute to Governor Stevens' great work, for which he was so eminently fitted, and which was so efficiently performed, the exploration of the Northern route for a railroad already referred to. This was a difficult work even with plenty of time to prepare, which there was not, but with almost incredible zeal and energy the organization was perfected, the transportation and supplies assembled on the frontier, and the work performed in a manner to command the approval of the Government and plaudits of the people. The Governor was at his best in this work, thoroughly equipped mentally and by education as well as by the untiring energy with which he carried forward all his work. It would have been a happy hour for him, had he received only this one appointment. Words can but faintly portray the debt of gratitude the country owes the man, who, like Stevens, severs his life-long political affiliations, cuts loose from all his old political associates, and in the darkest hour of our National existence throws himself in the breach to sacrifice his life that his country might live, as did Governor Stevens when he laid down his life on the bloody field of Chantilly, heroically struggling for the right.

CHAPTER XXXIII.

Point Elliott and Other Treaties.

The second treaty concluded with the Indians, that at Point Elliott, gave more general satisfaction, though it contained the germ out of which grew the worst outbreak of the war, the White River massacre, before mentioned. George Gibbs there acted as secretary. He had taken a census, reporting 3,959 Indians within the district described in the treaty, less than two-thirds of whom were present. The Governor and his party were taken to the treaty grounds by the large steamer Major Tompkins, which the settlers of that day looked upon as a marvel in luxurious appointments and safety. It certainly was a great improvement over the quite recent mode of travel by canoes, in the absence of any other method other than by oars, paddle or sail. The point selected for the main reservation, Tulalip, a township of six miles square, 23,040 acres, is a beautiful spot fronting on the Sound, with low shores adjoining, with some arable land and good fisheries, and was as well suited to the wants of the Indians as any one location that could be found. Three other smaller reservations were set apart for some of the smaller tribes—two sections at Port Madison, an island at the mouth of the Lummi River near our northern boundary, and two sections at the southeastern end of Perry's Island. These small reservations were set out to placate bands which either from fear or jealousy refused to be moved to the large central location, Tulalip. But Governor Stevens made the fatal mistake of ignoring the wishes of

the very tribe whose name the treaty bears, the
Duwamish, and the allied or adjoining bands or tribes
inhabiting the upper rivers that form the Duwamish.
These Indians were in deadly terror of the more powerful and allied tribes, the Snoqualmies and Snohomishes,
near whose places of abode the large reservation was
made, and where all the Indians were required, under
the terms of the treaty, to remove within a year. The
rascally chief, Pat Kanim, who had given the white settlers much trouble and had, in 1849, even attacked Fort
Nisqually, was at the head of these two powerful tribes,
and not only gave trouble to the whites, but domineered
over the weaker bands as no other chief dared do that
had permanent location on the Sound. These Indians of
the up-river country of the Duwamish were very much
dissatisfied. They were required by the terms of the
treaty to remove from their place of abode from time
out of memory to a new district, among strangers whom
they feared, give up all their associations, their hunting
grounds, their fisheries, to go where they were to be
herded, as they thought, until some final disposition
could be made of them.

So pronounced did their discontent become that Acting Governor Mason found it necessary to visit them
during the summer of 1855 to try and quiet their fears.
He really had no power. Governor Stevens, the superintendent, the only man who could treat with them,
was a thousand miles away beyond the Rocky Mountains, on the upper waters of the Missouri River, where
he had gone as before mentioned to assist in treating
with the Blackfeet Indians. It was on this trip of Mason's that Leschi and his brother, Quiemuth, accompanied him as interpreters; but they had grievances of
their own, and it is not to be doubted that they added
fuel to the burning discontent that possessed these Indians. The instruction from the Department of the
Interior was:

"Endeavor to unite the numerous bands and fragments of tribes into tribes, and provide for the concentration of one or more of such tribes upon the reservations set apart for their future homes."

The system as applied to these Indians was positively vicious, cruel and unnecessary, and if rigidly applied was certain to bring trouble.   However, if there had been a superintendent who had taken the pains to inform him-. self and the time to have intelligently applied his knowledge, and had been in condition of mind to have patiently investigated their grievances and exercised that "sound discretion" authorized by the letter and spirit of the instructions, there need not have been any difficulty with them.   Governor Stevens possessed none of the necessary qualifications, nor did he observe any precautions that should have been taken.

Governor Stevens always laid great stress upon the charge of perfidy on the part of the Indians for not observing the treaties, when, as a matter of fact, there were none except the treaty concluded at the Medicine Creek Council, that had been ratified by the United States Senate prior to the outbreak of the war.

It must also be borne in mind that our government reserved the right to repudiate the actions of its agent in making these treaties, and did so for years after they were signed, yet proceeded at once to appropriate the land, as though a binding treaty had been concluded and ratified.

None of the names of the head men of the upper White River Indians appear on the treaty, and it seems they were ignored altogether, as no provision whatever was made for them other than to require their removal to a distant reservation on the Sound.   They had no interest in common with the tribes on the Sound with which, under the terms of the treaty, they were bound to assimilate.   Their habits of life and consanguinity

both ran upon lines distinctly different; they lived by
the chase, the natural production of the soil, and the
river fisheries in close proximity to their place of abode.
The gap of the mountains, the Natchess Pass, gave them
ample opportunity to extend their field of exploration to
the east side of the great range, and had resulted in in-
termarriage, which brought about a semi-community of
interest with the powerful tribes of the interior.

Their relatives to the east had finally engaged in open
warfare. Agent Bolon had been killed and Major Haller of the regulars had been driven back to The Dalles
with his forces completely demoralized.

Slaughter, who had gone forward to meet Haller had
retreated and Maloney of the regulars, with Hays of the
volunteers, sent to support a second expedition from
The Dalles under Major Rains, were still in the pass and
retreating. Both these west of the mountains expeditions passed through the country occupied by the up-
river bands, the Muckleshoots and allied tribes, on
White and Green Rivers.

The consequence was that with these tribes there
came to be a regular hotbed of discontent, which was
fanned into a flame when they saw the troops marshaled
and traversing their country on the way to make war
on their relatives just beyond the mountains. They
were ripe for war by mid-summer of 1855, but could
get no allies west of the mountains; and besides, a winter campaign was what they sought. But when the second expedition under Captain Maloney and Captain
Hays, with both regulars and volunteers, passed
through their country and the Eaton rangers had driven
or frightened Leschi and the disaffected Nisquallies to
their vicinity they could be restrained no longer, and
the outbreak came like a clap of thunder out of a clear
sky. It was doubtless precipitated in part, like the
firing upon Fort Sumter to move the South to action.
So with these Indians. They rightly judged active hos-

tilities on their part would draw to their standard the wavering bands which they knew were in sympathy with them, and that once the war torch was lighted it could not be extinguished.

Settlements had been made throughout most of this district, and, as with the Indians in other districts already described, the settlers had been living in peace and neighborly friendship with them. There had been really but one disturbance, and that where the Indians alleged a settler had wantonly ploughed over some of the graves of their ancestors, at which they were greatly incensed. But as a general rule there had been no discontent until the treaties were made.

In the light of what is known, the neglect of the superintendent, or if not the neglect the mistake of that personage in not exercising his authority to give these people homes in their own country, came from the fact that either he did not know or did not care for the wants of these Indians. His action in either case was extremely reprehensible, especially so where the lives and fortunes of so many people of his own race were jeopardized, as well as those of whom he assumed the role of a ward over their destinies.

Two other treaties were made to complete the work on the Sound, one with the Clallams, reported by Gibbs 926 strong, the other the Twanas, set down as 290—a total of 6,068 Indians in the four treaties.

An effort to make a treaty with the Chehalis and Quinault Indians failed, principally because the Indians of those districts objected to having several tribes sent to one reservation. Governor Stevens, however, particularly blamed a young chief, Tleyuk, who held an appointment as sub-chief which the Governor had given him. Finally, when he gave up the attempt to have the treaty signed and was just ready to break up the council, the Governor gave him an angry scolding, took the chief's commission from him and tore it up before the eyes of all the Indians, immediately adjourned the council and broke camp for other parts.

The difference in the treatment of the Indians fifty years ago is well illustrated by the following account of what the Government is doing now with a part of these same Indians, who refused to treat as just related, and who never did enter into treaty stipulations with the Government.

The following telegram from Washington outlines a very different line of treatment:

"The fact that surveys are being made of the Quinault Indian reservation on the west coast of Washington has led many people to believe that the lands are soon to be opened to settlement, and in consequence many inquiries are being made at the Indian Office for information as to the proposed opening. To all such inquiries the department replies that under no circumstances will there be any opening of lands until the surveys have been completed and 80 acres of the land have been allotted to each man, woman and child properly on the reservation. The reservation contains approximately 224,000 acres of valuable agricultural and timber land, and this accounts for the interest that is taken in the contemplated settlement. After allotments have been made a portion of the remaining land will be set apart for the general use of the Indians, either for agricultural or grazing purposes. The Department has not yet determined whether the unallotted lands shall be thrown open to entry or reserved for the purpose of preserving the timber. The latter scheme has been suggested and will have due consideration, but will no doubt be opposed by the Indians themselves, who hope to receive something from the settlers who take up the surplus land."

This in the year A. D. 1904, fifty years after the Governor of the Territory had made the abortive attempt to restrict the amount of land for each Indian to less than four acres, as at the Medicine Creek treaty.

Thus it will be noticed the Government proposes:

1st. To let the Indians have first choice of land.

2d. That each man, woman and child shall be allotted eighty acres.

3d. After the allotments have been made a farther reservation is to be made "for the general use of the Indians."

An accurate census of the Indians is impossible, but taking the middle ground between the extremes, I have adopted the figure of 1400* as representing the number of the nine tribes treated with under the terms of the Medicine Creek treaty, where only 3,840 acres were set apart by Governor Stevens for the whole, equal to *two and seven-tenths of an acre* to each man, woman and child of the nine tribes. Applying the rule of eighty acres to each, we would have the aggregate of *one hundred and twelve thousand acres*. Nor does this yet show the enormity of the crime committed against these Indians under the terms of the Medicine Creek treaty. The Indians were not allowed to choose even that allotted to them, but were given the very poorest land for their use that could be found in the whole Territory. The tract of 1280 acres set out for the Nisqually tribe was the worst of all, utterly unfit for habitations, and yet remains as it was nearly fifty years ago, uninhabited by man or beast. Subsequent owners now even refuse to pay taxes on it.

It is to be noted that but few of the fish Indians, the Indians who lived on the Sound, went on the warpath. They did not care for land. As one of the Clallam chiefs put it, "he was willing to sell his land. All he wanted was the right of fishing."

Governor Stevens overlooked the fact he had two classes of Indians to deal with. It is no wonder he did,

*I do not forget that Gibbs set down the number at 893, but he did not have the time nor the opportunity to take an accurate census or to make a reliable estimate. The census of 1862 places the number at 1150, but we all know there were even more than that; but, taking Gibbs' estimate of 893 as correct, we would then have less than four acres to each person, and, even that pittance, the poorest to be found in the whole district.

as he was not only entirely unacquainted with the wants of the tribes, but of the tribes themselves, and refused to take counsel from those who did know. The fish Indians were easily satisfied as to their reservations, if such were but near their old haunts and convenient to the fisheries. Not so with the Indians living on the upper reaches of Green, White, Puyallup and Nisqually Rivers, where the occupants lived in great part by the chase and on the natural products of the soil, who were wide-awake Indians and were the tribes that went on the warpath.

As the result of the war very large additions were made to the reservations, or rather there were new reservations set apart under the executive orders of the President. Although the Medicine Creek treaty was promptly ratified, the original reservations set apart for the Nisquallies and Puyallups, respectively, in the treaty, were never occupied by the Indians, and in fact never surveyed as reservations for them, but finally again merged with the public land and disposed of to settlers as the remainder of the public domain. After the war was over a new reservation was given the Dwamish Indians, as they are called in the treaty, in their old haunts at Muckleshoot and vicinity, since when there has been no further difficulty with them, except as will be related in the chapter following.

CHAPTER XXXIV.

Defects and Results of Treaties.

Eight years after the events related in preceding chapters, and after the military reservation at Muckleshoot had been turned over to the Indians as a reservation, it had fallen to my lot to subdivide the township lying west of the reservation, where, many years before, only the township lines had been run. The line ran near the Muckleshoot prairie, and in the prosecution of the work it became necessary to retrace it. The survey alarmed the Indians, who feared that in some way the white man's compass and chain would endanger their title. They came to our camp to try to persuade me to quit the work, but I told them it was impossible to do so as I had contracted with the Government to survey the land and would be compelled to go on with the work. I was acquainted with nearly all of them, but that made no difference, as they could not understand what business I had to be surveying so near their homes, and I could not allay their fears. When, in the morning, the time came for running the line near their reservation, the Indians were out in force, but unarmed, and, discovering by the work of the axman the course, placed themselves in the way, all the while pleading for us to desist, but offering no violence. Finally several took hold of the chain, and by that means completely blocked the work. My boys wanted to take the chain to the camp, but I said, "No, leave it right where it is;" and we went to our camp and the Indians to theirs, a few hundred yards distant. No threats on either side had been made, but the Indians seemed determined to stop the survey.

Right then and there we had an object lesson which, if
it had been studied and acted upon before the war, would
have saved the Government millions in money and hundreds of precious lives; that is, to give the Indian
plenty of time to think and then reason with him. His
mind moves slowly; but give him time and repeat patiently, as you would to a child. If you are in the right,
ninety-nine times out of a hundred you will succeed by
persuasion. I simply staid in my camp and restrained
my boys from visiting the Indians. Finally, in the evening, several of their head men came to "talk." I repeated that my work would not endanger the title to
their land. They then wanted me to go and see the
Governor. I told them I had no business with the Governor; that he (the Surveyor General) had sent me to
survey the land, and that they would laught at me if I
went back to talk instead of being out in the field at
work. (Selucius Garfielde was then Surveyor General
and Marshall F. Moore was Governor.) The Indians
repeated they did not want me to survey, and I repeated
what I had said before, to take time to think. I could
only catch a word or two here and there in their native
tongue when they talked between themselves, but
enough to know they were canvassing what I had told
them. It took us three days to settle the controversy,
with a trip to Olympia, the Indians furnishing the transportation, with the result that their own men laid hold
with us on the work with a will, and we remained
friends for life.

There is a lesson in this transaction, if it could have
been studied and acted upon while making the treaties
with the tribe, which would have saved us from the horrors of that massacre, but a few miles distant, by these
same men. The Indians had forcibly interfered with the
work of a United States deputy surveyor, were clearly
in the wrong, and troops would have instantly been
sent to quell the uprising (?) (God save the word; I

have heard so much of it) if they had been called. A few Indians would have been chastised, perhaps some killed, and then what? The answer has been rendered a thousand times by the blood of innocent people.

As a result of the war, instead of 1280 acres of sterile bluff timber land for the Puyallup tribe, there was set out by executive order in the month of August, 1856, over eighteen thousand acres, two-thirds of which was the choicest of rich land in the Puyallup valley. How this was done is best described in the words of Hiton (Indian), previously mentioned, who was present and helped to get the new council together:

"Governor Stevens he asked, 'What do the Indians want?' The Nisquallies said they wanted eight miles square, where the fisheries are. (This included the Leschi and Quiemuth farms and homes they had coveted so much.) Governor Stevens he sat down on a log and he put his face in his hands a very, very long time. By and by he raise up his face very slow. He said, slowly: 'A-ll right. Now, what do the Puyallup Indians want?' 'They want six miles square in the Puyallup bottom down to the salt water.' Governor Stevens he say right away, 'All right,' and then they went to surveying"—gave the Indians the land they wanted at the outset and enough to satisfy them. Though vanquished in the field, they won what they went to war for.

A careful examination of these treaties will disclose glaring defects, and a candid review will expose the incongruity as a whole, particularly while taking into account the surrounding circumstances. With the Nisqually and Puyallup Indians, the reservations were so glaringly inadequate that the Indians did not believe the Government intended they should make their homes there. Article 6 of the Medicine Creek treaty (and the same provision was made in all the treaties) provides that the President of the United might remove them at any time without consulting their wishes. This arbi-

trary provision gave rise to the deep-seated belief that
the Government did intend to ship them off to another
land.   Without much stretch of imagination this could
mean a dark land, as the Indians were left entirely
helpless, with no voice in their destiny.   Article 4 provided for payments, but in fact were not payments, for
the whole matter was left to the discretion of the President as to what disposition he should make of the promised funds.

The expectations of the Indians had been raised by the
promise of presents at the treaties, but these were so ab-
surdly small as to create disgust and contempt in the
Indian mind—a couple of yards of calico here, a straw
hat there, some jewsharps for the children and black
strap (black molasses) for the women.   If that was to
be the measure of payments for their land, what was the
use of selling?   Might as well give it at once.   True, the
presents were not intended as a payment, but the idea
that they were could not be gotten out of the Indian
mind.   We must remember that Governor Stevens actually did make these treaties by interpreting in the
Chinook jargon, consisting of about three hundred
words.   Let any one conversant with that jargon try his
hand on any one of the articles to translate it; he will
instantly see the impossibility of the undertaking.   It
could not be done, and the Indians could not and did not
understand the treaties.   Admitting, for the argument,
they did understand.   What kind of an impression
would be made by the exacting of a total abstinence
pledge from the Indians while they had the example before their eyes of the government officials not practicing
what they preached?   Their condition might well serve
as a warning, but certainly not as an example.

There was, to say the least, a sort of grim humor in
Article 11, prohibiting slavery among the Indians, com-
ing as it did from a slave-holding race and a pro-slavery
Government.   Then the prohibition in Article 13 of for-

eign trade, while we of the superior race prided ourselves as a trading people, both at home and abroad. All
these provisions simply tended to confuse the Indian
mind, and accomplished nothing more, and therefore
were harmful.   The Indians held just as many slaves
(which never was many, nor slavery as we understand
the term), drank just as much whisky, and traded as
much in Victoria or elsewhere foreign with these provisions in the treaty, as if they had never been thought
of.   But the great grievance with the Indians that went
to the war was that the country had been taken from
them and no place given where they could build a house,
let alone have a home for themselves and children.   Out
of the several millions of acres within the whole district
covered by the four treaties, less than fifty-eight thousand acres were set apart for six thousand Indians—
eight acres to each.   Small wonder that war followed.
The great wonder is that a greater number did not enter
the hostile camp.

CHAPTER XXXV.

Gathering War Clouds.

The general discontent of the Indians, both east and west of the Cascade Mountains, following soon after the treaties, created great apprehension in the minds of many citizens. The fact soon became known that a number of men traversing the country east of the mountains on their way to the Colville mines, had been ruthlessly murdered, and finally A. J. Bolan, the agent, who had gone among the Yakimas to demand the murderers, shared a like fate, whereupon the expedition of Major Haller from The Dalles, as described elsewhere, was sent forward to enforce the demand, and of Slaughter from Fort Steilacoom.

On request of Captain Maloney, then in command of the United States troops at Fort Steilacoom, Acting Governor Mason, on the 14th of October, 1855, issued a call for two companies of volunteers to operate against the Yakima tribe of Indians, one company to be recruited at Olympia, the other at Vancouver. This was the first official act of the war on the part of the Territory, and was the direct result of the defeat of Haller by the Yakima Indians, and the consequent retreat of Lieutenant Slaughter from the Yakima country.

The companies to be recruited were promptly filled, and one of them, Captain Hays, was at once sworn into the service of the United States and entered into active campaigning, under Captain Maloney.

On the 22d of October Governor Mason again issued his proclamation, this time calling for four additional companies, giving as his reason for such action:

CHAS. H. MASON

"In order to make fully secure the lives and property of our inhabitants from any incursions or outbreaks on the part of the Indians, and to be prepared for any emergency."

This call also was responded to with alacrity, the companies organized and put into service. To go into the details of these volunteer organizations, and of others that followed later, would involve the history of the whole war, which is without the scope of this work. Mention is here made of this initial move to record the general unrest and anxiety pervading the minds of the people, as reflected by the Governor's action.

Secretary Charles H. Mason, then acting Governor, during the absence of Governor Stevens in the Blackfeet country east of the Rocky Mountains, was comparatively a young man, not having yet reached that mature period known as the prime of life. He was, however, well equipped by education, by temperament and by mental calibre for the duties devolving upon him. He was possessed to a great degree of that rare faculty of listening patiently to counsel, whether volunteered or invited, and then to weigh it and act upon his own judgment, while throwing all prejudice aside. He was a courteous gentleman, not headstrong, but firm; not opinionated, yet self-reliant; easily approached, nevertheless dignified in his bearing, while not in the least degree self-conscious as to his own importance in the difficult position in which he was so suddenly and unexpectedly thrown. Sorry was the day when this fine gentleman gave way to the luring tempetations of the cup and jovial companionship, which carried him off to an early and untimely grave a few years after the events of which I am writing.

One of the companies organized under the second call of October 22d was the Eaton Rangers, that took the field two days afterwards, and the same day undertook to apprehend Leschi, but which attempt failed and caused the two brothers (Leschi and Quiemuth) to flee from home to the hostile camp, actually leaving the plow in the unfinished furrow in Quiemuth's wheat field.

Governor Mason made a great mistake when he sent this force to the homes of these two influential Indians, who could not well leave home and go upon a reservation and turn their herds out on the prairies uncared for, a prey for evil-disposed men of both races. We cannot wonder at his action when such men as James McAllister, a known friend of Leschi, would write him to "be on the lookout for Leschi, as he didn't talk right," and other advice of like import. He made another blunder in sending orders for the arrest of prominent Snoqualmie Indians to hold as hostages for the good behavior of their chief, Pat Kamin. But for the discretion of Captain Sterrett, of the U. S. sloop of war Decatur, and the active intervention of Arthur A. Denny, there can be but little doubt the Governor's orders would have been executed, which would have driven that powerful tribe at once into the hostile camp; a very serious affair, when we consider their number (3,000) and discipline. This was the most warlike tribe of all the Indians within the western limits of the Territory. The chief himself was vain-glorious, unscrupulous and cruel, ruling with an iron hand. He alone, of all the prominent Indians on the Sound, had threatened the settlements, as he did on Whidby Island, and at an earlier date made his attempt to rob Fort Nisqually. The question of enmity or friendship of such a man was of vital importance. And yet we cannot blame Governor Mason for his act, when all the facts are known. Lieutenant Slaughter had in some unaccountable way come to believe the Snoqualmie chief was "dogging his tracks" in the Natchess Pass, and so wrote the Governor, when, as a matter of fact, there was not a particle of truth in the report. He was simply mistaken. Arthur A. Denny, in his "Pioneer Days on Puget Sound," says:

"Immediately after the White River massacre* Lieutenant Slaughter was ordered up the old military road to the Natchess Pass, and after reaching Porter's prairie he sent down an express to Governor Mason, stating that Pat Kanim was dogging him at every step and around his camp every night. On receipt of this dispatch Mason sent an express to Captain Sterrett, at Seattle, instructing him to immediately arrest two of Pat Kanim's brothers, with all members of the tribe who were then camping in Seattle, and put them in irons. Having previously stated to Captain Sterrett that I had received information from Pat Kanim that convinced me of his friendship and that of his tribe, the Captain did not feel willing to take so important a step without consulting with me, and sent for me to come on board the Decatur, when he stated what he was directed to do, and that he must make the arrest at once, for the Snoqualmies would certainly leave during the night.

"This was startling news to me, and I most earnestly protested, telling him I knew Lieutenant Slaughter was mistaken, and that we had enemies enough to look after without attacking our friends; but he was so much disposed to act on Governor Mason's orders that I finally proposed, if he would not disturb the Snoqualmies, I would be responsible for their good conduct and would prove to him that Slaughter was wrong by going to Pat Kanim's camp and bring him in. He very positively refused to allow me to leave town, but consented that I might send an express for Pat Kanim and stand responsible for them until their return, having a time agreed upon within which they would be back. Very fortunately for me, and probably for Pat Kanim, too, he was on hand within the time agreed upon. He had his women and children with him, and also brought a cargo of mountain sheep, venison, horns and hides, specimens of which he took on board and presented to the Captain, who expressed the greatest surprise and satisfaction with the conclusive proof which I had thus furnished of the good faith and friendship of the Snoqualmies."

---

*Mr. Denny is mistaken as to the time of Slaughter's departure. His command left Fort Stellacoom September 28th, just a month before the massacre, and had returned to Connell Prairie. Capt. Maloney's expedition, the second attempt to chastise the Yakimas, left on the 24th of October, four days before the massacre, and Slaughter's company formed a part of this second expedition, and it is this Mr. Denny probably had in mind, though even that was before the massacre.

CHAPTER XXXVI.

Beginning of the War.

The Eaton rangers hurriedly organized after the call for volunteers was made by electing Charles Eaton as Captain and James McAllister as Lieutenant. This company, nineteen strong, precipitated the war on the west side of the mountains by attempting to surprise Leschi and Quiemuth at their homes and force them to go to Olympia, where they might be under government surveillance.

The story is well told by a member of the company, J. W. Wiley, editor of the *Pioneer and Democrat,* an intensely partisan sheet published at Olympia. He wrote from Fort Steilacoom under date of October 30th, 1855:

"The company left Mr. Eaton's, nineteen strong, on the 24th inst., in quest of the whereabouts of Leschi, a Nisqually chief, half Klickitat, and whom, it was apprehended, had for some time been preparing his band for active hostilities against the settlements. Leschi is an Indian of more than ordinary wealth and power. He is in possession of farming land, which he has heretofore cultivated, near the Nisqually River, between Packwood's Ferry and the crossing of that stream at Yelm. He has some good, substantial houses on his place, and outward appearances would indicate that he might live there comfortably. As Eaton's command passed his farm under the pilotage of his half-brother, S'tahi,* expecting to find Leschi at his residence, evidence having been afforded at the Indian Department that he (Leschi) had assumed a hostile attitude towards the white settlers, the command found that the bird had flown, but that

---

*Brother-in-law.

the prairie around about abounded with his horses, and other evidence that his absence was only temporary.

"Suffice it to say, we found not the Indian or satisfactory information of his (Leschi's) whereabouts. We encamped on the evening of that day, and until morning, in Pierce County, near the house of a Frenchman of the name of Gravelle, about twelve miles from Steilacoom. Next day, after a short stay for persons who had joined the command— expecting them up and their not arriving at an appointed hour—the command left, nineteen in all, for the Puyallup River, crossed the river and encamped for the night about a mile on the eastern side of the house of Charles Baden (Bitting) ; good grass and water. Next morning Captain Eaton divided the company into two divisions—one under his own superintendence and the other under Lieutenant McAllister—with an object of making a reconnoissance of both sides of the Puyallup River, above the settlements about five miles, along which stream it was reported large bodies of Indians were engaged in fishing. Captain Eaton took the trail on the western side of the Puyallup, crossed the river at a ford, almost swimming, entered the settlements at the forks—a large prairie entirely deserted—and passed up the river some three miles, the trail crossing and recrossing the river, extremely rough and rugged, until a junction was formed with Lieutenant McAllister, who had scoured the other side most thoroughly. No sign of Indians was found of later period than two weeks, as was supposed. The whole command returned to their former camping ground somewhat late in the evening.

"Next morning, provisions being exhausted, we having only taking two days' rations from Mr. Eaton's, after consultation among the officers it was, as I suppose, deemed advisable for Captain Eaton to send Quartermaster and Commissary W. W. Miller to Fort Steilacoom for supplies and pack animals. At the same time, according to Indian reports, it was thought to be prudent on the part of Captain Eaton to assign Lieutenants Poe and Tullis to the recruiting service, and dispatch them, the former to Olympia and the latter to Mound Prairie, for the purpose of raising additional recruits. For the assistance of Mr. Miller in the ob-

taining of provisions and pack animals Captain Eaton detailed to accompany him two corporals and three privates.
Immediately after the departure of the above-named gentlemen Lieutenant McAllister applied to the Captain for permission to reconnoiter the military road leading towards
White River, at or near the crossing of which, it having
been reported that from two to five hundred Indians were
encamped, peaceably engaged in fishing, some twelve miles
distant from our present camp. Permission was given to
Lieutenant McAllister by our Captain, with an injunction to
return that evening. The reply of Lieutenant McA. was:
'I will return if alive.' And accompanied by Connell, a settler on White River, and two Indians, he left our camp.
An hour had elapsed, and Captain Eaton being informed
that a bad slough interrupted the passage towards White
River, about three-quarters of a mile from camp, and in
order to ascertain what amount of labor it would require to
repair the same, requested your correspondent to accompany him on a reconnoisance of it. After determining that
it would require not more than two men for two hours to
free from all danger horses passing over it, we started on
our way back to camp. When within about two hundred
yards of the house containing our baggage the sharp report
of a rifle was heard, followed immediately by a second. A
few seconds elapsed, bringing us to a standstill, after which
five additional shots were fired, when Captain Eaton coolly
responded to the shots: 'My God! Our boys are gone.'
We immediately hurried toward camp, Captain Eaton giving orders to the following effect: 'Boys, saddle up your
horses; get your baggage all in readiness, and above all
things keep cool.' "

As there has been some controversy as to the precise
date of the death of McAllister, I have printed this letter
of Wiley's in full, which, having been written almost
on the spot, by a man who was within the sound of the
first guns of the war, and a trained writer, ought to be
conclusive that McAllister and Connell were killed on
the 27th day of October, 1855.

The shot that killed McAllister was the shot that opened the war on the west side of the mountains, as the troops at that time struggling in the mountains, where they were going to chastise the Indians on the east side, had not molested them on the west. But the Eaton Rangers, to which McAllister belonged, was a different organization called together for a different purpose, said by courtesy to "apprehend" the Indians and place them on reservations. As already shown, their very first move was for Leschi's farm, to force him from his home. It is folly to say this was not war and that the troops were not the aggressors. It is true Leschi had been reported as having told his white friends and old neighbors he intended to go to war unless he could get his home, and had notified them they need not fear harm would come to them, but he had committed no overt act.* He was in the acting Governor's office in Olympia on the 22d of October, according to the testimony of Governor Mason himself. He was loth to go to the war, and did not go until the evening of the 23d of October, and only just in time to escape from the armed force that arrived at his place before noon of the 24th, and before the embers of the fire in the house were cold.

Leschi went in such haste that much of his stock fell into the hands of the troops, who later secured fifteen head of his horses and put them into service against him. Doubtless many of the tribe had already moved to a place of safety from arrest, in the vicinity of Connell's prairie, but Leschi and Quiemuth had lingered to the very last, it is fair to presume with the hope of somehow averting the catastrophe of war.† One thing in which Leschi was firm, and that was to have either a home or war. He had a large stock of horses grazing on the Nisqually plains near by, and he could not leave home with-

---

*While striving for peace, he doubtless made preparations for war, to be ready if finally driven to that dreadful and dreaded alternative.

†Indeed, we have Dr. Tolmie's letter showing that Quiemuth was actually plowing for fall wheat just before the Eaton Rangers visited their place, and that the two brothers fled in such haste the plow was left standing in the unfinished furrow.

out great loss, and if finally driven to the reservation
allotted to the Indians his accumulation of years would
be of no value to him; in a word, he would be compelled
to either sell or abandon them.

It was under such conditions that Leschi started from
home on the evening of the 23d of October, 1855.   He
did not begin his campaign by attacking and killing
settlers, but threw himself at once on the track of the
troops who had gone to fight his natural allies, the Yakimas, on the east side of the mountains.   Connell's
prairie and near vicinity, the point chosen for the battle
field, was the best of the whole country, affording grass
for the stock, shelter and salmon for his forces, and opportunities for striking in every direction or safe retreat if defeated.   Near by this chosen field the first and
last battles were fought, and in fact, we may say that
within a radius of five miles all the battles of the war
were fought, and where, in the near vicinity, the Indians
maintained themselves until March 10th, 1856.   By the
overwhelming force brought against them and with the
total failure of a supply of ammunition and food they
were finally defeated with loss and compelled to retreat
through the Natchess Pass to the east side of the mountains, which they did, without the loss of a man in the
retreat.

This chosen battle field furnished fortification in
every direction in the fallen timber and thick undergrowth, so thick in most places that a retreat of half a
dozen rods would completely conceal a warrior from his
enemy.

To the northwest, but two miles distant, White River
roared in the deep canyon where Leschi could easily
place his men on the opposite side, but which became
a formidable barrier to cross in the face of an enemy.
The Puyallup lay between his forces and the settlements,
except such as were in the valley of that name.   In a
word, the Indian forces were thrown into one vast forti-

fication suited for defensive warfare, where a greatly
inferior force might easily hold their ground and inflict punishment or change their position at will, and
confuse and annoy an enemy while safely escaping to a
new position if the exigency of the battle required it.
Seattle lay northwesterly from this field, thirty miles
distant, while Fort Steilacoom was but twenty miles
west, with only one wagon road leading into the country
from the west.

Immediately after killing McAllister and Connell the
Indians threw what force they could collect toward the
camp of the Rangers, which was in the Puyallup Valley,
three miles distant, and came very near capturing the
captain of the company, Eaton, and Wiley, editor of the
Pioneer and Democrat, who, as we have seen, barely
had time to reach their camp in the Puyallup bottom and
take shelter in a cabin with the remainder of the company not already sent on other duty. Here they were
besieged for a night without casualty, except the slight
wounding of private Wallace of Olympia, when the
Indians drew off, taking all their horses but one, thus
dismounting the whole company at the outset.

The killing of McAllister and Connell in the near
vicinity of the White River settlement, undoubtedly precipitated the outbreak in that valley, and resulted in
the massacre the next day, the very worst thing that
could have happened to the Indians for their own cause.
Just what happened in the camp of the hostiles now
gathering on Connell's prairie, within the next three
days, we are not fully advised, but know dissensions
broke out in camp at once on account of Leschi's stern
condemnation of the barbarous acts of the White River
Indians in massacring defenceless citizens, men, women
and children. It is tolerably certain that had not an
unexpected emergency overtaken the camp the divisions
would have become so serious as to have precluded any
co-operation between the assembled tribesmen.

The defeat of Haller, who had gone into the Yakima country from the Dalles of the Columbia River, in September, awakened the U. S. Military authorities to the seriousness of the situation on the east side of the mountains. Haller had gone from The Dalles, on the south, with one hundred men, while Slaughter was sent in from Fort Steilacoom through the Natchess Pass from the west with but forty-eight. Haller's forces were attacked by the Indians and sent headlong out of the country, with the loss of seventeen men killed and wounded, and narrowly escaped total destruction. Slaughter had arrived in the northern portion of the enemy's country when he discovered his danger, and retreated in time to avoid loss. His force both going and returning passed through Connell's prairie, where Leschi subsequently camped. Another attempt to chastise the Yakimas, although taken with a much larger force, proved abortive.

Captain M. Maloney, of the U. S. Regulars, from Fort Steilacoom and Captain Gilmore Hays of the Washington Territory Volunteers, with an aggregate force of two hundred and forty men, left Connell's prairie for the Yakima country via the Natchess Pass on the 24th of October. Major Rains was to co-operate by throwing a greater force against the Indians from the south over the route followed by Haller. This latter expedition being delayed until the 12th of November, left Maloney confronting the whole Indian force, whereupon this, the second expedition, fell back. An express rider, William Tidd,* had left Steilacoom for Maloney's camp on the 27th and in some unaccountable way passed over the road where McAllister and Connell lay and through the prairie unharmed, and safely delivered his dispatches

---

*William Tidd was a carpenter who lived at Steilacoom before and after the war. He was a quiet, unobtrusive man, the very last to have been taken for an express rider. He seemed to have had a charmed life. His hat was once cut with a bullet and clothing twice, but he went through the whole war without a scratch. He never talked boastingly of his exploits; in fact, not at all unless drawn out by suggestive conversation from others.

to Maloney on the 29th, who had already received warning and had prepared for retreat.

The intrepid express rider was not allowed to rest, but immediately turned his face westward again bearing tidings from Maloney. He was accompanied on his return trip by A. Benton Moses, who was aide-de-camp to Maloney, Joseph Miles, George R. Bright, ———— Bradly, Dr. M. P. Burns, nad A. B. Rabbeson. On the evening of the 31st of October, at 3 o'clock, these seven men, all save one belonging to the military service, drew up before the Indian encampment on Connell's prairie. It is difficult to say which party were the more surprised. It is certain the Indians did not expect any trouble to come from the east, and had no guards out in that direction, else the express riders would have been attacked before reaching the prairie. The attack on Eaton had been abandoned three days before, and a rear guard posted in the swamp a mile to the westward of the prairie. Burns, one of the party, a fool-hardy Irishman, wanted to kill an Indian right then and there, but his more level headed comrades stopped him. The Indians dissembled and professed friendship and so the conference soon ended, each party being too willing to be rid of the presence of the other. The one because they were not strong enough to make an attack, the other because of the close proximity of their families and the further feeling that the rear guard would destroy them.

The road leading from the prairie through the swamp was a narrow cut, barely wide enough for one wagon track, with much fallen timber and thick underbrush on either side. The mud and water were very deep for full three-quarters of a mile. It seems like a miracle that any of the party escaped, but five of them did, only Moses and Miles being killed. The ambuscade was on almost the identical spot where McAllister and Connell had been killed four days before, and whose bodies yet lay unburied when these two new victims were added to their number. It was for the shooting of Moses, as we shall see later, that Leschi was put on trial for his life, and for which after the war was ended, and after he had given himself up to Colonel Wright and had been promised protection, and after two trials and a third sentence he was finally hung on Friday, the 19th day of February, 1858.

CHAPTER XXXVII.

The White River Massacre.

On the very day (October 28, 1855) that Governor Stevens made his final start for home from the Blackfeet council grounds on the Missouri River, a thousand miles distant from his capital, and one day after the killing of McAllister, as related in the last chapter, nine persons were massacred on White River, about twenty miles south of Seattle. These people were peacefully living at their usual homes when the attack was made upon them. They were killed ruthlessly—men, women and children—with atrocities too vile to describe and mutilations of bodies so often seen in Indian warfare.

There were three parties that simultaneously attacked the three families so nearly destroyed, whose cabins were separated but short distances on the three claims occupied. The intervening timber shut out from view their neighbors' cabins, and each met their doom without the knowledge of the fate of their neighbors. Two of these families, Harvey H. Jones and George E. King, I had met on the Yakima crossing about September 8, 1854, and camped with them over night. As I was the first white man they had seen who had lived in the country in which they were just then arriving from a wearisome trip across the plains, they naturally plied me diligently with questions and acted upon my advice, and secured valuable claims in the White River valley exactly where I had recommended them to go.

An amusing incident occurred at the camp that evening of the day we met. I had just emerged from the mountains, going east in search of relatives. My only companion was a small, white, bob-tailed pony, my only food a sack of hard bread, and my only bedding my saddle blanket.

It was but natural they should invite me to accept their hospitality, to eat at their table and sleep in their tent. I had experienced great fatigue in the forced march to get out of the mountains, and naturally, after eating heartily, soon became drowsy and anxious for rest. But the desire for information about the country they were seeking, the conditions of the roads and numerous other matters, was not easily satisfied, and so the volley of questions continued until late in the evening. Finally a lull in the conversation came, and I thought my trial at an end, when suddenly Mr. Jones broke the silence with the question: "Can you see the sun rise in that country?" Thinking it was an idle question merely with a view to continue the conversation and feeling annoyed and perhaps half vexed that I had not escaped the continuation of the long series of questioning and perhaps with a view of putting an end to it, I answered, before taking a second thought how it would sound, that they could if they were up early enough in the morning. This answer, coupled with my manner and tone, brought an awkward pause and embarrassment, but the quick wit and tact of the lady, Mrs. Jones, came to the rescue by saying that they had lived in a deep canyon in Wisconsin, where the sun could not be seen until far above the horizon, ending the incident with a hearty laugh all round.

I never saw these people again, though afterwards have frequently traversed their settlement, and ten years later surveyed their donation land claims, and could even at that late date see the remains of their industrious year's labor. One of them had brought a lot of seeds across the 2,000-mile stretch of the plains, with which to plant a nursery. The remains of this nursery could be seen for years as a melancholy reminder of the tragic

THE RESCUED JONES-KING CHILDREN   MRS. HARVEY JONES

THE WHITE RIVER MASSACRE

event that cost these people their lives.   The others,
W. H. Brannan, wife and child, and Enos Cooper, who
lost their lives, had previously made their homes on an
adjoining claim.

Four of the King and Jones children made their
escape; three of them, shown in the illustration, speedily
reached Seattle by the help of friendly Indians.   The
larger of the three, shown in the group, that to the
reader's right, is the little hero, Johnny King, as the
pioneers have always spoken of him, who rescued the
two smaller children, brother and sister, as related by
the matured man, John I. King, in the graphic account
following.   This group was taken in San Francisco the
following spring after the massacre.

The other illustration on same page is the mother,
Mrs. Jones, who died unattended and uncared for, but
whose fortitude had not forsaken her, though wounded
and alone, whose dying words were: "Take the children and go to Thomas's; I can't live and you may save
them."   She was a bright, refined lady of superior intelligence, a typical pioneer of a class that deserves a
place in history and deserved a better fate.

The child by her side the reader will readily recognize as the same child, Johnny King, taken when
younger and before the trip across the plains.

The other, a child of 5 years, of the name of King,
but of another family, escaped from their cabin but
was held captive among the Indians until the following
spring, and then delivered to the military officers at
Fort Steilacoom.

The little fellow, George King, could not be properly
cared for at the fort, and the commanding officer sent
the child to me, where he stayed long enough to again
learn his mother tongue, which he had almost forgotten, and to cease speaking the Indian tongue, which he
spoke quite fluently when first brought in.

This is the child the Indian who saved him later made

an effort to find, with a view to will him his property, worth several thousand dollars, as related in full in another chapter, a mounment to the generous impulse of individuals of the native race. But he was too late. The boy was dead, and all his people.

The eldest of the three, John I. King, who was taken to Seattle, is now the only survivor of that terrible day. He was then 7 years old, and is the only witness we have, aside from the Indians, who almost always refuse to give out information about this affair.

We are fortunate in being able to get the story of this tragic event from the only living witness, written expressly for this work by Dr. John I. King, of Martel, O., whose memory has served him well all these years, as we know by many corroborating narratives from other sources. He says:

"The Indians were frequent visitors at our house. They were 'blanket' Indians mostly, and generally very uncouth, unkempt, untidy and repulsive. As the season of 1855 advanced there was an uneasy feeling along the White River valley. In fact, some two weeks previous to the massacre a few families did remove to Seattle. On the Friday preceding the outbreak Nelson, one of the chief men of the Indians of the vicinity, came early in the forenoon to visit us, and remained until nearly noon. I remember that that day he was unusually quiet and uncommunicative. Mother kept on with her household duties, passing before and around him, as occasion required. His talk was mostly in monosyllables, and then only in reply to some question or suggestion. Finally he left, and said in mixed Indian and English, that 'it would not be very long until Indian be gone and white man have all the land around here.'

"When my step-father returned we told him what Nelson had said. It was an enigma. It caused us an uneasy evening. I have sometimes thought he was trying as near as he dared to give us a warning, although some insist he was simply endeavoring to quiet our fears for the purpose of murdering us.*

"The Sunday following Nelson's visit was the 28th day of October, 1855. My step-father was not well and was in bed in the southwest bed room. His bed was in the northeast corner of the room. He is said to have had an attack of pleurisy. Mother, Enos Cooper, our hired man, my half-sister and my half-brother and myself were at the table eating breakfast. The table was set in the center of the large room. There came a sound from the door, a peculiar noise, but one which we remembered as being made by an Indian. As I remember, they never rapped at the door, but instead uttered a peculiar grunt or gutteral sound, until some one opened the door. Mother started for the door, and by the time she reached it we three children were beside her. As she opened the door there stood an Indian, but he was not standing at the door; he was standing a little to one side, and as the door was opened more widely he moved still further to the side. As his action attracted my attention I glanced past him towards the small log house, and was startled to see another Indian, who was standing back of one of the corners of the house, with his gun pointed out between the ends of the logs; his face was to the gun and his hand near the trigger. I shall never forget the sight! It seemed as though I was looking directly into the muzzle of the weapon.

"Mother must have observed it at the same instant, because before I could speak about it she screamed and at the same time seized us and threw us away from the door, which she closed violently and fastened. She did all this

*Those conversant with Indian character know from Nelson's actions, described by Mr. King, that he was trying to frighten those people away from their homes to save their lives. He knew of the gathering storm and doubtless was one of the stoutest advocates for war of any in his tribe, but he wanted to save his old-time neighbors if he could. He dared not tell them in plain words. If he had, the warning would have brought troops against his own people, and probably vengeance from other members of his tribe. To go there to the cabin, sit down in the way and act unlike his former self he thought would be warning plain enough to frighten the inmates without implicating himself. It is not probable any time had been set for the attack, but the encounter with the Eaton rangers, a few miles distant, the following day, precipitated matters, and so his friends were sacrificed. He doubtless wished the mother of the children should escape, as it would be incredible that she could get away from the cabin without being killed, other than by the design of the attacking party. There were none left at the other cabins to tell the story, and so all we know is the mute sight of the mangled corpses of the murdered people. Small wonder that a cry for vengeance went out from the horrified and frightened pioneers.

in an incredibly short time. It was evidently the intention
to shoot whoever should come to the door, and, of course, it
would have been natural for them to hope it might be one
of the male adults. They had skulked upon us while we
were at breakfast, because as soon as the door closed there
were guns fired and the warwhoop was given. I looked out
of the southeast window and saw the Indians coming toward the house, whooping and jumping and swinging their
tomahawks, and gesticulating in an excited manner. They
seemed to rise out of the ground. There were a dozen or
more in sight when I looked out, but there must have been
more a few minutes later. They were armed with flintlock
muskets, which carried an ounce ball and did terrible execution. They attacked the front of the house and began
firing through the door and windows. I shall never forget
the sickening sensation at the report of the guns, the sound
of shivering glass and my realizing sense of utter hopelessness of our situation. Mother got my step-father's five-
shooter and returned a few shots, but she soon discon-
tinued its use. After a time she took us into the northwest
bed room, and, bidding us to get into the northwest corner
of the room, as that was the farthest from the point of attack, covered us with a feather bed. She did this, I suppose,
to take advantage of the fact that it was a difficult matter
to send a musket ball through a mass of feathers, especially
the old flintlock musket ball. I became tired of my confinement and peered cautiously from beneath the bed. I noticed that the direction of the balls was more upward than
horizontal; they were coming through my step-father's
room, and tore huge slivers from the partition between the
rooms. These were mostly over his bed. Waiting a short
time I crept along the floor to the door, into the large room.
Soon my step-father came to his door and was leaning
against the left side of the door. Mother did not seem to
have known of his presence there. I was watching him
when I saw him stagger and lean more heavily against the
casing of the door. He said: 'Oh, God, I am shot!' Mother
turned quickly, and, advancing, said: 'Oh, Harvey, don't
say so!' and supported him in her arms. He opened his
shirt front and there was a huge wound near the nipple.

The ball had come through the front door. She helped him back to his bed. I returned to my hiding place. I shall never forget their parting. His prayers and advice were mingled with her sobs. After a time his moans ceased and I knew that he was dead. I never saw him again. In a short time I heard my mother and Mr. Cooper discussing the hopelessness of affairs. Mother told him that resistance was useless and advised him to attempt to escape. He came into the room where I was. With an ax he pried off a window stop and then moved the lower sash. I saw him hesitate; he looked one way and another, then leaped from the window.

"A short time after the escape of Cooper there was a lull in the firing. I noticed steps in the large room which were not my mother's. Looking again from beneath my hiding place I saw that the rooms were much lighter than before, and that the Indians had gained an entrance into the house, one of whom was carrying some bread in his arms. I was taken outside. One of the first I saw was Nelson, who was seated upon a cut from a log turned upon one end, a few feet from the door. He seemed to be directing the rest what to do. I was taken to him, as were my sister and brother a few minutes later. At first I was anxious and afraid, but he told me not to fear; that he could protect me. I trusted him implicitly, I remember, and assured the children there was no danger, because Nelson had said so. They were not as certain of this as I. When or how mother left the house I never knew, nor did I see her after she hid us under the bed until after the Indians left, after burning the house. Nelson was kind to me, and, as I remember, seemed to talk aside to me, as though he did not want the other Indians to hear him. Strangely enough, he told me to go to Mr. Thomas's, where I had gone to school. The trip was dangerous enough then, as there was only a path through the woods and the distance was some two miles. The Indians were carrying out blankets, clothing and other inflammable articles, and stuffing them beneath the house. They fired these, and thus the house was gotten well ablaze.

"Nelson dismissed all but one Indian, who, he said, would help me to get to Mr. Thomas's. After a time Nelson left, and we were then in the care of the Indian. When it pleased him he started with us. He had me by the hand, I held sister's, and she in turn was leading our little brother. I was surprised at his starting toward the southeast and demurred. He insisted and kept on. We began holding back. He partly led and dragged us to a low place in the fence near the barn, a few rods from the house. Here he suddenly let go of my hand, and we staggered backward and nearly fell to the ground. The Indian petulantly muttered something, which I have now forgotten. His manner was such as to lead me to think that he did not care what became of us. He soon disappeared, and I was alone with the children. I studied a time what was best to do. I concluded first to go to a nearer neighbor than Mr. Thomas. I remember how our house appeared. It was consumed, except some of the studding, which was erect and smoking. The little one-roomed building was burned also; the barn and outbuildings were standing when I left. Leading the children, I started for one of our neighbors living toward the south. I am not sure whether it was Mr. Lake's I had in mind or Mr. Brannan's, but I believe I went to Mr. Brannan's.

"As I went along I called long, often and loudly upon Mr. Cooper, hoping he might hear me, but I became alarmed at the echo of my calls from the woods, for fear I might attract the attention of any Indians who might be prowling about. I hadn't gone far until I became convinced I could get along better without the children. Looking around, I found a roundish depression in the ground, in which I placed them and covered them with brush, charging them to remain there and keep still until I should return. I hurried to the neighbor's, cautiously approaching after I came in sight of the house. As I came nearer I saw that the door was open; then that the windows were broken; and upon closer approach that the chairs, tables and other furniture were scattered about, and that the bedticks and pillows were ripped open and the feathers flying about here and there. I found no one, either dead or alive, and then made my way back to the children. I then took them back to the ruins of our home. We were hungry; we had been driven from the breakfast table. In the log building had been stored some potatoes and several firkins of butter. The potatoes were nicely roasted and there were streams of butter from the charred firkins. I dug some potatoes from the pile and spread some butter upon them, and thus made a satisfactory meal for all of us. I now thought of making my way to Mr. Thomas's. I went somewhat circuitously past the barn and woodshed. While here a half-grown pup, a great favorite and a very noisy fellow, too, came bounding to me. The children played with him, and I was at first disposed to comply with their wishes that we take him with us. On second thought, I knew it would not do, as he would certainly betray our presence should he see an Indian. I did what was very hard to do—took a stick and frightened him away. I shall never forget the expression upon the poor brute's face at this unexpected and unusual treatment. Going farther, I again called, 'Cooper! Cooper!' But the only answer I received was the pitiful echo from the woods.

"As I was passing along I unexpectedly came upon my mother, prostrate upon the ground, some hundred feet or so southwest from the remains of our dwelling. She was yet alive. I do not know how or when she came there, nor what was the nature of her injuries. She was pleased to know we were yet safe, but chided me for my delay in making my escape. She told me I must take the children and go to Mr. Thomas's (the same man that Nelson had named a few hours before). I did not want to leave her, but she told me it was best—that she could not live, and that I might save the children and myself. I wanted to remain. She explained that if the Indians would come back they would probably kill us all, and that I must go. With a sad heart and a courage inspired by mother's charge of responsibility, I made the attempt to do as she bade me. I never saw her again.

"Our route lay through heavy timber and dense undergrowth along a path narrow and winding, some two miles as I remember. When I came to where Mrs. Thomas lived, I went a fourth of a mile or so farther, to where I expected or hoped to find some white persons, but they were gone. I went still farther, but could not get near the house because

of a cross dog guarding the empty dwelling. I returned to
Mr. Thomas's, not knowing what to do next. Mechanically
I began retracing my steps to my home. The children were
a constant source of danger to me and themselves. My
little brother was inconsolable; he wanted to go home to
see his mother. He seemed to think I was out upon an expedition of my own and would not go home. I could keep
my sister quiet by saying 'Indians kill!' but my little brother
did not understand the meaning of this, nor how his crying might attract the attention of the Indians, should any
be near. I was becoming tired, as I had carried my brother
the greater part of the trip, over three miles or so. I lacked
about two weeks of being 7 years old, sister was not quite
4, and brother was not quite 2 years of age. It was getting
late in the afternoon of a day late in the fall. They, and I
too, were getting hungry, and I had nothing to give them
or eat myself, except bark and an edible root which mother
at one time showed me. I was in danger from Indians
and wild animals and as far as I knew, some twenty miles
from a white settlement. An almost overwhelming sense
of my danger and helplessness came over me as I thought
of the coming night. But I trudged on. Glancing along the
path, to my consternation I saw an Indian coming towards
us. From his manner I felt sure he had neither seen nor
heard us. My first thought was for the safety of the children. It flashed through my mind that they might be ran-
somed if captured. With this idea in mind I hastened
into the underbrush, secreted them, charged them to remain
quiet, and then ran diagonally back to the path nearer the
Indian than where I left. I hoped in case he killed me he
would spare the children. As we came nearer I recognized him as an Indian I had frequently seen while attending school at Mr. Thomas's. The school began the 27th
of July that summer. We called him Tom. I told him of
the massacre. He said he suspected something of the kind,
as he had heard firing in that direction. He told me that
I should get the children and take them to his wigwam,
adding that 'when the moon was high' he would take us
to Seattle in his canoe. His squaw was as kind and amiable
as could be, and did all in her power to make it pleasant

for us, but the children were very shy. She set out dried fish and whortleberries for our repast, but nothing she could do would induce them to go to her. Our hunger was so great that the various and penetrating odors permeating the food she had brought us was no bar to our relish for it as I remember.

"A short time after we went there I had left the tent. I heard a cracking of brush near by. I turned. The squaw had followed me to have me return to quiet the children. After I had gotten them calmed, she spread a huge bearskin upon the ground (floor), of the tent, and soon we were all sound asleep. Some time during the night I was awakened by some one tugging at my shoulder. Tom stood over me and said it was time to go. The moon 'was high,' because it was shining brightly down through the circular hole at the top or peak of the wigwam. I was sleepy, and the children positively cross; they were 'dead for sleep.' I made out to get them loaded into the canoe, and we started for Seattle. Near the mouth of the Duwamish River we were delivered to another Indian, 'Dave,' who headed for the sloop-of-war Decatur, lying in Elliot Bay, detailed there for the protection of that part of the Coast. She was a little over 500 tons burden, and carried sixteen guns. She was built in 1838, and at the time of which I speak, was in command of Capt. Sterrett. Dave delivered us to the marines, and we were taken on board by them. He laughed heartily at me as we came within hailing distance of the sloop, because I dropped flat to the bottom of the canoe, thinking I was to be shot. An officer had drawn a long glass on us for the purpose of making out what kind of an outfit we had. We were afterwards taken to a family in Seattle by the name of Russell, and Dr. Maynard appointed guardian. Subsequently a Mr. Buckley and a Mr. Neeley seemed to have us in charge. The children remained on shore while I was on shipboard. I daily went ashore and returned nights the greater part of the time we were in Seattle. About May 25, 1856, my uncle, John Smail, came and took us to our old home in Wisconsin.

"There was a large two-story block house in Seattle, and a stockade for the protection of the people against attack by the Indians. This building stood facing the hill back of Seattle, and had a door in the front left-hand corner. The back of the building faced the bay in front of the town. The sloop-of-war Decatur lay in the bay usually. As was my custom, I was ashore nearly all day every day. On Saturday, January 26, 1856, I came ashore as usual. A short time after I reached the fort that day the Indians attacked Seattle. They were principally upon the hill back of the town. I shall never forget the occasion. The people sought safety in flight into the fort. Small arms were being used on shore, and the Decatur was shelling the hill. The order came to keep clear of the port holes and of the door. One young man (a Mr. Holgate, I believe), defied the Indians and disobeyed orders, too, standing in the open door. In a short time he was shot in the face. I was terribly frightened, sick and faint with fear. I begged and pleaded and insisted on being taken to the Decatur. Finally, a small outlet was made at the back of the fort, and, giving my usual signal, a gig came to take me aboard. One saucy three-inch howitzer was planted on the beach, and the large guns of the Decatur were sending shot and shell over my head, but I preferred the crack of the small brass piece and the roar and boom of the guns to staying in the fort. Bullets occasionally dropped near us, but when on shipboard I was well beyond the range of the Indian muskets. When I came aboard the Decatur, in October, Capt. Sterrett was in command. A short time after this he was relieved, and at the time of the attack, in January, 1856, Capt. Ganzevoort was in command."

The following letter from Capt. C. C. Hewitt, supplies the sequel to this melancholy event:

"Seattle, Nov. 5, 1855.

"Mr. Editor: I have just returned from the scene of the late massacre, on White River, about thirty or thirty-five* miles from this place, and will proceed to give you a brief statement of the transaction.

"On Sunday evening, October 28, a young man by the name of Lake came to this place with two families (Mr.

---

*It is but twenty miles, being less than two miles from the town of Auburn, but the obstruction to travel was such as to cause one very reasonably to conclude that it was as far as Mr. Hewitt estimated.

Cox and Mr. Kirkland), and reported that he had been shot at and wounded while standing within the door of Mr. Cox, and heard guns and screams in the direction of some of the other neighbors. This was about 7 o'clock in the same morning. I immediately mustered forty men and four Northern Indians, and at 11 o'clock Monday morning started for the scene of action with such guns and outfit as we could command. After two days' hard work we reached the house of Mr. Cox, which we found robbed, confirming our suspicion that greater mischief had been done to the settlements farther up the river. We then proceeded to Mr. Jones's place, where we found our worst fears more than realized. The house was burned to ashes, and Mr. Jones, who was sick at the time, was burned in it. Mrs. Jones we found lying near the house, shot through the lower part of the lungs, face and jaw horribly broken, and mutilated apparently with the head of an ax. We found Mr. Cooper, who was living with Mr. Jones at the time, about 150 yards from the house, shot through the lungs, the ball entering the left breast. We buried the bodies and proceeded to the house of W. H. Brannan, a mile distant. Mrs. Brannan and child we found in the well, her head downwards. The mother was stabbed to the heart, the knife entering the lower part of the left breast, and also in the back and back of the head. She had apparently started to run with her child, an infant of 10 months old, in her arms, was overtaken and pitched into the well. The child was below her and bore no marks of violence on it. It was not dressed, showing that the mother had taken it from the bed and attempted to flee.

"Mr. Brannan was found in the house, literally cut to pieces. The left hand had two cuts, as though he had grasped a knife and had it pulled out, cutting the hand to the bone. There were also two stabs in the palm of the hand, as though he had attempted to ward off the fatal weapon. His arms and legs were badly cut, and I think there were as many as fifteen stabs in his back, mostly a little below the left shoulder. Everything seemed to show that he fought desperately, and I think he must have killed some of the devils from the fact that the fence, where they went out from the house, had the appearance of having something dragged over it, and the rails below were all smeared with blood.

"After burying them as well as circumstances would permit, we proceeded to the house of Mr. King, or, rather, where his house was, which we found burned to ashes, and where the most horrible spectacle of all awaited us.

"I am told by a black man, whom we met about three miles below our encampment, that, on reaching the opposite side of the river from where we stopped, he saw five Indians, part of whom he knew, from whom he learned that there were 150 Indians prowling about my encampment the evening before. The supposition is that they had collected their forces to make an attack. If they had done so, they might have done us considerable damage, as one-third of our guns were entirely inefficient. The next time I go up White River I shall be better prepared. Yours, etc.,   C. C. HEWITT.

"P. S.—Three children of Mr. Jones were saved. The elder, an adopted son about 7 years old, says that Nelson, a half-Klickitat, told him to take the other two and go down to John Thomas's, a distance of about two miles, which he did. Mr. Thomas and family having fled to Seattle, they were discovered by a friendly Indian and brought to town. The boy says he did not know any of the Indians but Nelson.   "C. C. H."

The following statement was found among the correspondence on file in the adjutant general's office at Olympia, without date or signature, indorsed as follows:

"Statement of Indian at Seattle, relation to murders committed on White River.

"Statement of Monish to me:

"I come to Seattle—Mr. Holderness had a bear, wanted something for it. Returned up the river a little above the Dutchman's; tied his canoe and slept. At midnight of the day he was at the fishery at Pupschulk (John Thomas,); went a little way up the road; saw the tenas man (young

Jones*), coming down the road (I may be mistaken as to
his being but one night on the river; he is positive as to
the being at Pupschulk at sitkum sun), (at noon). He
saw the Klickitats and was told Nelson killed with a knife
either William (Brannan), or William's wife, and that
Jones was killed in bed with an arrow. That the Klickitats
took his canoe, as Leschi was on horseback: that he stayed
at the fishery four days, and then came down on foot
through the woods to Alki; that the Indians would not
take him in their canoes, and that he stayed at Alki some
time, and a short time since got over to Capt. Howard's
mill."

The importance of this interview is that it fixes the
responsibility of the massacre in part at least on the
Klickitats, and locates Leschi "on horseback" a few
hours after the occurrence, and between the field of
the massacre and Seattle. To many this will fix in
their minds the responsibility of Leschi's participation
in this tragedy. Leschi, as we have seen, had established his camp on Green River three days before, after
his narrow escape from capture by the Eaton Rangers,
who were sent to his home for the purpose of forcibly
removing him to Olympia, and not more than eight
miles up that river, and doubtless within the sound of
the guns that destroyed the settlements, and he naturally would have ridden post haste to the field. Subsequent events have proven that he did not approve taking
the lives of noncombatants, and so we may reasonably
believe he did not participate in this outrageous destruction of innocent lives. But the reader can judge
of the probabilities as well as the author, having all
the facts obtainable before him.

----

*This was young King, the author of the preceding article; Jones was his
step-father, and it would be natural the lad should be called Jones by one
who was not intimately acquainted with the family.

CHAPTER XXXVIII.

The Flight of Settlers.

The news of the massacre on White River reached the settlements on the Puyallup and Nisqually plains during the night of October 28th, or rather in the early morning of the 29th. About two o'clock in the morning of the 29th, a loud knock at the door awakened the three families, father and two sons,* followed with the information that the Indians had broken out, had murdered all the settlers on White River, and would no doubt soon be out on the plains to murder the inhabitants wherever found. An Indian express rider had come out during the night, and had given the information to the people on the Puyallup, which lay right in .he path the Indians would come, and we thought that even at that moment the Indians were upon them, and that those whom we knew so well had yielded up their lives by the frenzied work of our old time friends.

The Puyallup settlement lay east from Fort Steilacoom from fifteen to twenty miles in the Puyallup Valley, and consisted at that time approximately of eighty persons, quite widely separated along the valley for twelve miles; each family in nearly every case shut out from view of their neighbors' cabin by the intervening timber and underbrush. We could readily see that if the Indians chose to follow up their work on White River it would be possible, and highly probable, that none would escape. While in our case we were but five miles from what was called Fort Steilacoom

---

*Jacob R. Meeker, Oliver P. Meeker, and the author, then living just beyond the confines of South Tacoma, south and five miles east of Fort Steilacoom.

(which was not a fort, but simply an encampment in log cabin and light board houses), yet we would be no safer there than in our own log cabins with our trusted rifles in our own hands, and in fact not so safe. The troops had nearly all been withdrawn to strengthen the expedition under Captain Maloney, then known to be well on the way, if not actually across the mountains, and probably at this time engaged in an active campaign against the powerful tribes east of the Cascades. My brother, O. P. Meeker, and myself stoutly contended we had best barricade the cabins and stay where we were, but the father and women of the household said "no" with such emphasis that the conclusion was soon reached that we must fly. The experience of our household was the experience of a hundred others, who had a like question before them to decide the latter part of that night and early morning of the 29th, and the final conclusion in each case seemed to be the same—to flee to the fort.

That was a busy night for all. Teams had to be gathered together; where possible, young stock as well as old turned out on the range to care for themselves; windows and doors barricaded, while what effects and provisions it was possible to care for were hastily loaded into the wagons and the start as hastily made. To this day I have not ceased to wonder at our actions. I believed then, and believe yet, we would have been safer at home in our cabins than in an open encampment, and yet our fears got the better of our judgments and impelled us to leave home. The same impulses governed elsewhere, and when we arrived at the Fort the scenes beggared description. Some came on foot and with scant clothing, and no food; some came with wagons piled high with household furniture, some with their chicken coops piled in promiscuously with other effects, some driving cattle, some sheep, some swine (property they could not possibly care for at the fort), some with horse teams, some with oxen, others with pack horses, while many a mother came packing the youngest child on her back and leading others. All day the never-ending stream came from the prairies near by, supplemented in the afternoon and until late in the night, and next day by the contingent from Puyallup and farther outlying settlements.

Small wonder that Lieutenant Nugen should write: "I have nearly all the women and children in the country at the post, and will of course protect them," and that he had detained Captain Wallace's company (just formed), to assist in protecting them.

A sorry mess this, of women and children crying, some brutes of men cursing and swearing, oxen and cows bellowing, sheep bleating, dogs howling, children lost from parents, wives from husbands, no order; in a word, the utmost disorder.

It would be a pleasure could I but know he was alive, to even yet thank that kind and considerate gentleman, Lieutenant Nugen, for his forebearance and energetic efforts to contribute to the safety and comfort of those panic stricken citizens. It is a source of deep gratification even at so late a day to bear this testimony to his memory, if perchance he may have passed to the beyond. By improvising some temporary quarters for his forces, most of whom, however, were placed on guard duty, room was provided in the soldiers barracks for the women and children, while the men were placed on guard with what few soldiers were left.

Of course, the hard floor of the barracks furnished the bed, supplemented by the bed clothing of the settlers, which too often had gone astray and could not be found by the rightful owners, the whole floor space packed closely from end to end of the building. We all soon adjusted ourselves to the new conditions, some building blockhouses, some entering government service, while others returned to their claims, and were not molested so much by the Indians as they were by the Governor.

The incident shows though, the discomfort and derangement of the industries of the Territory, as the great body of the settlers in the outlying district were unable to plant for the next crop season, and thereby lost a whole year besides what was lost by abandonment of their homes, which was, in many cases, very serious. But the Indians did not come. Not a settler was disturbed after this first outbreak until the war was virtually over, and then only one, before mentioned, William White, near Olympia.

It is absolutely certain a strong hand was laid upon the Indians in this matter of making war on defenceless women and children. Indian testimony is abundantly in evidence that it was Leschi's master hand that stayed the havoc. We have the testimony of those whites who came within his power during the war. It is certain I was in his power and remained unharmed; also Mrs. Dougherty and family, and were not molested; Peter Rinquist, likewise; John Swan twice, William Benson, Kishner, and many others aside from the so called treasonable settlers.*

Immediate measures were taken by the authorities to provide for the Indians who evinced a disposition to remain friendly, by sending them to temporary reservations under the care of agents, where, as soon as possible, food was provided, until finally four thousand such were dependents upon government bounty. The settlers, meanwhile, collected in groups all over the country, and built block houses, or removed to the small towns, and quite a number left the Territory never to return. General stagnation of business followed, except that closely connected with the war, and over half of the

---

*The "treasonable" settlers referred to, comprised a settlement on what is known locally as Muck Creek, about ten miles southeast of Fort Stellacoom, and consisted principally of discharged Hudson Bay employees, but who had become American citizens though most of them were living with Indian or half breed wives. Governor Stevens later charged these people with having given aid to the Indians and drove them from their homes, though no proof was ever brought forward to sustain the charge. The most plausible reason given was the fact that they returned to their homes soon after the outbreak and were not harmed by the Indians.

able bodied men joined the volunteer forces; some for general service, while others only as home guards. This last class, as we shall see later, caused a great amount of trouble. The pinch came hard on the pioneer settlers who had expended their all upon their farms. These found themselves thrown out of a home without money or credit and many of them without food. Employment might be had in the volunteer service, but there was no money with which to pay even small, incidental expenses. To add to the difficulty, winter was coming on with scant or inadequate shelter. Just how we did pull through it all is difficult to tell, but somehow, or someway, everybody came out in the spring without starving and some even made gain out of government work. Some people called the experiences hardships, some would say "it might be worse," but a response would be forthcoming that they "had not seen it," and it is quite within bounds to say the average reader of this day would, to say the least, call it roughing. It is safe to assert that all who had the experience do not care to go through another such an ordeal.

CHAPTER XXXIX.

Battle of White River.

Following the killing of McAllister and Connell, on the 27th, the massacre on White River the 28th, and the ambushing of the express riders on the 31st, there came a general concentration of the Indian hostile forces at Connell's prairie and Green River.

By this time fully one hundred and fifty fighting men had assembled and had to be fed, besides numerous women and children. Fish abounded in all the streams at that season of the year, and if interrupted at one place the women could find the salmon abundant elsewhere. Here was the spectacle of an army with strongholds as large as the field to be occupied, with food in all parts, even up to the most impenetrable forests of the foothills.

It is astonishing how abundant these salmon are found in the small streams and even rivulets of the headwaters of the greater rivers below. Besides, at this juncture, the Indians had abundance of stock, driven from the farms in the valley below.

One thing only disturbed the Indians for the time being. They were short of ammunition and deficient in effective arms, and these could not be replenished. The food could be obtained for many months, and even a supply accumulated for the later season when the salmon would disappear from the streams. When the final end came considerable supplies were captured and destroyed, silent witnesses of the industry and determined co-operation of the women in, to them, this great struggle.

Another element of weakness was the lack of any
central authority to unify the forces. Three main tribes
contributed the greater number of warriors; the Nisquallies, Puyallups, White River or Duwamish Indians.
Besides, each of these tribes was divided up into numerous bands or families, that acknowledged no central
authority, or if any, at best but the most shadowy.

The morale of this little army at its incoming gathering was high, as the Indians were flushed with what
appeared to them as victories; many of them not realizing the serious work before them. The efficiency of the
individuals comprised in the gathering was very low.
Only about one-third of the number, not over fifty in
all, were to be relied on for effective work. The fish
Indians, as a rule, are poor shots, arrant cowards and
desperate shirks. Like Dr. Burns, who, when he was
found with his head stuck in a barley stack, broke forth
into a volume of brag, insisting he had killed seven
Indians, and exhibited a piece of salmon skin for a
scalp; so with the cowards of the Indians, they could
talk loud without the presence of an enemy, but run
fast where danger was apprehended, or shirk in the
brush on the most trivial pretense.

Leschi had a serious task before him to organize this
force into any sort of a fighting machine. He had but
thirty-one of his own tribe. I have secured the names
of all but one, and all are dead but three. They comprised a force that would obey his command, execute
his orders with alacrity and remained faithful to the
last. His brother, Quiemuth, was of this force. His
brother-in-law (Stahi), was killed in battle and the only
one of this company lost during the whole war. Daniel
Mounts, yet living, had the charge of these Indians for
five years after their return, and is authority for this
remarkable statement and which is doubtless true. This
one instance alone will illustrate better than words could
paint the enormous disadvantage under which troops

labored working an aggressive campaign. An Indian could fire from behind a log or tree or an upturned root, drop to the ground, and be completely concealed by the low brush (the sallal), so general in this country. Their policy from the start was that of a defensive war. This was a wise course to adopt, but difficult to enforce when the enemy drew off and left the field, as occurred so soon. It is doubtful if the force collected at this time would have ever been consolidated had not an unexpected and serious emergency suddenly confronted them. ·While the jealous wranglings between petty chiefs were at their height, and discontent arising from Leschi's stern rebuke for the massacre on White River, there suddenly came upon them the vanguard of Maloney's returning expedition. The Indians barely had time to get their main forces across the river before Maloney's command of 243 men were in full possession of the prairie without firing a gun. This was on the second of November, two days after the express riders had been ambushed and two of them killed.

The contention of the chiefs suddenly ceased, and many of the men skulked to the brush. All eyes were turned to Leschi. He became commander of all the forces without a formal agreement. When the time came he went to the front in person, and asked no one to take any risks in which he and his immediate followers were not willing to share. The testimony of the Indians to this is unanimous. He was a good shot and always calm in the presence of the enemy, and inspired confidence among his followers by his example. After the first battle, presently to be described, there were no more questions raised as to who should command, as all were only too willing to have him take the lead.

On the 3rd, Maloney sent fifty regulars under Lieut. Slaughter, and fifty volunteers under Capt. Hays, to track the Indians, and soon found them posted on the right bank of White River.

The river at this point for miles, both above and below, in a roaring torrent, impossible to ferry, and could not be forded except in very few places, and at these, not when the river was high, as it was at that time. The valley is narrow, filled with drift wood on either side the river, and without soil—a barren waste of rounded boulders and sand with numerous sand bars.

An attempt made to fall a tree upon which to cross resulted in the loss of a man, shot dead upon the spot, and was abandoned as the Indian sharp shooters could not be dislodged, or in fact, discovered. The firing at long range became quite general, the aim usually into a brush patch from which a puff of smoke had been seen. The Indians made a very poor showing, as many of their men were skulking in the thickets and did not come on the firing line at all.

The bluffs on either side of the river are five or six hundred feet above the water level, are very steep, and in some places almost perpendicular. To the rear of the Indians two miles distant, the Green River runs in as deep a cut as the stream upon which the opposing forces were contending. Four miles above the battle ground a good crossing of White River was known to both forces, on the only wagon road in the near vicinity. A good trail led down parallel with the right bank of the river, but on the bluff to the rear of the Indians under the steep hill. Towards noon the Indians began to draw off from the firing line and go up the hill, where there was something for them to eat, but these forgot to go back and skulked. It may well be doubted if Maloney knew of this trail, or if he did if he thought it worth while to make such a flank movement, involving the division of his command without the hope of speedy junction in the case of disaster. Leschi doubtless had fears of attack in the rear all day, and so, in the afternoon, after nearly all his men had drawn off, ceased firing except an occasional shot, and with seven men

CAPTAINS C. C. HEWITT   GILMORE HAYS
INDIAN WAR VETERANS, 1855.

held the drift in which they had fought, until it was too late in the day for his enemy to cross, or if he did, to follow up with his forces.

And so, as we shall see later, the first day's battle resulted in the expenditure of a good deal of ammunition, but not much blood, and caused a good deal of merriment on the part of the Indians. At 3 o'clock, Maloney's forces turned their backs on the battle field, while the Indians were retreating on the opposite side; the first to climb the hill to their camp on the prairie near by, while the Indians continued their retreat to their camp on Green River, some three miles distant from the battle field.

In the light of what has since been learned, the official reports of Captains Maloney and Hays are amusing. No doubt they were sincere in what they wrote, but we now know, and could have then known had they stopped to think a moment, that their reports were grossly incorrect as to the number of the Indians killed. Capt. Maloney says: "They had the advantage of the ground, but still there were over thirty killed and I don't know how many wounded." Hays reported "we estimate their loss at thirty men."

The official reports received by the commander at Fort Steilacoom and by him transmitted to the authorities at Olympia, show to what extent men may be led while acting under the strain of excitement, and show how easy it is for the best and bravest of men to be mistaken as to their information. No one doubts the honesty of either Captain Maloney or Hays, or for that matter that of the men posted on the hill who saw the Indians fall, from whom the information was gained that thirty Indians had been killed. The following report was forwarded:

Fort Steilacoom, Nov. 4th, 6 P. M., 1855.

James Tilton, Adjt. Gen. W. T. V., Olympia.

Sir: I have just received an express from Capt. Maloney informing me that Lieut. Slaughter, with fifty regulars and Capt. Hays, with fifty volunteers, had met the Indians yesterday about 8 A. M. They had taken a position on the right bank of the river, and opposed the troops crossing. The river was too high to ford, and the Indians behind logs firing, so the fight became general, and lasted until about 4 P. M. Thirty Indians were killed, and no telling how many wounded, as they were carried to the rear. Slaughter had some men posted on a hill in the rear of his position, where they could see and count every Indian who fell. Slaughter killed one, and Lieut. Harrison killed two.

Our loss, one soldier killed, who was falling a tree in order to cross the stream; one soldier wounded severely, and one volunteer wounded. * * *

JOHN NUGEN,
Lt. 4th Inf. Com. Post.

This was the first battle of the war on the west side of the mountains, and naturally all parties on both sides would be laboring under excitement.

I happen to have Puyallup Tyee Dick's account of this battle, who was at the front the whole day, and he says they lost but one man. At first, the Indians were quite nervous and inclined to fall back from the river, but as the hours passed and they remained under cover in the drift and no one was hurt, they became more confident, and finally jubilant. He described the battle as "hi-ue he-he, hi-ue he-he" (lots and lots of fun).

The Indians soon found that if any object was shown from under cover, the troops on the opposite side of the river would fire at it from various points, and so they began to push up hats and sticks until it came into sight, and bang, bang, bang, would go the guns of the enemy, down would go the hat and another Indian reported killed. This thing went on until it became a standing joke and brought yells of delight from the Indians all along the line.

A full confirmation of this story from another source convinced me that Dick was telling the truth. Daniel Mounts, before referred to, was with Capt. Hays in the battle. Hays reported having seen six Indians killed in one particular spot, and that he (Mounts) saw two of them fall himself, or at least saw their heads suddenly disappear from sight immediately after the volunteers had fired. At the same time, he believed they were killing Indians right and left, but wondered how it came that so soon after an Indian was killed, another would take his place in the identical spot.

Subsequently, Mr. Mounts was appointed agent on the Nisqually Indian reservation, and had charge of the Nisqually war party, upon their return, for five years. These Indians told Mr. Mounts the same story told me by Indian Dick. The corroboration of the story lies in the fact that of the thirty-one Nisquallies that went on the war path under the leadership of Leschi, thirty came back unharmed—only one of the whole number wounded or killed during the war.

Nor is this to be wondered at when we take into consideration the splendid cover under which the Indians could fight, with their rear always fully guarded by the impenetrable forest and thickets that covered the whole country round about the district of active hostilities.

These figures by no means are given to belittle the efforts of the volunteers and regulars in this war. They show, however, what a great task lay before them, and had we had a desperate and able foe like the Modoc warriors, there would have been many more lives lost, much more treasure expended, and the time for the final ending of the war greatly delayed. The material for the volunteer forces was the best the country afforded. A majority of the men were sturdy pioneers who went to the war from a sense of duty, knew no fear, nor shirked a duty. As with all such bodies, there were sure to be some poltroons, some whose acts were reprehensible, but such were no more a reflection upon the good name of the volunteers than the same individuals were upon the community from which they were drawn. It is well for the reader to bear these remarks in mind while perusing these pages containing accounts of wrongs perpetrated upon the Indians. It is lamentable that cruel murders were committed, but because the criminals belonged to the white race is no reason why we should screen them from view and from condemnation.

CHAPTER XL.

Green River Skirmish.

On the morning of the 4th, Capt. Maloney made an early start for the battle ground of the day before (described in the preceding chapter), with one hundred and fifty men, but found no Indians at the river crossing where the struggle had ended the previous afternoon. The Indians had withdrawn their whole force to Green River Valley, where their main supply camp had been established. To reach them from Connell prairie it was necessary to march nearly two miles from the encampment on the prairie to the brow of the bluff, descend fully six hundred feet into the narrow canyon of White River, ascend the opposite bluff to the same level of the prairie, then march a mile and again descend five hundred feet or more by a very steep, crooked trail into the Green River Valley. The whole distance, except the first mile, could be traversed only by following a crooked, narrow, slippery Indian trail. The movement over such a trail was necessarily slow, which, coupled with the necessary detention at the river crossing, made it late in the day when the Indians were finally encountered in the Green River Valley. All that Capt. Maloney says of this last day's operations are these words:

"Next day I started a command after them, and found them on the opposite side of Green River. They showed but little fight. We had two wounded; I can't say how many Indians were wounded."

Capt. Hays says of this affair:

"I ordered Lieut. Hurd to charge them on the left, over a deep slough, the river on the right being too deep, but

afterwards countermanded the order, knowing full well
that in the charge we would lose more men than the
enemy. They were prepared to fire and run. We returned
to camp."

By this time Captains Maloney and Hays began to
realize it was no fun to fight Indians in the brush
on a rainy, wintry, November day or night, without
camp equipage or food supplies, where any bush might
conceal a gun, and in any event if touched, turn a shower
of accumulated rain on the bush upon the devoted heads
of their troops. It was impossible to move about in
any direction without being drenched to the skin and
chilled to the very marrow, the Indians meanwhile lying
-concealed, awaiting their opportunity to catch their
victim. And so, as they had marched their troops up
and down the hill to find an enemy, and found him,
they concluded it was best to reverse the order and
march again up and down the hill towards their own
camp, which they did.

I mean no reflection upon the two captains for they
both were brave, capable men, but the fact was they
were undertaking an almost impossible task to chastise
the Indians during a rain storm in the dense forests
of Western Washington, and in any event, certain to
receive greater punishment than they could inflict. The
Indians have been roundly berated for their method of
warfare, but it is certain they could not do otherwise
with any hope of success.

Fun will crop out under almost any circumstance,
whether in danger or in safety. The deep slough
referred to by Capt. Hays in his report, afforded the
opportunity for a good deal of merriment. While attempting to cross the bar and slough, the Indians began
to pepper away at the horsemen while crossing, whereupon, the men jumped off into the water crotch deep,
making breast works of their faithful animals. One
young Irishman, named Murphy, not being satisfied with

his cover, made a bee line for the brush, stirring up the water in great shape while he ran, making only "one long streak" in his swift retreat, the men afterwards said. The long strides, the speed, coupled with the oddity of the performance, set the company in a roar of laughter, but when Murphy bawled out from his safe retreat to "tell that man with the dog to bring my horse over" there was an explosion all along the line. A merciless wag bawled at the top of his voice, "why in h—l don't the lubber go and get his own horse," and then again there came another roar, but nobody was hurt.

The "man with the dog" was Peter Smith, to whom I am indebted for the anecdote. Smith is now eighty-six years old, hale and hearty, and laughed immoderately while relating the incident.*

Smith to this day believes the Murphy who called to him was John Miller Murphy, the veteran editor of the Standard, but he stoutly denies the charge and says he was not hunting Indians at the time.

Notwithstanding the enormous difficulties encountered by Captains Maloney and Hays, it was a great blunder for them to withdraw their forces as they did and give the Indians a breathing spell. The main camp of the Indians was but a few hundred yards distant, in which were all their camp equipage, women and children, and what accumulation of food they possessed. This would have been all, or measurably all, lost to the Indians had the two captains camped where they were and pushed their advantage. They made the singular mistake of leaving an enemy immediately in their front to withdraw to their own camp on the prairie, four miles distant, and the very next day (Nov. 5th), to start an expedition of a hundred men in almost an opposite direction, to South Prairie, six miles distant from their camp, in search of Indians. The Indians were found,

*Again I am compelled to note the death of another pioneer since the writing of the incident. Smith died a few short weeks ago, after rounding out a long and honorable life in his chosen home.

five white men were lost, and immediately the force was withdrawn without inflicting any punishment upon the enemy.

, On this last expedition the force was divided, fifty men in each detachment, one going by a direct trail of six miles, the other by Finnell's prairie. As afterwards ascertained, there were but four Indians (scouts), near the prairie, and each "got his man," that is, each of their shots took effect, and in fact one shot killed one man and wounded another. When their fire was delivered, the Indians withdrew a little farther in the brush, and were not seen at all by the troops. The troops marched back the same day to their camp on Connell's prairie without accomplishing anything, except as we have seen, losing five men and gaining a rousing appetite for supper.

Small wonder the thought occurred to Capt. Maloney to call a halt. On the 6th, the Captain wrote Governor Mason: "What do you think of my falling back?" A very pertinent question.

Without waiting for a response to his suggestion to Governor Mason, Capt. Maloney on the 7th, began his retreat from the enemy's country, and on the 9th arrived at Fort Steilacoom with the bodies of the dead and wounded.

The casualties from the 27th of October to the 6th of November were as follows:

Oct. 27th, killed, James McAllister, 1st Lieut. of Eaton Rangers; Oct. 27th, killed, ——— Connell, citizen, accompanying Lieut. McAllister; Oct. 28th, killed in massacre on White River, nine persons, as follows:

Harvey Horace Jones, Mrs. Eliza Jane Jones, Enos Cooper, W. H. Brannan, Mrs. W. H. Brannan and infant, George E. King, Mrs. George E. King and child; Oct. 31st, A. B. Moses, Joseph Miles; Nov 4th, 1 regular killed; Nov. 4th, 1 volunteer wounded; Nov 5th, wounded, Andrew Burge, in the leg, on Green River; Nov. 6th, killed, John Edgar, South Prairie; wounded, Ad. Perham, South Prairie;

wounded, two regular privates; wounded, Corporal Moeyck. South Prairie.

Thus it is seen that thirteen were killed and six wounded in eleven days' time after the outbreak. Small wonder there should be a gloom settle on the minds of the little group of pioneers who, with their families, were exposed to a like fate.

On the 9th Lieutenant Nugen wrote from Fort Steila-coom:

"* * * The Indians on the lower Puyallup have broken out, so there is more work.

"Capt. Maloney's pack train is coming in, and will reach this post to-day. The train brings the remains of Moses, Miles, and McAllister. I wish to know whether the bodies are to be sent to Olympia or to be interred here. Let me know by return express.

"Capt. Wallace comes in with the pack train.

"A company of seventeen men, under Capt. Carson, raised here, started yesterday for the lower Puyallup."

It does seem that men at times will do things that are the very essence of folly without thought of the danger incurred, which they would shrink from had they but stopped to consider the probable consequences of their rash acts. The seventeen men referred to in Lieut. Nugen's letter were seventeen pioneers,* nearly

---

*This company started for the valley within twelve hours after the organisation, and disbanded at once upon return to Fort Stellacoom.

The names were, as near as the survivors' memory serves them, are:

John Carson, Captain	Puyallup
Robert Moore	Puyallup
James Bell	Puyallup
Henry Whitesell	Puyallup
R. Nix	Puyallup
Frank Wright	Puyallup
Israel H. Wright	Puyallup
John F. Kincaid	Puyallup
Edward Lane	Puyallup
———— Hayward	Puyallup
William Benson	Puyallup
Willis Boatman	Puyallup
Albert Balch	Stellacoom
Abraham Woolery	Puyallup
Isaac Woolery	Puyallup
Daniel E. Lane	Puyallup
Byrd Wright	Puyallup
O. P. Meeker	Puyallup Plains
E. Meeker	Puyallup Plains

all of whom had but recently left their homes on the Puyallup in such haste as to preclude bringing their household goods or provisions with them. Ten days had passed since their flight in a panic to save, as they thought, the lives of their families, and enough time had elapsed to bring the pinch of hunger and intensify the discomforts of virtual prison life at the fort. These people had an abundance of food and raiment with much stock at their homes on the Puyallup, fifteen miles distant, and so this company was formed with John Carson of Puyallup, as Captain for the purpose of going to get the property so much needed by their families. Three of us, not residents of the valley, joined the party, and this being the author's sole military record, the reader must pardon the prominence given so small an expedition. This company was formed for this special trip, not to fight Indians, but with a view to save property, but it was well understood that all must go armed, and fight if we had to.

The theater of active hostilities lay beyond the Puyallup some six or eight miles, where, at the time the start was made, it was supposed Maloney would stay with his force, then augmented by reinforcements, to over three hundred men. There are two roads leading from the prairie through the wide belt of timber bordering on the Puyallup, about six miles apart and running almost parallel, the lower intercepting the Puyallup River near where the thriving city of Puyallup is now located; the other, six miles farther up the river. We took the lower road, while that very day, Maloney marched out by the upper road. We were in blissful ignorance of this move until the fourth day, but did not return until the sixth, just in time to stop the whole of Maloney's force from marching to our relief. We saw no Indians, though there were Indian signs. The property had not been destroyed and all of it was secured as well as most of the stock running at large. And now for the sequel as to our escape.

Hayward, one of the settlers, lived with an Indian woman who it was known was skulking in the woods near by their home. The second day he was missing from the party a long time and well into the night. There was profound distrust in the minds of most of us as to his motives, and a close watch was set upon his actions. Subsequently, though, we all believed he communicated with his wife, and she in turn with the hostiles near by, and saved the party from destruction. A number of the Indian friends of the settlers were known to be in the hostile camp and had doubtless saved the property from destruction.

This was the beginning of the discrimination of the Indians in favor of the non-combatants, which became so pronounced as the war progressed. From the day of the battle on White River to the killing of William White near Olympia in March, as the Indian forces were disintegrating, not a single white non-combatant was hurt.*

*Northcraft, who was killed in March (1856), just before White, and in the near vicinity was in the employ of the volunteer service as teamster and was armed when killed.

CHAPTER XLI.

Death of Lieutenant Slaughter.

On the 24th of November, Lieut. Slaughter with fifty regulars and two companies of volunteers, Captain Hays and Wallace's commands, moved to Puyallup, camping on the same ground where the Eaton Rangers had been previously besieged. At nightfall of the 25th, the camp was surrounded by Indians, the night made hideous by their yells, and some shots fired into camp without harm. The Indians succeeded in running off a part of the horses of the command. The next day one man was wounded, and the camp kept under arms at night by occasional shots, after which the Indians drew off, and were seen no more at that camp.

The whole attack, on the part of the Indians, consisted more in yells than of bullets, and seemed ludicrous after the affair was ended.

A curious incident occurred during this affray. The horse ridden by Dr. Burns on the 31st of October, through the swamp when Miles and Moses were killed, came into camp with saddle, saddle bags, sword and everything just as he was when Burns abandoned him nearly a month before. The superstition of the Indians had doubtless deterred them from touching the outfit, and saved the horse to be again "shot down from under him," as previously reported by the eccentric doctor.

The Indian, Kanasket, was mortally wounded during the evening and brought into camp defiant to the last, exciting the admiration and pity of his foes. He said he knew his time had come but that he was willing to die; that if he had the power to do so he would renew the

fight and never make peace as long as there was breath
of life in him. He was one of the most fearless of his
tribe. His loss was keenly felt and doubtless caused
the early withdrawal of their forces from the field, as he
was one of their leaders.

Slaughter's command moved down the Puyallup a few
miles to near the mouth of Stuck. Here, forty of the
volunteers under Lieutenant Moore, of Wallace's company, were left in camp while Slaughter, on December
4th, pushed on over to White River, and camped near
the ground of the recent massacre, two miles below the
mouth of Green River. While consulting in an open
cabin at night fall with Captain Hewitt, who had moved
his company from Seattle to a point near by, the Indians
made a sudden rush, killed Lieutenant Slaughter and
Corporals Berry and Clarendon of the volunteer force,
and wounded four privates of the regulars, one of whom
soon after died.

Captain Keyes hastily summoned Captain Hays
company to extricate the forty men camped on the Puyallup, and again the country was evacuated, Slaughter's
contingent going out down White River to Seattle, while
the Puyallup command returned to Steilacoom by the
same route they had gone in on.

The utter futility of attempting to prosecute a winter
campaign became so apparent that no further move
was made for over two months.*

With reference to the movement of the troops, Governor Mason, in his message, delivered to the legislature
December 7th, 1855, said :

*On December 7th, Capt. Keyes wrote Gov. Mason : "It is reported on all
hands that it is impossible to operate against the Indians with any effect in
the country on the White, Green, and Puyallup Rivers, at this season of
the year, and I know it to be so from personal observation. To continue
such a course will break down all our men and effect no harm to the Indians.
Our pack animals are broken down, and we must establish our forces on
our own ground in places where they will not suffer at night, and where
they can protect the settlers. As you must be far better acquainted with
such points I would request that, if convenient, you will come and see me
tomorrow."

"The disposition which has been subsequently made of the troops in the field in this portion of the Territory, has been with the design—while at the same time to keep the hostile Indians in check, adequate force should be moving on the outskirts of the settlements—that the farmers might be enabled to return to their claims to provide for the coming year's subsistence."

This was a very different policy from that adopted by Governor Stevens a few months later, when he actually used a part of the volunteer force to drive settlers off their claims instead of protecting them. Governor Mason continued this humane policy until Stevens' return to Olympia, Jan. 19th, 1856.

Mason in his message paid a handsome tribute to Gov. Douglass. He said:

"I deem it my duty here, to make public acknowledgement of the services rendered by his Excellency, James Douglass, Governor of Vancouver's Island. Upon the alarm naturally attendant upon a serious Indian outbreak, almost within arms length of us, and owing to the scarcity of fire arms and ammunition, application was made to him for such an amount of these munitions of war as he could possibly furnish. That application was promptly and cordially responded to, to the extent of his power; he at the same time regretting that he had at the moment no vessel of war at his disposal, and that his steamers, the Otter and Beaver, were both absent, but upon the arrival of either, she should be dispatched to the Sound, to render such service as might be required of her. Since then the Otter has visited this place."

Let us recall the famous saying that "blood is thicker than water."

Pursuing this subject a little further, the following letter from R. S. Robinson, who was Quartermaster and Commissary of the Northern Battalion, with headquarters at Port Townsend, will be interesting reading:

"Our volunteers in the field were short of supplies. Governor Stevens requested me to go to Victoria, and, if possible, get what supplies were needed of the Hudson Bay Company.

"I went over to Victoria and presented my letter to the company. Governor Douglass was friendly from the first. The company would furnish the supplies if Governor Stevens would draw direct on the Treasurer to pay for the goods. I told them the Governor could not draw on the United States Treasurer for there was no appropriation to meet this emergency.

"Governor Douglass said: 'You shall not go back without some supplies.' He then wrote an order on the H. B. Co. to let me have $5,000 worth on his account. I presented this to the company. They saw the Governor was not afraid, and asked me for a statement of everything I wished from them, and I received the supplies to the full extent required."

Governor Stevens neglected to mention this generous act in his message to the next legislature. In looking over the old papers and books of accounts at Fort Nisqually, I found that at that post $27,304 worth of goods were supplied to the volunteer forces, and from the private correspondence it becomes manifest the management both at Nisqually and Victoria were very loth to give up the goods for scrip, and did it only as a sense of duty. Governor Douglass wrote:

"* * * I must cordially acknowledge the moral obligation which binds Christian and civilized nations to exert their utmost power and influence in checking the inroads of the merciless savage, and it is a cause of sincere regret, on my part, that our means of rendering you assistance comes infinitely short of our wishes."

This letter was in response to the first request for help, but later the amount ran so large they doubted the wisdom, as a business venture, of letting so large a sum go, rightly saying that the emergency had passed and that the American Government could provide for the troops.

November 14th, 1856, Dr. Tolmie wrote the Board of Management of the Hudson Bay Company, Western Department, Victoria:

"* * * I am happy to inform you that commissioners residing in Oregon have been appointed to investigate the scrip liability incurred during the Indian troubles. Governor Stevens has taken a new position in framing his excuses for the Indian war, and has publicly declared that arch enemy, the Hudson Bay Company, is the only cause why the Indians would not observe the treaties made with them."

Of course the management were very much puzzled to account for such action on the part of Governor Stevens, not realizing the influences that were leading his mind astray, and that he so often was not responsible for his words.

Another incident Mr. Robinson narrates, which is worthy of record:

"Some time after Lieut. Slaughter was killed the settlers on the Sound were alarmed, not knowing when their time would come, being mostly housed up in block houses. It was then the Puget Mill Company offered to furnish a vessel, arm it and supply it with men and provisions, and present it to the Governor for protection of the Sound. I represented the facts to Quartermaster General Miller at Olympia. He consulted with Gov. Stevens. They represented to me that they felt under deep obligation to the Puget Mill Company for their generous offer, but did not consider the situation sufficiently alarming to warrant acceptance of the offer.

"The above incident was never published. It seems to me it was of sufficient importance to be preserved. The P. M. Co. certainly deserves credit for so generous an offer. Capt. Keller was superintendent at the time."

CHAPTER XLII.

Peace Negotiations.

After the death of Slaughter a month passed without any incident transpiring connected with the war. No depredations had been committed by the Indians. It was definitely known that many of their leaders were anxious for peace, as well as most of their rank and file. The hopes and prayers of the settlers went out for peace. General Wool had given out that while he was in favor of peace, yet he would be prepared for war, and that soon a thousand more regulars would be added to the forces already in the field, and so the peace talk became general. But there was one great obstacle in the way. It was known the Indians in the hostile camp could not be forced to go on the reservations allotted to them. They simply could not live there even if disposed to go, which they were not, as all reports indicated their firm determination to demand new reservations as a condition of peace. No person in the Territory was authorized to grant this demand. Governor Stevens, if present, could only recommend. The power lay with the President of the United States only. He alone, by executive order, could grant additional reservations, which as we shall see later, was finally done by granting 25,000 acres,* a large proportion of which was

---

*I include the Muckleshoot Reservation in this. Although it was alleged these Indians joined in the treaty at Point Elliott, and their homes described as a part of the land ceded by that treaty, yet when a reservation was set out for them by executive order at a later date, as a result of the war, it was done under the Medicine Creek treaty, with which these Indians had nothing to do. They not only lived without the boundary of the Medicine Creek treaty, and were not described as one of the tribes treated with in that council, yet were allotted a reservation under it, while there was no pretense of their ever having signed the treaty, a curious incident, showing what loose management the Indian affairs had reached.

rich land in lieu of the 4,000 acres of sterile, timber land set out for them in the treaty.

The regulars, under the inspiration of General Wool, favored a peace policy, but were handicapped by the fact of a victorious foe with arms yet in their hands. At this juncture a sudden emergency came. The account of what happened is best given in the words printed at the time in the Puget Sound Courier, published at Steilacoom, under the heading "Leschi."

"On the afternoon of the 5th inst. (Saturday, Jan. —, 1856), our town was thrown into a high state of excitement by the arrival of a canoe from the Indian reservation (Fox Island, three miles distant), opposite this place, with the intelligence that Leschi, chief of the Nisquallies, accompanied by a band of his warriors, was then on the reserve and had Mr. John Swan, the gentleman in charge of the friendly Indians, a prisoner. With that activity which has ever been displayed when opportunity offers, Captain Keyes dispatched a messenger to Dr. Tolmie, at Fort Nisqually, asking for the steamer Beaver, then lying at Nisqually landing, which favor was immediately granted and the steamer placed at the disposal of Captain Keyes, who detailed Captain Maloney, with a command of thirty men, to proceed to the rescue of Mr. Swan. Owing to some unaccountable delay, the steamer did not leave until the next morning, when she proceeded to the reservation. Judge Lander, Captain Balch, and several citizens accompanied the command. From a person on board we learn the following particulars:

"That on arriving at the encampment the whole band of hostiles were plainly recognized, foremost among them Leschi. Soon after Mr. Swan was observed coming off to the steamer alone. After some conversation with Capt. Maloney, he returned to the shore, and after another 'talk' again returned to the steamer; he was entreated to remain on board, but refused, saying that he had been permitted to visit the steamer by promising to return, and as a man he could not break his word.

"Capt. Maloney not deeming it advisable to land his men (as the steamer had but one boat, which would carry four

or five men), and the whole band of hostile Indians numbering some thirty-five or forty men, all well armed, lined the
beach, rendered such a thing impossible. The steamer returned; consequently, Leschi had every opportunity to
escape.

"P. S. Since the above was in type, we have had a conversation with Mr. Swan, from whom we learn that about
the middle of the afternoon on the 5th, he was surprised
by seeing six large canoes landing on the beach in front of
his house. He recognized Leschi, and several of the leading spirits of the men. Leschi advancing, saluted Mr. Swan,
and told him that he did not wish to harm him; that he
(Swan) had always been kind to the Indians, and reassured
him that he would not harm him.

"Leschi stated that he had come to take Mr. Swan up to
his country; that his people would work for him; that
he had come to say that if the whites wanted peace he was
ready to 'talk', but that he would not see Mr. Simmons,
who, he says, is the cause of the war, and toward whom he
entertains a most deadly hatred; saying that if the 'Bostons' would replace Col. Simmons all would be well, and
that he would then treat with some good man. He further
added that he had been driven into the war, but that his
heart was sick now, and he would make peace. All he
wanted was land enough to raise a few potatoes. He did
not care if the whites took all the rest, only let him have
enough for that. He disclaimed murdering the families on
White River, saying it was done by some 'cultus' Indians
and not by his orders. He appeared to have but a poor
opinion of the soldiers, and gave a description of the
Indian mode of warfare. He also informed Mr. Swan that
they had a white boy prisoner (George King), and intended
to make a chief of him when he grew up, and that his
parents were killed on White River. Mr. Swan states that
the band intended visiting Mr. Simmons' reservation, but
that he persuaded them from doing so as he was alarmed
for the safety of that gentlemen.

"After remaining four or five hours after the steamer
left, and some thirty hours in all, the whole party left for
the Puyallup, after informing Mr. Swan that if the whites

would send him they would 'talk.' Considerable disposition
was manifested among them to take him along with them."

The Courier said editorially:

"In today's paper will be found an account of Leschi's
visit with some thirty or forty of his warriors to the friendly
Indians opposite to this place (about four miles distant).
It is in vain that we look for a parallel case of bravery in
the annals of Indian warfare to the one in question; which
proves to us that we have sadly underrated the courage
and daring of the Indians on the Sound.

"Mr. Swan's conduct is deserving of the highest praise,
as by remaining on the reserve, his influence tended greatly
to counteract the evil consequences of Leschi's visit, by
keeping the friendly Indians from being led away. Well
would it be for us if those who have had dealings with the
Indians had kept their word as did Mr. Swan, who would
not, after being taken prisoner, break his parole with them.
Had we a few such men in the Indian Department we would
not now have cause to lament the existing state of things."

Truths well spoken.

In passing through the Puyallup Valley going to the
reservations, Leschi's party suddenly came upon William Benson, one of the Puyallup settlers, who had ventured on his place for a season. Leschi could not well
take him along, and would not trust him free to give the
alarm to the fort, sixteen miles distant, so he detailed
two of his men to hold Benson prisoner in his own
house until the return of the party. Benson was an
ex-Hudson Bay man, had an Indian wife, who was on
the reservation, and was not much concerned for his
own safety.

Not so with three men whom Leschi encountered soon
after leaving the reservation on his return trip. These
men, Peter Rinquist, Jacob Kishner, and a black man,
were returning from the mouth of thePuyallup with a
canoe load of potatoes, and met the war party in their

canoes in the "Narrows," a few miles below (north), Steilacoom, and were taken prisoners by them.

"I tell you, sir, that nigger's wool turned as white as the top of Mount Rainier; it did, for a fact, sir, and no mistake," Rinquest said when they returned to Steilacoom.

"Well, yes, I guess we're all skeered a little, well, a good deal, for we fellers couldn't tell what the buggers might take a notion to do, for a fact, sir, and no mistake. They just turned our canoe around and took us along with them; that they did for a fact, sir, and no mistake."

But they did not take them very far—just far enough to transfer enough potatoes to their own canoes for a supper for their party, and told them to go their way, for they would not harm them.

"Golly, but didn't we paddle; feared the buggers might change their minds, for a fact, sir, and no mistake," but they did not, and kept right on their course for the mouth of the river, and disappeared, releasing Benson on their way.

Benson is the man that was made the scape-goat for the so-called treasonable settlers we presently shall hear about, but there was nothing proven against him except of having used intemperate language, and that by a witness of doubtful credibility.

The next and last attempt Leschi made to open negotiations for peace was a month later than the incident just related. He did not come with so strong a force as before, nor to so dangerous a point.

On February 4th, Leschi and Kitsap with fifteen of their armed followers appeared at John McLeod's farm, a few miles from Camp Montgomery, to renew the offer of peace, as will be seen by the following:

From the Puget Sound Courier, Feb. 8th, 1856. (Editorial.)

"On the evening of Monday, the 4th inst., a few of the hostile Indians paid a visit to some of the settlers of Muck and vicinity; in fact, spending nearly the whole night in calling at the houses of King George's men who still live upon their claims. These Indians numbered seventeen, and among them were Leschi and Kitsap, the two chiefs who are considered the instigators and leaders of all the Indians this side the mountains who are in arms.

"Their professed object in coming upon the plains was to get a message to the Commander of the military forces at Fort Steilacoom, that they wished to have a talk for peace. At Mr. McLeod's house they stopped several hours, and Leschi, who did most of the talking, spoke with savage earnestness of the wrongs that he and his people had suffered. He spoke bitterly of Governor Stevens; accused him of having deceived them in the treaty, and said he would like to have two pieces of paper taken, on one to be written the wrongs done by the Indians; on the other the wrongs the whites have inflicted upon them. Let these two papers, said he, be sent to the Great Chief, and let him decide who is the most to blame—the Indian who has had his lands taken from him, or the white man who has deceived him? Leschi denied that any of his band were at the so-called attack on Seattle, and expressed considerable contempt for those white braves who defended the town on that memorable occasion. Leschi was anxious that Mr. John Swan, sub-Indian agent of this town, might be allowed to come to their camp on the Puyallup (Green River), and have a talk, and Col. Casey, now in command at Fort Steilacoom, dispatched him yesterday to the Indian country to bring in any proposition they may have to make. The duty of Mr. Swan is perilous, and there are few who would like to undertake it, but from his long intercourse with them, and the confidence with which they regard him, he will probably return to us unmolested. Of course, it cannot be expected that any terms of peace will be proposed that can be accepted. Prudence and policy require that first of all they should be punished. They may have been wronged; we believe that they have been; that the Executive of this Territory has most grossly imposed upon them, but as one wrong does not justify another, however much the Indian can say in his own behalf, justice requires that a proper atonement shall be made for the lives of the men, women and children who were massacred at White River before a peace can be thought of."

From the Puget Sound Courier, February 15th, 1856.

"News from the Indian Camp:—In our last number we stated that Mr. Swan had been sent to the camp of Leschi and other chiefs to learn if they would lay down their arms and give themselves up as prisoners of war, as they had sent in word they were anxious to make peace.

"We are happy to chronicle Mr. Swan's safe arrival back, and, although he brings no intelligence of great importance, it is, nevertheless, interesting. From Mr. Swan we learn that the main camp of the hostile forces is in a large swamp near Green River, where they have their women and children. This swamp is near the base of the mountains, difficult to reach and almost impenetrable, and all its approaches are watched by spies. A trail leads from the swamp into the mountains, on which they would doubtless try to retreat in case of an attack.

"The number of warriors present was about one hundred and fifty, and these, with the small number of spies out, undoubtedly comprise all the force in arms. Leschi is anxious for peace, but he wishes a guarantee that his people shall receive no punishment, and that a new reservation shall be set apart for their use. He fears that if his people lay down their arms private citizens may take their lives for what they have done in war.

"Among this band there were a very few Klickitats from east of the mountains, less than twenty in number, and the chiefs all said that these were the only ones who had come over, although certain parties try to make it appear that there were 700 in the attack on Seattle. We will not here repeat the Indian version of that affair, for it may not be correct, and we are unwilling to throw any imputation on the character and courage of those white men who were engaged in it, but from information that reaches us from this

and other sources, we are convinced that on our part the
matter was very badly managed.

"Mr. Swan stopped at the Indian camp two nights and
one day, and as far as he could observe, provisions and
ammunition were getting scarce and the Indians were quar-
relling among themselves. Leschi mentioned as a base
act of ingratitude that some of his Duwamish friends had
visited him, and on returning had stolen and taken away
his horses. Our next news from that camp will probably
be of a more warlike character."

Nothing came of this attempt, and the trip of Agent
Swan to the hostile camp that followed, except to intensify the feelings of settlers who were beginning to
feel the heavy hand of the gathering volunteer forces,
and likewise, laying bare the weakness of the situation
in the hostile camp. The senseless attack upon Seattle
had but recently been made and failed, leaving the
camp demoralized and broken up into factions. Mr.
Swan's observations are of importance as to the number
of warriors in the camp, as they were doubtless all there
with the exception of the few mentioned, and completely
confirmed the previous estimate of two hundred all told,
made by the officers of the United States Army, Governor Stevens, and volunteer officers in the service. Mr.
Swan's observation also disposes of the wild story of
Navigator Phelps (afterwards Rear Admiral), about
the attack of from one to two thousand Indians on the
devoted village of Seattle, where he and his gallant comrades, amidst the "storm of bullets filling the air like
swarms of bees" held the savage hosts at bay for so long
a time.

But we must not anticipate further, for on January
19th, 1856, Governor Stevens had arrived at Olympia,
and was greeted with the thunder of thirty-eight guns,
"the cannon charged to the muzzle," where "all was
joy and gladness on the occasion, and our citizens seemed
to look upon him as their deliverer—their hope"—

where "in the coure of his (Stevens') remarks he made the declaration that *the war shall be prosecuted until the last hostile Indian is exterminated,* and our word for it he will endeavor to carry that declaration into effect." (Pioneer and Democrat, Jan. 25th, 1856.)

One noticeable feature of the partisan press of that time, the principle paper, the Pioneer and Democrat, the mouthpiece of the Governor, was that it ignored all overtures for peace and did not publish a line to enlighten its readers, doubtless fearing such information would weaken the war feeling among the people of the Territory.

CHAPTER XLIII.

Stevens-Wool Controversy.

Everything had been running smoothly between the volunteer forces called into the field by acting Governor Mason and the officers of the United States regulars in charge of the conduct of affairs in Western Washington. A majority of the volunteers had been sworn into the regular service, hád drawn their rations and supplies from Fort Steilacoom and had acted under the orders, and of necessity in concert with the United States forces. Nearly three months had elapsed since the first outbreak. The subsequent acts of the Indians had been governed by what may be properly termed the rules of war. No settlers had been attacked or molested. The Indians had repeatedly made overtures for peace. The troops had been virtually resting upon their arms for six weeks. Meanwhile, reinforcements of United States regular troops had begun to arrive at Forts Steilacoom and Vancouver. Intelligence had been received that a thousand more regulars were on the way (of whom eight hundred arrived during the month of January), bringing the whole force to over seventeen hundred and thought by the military authorities ample to control the situation. Accordingly the notice following was given Acting Governor Mason that at the expiration of the three months' service no more rations would be issued to volunteers.

"Headquarters Puget Sound District,
"Fort Steilacoom, W. T., Jan. 10th, 1856.

"Hon. C. H. Mason, Acting Governor W. T.

"Sir:—On the 4th instant, I had the honor to inform you that I had neither law nor instructions to warrant me in giving orders to volunteers. I have none yet, but I will furnish provisions till the end of three months. I cannot give them further orders with propriety.

"I have heard directly and indirectly from Leschi, and the temporizing course I am pursuing, I feel certain, is the reason why he and the hostiles have ceased their depredations. I have repeatedly stated in my letters that this war cannot be effectually prosecuted without first establishing posts in the enemy's country, so that the men may go out without pack trains, and may generally sleep dry. My men who were out with Lieut. Slaughter have many of them since been disabled with rheumatism. I deem it necessary to record my opinion that a forward movement at this time would not hasten the termination of the war, but might and probably would, induce the hostiles to recommence their depredations. I hope soon to get reinforcements, and then operations will commence at once.

"Very respectfully, Your obedient servant,
Signed: E. D. Keyes, Capt. 3rd Artillery, Commanding.

I have always been curious to know why, if Capt. Keyes had authority to issue rations, he did not have "law nor instructions to warrant me in giving orders to volunteers." He had been giving orders to volunteers during the previous month, but why this sudden discovery as to his powers we are not advised. We suspect he had recently received missives from Commanding General Wool to cause him to call a halt in his dealings with the volunteer forces.

This was the situation when Governor Stevens arrived at Olympia. Capt. Maloney had likewise given it as his opinion that a winter campaign against the Indians was impracticable in the timber region west of the Cascade Mountains. The season had been unusually severe, coupled with snow fall to make matters still worse. The same condition existed east of the mountains. Col. Nesmith wrote of the Oregon volunteers three weeks' campaign in the Yakima Valley with Major Rains, that:

"Many of the men were frost-bitten and can hardly be said to be fit for duty. An inspection of the horses has been had at camp, and about one-fourth (only), of the whole number were found fitted for present duty. The command suffered intensely."

This campaign, it must be remembered, was long before the real cold weather set in. The testimony of the officers at Vancouver was unanimous against the policy, and in fact, the possibility of a winter campaign.

It was at this juncture of affairs that Governor Stevens wrote his famous "plan of campaign letter" upon his arrival at Walla Walla, December 28th, 1855, to Major General Wool who was then in command of the United States troops on the Pacific Coast. It was a very long letter and almost dictatorial in tone. He, in any event, essayed to plan the campaign, as will readily be seen by the perusal of that document, too lengthy to publish here in full, but the extracts following will give the reader a general idea of its import. This letter brought out the laconic reply of the General "that he had neither the resources of a Territory nor the United States treasury at his command." Governor Stevens wrote:

"I will recommend that you will urge forward your preparations with all possible dispatch. Get all your disposable force in this valley in January; establish a large depot camp here; occupy Fort Walla Walla and the Yakima country, and be ready early in February to take the field."

After suggesting that a stern wheel steamer could be put on the Columbia River to run from the mouth of the Deschutes River to above Walla Walla, he continues:

"The plan of campaign which occurs to me as possible, is as follows: Occupy the Walla Walla Valley in January; establish a large depot camp in the Touchet; hold Fort Walla Walla; get up supplies by a line of barges on the Columbia; have an advance post on the Tucanan, and pickets at the crossing of the Palouse, and opposite the bend of the Tucanan. * * * In February cross the Snake; attack the enemy on the Palouse; establish a depot

camp at the first wood; occupy the forks of the Snake;
establish the line of barges up the Snake to the mouth of
the Palouse, and push forward a column to the Okanogan."

**To which General Wool replied under date of Feb.
12th, 1856:**

"* * * In presenting, however, your plan of campaign,
which is a very extended one, you should have recollected
that I have neither the resources of a Territory nor the
treasury of the United States at my command. Still you
may be assured that the war against the Indians will be
prosecuted with all the vigor, promptness and efficiency
I am master of, at the same time without wasting unneces-
sarily the means and resources at my disposal, by untimely
and unproductive expeditions. With the additional force
which recently arrived at Vancouver and at The Dalles,
I think I shall be able to bring the war to a close in a few
months, provided the extermination of the Indians, which
I do not approve of, is not determined on, and private war
prevented, and the volunteers withdrawn from the Walla
Walla country. * * *

"I have recently sent to Puget Sound two companies of
the Ninth Infantry. These, with the three companies there,
will give a force of nearly or quite four hundred regulars,
commanded by Lieut. Col. Casey. This force, with several
ships of war on the Sound, to which will be added in a few
days, the United States Steamer Massachusetts, it seems
to me, if rightly directed, ought to be sufficient to bring to
terms two hundred warriors. Capt. Keyes in his last report
received, says 'there are not quite 200 in arms in that
region.' "

The quotations from these letters fairly show the difference between the policy of the two men. The Governor wanted to move at once upon the Indians and ex-
terminate the hostiles, while General Wool and all his
officers believed an immediate move impracticable,* and
further, that peace was in sight without further loss of
life.

---

*In fact, the Columbia River was, soon after this correspondence passed,
closed by ice for several weeks.

CHAPTER XLIV.

Policy of Extermination.

The reader must not conclude that I misrepresent Governor Stevens when asserting in a previous chapter that he advocated the policy of extermination of the hostile Indians. The Pioneer and Democrat, a paper published at Olympia, the mouthpiece of the Governor and a partisan supporter of all his measures, printed in its issue of January 25th, 1856, a report of the Governor's speech, in which occurs this remarkable passage italics and all:

"On Saturday evening he (Governor Stevens) delivered an address at the hall of the House of Representatives to an immense audience, which was listened to with marked attention, but frequently interrupted with deafening cheers. In the course of his remarks he made the declaration 'that **the war shall be prosecuted until the last hostile Indian is exterminated,**' and our word for it, he will endeavor to carry that declaration into effect."

Again, in the Journal of the House of Representatives of the Territorial legislature for the session of 1855-56 is published a message signed "Isaac I. Stevens, Governor, and Supt. Ind. Affs., Wash. Ter.," in which this remarkable sentence is found (page 155):

"I am opposed to any treaties; I shall oppose any treaty with these hostile bands. I will protest against any and all treaties made with them:—nothing but death is a mete punishment for their perfidy—their lives should pay the forfeit."

This message was delivered two days after the speech quoted, and so it became known that it was the deliberate policy of the Governor to prosecute a war of extermination against the hostile Indians in arms, and it is a lamentable fact he adhered to this policy until his power was completely broken. The open advocacy of such a policy did great harm by encouraging crime that followed.

Right truly was it said that it would have been better if the Governor had gone from the Blackfeet council direct to New York and absented himself from the Territory altogether until the war was ended, and many went further and said for all time.

On January 23rd, the Governor issued his proclamation calling into service six companies of volunteers for six months service. This call was not responded to with alacrity, but finally the companies were organized, though not all full, and eventually recruiting officers were sent to Salem, Oregon, to enlist men.

Colonel Casey all the time insisted there was no necessity for more volunteers, but the Governor would give no heed to his advice and thereby unquestionably prolonged the war, as will appear later.

Lieut Colonel Casey wrote Gen. Wool, under the date of June 2d:

"There are but few hostile Indians in this district at present, and the war is certainly finished. * * * There is no necessity for the independent military organization in this district."

Following this Casey sent two companies of troops to Colonel Wright east the mountains via the Columbia River.

"Since taking the field on the 13th of February," Casey wrote further, "I have sent to the reservations about three hundred Indians, including men, women and children, besides those killed in battle and the prisoners now confined in the guard houses."

On the 6th the Colonel again wrote of the murder of an Indian in the town of Steilacoom, one at Fort Nisqually, and two near Seattle, and expressed concern as to the probable effect upon the friendly Indians.

On June 20th, he wrote:

"Governor Stevens still retains a portion of the volunteers in service in this district. I signified to him, some time since, my readiness to occupy all those points now held by his men, and which I consider in any way necessary for the protection of the country within the region of recent hostilities. I do not consider the service of any volunteer as having been necessary for more than two months past."

The Colonel then notes the murderers of the three friendly Indians near Seattle are yet at large and tells of another Indian murdered by a volunteer near Mound prairie.

"Headquarters Puget Sound District,
"Fort Steilacoom, W. T., July 21st, 1903.

"Major:—I have the honor to enclose for the information of the general commanding the department, a copy of a communication received by me from Governor Stevens on the 18th inst., with a copy of my reply.

"I will reiterate what I have already communicated to the department headquarters, viz: that there has been no necessity for any volunteers in the Puget Sound District for several months past; and further, that there never has been, since my arrival here on the 31st of January last, any necessity for more than two companies of those troops, had they been organized according to the infantry of the regular army and mustered into the service of the United States.

(Signed)　　　　　　　　SILAS CASEY.

"Lieut. Col. 9th Infantry, Com. Puget Sound District.
"Major W. W. Mackall, Benicia, Cal."

In the message of the Governor, printed after the close of the war, we find this item:

"In the six months organization" (under call by Stevens), "the force consisted of eighteen companies, twenty captains, twenty 1st Lieutenants, eighteen 2d Lieutenants, 1002 non-commissioned officers and privates, giving a force of 1060 men, and an aggregate of 133,259 days' service of a single man. There has been issued the sum of $1,019,090.20 in scrip, of which $132,721.09 has been cancelled by sales. About $40,500 remains to be issued."

It will be seen that through this organization the Governor acquired greater power than ever throughout the Territory.

The second day after delivering his message to the legislature, the Governor took his departure from Olympia in the United States Steamer Active for a cruise on the Sound. Rear Admiral Phelps, then navigator on the war sloop Decatur lying in Seattle harbor, wrote:

"On the 24th, the Active came into the harbor, bearing Governor Stevens and staff, accompanied by Captain Keyes and Indian Agent Simmons.

"The Governor, recently returned from visiting the Coeur d'Alenes and other transmountain tribes, scoffed at the idea of Indian troubles, and on the evening of the 25th concluded a speech addressed to the settlers, with these emphatic words: I have just returned from the countries of the Nez Perces and of the Coeur d'Alenes. I have visited many tribes on the way, both going and coming, and I tell you there are not fifty hostile Indians in the Territory, and I believe that the cities of New York and San Francisco will as soon be attacked by Indians as the town of Seattle."

The Governor was entertained on board the Decatur and used his utmost endeavors to persuade Commander Gansevoort to leave the Seattle harbor with his ship and cruise elsewhere on the Sound. This the Commander positively refused to do, and Stevens went his way, leaving Seattle on the 25th and only about fifteen hours prior to the attack on the town by the Indians.

The aberration of Governor Stevens' mind could only be accounted for in one way, the cause of which has been related in a previous chapter—a lamentable condition that at any moment might cause great harm to the citizens of the Territory.

It seems that when the mind of the Governor became set in an opinion nothing could change it. After making his visit to the reservation he returned to the Seattle harbor, after the attack, and, while the Decatur was crowded with women and children, still insisted there was no danger.

Hearing that Hon. C. H. Hanford, now United States Judge for this district, then a child, was present at the interview referred to by Admiral Phelps, I have the reply to a letter of inquiry with reference to an occurrence on board the Decatur, which to my surprise, is a subsequent interview to that related by Phelps.

, Judge Hanford writes:

"The occurrence referred to in your letter of the 17th inst., was on board the Decatur, after dark the evening of the day on which the attack was made on Seattle. Governor Stevens and Capt. E. D. Keyes came into the cabin of the vessel and talked with Capt. Gansevoort. I watched them with intense interest, and a deep and lasting impression was made on my mind, but I did not attempt to memorize any particular remark or expression. I can only remember that Stevens was emphatic in disputing the fact that an attack had been made, and in denying the presence in the vicinity of any considerable number of hostile Indians. Just before leaving the vessel, Stevens asserted that he would or could, with ten men, gather up and bring into the town all the Indians then in the woods between Seattle and Lake Washington.

"I was on board the Decatur at that time, because about noon that day all the women and children were taken on board for their protection, and I suppose that I was permitted to listen to the conversation because I was then too small to be noticed."

When the Governor arrived in Olympia the next day, however, he authorized the enlistment as home guard of Company A, that became famous through the attempt soon after to order them to other parts of the Territory for service.

Mr. Denny was suspended for alleged insubordination and charged with disobedience of orders. After the war was closed a legislative investigation resulted in the vindication of Mr. Denny and the condemnation of the Governor's action.

CHAPTER XLV.

The Attack on Seattle.

The impending attack had been known to the inhabitants of Seattle several days before it occurred. Friendly Indians encamped in the town had been approached by their friends in the war camp to enlist their aid, some of whom doubtless lent a willing ear. The sympathies of all the Indians were with the struggling hostiles. There can be no question of that, although individuals no doubt were true to their particular friends among the whites. Through this source several leading citizens had notice each by their particular favorites who were anxious to save their patrons yet could not withhold their sympathy from their race, and so it became positively known that preparations were made for an attack, but no one could even guess when it would occur.

So stealthily had the Indian forces been gathered to the near vicinity of the town that on the morning of the 26th, an hour before the outbreak, the marines had gone on board the Decatur with their hammocks and were at breakfast when the first gun was fired.

The actual fighting (if it may be called fighting) was precipitated by the Decatur dropping a shell in "Tom Pepper's house," where a friendly Indian woman reported the hostiles had gathered. The house which was in the southern outskirts of the town near the tide flats and on tide level, afforded an opportunity for either an advance or retreat but was not chosen as the particular point of the main attack.

The town then consisted of a few straggling houses near the water front and two two-story block houses.

These last had been erected immediately after the outbreak on the 28th of October of the previous year, and were of size sufficient to accommodate the whole population at night, the women and children occupying the upper stories while the men slept or kept guard below. So secure did the people feel that there was no danger of an immediate attack that almost all the families occupied their own houses during the night of the 25th, and on the morning of the 26th (of January, 1856), were either preparing or eating breakfast, when the alarm was sounded and the people rushed pell-mell into the block houses.

Captain C. C. Hewitt's company, seventy-two strong, had been mustered out of the service on the evening of the 25th and had stacked their arms, but the men were all in the town, most of them being residents. This force, if organized, would have been sufficient to have defended the block houses, but from accounts written at the time a part of the men refused to take up their arms again the next morning and crowded into the block houses ingloriously for safety.* All of the citizens of the company resumed their guns and went on duty the same as if their discharge had not been granted.

Capt. Gansevoort had ninety men on shore and others on shipboard to man the guns. At no time was there any danger after the people reached the block houses had common, · ordinary prudence been observed. Milton Holgate, a lad of sixteen years, thoughtlessly exposed himself at the northern block house door and was shot and killed early in the day; the only casualty at or near either of the block houses. Robert Wilson was

---

*Admiral Phelps, in his long-drawn-out account of this affair, written many years afterwards, openly charges cowardice upon the recently discharged volunteers. But we must make allowance for his evident bias, beside the manifest desire to magnify the part he and his men played in repelling the attack. However, there is no doubt but some poltroons were willing to shirk, but Mr. George Frye, yet living in Seattle, says that all of the company that had any interest in Seattle took up their arms again.

killed on the beach while exposing himself to procure water. None were wounded during the whole attack. The real danger was not great when we consider how weak the Indians were when making the attack. They would not expose themselves as a target for an enemy, and but very few Indians were seen during the whole day and then only while skulking in the forest near by or moving stealthily from cover to cover. The reader will remember the bungling work of these same Indians on the inmates of the cabin, as described by Mr. King in a previous chapter, at the time of the massacre on White River. Had there been even two resolute armed men it is not probable the attack on the cabin would have succeeded. With two hundred men in the town, most of them either with arms or arms easily obtainable, the Indians would not venture from under cover and contented themselves with the robbery or destruction of houses on the outskirts and of firing at the block houses or marines on the beach at long range. In the dense forest skirting the town* the Indians were as safe from attack as the whites in the block houses. When they tired of firing, their forces withdrew a short distance to leisurely partake of their dinner that had been taken in part from the breakfast tables of the frightened families, and again return to renew the harmless and senseless expenditure of ammunition. I say senseless, for the reason that there never was the least possible show for the Indians to take the town and profit by their raid, and the only result to them was the waste of ammunition which they could not replace, and to demoralize their forces by their failure while strengthening the hands of their enemy in hastening recruiting under the call for volunteers previously made by the Governor.

Moses Quiemuth tells me that Leschi opposed the

---

*There was heavy standing timber where the New York block now stands on Second avenue, while the north block house and north end of the stockade was at the foot of Cherry street, not much, if any, more than 300 feet distant.

move as unwise, but he thinks he went with the forces.* He (Moses) did not go, and many others, so that it is not probable there were more than one hundred and fifty in the attacking party. The grotesque account of the young Navigator Phelps, where "bullets were flying in the air as thick as bees from the hive," and where he numbered the foe "from one to two thousand judged by their yells," must be set down as either pure fancy or else a desire to magnify the prowess of his troops by the representation of the great numbers opposed to them. And yet this statement will doubtless bring out hot rejoinders from some of the participants, who, to this day, will not believe there were less than a thousand Indians of the attacking party. No doubt their yells were terrifying and we have no reason to wonder that stout hearts quailed at the spectacle presented to them, not taking into account the lack of discipline among the Indians and utter absence of means to make a successful attack upon the strong block houses of the town.

Arthur Denny wrote of the conditions surrounding Seattle and of the attack:

"After the White River massacre it was determined to prepare for defence in case of an attack on the town (Seattle). At the time there was a large amount of hewn timber on hand twelve inches square, which was well suited to the purpose. Two houses were built of this timber, with sufficient capacity to hold the entire population at one time. One was located at the junction of Front and Cherry Streets, and the other at the junction of Main and South Second Streets, and the two joined by a stockade which also ran from each westward to the bay, and was well calculated for protection on the land side of the town, from whence all attacks were likely to come. Early in the morning of January 26th, 1856, the town was attacked by the

*Agent Swan, who was taken prisoner at Fox Island and released, and who afterwards visited the hostile camp on Green River, says Leschi told him that he not only counseled against the attack, but did not go with the attacking party. Tolmie corroborates this in a published letter in 1858.

Indians. They had congregated during the night and taken their position under cover of the timber along the face of the hill, in readiness to make the attack as soon as the people began to stir, but their presence was made known by friendly Indians before the attack was made, and a howitzer was fired by order of Captain Gansevoort in the direction indicated by friendly Indians, which was promptly followed by an answer of musketry all along the woods in the rear of the town, fully demonstrating the fact that the place was really surrounded by the hostiles.

"Fortunately, all the whites who were sleeping outside of the stockade escaped to the block houses without injury. The firing was kept up all day and two whites were killed; one, Robert Wilson, fell near the southern block house, and the other, Milton G. Holgate, brother of Mrs. E. Hanford and Lemuel J. Holgate, who still reside among us, was shot while standing in the door of the Cherry Street block house. Two houses were burnt during the day, one near where the gas works now are, and the other the dwelling of Mr. Bell. Several other houses, my own among the number, were plundered during the evening and everything of value carried off.

"It is a mere matter of opinion whether the town without the aid of the Decatur would have been able to withstand the attack, but with the help of the marines on shore and the guns of the Decatur in the harbor, it was quite a different matter."

CHAPTER XLVI.

End of the War.

The inactivity of the troops continued after the assault on Seattle, though that event greatly accelerated the movement for enlisting volunteers. By this time the military arm of the Government, as well as citizens, began to respect the common foe as one more than a mere uprising of a few dissatisfied Indians bent on murder and rapine. A force that would in broad day light boldly come out of their stronghold and attack a town right under the guns of a ship of war, it was agreed, was such a menace as to call for the utmost exertion to overthrow. We heard no more talk like that of McAllister, "that he would take his cane and drive the whole band in," or of Clark, "that a dozen men could run the whole lot into the Sound," and like expressions at the beginning of the war. Opinions ran to the other extreme and the prowess of the Indians was magnified as far beyond their real power to harm, as before it had been underrated. Had the attack on Seattle not been made it is quite doubtful if the call for volunteers would have been filled. At best the number called for could not be had in the Territory, and recruiting officers were sent to Portland, Salem and elsewhere in Oregon for men to fill up the ranks.

The Indians were weak, not strong, as the result of their attack on the embryo city showed, as likewise appeared wherever they had undertaken an aggressive movement, except in the one instance when Slaughter was killed. Their forces could not be much longer held together. The pinch of hunger had begun its work. The salmon run was over. The cattle, taken from the settlers of White River and Duwamish at the outset, were all gone. Their horses were unfit for food, and besides, most of them had perished or had been stolen or strayed from them. Their ammunition was well nigh exhausted, and they could not replenish it, neither could they gain accessions to their force even if it were possible to subsist them. The waiting policy had done its work; dissensions pervaded the camp, and the work of disintegration had already begun. Thirty warriors are known to have withdrawn from the hostile camp, if indeed, they ever rejoined it after their failure at Seattle. These were secreted and scattered around and near Lake Washington only waiting a chance to safely get to the reservations where government food was abundant. A like camp or rendezvous had been selected in the swamps of the Stuck Valley for a like purpose, the occupants of which soon obtained protection from the regulars who ran across them when the forward movement was made in February. Instead of a strong foe, as many believed the attack on Seattle indicated, the truth was that sheer desperation drove the Indians to it.

We have come now to the last stage of the war west of the Cascades, and short work there was made of it when once the move was inaugurated, for within a month after the troops were set in motion, the U. S. regulars were quietly planting garden at Muckleshoot right in the heart of what had been the Indian stronghold from the beginning.

On the 13th of February, the regulars began the movement from Fort Steilacoom, and by the 26th had four companies in the field, 246 men, under the command of Lieut. Colonel Casey in person. Simultaneously with this movement three companies of volunteers, 140 men, moved to Puyallup and began erecting a block house, and soon afterwards to Connell prairie, where also a block house and store house were built. A party of fifty-five Indians belonging to the Snoqualmie tribe, with their chief, Pat Kanim, as captain, in charge of Major Van Bokkelin, was sent in from the north, making a grand total but little short, if any, of 600 men in the immediate vicinity of the Muckleshoot prairie.

A band of Chehalis Indians was also organized and sent into the field under Capt. Ford. Many other companies were stationed in different parts of the district from the Columbia River to the northern boundary, between four and five hundred in all, that did not get the smell of gunpowder.

Block houses had been built all over the country, enumerated as sixty by the volunteer forces alone, but many more were erected by the regulars and settlers, the whole aggregating nearly, if not quite, a hundred. Small wonder that Stevens should write "this is emphatically a block house war"; and so it was.

It may be well doubted if at this time Leschi could muster 150 available men. Besides, he was encumbered by the families of many of his warriors, who, by this time had became clamorous for peace. He could not retreat farther into the mountains without starvation staring him in the face, unless he took the pass and went east of the range; a perilous undertaking that early in the season. This is what he did with eighty of his following, as will be related later.

The regulars separated just north of the upper crossing of the Puyallup. Lieut. Colonel Casey, with one division, following the wagon road direct to Connell's prairie and thence to the crossing of White River above Muckleshoot, while the remainder of the troops under Lieut. Kautz made a detour to the left parallel with the Stuck Valley, and thence by the trail to the Muckleshoot prairie direct. This, the last battle of the regulars had with the Indians is best told in Lieut. Kautz's own words, he being on the spot and in command of part of the forces. It will be noticed the Lieutenant says nothing as to the punishment inflicted upon the Indians. He probably did not know and was too experienced a soldier to venture a guess, but the Indians must have put up a pretty stiff fight to have killed one man and wounded nine others as reported.

"Our objective point was Muckleshoot prairie, between White and Green Rivers. It was regarded as the heart of the country occupied by the hostiles. The troops separated at the Puyallup block house. From there I marched on with that portion of the command which went direct to Muckleshoot prairie. Colonel Casey, who was in command of the other detachment, went by the Lemon prairie route to Muckleshoot. My command reached the prairie about the last day of February. On that day I received a dispatch from Colonel Casey requesting me to send a detachment to the crossing of the White River to meet him. On the next day, the 1st of March, I started out with a command of fifty men. When we arrived at the ford of the White River the Indians appeared in our rear and threatened an attack. I at once sent a dispatch to Colonel Casey telling him the Indians had made their appearance, and that I would endeavor to hold the ford until he arrived. I made disposition of the men on a bar of the river, among some drift wood, to await the coming of the troops. The Indians worked their way around us on both sides of the river, but were not able to make any impression on the troops lodged as they were behind logs and driftwood.

"At three o'clock in the afternoon, Capt. Keyes arrived at the ford with about 100 men. We then moved against the Indians and they retreated. Later, as we were marching to Muckleshoot prairie, they gave us a volley from a bluff where they were stationed. They then disappeared and we went into camp. One man had been killed and nine men, including myself, wounded. This was the last fight the regulars had with the hostiles."

Meanwhile, the volunteers moved to Connell's prairie by the wagon road and camped there to build a block house and establish a depot of supplies.

On the 10th of March, the pioneer company, under Capt. White, were ordered to move out from the prairie towards the crossing of White River, and while but half a mile from their camp engaged on road making, were attacked by the same Indians who had been, on the first of March, driven by the regulars out of their stronghold on the right bank of the White River near the Muckleshoot prairie and across the river near Connell's and the volunteer camp. The account of the battle, the "Appomattox" of the war can be best given in the words of Capt. White, though written under the strain of excitement incident to his new experience, his first and last battle, and swelling with pardonable pride upon the achievements of his men.

Although this account by Capt. White is not official, I prefer to rely upon it for the facts rather than the very long and manifestly inaccurate and exaggerated official account sent by the commander of the volunteer forces, who sent Capt. Henness with 20 men, Lieut. Martin with 15, Lieut. Van Ogle 15, and 12 under Capt. Rabbeson, 62 men in all, to Capt. White's assistance, holding the remainder of his forces in reserve on the prairie near by.

Captain White wrote on the 10th of March:

"Early this morning I started with my command armed with rifles, axes, crosscut saws and scribing awls, for White River, in accordance with the command of the Governor, for the purpose of erecting a block house and ferry at the crossing. After gaining the edge of the timber and going down a steep descent, my advance guard, commanded by Lieut. Hicks, was suddenly and furiously attacked by between 50 and 100 Indians, from the top of the hill we had descended. At the same instant, I, with the rest of my company, received a murderous fire from the same devils— all within 'point blank' shot—and not over 100 yards from us. I ordered my men to take shelter behind logs and trees, and stand their ground, which was done, admirably. We immediately returned the fire with such firmness and deliberation that the Indians soon found we were ready for the emergency, and which told to them that we were as well skilled in making a mark with our guns as we were with a scratch awl, and that when we strike **a line** it is sure to be pretty straight. We maintained our position for perhaps half an hour before assistance could reach us from camp, it being nearly a mile off. As soon as I learned assistance was at hand, I ordered a retreat back up to the top of the hill. On gaining the top I found we were, and had been, nearly surrounded by the Indians. I again ordered my men to seek shelter, and, while doing so, the Indians supposing we were retreating back to camp came out in full view and poured a storm of bullets and shot at us. Upon examination I found that several of my men were pretty badly wounded, when I dispatched for assistance to camp, and resumed my stand. Most of the other companies had by this time gained positions, and the battle raged hot and furious. The Indians soon found they were badly mistaken at our movement, as numbers paid the penalty of their lives for their rashness. The remaining and unhurt portion of my company were up and doing all the time, either in deliberate firing or making and conducting charges upon them in their strongholds.

"The fight continued until about 3 o'clock in the afternoon, and, considering the great advantage the Indians had over us, I consider it one glorious victory. We completely routed them with great loss on their part, while with us, we lost none and had but a few wounded. Three men of my command were pretty badly wounded, but none dangerously. I think the Indian force must have been near 150 strong—ours all told, did not exceed one hundred."

And thus really ended the war west of the Cascade Mountains as no more fighting occurred and but two or three shots were subsequently fired by the Indians.

CHAPTER XLVII.

Leschi's Retreat Through the Natchess Pass.

After the battles of White River with the U. S. regular forces and at Connell's prairie with the volunteers, described in the last chapter, resulting in defeat in both cases, the situation became desperate. Three courses were open to Leschi, neither of which gave hope for further continuation of the struggle. His cause was lost. His forces had been defeated in two battles and were now hemmed in by two vigilant enemies, either of whom were vastly superior to him in equipment as well as in numbers. He might surrender or his force could be divided up into small parties and for a season go into hiding, or he might possibly by a bold move reach the open country east of the mountains where he could continue the contest.

The first suggestion was not to be thought of by the leaders and by many of the rank and file, as they had heard of the Governor's declaration for extermination. The second would be adopted to a degree by individual families or groups, with or without the consent of Leschi and those whose fortunes were closely allied with him. The third proposition, to leave the country west of the mountains and make the attempt to pass the summit of the mountains, was instantly adopted, and the movement up White River began at once after the battle of the 10th at Connell's prairie with the volunteer forces.

Fortunately for the Indians, the weather was clear, the nights cold and water low. The path lay up the White River which they must cross several times within a dozen miles or so, after which the road lay on the north bank to Green Water (not Green River), and up this water course to near the Summit prairie, a distance from the battlefield of over forty miles.

The fleeing Indians reached the foot of the Summit Hill, or mountain—made famous by one of the incoming immigrant matrons, Mrs. Hines, denominating it as the "end of the world; the jumping off place"—the following evening without rest, without food, without blankets, and without shelter. Here the party encamped from sheer exhaustion. A skeleton of a horse slaughtered for the occasion furnished a scant supply of food to give strength for the next day's trial over the summit.

"How did you get over through the deep snow?" I asked the younger Quiemuth, then a lad of fifteen, now an old man and known as the Priest Moses Leschi.

"You see there had been some warm weather, and the snow had settled and that night was cold and so we went right over."

"Solid was it?" I queried.

"Hard as that stove," pointing to the cook stove near by in his brother George's cabin.

"The horses walked right on the snow the same as on a hard road," interposed George (his brother), who was along but was younger, who, however, had a vivid recollection of the trip.

"The worst part of it all was wading the Natchess River so often,"

What they said I could readily realize, having myself but the year before crossed the same river no less than thirty-two times in going through this same canyon. I had seen that same hill and camped alone near it with my saddle blanket for my bed, and I, too, had a vivid idea of what such a trip would mean under such conditions.

"But we got out into the open country in two days more, and found some roots like this (sending his wife to bring a string of dried roots they had for a keepsake). The

Indian name is 'Adopasch.' It doesn't grow on this side
of the mountains, but comes very early—the first of any over
there—and I guess it saved us from starving."

He added, with a shake of the head, as the old man
recalled his boyhood experience.

"Kamiakan he killed some wild horses for us as soon as
we got to him. He helped us right along until we could
take care of ourselves."

"And what became of Leschi?" I asked.

"Oh, after awhile Leschi and my father and two other
men they went to see General Wright (Colonel Wright).
Kamiakan told them to go; and they told Wright they
didn't want to fight no more, and General Wright told them
he wouldnt' fight them and that he wouldn't let anybody
hurt them, and to stay where they were for the present."

We will have a confirmation of this in Colonel
Wright's own letter to be found in a later chapter. Leschi and all his party were promised protection upon
the sole condition that they would lay down their arms
and cease to make war against the whites, which they
did.

Four days after the battle of the 10th and flight of
Leschi and his party, Capt. White's men were fired on
at long range from a bluff while at work building a
block house at the river crossing, and one man was
wounded, but the Indians immediately withdrew without waiting for a return fire. This was the last gun
of the war on this side of the mountains by the Indians.
From that date forward, as reports came in from the
field, "there is no fight in them," and in fact, there were
but few left together. The congregated bands had vanished as mysteriously as they had been drawn together
five months before.

On the 15th more reinforcements for the regulars
arrived at Fort Steilacoom, reported 150 men, and Colonel Casey, as we shall see, had more men than he

needed, and on May 28th sent two companies overland
to Vancouver.   Ten days later Governor Stevens dispatched Colonel Shaw through the Natchess Pass with
all available force to the Yakima country.   He arrived
on the 20th of June, to find his occupation gone.   Col.
Wright was there in force before him and had received
the submission of the Indians, including that of Leschi
and his party.

On the 24th of February, the Indians waylaid and
killed William Northcraft, a teamster in the volunteer
service, while passing through Yelm prairie.   The body
was secreted and not discovered until the 2d of March.
On this latter date William White, a respected citizen
living about twelve miles easterly from Olympia, was
overtaken by seven Indians and murdered in cold blood,
while he, with his wife and Mrs. Stewart, were returning home from church.   We know nothing of the particulars of the killing of Northcraft, as no one was left to
tell the story, but in the case of Mr. White we have the
story of the two ladies, who escaped unharmed, except
an injured ankle caught in the cart wheel.

The women were riding in the cart while Mr. White
was walking behind with the lines in his hands driving,
when the Indians emerged on foot from a point of timber
a little ahead of them.   The aim seemed to be to kill
Mr. White, but in the fight that followed, the horse became frightened and ran away.   Part of the Indians
ran alongside the cart trying to head the horse off the
road or get ahead of him, but failed, and after making
the race to within a few hundred yards of the block
house, gave up the chase and returned to their comrades,
who, in the meantime, had killed the poor man.   But
not without a desperate struggle as shown by visible
signs left on the ground.

The next day, A. J. Baldwin, of Olympia, while passing near the scene of this murder, was suddenly confronted by four Indians on horseback as he rounded

a point of timber.   They immediately drew their guns upon him, when one of them spoke loud in their native tongue to the others, and their arms were lowered without firing.

"Jack Baldwin?" the spokesman said.

"Yes, that's my name."

"You out to fight Indian?"

"No. I am carrying an express to Yelm for pay."

"You remember the bucket of water at Olympia?"

Baldwin, who related this circumstance to the author, said it then flashed upon his mind what Indian it was that was talking. The year before this Indian was filling his bucket from a flowing spring in Olympia, when a brute of a white man came along, insolently removed the Indian's bucket, pitched it into a mud hole near by, and put his own under the spout, whereupon he (Baldwin) interfered and pitched the ruffian into the mud hole after the Indian's bucket. The fellow confronting Baldwin remembered him.

"Go on," he said, "we don't kill you," and go he did unharmed without further ado.

The last depredation of which we have any record or knowledge followed shortly in the burning of Glasgow's barn, a few miles south, after which the Indians disappeared and were seen no more with arms in their hands.

The parties engaged in this foray consisted of only seven Indians with Wa-hoo-lit, known as Yelm Jim, at their head. They spread such consternation that in the current publications of the day the number soon ran to forty or more. This was the first depredation of any kind south of the Nisqually River during the whole war, and made such an impression on the mind of the Governor as to change the whole plan of the campaign. Maxon's company from near the Columbia was ordered to Olympia immediately; Shaw, who with his command was moving up the Columbia River, suddenly turned around and was on the way to the Sound. Energetic measures were inaugurated for scouting the whole country, but to no purpose, as the Indians had disappeared as suddenly as they had come.

Old Wa-hoo-lit (Yelm Jim, as we call him now), was then a young man, unmarried, fearless and of a morose disposition, and age has not improved his temper very much. He has lived near neighbor to the author now for forty years, but I have never known of any other lawless act committed by him. He was tried, convicted and condemned to be hung for the murder of White, but was reprieved the day before he was to be executed and sent at midnight to his friends without previous warning. When I saw him in the preparation of this work, he was more intent upon selling hay than of talking about old war times, and with a significant passage of his hand across his neck, said he "didn't like to talk about it, but if I would give him five dollars he would tell me the whole story."

It would be uninteresting and unprofitable to undertake to follow the movement of the troops, to relate the numerous scouting trips, block houses occupied, surrenders of parties and families, but the work went steadily on, the Indians avoiding the volunteers as much as possible and giving themselves up to the regulars.

CHAPTER XLVIII.

Insubordination at Camp Montgomery.

On the 21st of May (1856), an Indian was shot near Fort Nisqually while peacefully cutting wood by the road side and died soon after. The incident became prominent from the fact that he was in the employ of the Puget Sound Agricultural Company and under the protection of W. F. Tolmie, the agent of both the Hudson Bay and Puget Sound Agricultural Companies at Fort Nisqually. These two companies had assisted financially in the prosecution of the war against the Indians to the extent of forty thousand dollars, and felt they had a right to protection instead of being attacked.

Upon the solicitation of Lieut. Colonel Casey commanding at Fort Steilacoom, Dr. Tolmie reported in full the incidents attendant upon the murder and upon' invitation of Colonel B. F. Shaw, Commanding the volunteers at Camp Montgomery, visited that camp to point out the murderer with a view to his punishment.

What followed is best told in his letter to Colonel Casey, kindly furnished me by Edward Huggins, one of the participants. The letter follows:

"Ft. Nisqually, W. T., May 27th, 1856.

"Colonel Casey, 9th Infantry, U. S. A., Commanding Puget Sound District, Fort Steilacoom, W. T.:

"Sir—On the 23d inst. I addressel you, detailing the circumstances of the murder at this place, on the 21st inst., of a friendly Indian by a passing volunteer, and have now to inform you what has subsequently happened in relation to that unfortunate affair.

"On the 22d inst. I saw at Camp Montgomery Colonel B.
F. Shaw, commanding the Northern Battalion of Volunteers, when I mentioned to him the murder that had been
committed the day before. The Colonel thereupon requested me to return the following day, accompanied by witnesses able to identify the supposed murderer, and in reply
to an inquiry on my part as to whether it would be safe to
bring Indians to camp to testify against a volunteer, he
stated that it would, and was supported in his opinion by
other officers, all agreeing that no one would sympathize
with the perpetrators of such a foul and unprovoked murder as that to be investigated.

"I acordingly, on the 23d inst., went to Camp Montgomery, accompanied by three white men, one Sandwich Island-
er and four Indlians amongst them, able to substantiate all
the statements set forth in my letter to you of the 23d inst.
reporting the murder On our arrival at camp two companies of volunteers were paraded for inspection, and in one
of them the man Lake was recognized at a glance as the
volunteer who had passed Ft. Nisqually about 2:30 P. M.
on the 21st inst. His perturbed and guilty look while
standing in line betrayed him to myself and others to whom
he was personally unknown.

"I heard Colonel Shaw then give orders to have Lake deprived of his gun and arrested, which I believe was done.

"Very soon after a large number of volunteers tumultu-
ously declared that Lake should not be molested. They
spoke of murdering the Indian witnesses, and of lynching
one or two persons they supposed had given information
regarding Lake's position in the line of volunteers paraded
for inspection. They also, I am informed, spoke of shooting me, but as I remained with the Indians in front of Colonel Shaw's tent until the commotion had nearly subsided,
I did not myself hear any threats uttered. Being at length
called into the crowd to exonerate Dr. M. P. Burns of the
volunteer force from the charge of having given information
regarding Lake's position, I was lectured in a loud voice by
one of the volunteers on the impropriety of bringing a
charge against any volunteer at the suggestion or by the
wish of their officers, for whom, Colonel Shaw and Gov-

ernor Stevens included, he in emphatic terms said they did not care.

"The last act of the volunteers that I witnessed was the getting of Lake into their midst and saluting him with repeated cheers. Very respectfully, your obt. servant,

"WILLIAM F. TOLMIE."

No doubt when Colonel Shaw advised Dr. Tolmie to bring witnesses to his camp to point out the murderer of Indian Bob, he was sincere in his intention to have the man punished. Neither have we any reason to doubt that he intended to enforce his order to arrest the murderer, but we know he did not; that Lake went Scott free and that neither Maxon nor any of his men were punished or reprimanded for their acts of insubordination. We know, on the other hand, that Maxon was promoted and given important duties to perform and was treated as one of the trusted Lieutenants of the Governor; that he was given the awful charge to turn the guns of his men against citizens and to "at all hazards" arrest the Judge (Chenoweth), which meant the shooting of citizens in the event they did not submit to his will; this too, in the face of the then known fact of the brutal massacre by Maxon and his men of from seventeen to thirty Indians on the Michel, fifteen out of the seventeen being positively proven to be women and children. The Indians had fled far into the mountains, were unarmed and engaged in fishing when pounced upon by Maxon.

Several years ago, Hon. James Wickersham, then a practicing attorney of Tacoma, now a United States Judge for Alaska, looked up the testimony as to this humiliating and brutal affair, embodied the facts in a paper filed with the State Historical Society at Tacoma, Oct. 30th, 1893, from which I quote:

"* * * Colonel Shaw returned to Camp Montgomery while Maxon's company again turned south and east and

went up the Nisqually to near the canyon, where they discovered a large fishing camp, and here they murdered
everyone—men, women and children. But Mr. Evans
says, where is your record? Such as it is, is on pages 307-8
of Governor Stevens' war message (letters), which lies
open before me. Here is all there is of it: 'We (Maxon)
continued our returning course next on the trail, being generally in a south and east direction. * * * * Again arrived at Michel prairie. * * * * Having no provisions,
I have come to this place, where I await orders. Signed,
H. J. G. Maxon, Capt. Com'd'g Mounted Rifles.'

"Now, read those eight asterisks and you have the massacre. The record is mutilated—it is wanting in complete-
ness. When Governor Stevens printed his message with
appendix, he found it too vile in this spot and cut out the
account of the massacre—at any rate it should be in this
very spot under date of April, 1856. But it is not there and
we must supply it."

"Under date of Sunday, August 21, 1892, James Longmire's (an intense partisan of Governor Stevens) account
of early days was published in the Ledger and from that I
quote one paragraph:

"About this time Governor Curry of Oregon sent a company of troops to our assistance, under Captain Miller. Indians were still stealing horses and killing cattle. A band
of these robbers were followed by Captain Maxon to the
Michel River, where the last one of them was killed.

"Robert Thompson, who now lives at 24th and South C
Street, Tacoma, was present when Maxon's company attacked this camp and I quote a letter from him on this subject:

"Tacoma, Oct. 29th, 1893.

"James Wickersham.—Dear Sir: I know about the killing of the Indians by Maxon's company on the upper Nisqually. They killed about fifteen to seventeen, maybe more.
[We know from other sources there were nearer thirty.—
E. M.] I saw the dead ones—two in the river. There were
but two men among them.

(Signed)   "R. THOMPSON.

"Mr. Thompson is known by all old settlers to be reliable, and in this matter he absolutely refused to state a number above those actually seen by him dead on the ground and the two in the river.   The whole truth is that about thirty or more were cruelly massacred, nearly all being women and children.

"Maxon was Captain of the Washington Mounted Rifles, and on page 292 of Governor Stevens' war message is the copy of the order under which Maxon made his raid to the upper Nisqually.   The last clause in this order reads 'all Indians found in your field of operations except those before described (Lieut. Gosnell's Indian Company), are to be considered as enemies.'

"Do you know what that meant?   It meant kill every Indian you find!   How well this was done appears from the asterisks in Governor Stevens' message and from the statements of Longmire and Thompson."

Governor Stevens, in his message advocating extermination of the Indians, had "sown the wind" and now reaped the whirlwind and could say naught against the actions of Maxon, as his own official utterances came home to plague him.

CHAPTER XLIX.

Controversy Between Stevens and Wool.

The close of the war with the Indians, related in preceding chapters, by no means closed the vigorous war of words that had been waged with great virulence between Governor Stevens and Major General Wool, Commander of the U. S. regulars in the Department of the Pacific. As the expiring embers of the one were dying, the lurid flames of the other seemed to blaze with intensified and increased fury. So acrimonious had this become that the General was ready to turn the bayonets of his soldiers against the volunteers, while the legislatures of the two Territories and the two Governors exhausted the vocabulary of invective against his devoted head. In letter writing the General had the better of his opponents. He was as vigorous a writer as he had been proficient as a soldier and held his own well. Think of it! Three to four thousand words launched by Governor Stevens in one epistle, while the General would come back to the combat with a thousand or more.

This was carried on during the hostilities against the Indians, and continued for many months after. To give the reader a faint insight into the virulence and scope of this unfortunate controversy, a few extracts from the correspondence is here given. The whole correspondence would fill a large volume but would not interest the general reader. Wool to Casey:

"Nov. 19th, 1856.

"Sir: Your several communications and your correspondence with Governor Isaac I. Stevens, relating to the surrender of Leschi and several other chiefs, for trial, were received yesterday and laid before Major General Wool. The following is his reply:

"He approves of your course in not complying with the requisition of Governor Stevens. 'It is evident,' he says, 'that Stevens, in persisting in demanding the surrender of Leschi and others for trial, is dictated by a vindictive spirit, caused by his recent attempt to renew the war in the Walla Walla country.' * * * * He directs that you will not fail to give protection, if necessary, to Leschi, and all other Indians peaceably inclined to the whites. * * * * If an attempt should be made by Governor Stevens or other persons to renew the war on Puget Sound, you will resist it to the extent of your power. Should the whites attack the Indians, the power of the Indian agent ceases, and the whole power of peace and war will be vested in yourself, under the instructions of the commanding General, and none other. Volunteers will in no wise be recognized, and should any be sent into the field to make war on the Indians they will, if you have the power, be arrested, disarmed and sent home."

Stevens to Wool:

"* * * In conclusion, it is due to frankness that I should state that I have determined to submit to the department the course taken by the military authorities in the Territory of Washington for my relief. No effort was made, although the facts were presented, both to Major General Wool and Major Rains, to send me assistance. The regular troops were all withdrawn into garrison, and I was left to make my way the best I could through tribes known to be hostile. It remains to be seen whether the commissioner selected by the President to make treaties with the Indians in the interior of the continent is to be ignored, and his safety left to chance."

, Wool to Stevens:

"* * * I need not say, although I had previously instructed Colonel Wright to take possession of the Walla
Walla country at the earliest moment practicable, that I
directed him to give protection as soon as he could to the
friendly Cayuses from the depredations of the volunteers.
* * * * In your 'frankness' and determination to represent me to the department, I trust you will be governed
by truth, and truth only. Perhaps it is equally due to frankness on my part to say that your communication is the first
I have received in relation to yourself, or on any subject
whatever touching the Indian war, from any civil functionary, either in Washington or Oregon Territories; and I
have received but one from the military, and that was from
Colonel Nesmith, who requested me to furnish him with
two howitzers, which I refused. I have only to add that I
disbanded no troops raised for your relief; and your communication gave me the first intelligence that any were
raised for such a purpose."

Stevens to Davis, Sec. War:

"Mr. Secretary: Major General Wool, commanding the
Pacific Division, neglected and refused to send a force to
the relief of myself and party, when known to be in imminent danger, and believed by those who are best capable
of judging, to be coming on to certain death; and this when
he had at his command an efficient force of regular troops.

"He has refused to sanction the agreement made between
Governor Mason and Major Rains for troops to be sent to
my assistance, and ordered them to be disbanded. It was
reserved for the Oregon volunteers to rescue us. There has
been a breach of faith somewhere. I ask for an immediate
investigation into the whole matter.

"The only demonstration made by Major Raines resulted
in showing his utter incapacity to command in the field. As

has been heretofore said, his expedition against the Yakimas effected nothing but driving the Indians into the very country through which I must pass to reach the settlements. I have, therefore, to prefer charges against General Wool. I accuse him of utter and signal incapacity, of criminal neglect of my safety. I ask for an investigation into his conduct, and of his removal from command.' '

Wool to Stevens:

"Whilst I was in Oregon it was reported to me that many citizens, with a due proportion of volunteers, and two newspapers, advocated the extermination of the Indians. This principle has been acted on in several instances, without discriminating between enemies and friends, which has been the cause in Southern Oregon of sacrificing many innocent and worthy citizens. As in the case of Major Lupton and his party (volunteers), who killed twenty-five Indians, eighteen of whom were women and children. These were friendly Indians, on their way to the Indian reservation, where they expected protection from the whites.

"* * * In regard to the operations east of the Cascade Mountains, if Governor Curry's volunteers have not driven the friendly Cayuses and the Nez Perces into the ranks of the hostile tribes (and they should be withdrawn from the Walla Walla country), I have great hopes that I shall be able to bring the Indians in that region to terms, notwithstanding the volunteers killed the chief, Pee-Pee-Mox-Mox, scalped him, cut off his ears and hands, as reported by volunteers, and sent them to their friends in Oregon. All this, too, after he met them under a flag of truce, declaring he was for peace; that he did not wish to fight; that his people did not wish to fight, and that if any of his young men had done wrong he would make restitution, while he at the same time offered the volunteers cattle for food."

What are we to say or to think of the imbecility of the administration at Washington to maintain in power two such warring factions of the two separate arms of the service, both under the control of the one head, the President of the United States? General Wool in other instances gave as explicit orders for the regulars to attack the volunteers, as is here reported, and was balked by the sound discretion of the officers in the front, while Governor Stevens was just as insistent and positive in his orders to his subordinates to continue the war against the Indians. Happily no clash of arms came, but it must in candor be said both were willing if not eager for the fray.

While Governor Stevens had these two wars on his hands, a third, the most virulent of all, broke out when he turned his guns against the citizens and the courts of the Territory, the particulars of which must be left for another chapter.

CHAPTER L.

Troubles in Pierce County.

I witnessed what but few American citizens have ever seen when, on the 7th day of May, 1856, at Steilacoom, I saw twenty armed men, acting under the orders of the Governor of the Territory, enter the court house and forcibly remove a United States Judge from the bench, arrest the clerk, and with him carry off the court records. That was what I saw while standing in the court room with arms in my hands, called there in common with other citizens by the sheriff as a special posse to protect the court from threatened indignity and arrest of the Judge.

Before reciting what happened, we will go back to inquire what it was that caused this uneasiness on the part of the court, and why the Governor of the Territory should want to break up the courts of the commonwealth, instead of protecting them.

As has been told in previous chapters, there had, prior to the 7th of May, been an Indian war in progress for nearly five months in a small district of the country west of the Cascade Mountains. This struggle had been confined within narrow limits, the power of the Indians broken and their forces disintegrated nearly two months before the incident mentioned.

Beyond the Puyallup River to the south, comprising Pierce and Thurston Counties, not a life of a non-combatant had been lost, except that of William White, near Olympia.

Many of the farmers were living on their claims in all this region south of the Puyallup valley to the Columbia River, and had been for months, and none was molested, except the one mentioned. Some had con-

structed block houses, others had not. Almost all of the
pioneers believed the Indians when they said war would
not be made on their old neighbors, especially so when
it became known that some of them had been within the
power of hostile bands and remained unharmed, and
that for months none had been molested. I had, either
myself or some of my people, been daily with our stock
on the range, and was not disturbed. Once a band of
eleven Indians, with Leschi as leader, had passed near
by W. P. Dougherty's place in the dusk of evening,
and close to where I was milking cows, and neither of
us were molested. Leschi had sent word to Thomas M.
Chambers, a prominent citizen of the community, that
he would not be harmed, or any of the old settlers. He
in turn gave out the word to others, among whom was
his daughter, Mrs. Dougherty (and who still lives on
the same spot where she was living then). Dougherty
and his family returned to their home in less than a
month after the outbreak and lived there all winter, and
others did the same.

Southeasterly from Fort Steilacoom, about twelve
miles distant, is a creek called Muck that runs south-
westerly and parallel to the timber belt, which is a mile
or more to the east. Along this creek a tier of claims
were occupied by thrifty farmers and stock raisers, most
of whom had been employees of the Hudson Bay Company in earlier times, who had taken to themselves
as wives Indian women or half-bloods. They all had,
long before, become American citizens, were voters, and
had taught their children the English tongue. It was an
American settlement, although of foreign blood. In the
near vicinity were stations of the Puget Sound Agricultural Company, where there were large flocks of sheep
cared for—several thousand head—all under the immediate supervision of Hon. Edward Huggins, who lived
with the flocks all through the war, and who still lives
on the site of old Fort Nisqually. Mr. Huggins then

was of English citizenship, but long since has become an American citizen and held honorable positions of trust under our government.

Such was the condition of affairs when Governor Stevens, on the 8th of March, ordered Isaac W. Smith, Acting Secretary of the Territory, to take twenty men and "march to the settlements occupied by the French and other foreign-born settlers, and remove them to Fort Nisqually."

This was the beginning of the war on the settlers. On the 11th Smith reported:

"The shepherds of the Puget Sound Agricultural Company could not be removed without danger to the large flocks of sheep under their charge.* About six miles from Montgomery Station is a settlement of English and half-breeds. The names of the men composing it are Wren, two Smiths, two Murrays, McLoud and Gravelle. Their teams being in the volunteer service, it was necessary that they should await their return in order to remove their large families and household furniture. * * * They will turn over to the Quartermaster and Commissary General such stock, provisions and grain as they may not need for private use."†

The alleged reason for this wholesale removal of settlers is shown in the following extract from Governor Stevens' message to the Legislature:

"I refer to the so-called neutrals in the war, who remained on their claims unmolested, when our patriotic citizens were compelled to live in block houses. There is no such thing, in my humble judgment, as neutrality in an Indian war, and whoever can remain on his claim unmolested is

---

*But he did not indicate how the settlers' stock was to be cared for. These people all had flocks of sheep and cattle, as well as many horses, besides other property, including their crops. In a word, they were well-to-do farmers of a most advanced settlement of the Territory.

†This last significant sentence carried a world of meaning. Governor Stevens had not hesitated to order not only the impressment of men and teams, but also provisions and property, shown in the official correspondence elsewhere. This at a time when the United States regulars were in possession of the hostile zone, the Indians scattered and notice given that the volunteers were not needed. In fact, the regulars then had garden stuff planted at Muckleshoot.

an ally of the enemy and must be dealt with as such. These
men I ordered into the towns, giving them the choice of residence at Olympia, Nisqually, or Steilacoom, and on returning to their claims in violation of orders, I caused them to
be put in close confinement."

This is the sum and substance of the charges against
these settlers, who, soon after their removal returned
to their claims, and were again arrested and held as
prisoners. No crime was alleged against them, and
they were deprived of their liberty without due process
of law. They immediately employed counsel to procure
their release by application to the court for a writ of
habeas corpus.

The following is a sample of reports sent to the Governor:

"Major Maxon, who was in pursuit of the Indians, informed the Commander-in-Chief that, unless these men
were removed from their claims and cut off from all communication with the Indians, it would be idle to carry on
the war, and his whole battalion would be compelled to
leave the field."

This was a bald, senseless subterfuge, as there were
no Indians in the vicinity to fight, and if there had been,
if these men on their farms could induce the Indians to
come out from their cover, what better chance could the
volunteers want? Like, as at the salt lick, stalk their
game? Fort Montgomery was but a few miles distant.

As we have seen, these farms could not be reached
without crossing a wide stretch of prairie. How much
better it would have been for the volunteers to have
watched and turned their guns on the Indians, if there
were any, than upon the settlers! As I write, to this
day, knowing all the circumstances as I do, it seems
incredible that such action should be taken upon such a
flimsy pretext; but we know the arrests were made, and
so must needs record what followed.

I was myself at that time in open violation of these

orders, going where I chose over the prairies looking
after stock, as likewise were many others, peacefully
and safely occupying their farms and pursuing their
usual occupations. There were no hostile Indians in the
vicinity, and had not been during the whole period of
the war, except, as heretofore related, when on missions
of peace.

This man Maxon requires more than passing mention. He was a jolly wit, with a stomach entirely out
of proportion to his brains, but of such address as to
gain the full confidence of his men. Coupled with this
jolly disposition there lurked a low cunning and brutal
instinct, as we know from the horrid massacre on the
Michel, which is related elsewhere, and from his insubordination, that ended only with the war. Notwithstanding all these defects in his character, he was a
strict disciplinarian with those under his command,
was brave almost to the point of rashness, and reputed
as "one of the best Indian fighters in the volunteer service." He was one of the trusted lieutenants of the Governor, and if, at the time, Stevens understood his character he seemed inclined to condone his faults, which
later brought him into disgrace and his whole company
into trouble by their insubordination in the face of the
enemy, east of the Cascade Mountains.

Major Maxon was the man who asked his men significantly if they were going to submit to have one of
their number arrested for killing an Indian at the instance of a Hudson Bay Company agent, while Colonel
Shaw, the commanding officer, was in his tent writing
an order for the arest of Lake for the murder of Indian
Bob at Fort Nisqually.

Upon this call of Maxon his company turned upon the
witnesses and defied their commander, Colonel Shaw,
and caused the sudden departure of the party that had
come to identify the murderer, to save themselves from
violence.

Major Maxon at that time was one of the five volunteer officers selected by Governor Stevens to sit in judgment at the trial of citizens arrested upon the charge of
treason, which meant the forfeiture of their lives if
found guilty, and for which the Governor had charged
Maxon to "at all hazards" enforce martial law, to the
end that the courts of the Territory be broken up and the
trial of citizens be brought before the court martial, of
which this man Maxon was a member. Notwithstanding this act of insubordination and open espousal of the
cause of the murderer and defiance of the order of his
superior in command, Maxon was continued to the end
as a member of the court martial, and, so far as the records show, was never reprimanded for his conduct. On
the contrary, Lake went free, was continued in the service, and never was punished. Finally we find his name
as one of the four hundred signers endorsing the policy
of the Governor in proclaiming and enforcing martial
law, alongside that of Maxon and the remainder of his
company. Lake had just committed a murder in Olympia, there killing an Indian, and had boldly left the town
for the volunteers' camp at Montgomery. He was arrested upon his arrival in camp, but was immediately
discharged. He was never punished for either crime.

Many people thought Governor Stevens would take
energetic action to punish the criminal, but he did not,
and, in fact, could not; he had himself sown the seeds
of lawlessness by his advocacy of the policy of extermination, and could not control the lawless element
within the body of his armed supporters. When Maxon
wrote the Governor that his battalion would be compelled to leave the field unless the suspected citizens
were arrested, it was not an idle threat (at least the
Governor took it seriously), and spurred him on to the
acts of desperation elsewhere related under the heading
of martial law.

It should be noted that Maxon's company came from
the Columbia River district, the Southern Battalion, as
designated by the Governor, and contained a goodly
number of men enlisted in Oregon.   I would by no
means intimate that the men from the southern part of
the Territory and Oregon were, as a class, worse citizens when at home than those living near the seat of
the war. We can hardly lay such a claim, while considering the fact that the man Lake, who had caused this
trouble, was one of our own nearby citizens; but the
motives of the men who had enlisted in Maxon's company, at least to a considerable extent, differed materially from those who had volunteered to defend their
homes, as they supposed, from the attacks of Indians
in the near vicinity.   Enlistments had been made far
and wide in Oregon Territory, as well as in the
southern part, and elsewhere, in Washington Territory, and the company roll had been filled only after
a long canvass and by the acceptance of adventurous
spirits that cared but little for the cause.   However,
whatever may be the explanation, the facts are as related—that the mob spirit took possession of a portion
of the volunteers at Camp Montgomery; that the officers
were defied, a criminal protected, and the executive of
our Territory, the Commander-in-Chief, was either in-
timidated or became a participant in the crime.   The
incident also illustrates the dangerous condition of affairs when thirty of these same men were sent by Maxon
to Steilacoom, with orders from the Governor to "at all
hazards" prevent the holding of a regular term of the
United States Court by a United States Judge, holding
his appointment from the President, where, as related
elsewhere, bloodshed was avoided only by the exercise
of a sound discretion by Lieutenant Curtis when confronted by a superior force of citizens prepared to defend the court.   .

CHAPTER LI.

Martial Law.

The citizens arrested by order of Governor Stevens upon a charge of treason, as related in previous chapters, were sent to Colonel Casey to be confined at Fort Steilacoom, Governor Stevens alleging as a reason that there were "no jails in the Territory, otherwise I would not put you to the trouble. Even if the evidence should fail to convict one or more of them, the peace of the county requires that those not convicted be kept in close confinement till the end of the war."

Casey responded:

"In view of the reasons assigned by you for not confining them in some jail of the Territory, I consider it my duty to comply with your request."

April 2d, 1856, Frank Clark and W. H. Wallace left Steilacoom in search of Judge Chenoweth, to procure a writ of habeas corpus, whereupon Governor Stevens, on the 3d, issued his proclamation of martial law:

"Proclamation: Whereas, in the prosecution of the Indian war, circumstances have existed affording such grave cause of suspicion, that certain evil-disposed persons of Pierce County have given aid and comfort to the enemy, and that they have been placed under arrest and ordered to be tried by a military commission; and whereas, efforts are now being made to withdraw by civil process these persons from the purview of the said commission; therefore, as the war is now being actively prosecuted throughout nearly the whole of the county, and great injury to the public service will result, and the plans of the campaign frus-

trated if the alleged designs of these persons be not averted,
I, Isaac I. Stevens, Governor of the Territory of Washington, do hereby proclaim martial law over the said County
of Pierce, and do by these presents suspend for the time being, and until further notice, the functions of said civil officers in said county.

"Given under my hand at Olympia, this 3d day of April,
eighteen hundred and fifty-six, and the year of independence of the United States the eightieth.

"ISAAC I. STEVENS."

A copy of this proclamation was sent to Fort Steilacoom on the 2d of April, with a letter explaining the
object, whereupon Colonel Casey notified the Governor:

"I doubt whether your proclamation can relieve me from
the obligation to obey the requisition of the civil authority.
I request, therefore, that you will relieve me from their
charge."

He referred to the prisoners just mentioned.

Judge Chenoweth being sick and at his home in the
northern part of the Territory, no action could be taken
before the court for a month. Meanwhile the prisoners
were held, but no charges were preferred against them.

The time arriving for the regular term of court in
Pierce County, Judge Chenoweth remaining sick, Chief
Justice Edward Lander arrived at Steilacoom to hold
court in Chenoweth's place. Colonel B. F. Shaw, then
a young man of twenty-three, waited on the Judge, and
learning that he intended that day to only open court
and adjourn, he wrote to Governor Stevens, "under
these circumstances I 'permitted' him to go to the court
house."

Think of the indignity to a United States Judge of
mature years, to be under the surveillance of a young,
irresponsible volunteer officer, to "permit" him (the
Judge) to open and adjourn court!

. On the 4th Governor Stevens wrote to Shaw: "Your express is just in. *Enforce martial law.*"

On the 5th Lander wrote to Stevens of the "imminent danger of collision between the civil and military authorities," telling him that he felt it his duty to hold court and asked him to abrogate martial law, "especially as the present conditions of the county seem not to require it as strongly as before, and it can make no difference in regard to what has been done," but Stevens responded on the 6th to Shaw, *"martial law must be enforced,"* italicizing the order.

Meanwhile four deputies were sent out, by order of Judge Lander, with capiases to summon every male citizen over the age of sixteen years to attend the court on Wednesday, the 7th.

It became patent to all that Governor Stevens intended to sustain his proclamation, even if bloodshed followed. A large number of citizens did not obey the summons and threw themselves on the mercy of the court for contempt proceedings, rather than to face the guns of the volunteers at short range within the confines of the court room. Some did not have arms and could not procure them, and, of course, could not be expected to attend. I shall never forget the day. It seemed like walking right into the jaws of death. About thirty citizens attended, though, with arms ready for use. Colonel Shaw marched into the court room at the head of a file of twenty volunteers. If the order had been given to clear the court room Shaw would have gone down at the first onset. The citizens had counseled together enough to conclude that to make the shortest work of the affair would be by taking the leader first. If the order had been given to clear the room it would have been done, as side arms could have been used more effectively at arm's length than muskets. At the last moment Judge Lander submitted, was removed from the court house a prisoner in the hands of the volunteers, and taken to Olympia. He was not held very long, for we find that on the 13th another proclamation was issued declaring martial law over Thurston County. A whole company of volunteers, Captain Miller, was ordered to move to Tumwater, and on the 14th, at 7 o'clock, to Olympia, whereupon Lander was again arrested, this time for holding court in his own district, and sent as a prisoner to Camp Montgomery.

Mrs. Lulu Packard, whom I knew well, had the experience of having the custody of Chief Justice Lander for one night while on this trip. She said:

"The Judge's eyes fairly flashed fire at the indignities heaped upon him as he dismounted in front of our cabin at the Nisqually crossing and entered the house, and the guard turned to go to the block house near by. I gave him the best we had in the house and the best bed we could, but I wouldn't lock the door.

"Next morning I remember putting some apples on the table. Such a delicacy was very rare in the country at the time, and it seemed to touch his heart like no other act of kindness that I could do. He was greatly cast down and seemed humiliated at the treatment he had received from the military authorities, and doubtless was in a mood to more appreciate any little act of kindness than he would under ordinary circumstances."

Judge Chenoweth now appeared on the scene. On the 21st Stevens writes Shaw: "Martial law must be enforced at all hazards in Pierce County." Chenoweth summoned fifty men. Again Stevens wrote Shaw, on the 22d: "The prisoners must at all hazards be tried by the commission now sitting at Montgomery's," and to take measures to arrest the Judge if he attempted to hold court.

Lieutenant Curtis, of the volunteer force, was sent from Camp Montgomery by Major Maxon, with thirty men, to arrest the Judge in the event he attempted to hold court. On the evening of the 23d Judge Chenoweth

held a conference with the sheriff and notified him that
he would be expected to use force in the event of any
molestation of the court by the volunteers, and to prepare himself accordingly; that he (Chenoweth) intended to resist to the last, and suggested to the sheriff to
strengthen his force, which he did. When Curtis arrived he could see armed men. He could see more armed
men to oppose him than he had himself. There is· no
doubt but the Lieutenant stood appalled at the prospect
before him. He and his men had enlisted to fight Indians, not his neighbors and kinsmen. The orders were
positive to "at all hazards" arrest the Judge in the
event he attempted to hold court. Stevens was in Olympia and could not be reached. It was in the air that the
regulars would take a hand the moment there was bloodshed. Colonel Casey had come down in person,* though
he sent no troops. His men were but a mile distant and
could be gotten on the ground in half an hour. By this
time it had become known in Camp Montgomery that
the court martial collected to try these men, Wren,
Smith, and others, who had applied for the writ of
habeas corpus, would not try them; that a majority of
the men appointed by Governor Stevens utterly refused
to stultify themselves by assuming to consider the accu-
sations against the prisoners charged with treason. The
current talk of the hour was that Governor Stevens' own
officers had gone back on him.

*Fort Stellacoom, May 24th, 1856.—Sir: From a note just received from
the sheriff, and from what I have just learned from his deputy, there must be
a collision between the citizens and the volunteers, both of which are now
assembled at Stellacoom, and a scene of bloodshed will be inevitable. I
therefore respectfully ask you to furnish a sufficient number of United States
troops to preserve the peace and prevent bloodshed.
                    (Signed)   F. A. CHENOWETH,
Lieutenant Colonel Casey.   Judge Third Judicial District.
    Colonel Casey replied that he could not send a force as requested, but
would go in person to see the officers in command of the volunteers, which he
did.
    Casey promptly reported the case to the Adjutant General at Washington,
D. C., in which he says: "I trust it may never be my fate to witness bloodshed in a civil controversy," and adds: "It may not be expected that I
should enter into the merits of the case, but, nevertheless, it appears to me
that nothing can justify an executive in suspending the writ of habeas corpus
but an overruling necessity, and in my opinion that necessity did not exist in
this case." But Casey did have to witness rivers of "bloodshed in a civil controversy."

The following report of the proceedings of the court martial for that day tells the whole story:

"Camp Montgomery, Washington Territory, 1 o'clock P. M., May 23d, 1856.

"Court met pursuant to adjournment.

"Present, all the members, Supenumerary, Judge Advocate, Recorder, and L. A. Smith.

"The court was cleared for deliberation, and after mature consideration the court gave the following opinion, viz.:

"The charge against Lyon A. Smith is 'aiding and comforting the enemy.' We are of the opinion that such an offense constitutes the crime of treason, and that this court has no jurisdiction as a military court to try and punish a prisoner for such an offense.

"We are, however, of the opinion that this court was ordered by a competent authority, and that it is legally and constitutionally created, and has jurisdiction of such crimes as are cognizable by military tribunals.

"The court then adjourned until Monday, May 26th, 1856, at 1 o'clock P. M.

(Signed)   "JARED HURD, President, M. C.
"H. J. G. MAXON, Major, S. B.
"C. W. SWINDALL, Capt., W. T. V.
"W. W. DE LACY, Capt., W. T. V.
"ANDERSON SHEPHERD."

As soon as the record could be written up Quincy A. Brooks was dispatched to Olympia to acquaint the Governor with the result, and bore the following letter from Victor Monroe, who had been appointed by the Governor as Judge Advocate:

"Fort Montgomery, May 23, 1856.

"Gov. Stevens: Mr. Brooks will deliver to you the record in the case of L. A. Smith, and you will see the position of the case. Smith, Wren, and McLeod are still in custody awaiting your action. If the specifications can be made in the form of charges they can yet be tried.

"Brannen and Lake are here, but no charges have been preferred, and I am uncertain what to do with them. If you desire them to be tried, please have the charges preferred and send them to me. I have talked with Mr. Brooks and he will give you my opinion in the premises.

"Yours, &c.,   V. MONROE."

Lieutenant Curtis saw that an attack on the court meant bloodshed and certain defeat if he made the attempt to arrest the Judge with the force under his command. His men would have gone into a fight with citizens half-hearted, if indeed they would have obeyed orders at all to shoot down the defenders of the court. On the other hand, the citizens were determined and confident, and would have made a stubborn resistance, and were prepared to make their defense effective. The Lieutenant halted his men outside the court house and dispatched a courier post-haste to Governor Stevens, who was in Olympia, with the following letter:

"Steilacoom, May 24.

"Sir: I was ordered by Capt. Maxon to Steilacoom with a detachment of men to arrest Judge F. A. Chenoweth for violating martial law by officiating as Judge.

"On my arrival here I find the citizens of the town and country about warned by the sheriff to defend the court which is to sit at one o'clock. They are here in force. I see fifty or sixty about the town. The Judge is at the military station and I suppose that the commander of the post is called upon to protect the court. I have sent an express to Major Maxon at Montgomery Station to give him information in the case. I shall make no forcible attempt to arrest the Judge until I receive further orders from Capt. Maxon or some higher authority.

"I will try to prevent a collision till I hear from you.

"Yours with respect,

"SILAS B. CURTIS, 2d Lieut. W. M. R."

As shown by his letter, Curtis also posted an express rider to notify Maxon at Camp Montgomery, twelve miles distant, and so matters stood on the afternoon of the 24th, when Judge Chenoweth convened court..

I do not recall meeting Lieutenant Curtis except on this one accasion, but was then favorably impressed with his frank, open countenance and apparent sincerity of purpose. He was of medium stature, rather light in weight, with clear, light-blue eyes, which, coupled with a light complexion, marked him intellectually far above the average of men. He was a citizen of Clarke County and had enlisted at Vancouver, where he had taught school at intervals. He was not a place seeker. It is told of him that his companions in arms at the outset wished to elect him lieutenant, but he said "no, not until I get some experience that will qualify me to understand the duties of the office," and was elected as corporal, in which capacity he served for a time, and was finally promoted to the second lieutenancy. His action unquestionably averted bloodshed and saved Governor Stevens from the very serious consequences that would have followed a clash of arms between citizens and volunteers. Such an event would not only have sealed Governor Stevens' political doom, but likewise would have subjected him and all his subordinates to criminal proceedings, doubtless with grave results.

The two couriers, one from Curtis, the other from Monroe, delivered their dispatches to the Governor the same day, or rather during the day and night, for Brooks did not arrive until after midnight and immediately aroused the Governor from his slumber, so urgent did he feel the business in hand to be.

The Governor was up against a barrier as solid as a stone wall. His own officers had refused to try the prisoners on the charges preferred. The United States Court was in session in spite of his utmost efforts to prevent it. Something must be done, and that at once.

On Monday the court martial would be in session again.
New instructions must be sent. Catching at the suggestion in Monroe's letter, "if new specifications can be
made in the form of charges they can yet be tried," some
new charges were submitted; but we are left to con-
jecture what they were. I have searched the records diligently among the state and court files, and if any such
exist they have been overlooked. We know by what followed at the convening of the court at Camp Montgomery, on the 28th, that amended charges were filed, as
shown by the proceedings following:

"Camp Montgomery, Washington Territory, 1½ o'clock P.
    M., May 28th, 1856.
"Present, Major Maxon, Capt. Swindal, Capt. De Lacy,
Lieutenant Shepherd and Lieut. Curtis.
"Present also, the Judge Advocate and Recorder, and
John McLeod and Charles Wren, the accused.
"The court room was then cleared for deliberation, and
after mature consideration the court gave the following decision, viz.:
" 'The court decides that courts martial have a right under articles 56 and 57 of the articles of war to take cogni-
aznce of offense committed by citizens of the United States,
and that this court has jurisdiction of the offenses mentioned in the amended charges and specifications, as filed
against John McLeod and Charles Wren. Wherefore, the
court overrules the plea of the accused to the jurisdiction,
and orders the said John McLeod and Charles Wren to answer over.'
"The Judge Advocate, addressing the accused, John Mc-
Leod and Charles Wren, said: 'You have heard the charges
preferred against you; how say you—guilty or not guilty?'
To which each of the accused answered, 'Not guilty.' The
Judge Advocate then read the following paper, marked K,
viz.:
" 'Mr. President and Gentlemen of the Court: Believing
that the further prosecution of the charges against John
McLeod and Charles Wren involves the absence of many
valuable officers from the command of the troops, and is

thereby seriously interfering with military operations, and as martial law has been abrogated in this county, I desire no further proceedings be had before the court against the said accused, and that they be turned over to the civil authorities.'

"Hereupon the court room was cleared for deliberation, and after mature consideration the court announced to John McLeod and Charles Wren that they were discharged from any further proceedings, and were turned over to the civil authorities.

"Signed by all the members of the court."

"Headquarters W. T. Volunteers, Olympia, W. T., May 29, 1856.

"The proceedings and findings of the foregoing general court martial are hereby approved.

"ISAAC I. STEVENS,
"Gov. and Commander-in-Chief."

And so ended this court martial that commenced on the 20th of May and adjourned on the 28th; that decided first they did not have jurisdiction over the prisoners for the crime charged against them, and when the charges were changed so the conclusion was reached they had a right to try them, then suddenly decided they did not have the time.

The prisoners were not "turned over to the civil authorities," but were discharged and went straight to their homes, only a few miles distant from Camp Montgomery.

CHAPTER LII.

Martial Law—Concluded.

Two years after the event Judge Chenoweth wrote an account to Governor Fayette McMullen of the attempt to break up his court, in response to a request from that official, who for a brief period, without much credit to himself, filled the chair previously occupied by Stevens. The letter follows:

"March 6th, 1858.

"His Excellency Fayette McMullen,
 "Governor of Washington Territory.

"Sir: At your request I proceed to make a plain, brief statement of the part I took in the exciting matter of martial law. It is true, as has been suggested, the whole truth does not appear in the published account of that transaction. The only permanent press of the Territory at that time was under the control and in the interest of the Governor and gave but one side of the case. The facts then are briefly these: I was sick at home at the time my court was to have been held at Steilacoom. I requested Judge Lander to hold my court, which he did or attempted to do, and as to how his court was broken up and he made a prisoner you have already learned. But as you are anxious to know the particular part I took in the transaction, I will say that at the request of the members of the bar I went to Steilacoom as soon as my health allowed me and did up such business as could be done at 'Chambers' while martial law was still in force. On arriving at Steilacoom I learned that an effort would be made to arrest me and break up my court, and make me a prisoner as was done with Judge Lander, but I determined to stand upon my rights and pursue my duty regardless of consequences. I accordingly ordered the sheriff to summon from the body of the county fifty men to pro-

tect the court, which was done. The men appeared in court
in obedience to the summons. As to how well they were
armed or whether they were armed at all I could not tell.
They had no arms that were visible, but I was assured by
one of the deputy marshals that they were armed, and I had
no reason to doubt but what a pitched battle would take
place and I was fully determined to defend myself with my
life. I believed I was in the discharge of my duty, and was
willing to risk my life in it. Capt. Curtis with thirty men
was sent from Camp Montgomery to arrest me. Capt. Curtis, on finding that I had a strong posse, sent back for a
reinforcement, and I applied to Col. Casey of U. S. A. for
troops to protect me. The Colonel declined to furnish them
at that time, but intimated that a state of things might arise
in which he should interfere, and remarked that he would
go and talk with Capt. Curtis, which he did and the result
was Capt. Curtis withdrew his men and the court was not
disturbed, and on that night martial law was abrogated.
The business transacted that day was the hearing of a cause
in Admiralty, Dun and others vs. the Steamer Water Lily,
and the granting attachments in the matter of the habeas
for the body of Edward Lander, Chief Justice, and others.
The opinion given in that case you have seen. On the following day the attachment was returned by bringing Col.
Benjamin F. Shaw before me, and as he refused to make the
return according to law, I committed him to prison and ordered the marshal to keep him in close confinement without bail until he made the return. As martial law had now
been abrogated, and Governor Stevens seeing I was determined to enforce the law he addressed me a respectful note
asking me to dispose of the matter by a fine or accept bail
in Col. Shaw's case and allow him to return to his command.
This letter was so different from the haughty and dictatorial
language that had been held up to that time that I determined to do what I could to comply with the request, for
while I was determined to do my duty I did not wish to
widen the breach between the judiciary and the executive;
so I informed Col. Shaw that if he would order the prisoners
to be turned over to me and give me his parole of honor to
appear at the next term of the District Court and submit to
such orders as I might then make I would discharge him, to

which he agreed and was discharged. I may be allowed here
to state briefly the reasons why I think and have always
thought there was no manner of necessity for martial law.
As far as I could see the Indians were conquered at the time,
especially those on the west side of the mountains. The
people had begun to feel secure and return to their farming
and other occupations in the county. The reasons assigned
by Governor Stevens for this extreme measure have been so
various and contradictory as to show clearly that it was a
desperate struggle to save a sinking cause. The reason that
has figured most prominent is that previous to martial law
the enemy could not be found, but that afterwards they were
'frequently struck and readily subdued.' Now where are
the facts to support any such argument as this? The only
two battles that were ever fought in Pierce or Thurston
Counties were the battle of White River and the one on
Connell's prairie, both of which were fought before the
proclamation of martial law. (I respectfully call your attention to Governor Stevens' reports of these battles). No
engagement of any description took place after the proclamation of martial law except the little party met by Major
Maxon that only numbered 5 or 6 men and some women, in
which the Major killed a portion of this small party and took
the remainder prisoners. Whether this argument is good
for anything or not I will not pretend to say, but one thing
I can say, that the facts on which it professes to be founded
are not true. Again, at the time martial law was proclaimed,
these suspected persons were in prison at Steilacoom—five
in number. Pierce and Thurston Counties were both placed
under martial law, both large and populous counties, embracing at least one-third of all the inhabitants of the Territory. Now why could not these prisoners have been taken
to the head quarters at Camp Montgomery, and have been
placed under the same guard that was placed over Judge
Lander and other citizens that were held as prisoners, and if
martial law was necessary for the safe keeping of these
prisoners it could have been confined to the camp and need
not have interfered with the people generally. There were a
large number of troops employed in enforcing martial law in
the two counties for no other purpose than to prevent the
release of these prisoners. Now who can seriously say that

this was necessary? Who will say that these men could not have been just as safely kept at Camp Montgomery? And that if martial law was necessary at all it was only necessary to extend over the camp that contained the prisoners?

"Again, did Governor Stevens know that these suspected prisoners would be released? He surely had no reason to think so if there was evidence of their guilt. Would it not have been better to have waited and seen whether the District Court was likely to discharge them? He could have had his troops near the court house door, and if they were improperly discharged could have arrested them again. The Governor complains of no distemper in the community at large or any general treasonable plot. Simply, these five persons labored under suspicion. The people did not seek to screen them if guilty. The people all had one common interest in subduing the Indians and in protecting themselves. These, sir, are the principal facts of the case.

"I might refer you to the correspondence with the Secretary of State under the former administration for a more full exposition of the matter.

"I am, sir, very respectfully,
"Your obedient servant,

"F. A. CHENOWETH."

And now it is pertinent we should inquire what is this so-called martial law, and why was Gocernor Stevens so persistent and so anxious to have his way? As has been clearly shown, there was no impending danger hanging over the commonwealth. The so-called martial law was not law—it was the attempted subversion of all law, by substituting the will of one man for that of statute law. It was clearly illegal and depended entirely upon immediate and present physical force, and so long as that force could be made effective the deliberate judgment of the people, as reflected by their statute laws and constitutional guarantees were set aside and the whim, or passion, or defective judgment of the one will put in their place. Such proceedings were a positive danger

to the peace and quiet of the community, and we have
seen how narrow the escape from bloodshed and actual
civil war, that the incident should stand as a warning
against such excesses.

After all, Governor Stevens himself was the greatest
sufferer of all. We have not done with telling the trials
and difficulties surrounding him. He was condemned
by all thinking men both local and national, except his
immediate partisans, by the legislature of his own Territory, by the President of the United States, by the Senate to the extent of refusing further appropriations for
the Indian service in Washington Territory until the
Governor should be superseded and have no part in
handling the funds or control of the Indians—a curious
way of wreaking their vengeance, as the Governor had
in no wise been accused of misappropriating funds that
had been entrusted to his care—but for the sole alleged
reason because he had declared martial law. This was
done by consolidating the Oregon and Washington
superintendencies, leaving the Governor out in the cold
with his occupation gone. Why they did not turn their
guns on him as Governor was an enigma at the time
and remains so to this day, probably though because
the President would not remove him and they could not
punish him in any other way than by compelling his
removal from the Indian superintendency by withhold-
ing appropriations, or by impeachment.

The following extracts and publications will only in
part show the general condemnation that followed in
the track of the Governor's rash action:

"JOINT RESOLUTION

"Relative to the proclamation and enforcement of martial
law over the counties of Pierce and Thurston.

"Whereas, Isaac I. Stevens, Governor of this Territory,
declared martial law over the counties of Pierce and Thurston for the express purpose, as shown by his proclamation

and vindication, of suspending the writ of habeas corpus—interfered with, and broke up the courts of said counties and attempted to try citizens òn the charge of treason before a military commission.

"And Whereas, in his message to this body, he 'invites a rigid scrutiny into the necessity of his proclamation, and the measures taken to enforce it;' therefore

"Be it resolved by the Legislative Assembly of the Territory of Washington, That, in thus attempting to suspend the writ of habeas corpus, the Governor undertook to exercise a power conferred by the constitution of the United States on Congress alone.

"That, in any attempt to interfere with our courts of justice, or to try citizens before a military tribunal, he aćted in direct violation of the Constitution and Laws of the United States, and that any such attempt to exercise unconstitutional power, tends to the subversion of our institutions, and calls at our hands for the strongest condemnation.

"Passed, January 24th, 1857."

The conclusion of Caleb Cushing, Attorney General of the United States during Pierce's administration, to whom the Secretary of State, William L. Marcy, had referred the matter of martial law proclaimed by Governor Stevens, is summed up briefly as follows:

"Under the Constitution of the United States, the power to suspend the writ of habeas corpus belongs exclusively to Congress.

"The power to suspend the laws and substitute military in the place of civil authority, is not within the legal attributes of a governor of one of the Territories."

These brief conclusions are supplemented by an exhaustive examination of the subject, or more accurately speaking, rather the result of such investigation.

One note of warning sounded is well worth reproducing here as there seems to be such general confusion of opinions and which if erroneous conclusions are reached and our people taught to submit to martial law without protest, place us on dangerous grounds and on the road to the final subversion of our liberty.

In considering the subject Mr. Cushing says:

"Permit me to say, before leaving the case, that the extreme indeterminateness and vagueness of existing conception, on this particular subject, are a matter of regret, and the removal thereof a desideratum in our constitutional jurisprudence."

A few extracts from this elaborate opinion will be interesting reading in considering the case in hand.

Mr. Cushing says:

"Martial law is a thing not mentioned by name, and scarcely as much as hinted at, in the Constitution and Statutes of the United States."

Speaking of our army in a foreign country:

"Thus, while the armies of the United States occupied different provinces of the Mexican Republic, the respective commanders were not limited in authority by any local law. They allowed, or rather required, the magistrates of the country, municipal or judicial, to continue to administer the laws of the country among their countrymen,—but in subjection always to the military power. * * * * In England, as we have seen, Earl Grey assumes that when martial law exists, it had no legal origin, but is a mere fact of necessity, to be legalized afterwards by a bill of indemnity, if there be occasion. I am not prepared to say that, under existing laws, such may not also be the case in the United States. * * * *

"In the Constitution there is one clause of more apparent relevancy, namely, the declaration that 'the privilege of the writ of habeas corpus shall not be suspended, unless when in case of rebellion or invasion, the public safety may require it. This negation of power follows the enumeration of the powers of Congress; but it is general in its terms; it is in the action of things denied, not only to Congress, but to the Federal Government as a government, and to the

States. I think it must be considered as a negation reaching all the functionaries, legislative or executive, civil or military, supreme or subordinate, of the Federal Government; that is to say, that there can be no valid suspension of the writ of habeas corpus under the jurisdiction of the United States, unless when the public safety may require it, in cases of rebellion or invasion. And the opinion is expressed by the commentators on the Constitution, that the right to suspend the writ of habeas corpus, and also that of judging when the exigency has arisen, belongs exclusively to Congress."*

Speaking further as to states and citing several cases, Mr. Cushing says:

"And it may be assumed, as a general doctrine of constitutional jurisprudence in all the United States, that the power to suspend laws, whether those granting the writ of habeas corpus, or any other, is vested exclusively in the legislature of the particular state.

"How intimate the relation is, or may be, between the proclamation of martial law and the suspension of the writ of habeas corpus, is evinced by the particular facts of the case before me,—it appearing, as well by the report of the Governor as by that of Chief Justice Lander, that the very object, for which martial law was proclaimed, was to prevent the use of the writ in behalf of certain persons held in confinement by the military authority, on the charge of treasonable intercourse with hostile Indians. That, however, is but one of the consequences of martial law, and by no means the largest or gravest of these consequences, since, according to every definition of martial law, it suspends, for the time being, all the laws of the land, and substitutes in their place no law; that is, the mere will of the military commander."

The concluding paragraphs of Mr. Cushing's able paper are well worth a study by every citizen who values his political liberties and the liberties of his country.

---

*Story's Comm., 1342; Tucker's Bl., Vol. 1, p. 202.

"There may undoubtedly be, and has been, emergencies of necessity, capable of themselves to produce, and therefore to justify, such suspension of all law, and involving, for the time, the omnipotence of military power. But such a necessity is not of the range of merely legal questions. When martial law is proclaimed under circumstances of assumed necessity, the proclamation must be regarded as the statement of an existing fact, rather than legal creation of that fact. In a beleagured city, for instance, the state of siege lawfully exists, because the city is beleagured, and the proclamation of martial law, in such case, is but notice and authentication of a fact,—that civil authority has become suspended, of itself, by the force of circumstances, and that by the same force of circumstances, the military power has had devolved upon it, without having authoritatively assumed, the supreme control of affairs, in the care of the public safety and conservation. Such, it would seem, is the true explanation of the proclamation of martial law at New Orleans by General Jackson.

"As to the present case, therefore, it suffices to say, that the power to suspend the law and to substitute the military in the place of the civil authority, is not a power within the legal attributes of a governor of one of the Territories of the United States."

The President, after consulting Mr. Cushing's opinion, directed the Secretary of State to notify the Governor of the disapproval of his action, which he did in words as follows:

"Department of State, Washington,
"Sept. 12th, 1856.

"His Excellency, Isaac I. Stevens, Governor of the Territory of Washington,

"Sir: I have laid before the President all the documents and papers which you have transmitted to this department in explanation of your course in declaring martial law in some parts of the Territory of Washington. After a full consideration of them, he has not been able to find in the case you have presented a justification for that extreme measure. Whether in any circumstances whatever, the Governor of a Territory can resort to such a measure, unless under express authority given by legislation is a question which it is not proposed now to discuss or decide. It is quite certain that nothing but direful necessity, involving the probable overthrow of the civil government, could be alleged as any sort of excuse for superseding that government temporarily and substituting in its place an arbitrary, military rule. The recognition of such an inherent power in any functionary, whatever be his grade or position, would be extremely dangerous to civil and practical liberty. While the President does not bring into question the motives by which you were actuated, he is induced, by an imperative sense of duty to express his distinct disapproval of your conduct so far as respects the proclamation of martial law. Were the President able to adopt the conclusion that martial law could in any case be established without express legislative authority, he could find no such case in the state of things in Washington Territory, as you have presented them. Where rebellion, or a formidable insurrection, had in effect overthrown the civil government, martial law has been occasionally resorted to as the only means left for its re-establishment. Martial law has also been resorted to in aid of the Government, when in imminent danger of being overpowered by internal or external foes. In such cases the measure has been regarded as excusable, but it never can be excusable where the object in resorting to martial law was to act against the existing Government of the country or to supersede its functionaries in the discharge of their proper duties. The latter seems to have been the principal grounds you had for proclaiming martial law. Your conduct, in that respect, does not therefore meet with the favorable regard of the President.

"I am, sir, your obedient servant,

"WM. L. MARCY."

Severe condemnation by the United States Senate followed, as shown by the proceedings (January 31st, 1857), where the Governor's political associates scored him with scathing words of condemnation and refused 'further appropriations for the office of Superintendent of Indian Affairs unless he was deprived of the Superintendency.

Students of history will find a full report of these proceedings in the Congressional Globe of the date mentioned, but are too volumnious to reproduce in this work.

CHAPTER LIII.

Governor Stevens' Characteristics.

The eccentric actions of Governor Stevens on so many occasions have puzzled many who attempted to study his character. Aside from the unfortunate habits of life, adverted to elsewhere, we know there must be some other underlying cause that led him into such unusual actions.

His conduct in proclaiming martial law on such slight pretexts; of following it to the bitter end, even to the willingness of shedding the blood of innocent citizens if need be to carry his point; his stubborn contest in the court proceedings that followed, even to the issuance as Governor of a respite to himself as prisoner before the bar; his actions at the Medicine Creek Treaty; at Seattle before and after the attack on the town; and numerous other anomalous incidents, all pointed to some great defect in his mental balance unfitting him for the high position he held. Blaine's estimate of Andrew Johnson's character, in his "Twenty Years of Congress," so aptly describes the characteristics of Governor Stevens that I am tempted to quote his words. He says:

"It is not to be forgotten, however, that Mr. Johnson's course was marked by the inherent qualities of his mind. He had two signal defects, either of which would impair his fitness for executive duty; united they rendered him incapable of efficient administration—he was conceited and he was obstinate. Conceit without obstinacy may be overcome by the advice of judicious counselors; united with obstinacy it carries its possessor beyond the bounds of prudence, almost beyond the control of reason. Obstinacy united with good judgment is softened into the virtue of firmness. It has often been said that self made men as they are termed, are necessarily conceited. Like all aphorisms, this must be taken with numberless exceptions, but it was singularly applicable to Johnson, who in all respects, was a self made man. His great career was never absent from his thoughts, and he was always looking at himself as he fancied he would appear in history. He came to regard himself as the hero upon a remarkable stage of action, and naturally made the reflection that if he could have had, in his early years, the advantages which so many possess without improving, he would have made strides in life which would have left him without rivals. It would be impossible to gain a full and correct appreciation of Mr. Johnson's character without taking into account these qualities—qualities which were both the remote and immediate cause of his extraordinary career as Chief Magistrate."

Stevens, like Johnson, was both conceited and obstinate. Stevens had an honorable ambition but it was so unbounded that he was always led into controversies with his superiors. He quarreled with the United States military authorities because they would not act upon his advice; with the Judiciary of the Territory because they would not submit to his dictation; with Cummings, Co-Commissioner at the Blackfeet Council; with Palmer at Walla Walla,—or rather, there, *would* have *his* way, and everywhere the same, his word must be paramount. With unbounded confidence in himself, it is not to be wondered at that he wanted to have his way. He undoubtedly was honest in his convictions as to his abilities and he was not slow to assert them on any or all occasions where he thought his aspirations might be advanced by so doing. Be it said to his honor, that Stevens was not a corrupt man. He did not aspire to place for peculation. Acquired power that tickled his vanity was sufficient compensation for him. He had marked ability as an engineer. His work on the great

exploration for a Northern route for a railroad entrusted to him, is a monument to his fame that will last
so long as that work is contemplated.   He was tenacious
as to his political principles.   He was a Democrat first
and an American afterwards until treason showed its
head and then he was for his country first, last, and all
the time, until he laid down his life that his country
might live, and deserves the tender regard of all succeeding generations for his brave acts, for it must be remembered that it took courage of high order to come out
from the demoralizing affiliations surrounding him at
the outbreak of the great rebellion, as well as to meet
the awful responsibilities of the battle field.   He had
the mental capacity to have carried him high in the
councils of the nation had he been possessed of the
mental balance to have controlled his actions.   But
he had not.   His idiosyncrasies were such as to render
abortive to an extent the greater powers of his mind and
to lead him constantly into turmoil and strife.

CHAPTER LIV.

Governor Stevens' Trial.

The day of reckoning was at hand. Martial law had been abrogated and now there could be no pretense but that civil law must be obeyed. Before Judge Lander's arrest in Olympia, a warrant had been issued for the arrest of the Governor for contempt of court. The marshal had attempted to execute the warrant and had been ejected from the Governor's office by force in which the Governor himself took a hand. A scuffle ensued, while eight of his followers were in the office where the attempt was made to arrest him. One, A. B. Rabbeson, joined with the Governor to resist the marshal, while the others refused to obey the summons of that officer for help and so the arrest was not made at that time.

Now all was changed and the Governor submitted to arrest. He was accorded ample time to procure counsel, prepare an answer and to put in pleadings, but all to no avail. The judge was inexorable but not vindictive. He might have inflicted a heavy fine and imprisonment, but instead, he assessed the nominal fine of fifty dollars to establish the principle that the civil law was supreme. Stevens refused to pay the fine and came into court with one of the most remarkable documents to be found in the annals of American jurisprudence, no less than a respite for himself, by himself, in words that follow:

"Respite.—To all persons to whom these presents shall come, greeting: Know ye:

"That, Whereas, on the tenth day of July, A. D. 1856, in a case pending before the Hon. Edward Lander, Chief Justice of Washington Territory and presiding Judge of the

Second Judicial District of said Territory at Chambers, in the county of Thurston in said Territory, for an alleged contempt of court, wherein the United States is plaintiff and Isaac I. Stevens, defendant; the said Edward Lander, a Judge as aforesaid, adjudged the said defendant to be guilty of a contempt and imposed a fine upon him of the sum of Fifty Dollars, together with the costs of the attachment.

"That I, Isaac I. Stevens, Governor of the said Territory, by virtue of the authority vested in me as Governor, as aforesaid, in order that the President of the United States may be fully advised in the premises and his pleasure known thereon, do hereby respite the said Isaac I. Stevens, defendant, from execution of said judgment, and all proceedings for enforcement and collection of said fine and costs until the decision of the President of the United States can be made known thereon.

"In testimony whereof, I, Isaac I. Stevens, as Governor of the Territory of Washington, on the tenth day of July, A. D. 1856, at Olympia, in said Territory, have set my sign manual, and have caused the seal of said Territory to be affixed.

"By order of the Governor,
                    "ISAAC W. SMITH,
                        "Acting Sec'y Wash. Territory.
                    "ISAAC I. STEVENS,
                        "Gov. Wash. Territory."

Judge Lander refused to be governed by the so-called respite, ordering the Governor into the custody of the marshal and to close confinement, whereupon the fine was paid by the Governor's friends.

The proceedings in the case are very voluminous, particularly in the answer which cites the proclamation of martial law, the proceedings of the eight days' session of the court martial at Camp Montgomery, and an argument against the right of the civil authority to ignore martial law. The closing scene is best told by the record, which, so far as civil proceedings in the Territory, ended this unfortunate incident.

"Thursday, July 10th, 1856.

"UNITED STATES OF AMERICA
vs.
"ISAAC I. STEVENS.

"Attachment for contempt in refusing to make return to writ of habeas corpus

"And now, to-wit, on the 10th day of July, 1856, the argument of counsel having been heard and the said cause having been duly considered, it is ordered and adjudged by the Court that the said Isaac I. Stevens be committed to the custody of the marshal until he shall have fully satisfied and discharged the sum of Fifty Dollars fine and costs of the attachment of which he stands convicted, as for a contempt in refusing to make return to the writ of habeas corpus heretofore issued against him at the instance of Charles Wren, Lyon A. Smith, Henry Smith, John McLeod, and John McFeel.

"And therefore said defendant files in open court a respite by Isaac I. Stevens, Governor of the Territory of Washington, and moves the court that all further proceedings in this case be suspended until the decision of the President of the United States can be known, which motion the Court do overrule.

"And afterwards it appearing that the fine and costs herein are paid and discharged, ordered that said defendant be discharged and go hence without delay."

A diligent search for the original of this unique respite failed to discover it. Subsequent information obtained disclosed the fact that the paper in question had been abstracted from the files and was for a long time in the possession of a prominent citizen of the Territory; that while exhibiting it to a friend the precious document was whiffed aside, brought to Seattle and finally burned in the great conflagration of 1889 that so nearly destroyed the city. It did not seem to be a case where "there was honor among thieves," yet neither profited by their respective thievery.

CHAPTER XV.

The Unrelenting Foe.

Leschi surrendered himself and immediate followers to Colonel Wright and was promised protection with the remainder of the Indians then in the Yakima country. During the summer of 1856, he remained in quiet seclusion east of the Cascade Range, and committed no acts of war. He was at peace with the whites. He had lost his home, all his property, and was an outcast. While he was at peace with the whites, not so with Governor Stevens, commanding the volunteers with him, who was unlelenting in his efforts to wreak vengeance upon his fallen foe.

The Governor clamored to gain possession of his body and that of his brother Quiemuth to put them on trial for their lives for acts committed during the war.

As soon as the Governor emerged from his perilous ride from the Blackfeet Council, he began a correspondence showing a relentless spirit which was maintained to the last, by his official utterance at Olympia in advocating the extermination of the hostile bands.

To Manypenny, the Commissioner of Indian Affairs, he wrote from Walla Walla under date of Dec. 22, 1855:

"My plan is to make no treaties whatever with the tribes now in arms; to do away entirely with the reservations guaranteed to them; to make a summary example of all the leading spirits, and to place as a conquered people, under the surveillance of troops, the remains of these tribes on reservations selected by the President, and on such terms as the Government in its justice and mercy may vouchsafe to them."

To Colonel Wright he wrote June 18th, 1856, as follows:

." * * * I will, however, respectfully put you on your guard in reference to Leschi, Nelson, Kitsap, and Quiemuth from the Sound, and to suggest that no arrangement be made which will save their necks from the executioner. * * * *"

To Colonel Casey, Oct. 27th, 1856:

"The operations on the Sound have been, from the beginning, on the part of the Indians, those of murderers and outlaws—no tribe as such having broken into hostility—and they are, therefore, entitled to none of the rights of war. Yet, that great lenity has been shown them by the Territorial authorities, I presume that I could have no better witness than yourself."

This in response to a letter from the Colonel, under date of October 21st:

"Those whom you wish my assistance to take, delivered themselves up to Col Wright, made peace with him, and were promised protection.

"I would suggest that the better way would be to consider that we have been at war with these Indians, and now we are at peace."

These were amazing statements for the Governor to make as to the Indians in arms being outlaws, and were not true, as one can see by his own writing, at the time, advocating the policy "to do away with the reservations, *with the tribes now in arms."* But he persistently followed up this unrelenting policy to the very last day of his official life in the Territory.

Colonel Casey anl Colonel Wright were both trying to make peace with the Indians who were willing to lay down their arms, the one west, the other east of the the Cascade Mountains, and Wright had actually received Leschi's submision and had promised him protection.

Colonel Wright wrote from his camp on the Natchess, June 11th, 1856:

"On the evening of the 8th, two men came to me from the Chief Ow-hi, saying, that himself and other chiefs would come in on the next day. The man remained with us, and on the evening of the 9th, Ow-hi, Kam-i-ak-an and Te-i-as encamped on the opposite side of the river. After awhile Ow-hi and Te-i-as came over and we had a long talk about the war, its origin, etc. Ow-hi related the whole history of the Walla Walla Treaty, and concluded by saying that the war commenced from that moment; that the treaty was the cause of all the deaths by fighting since that time. Ow-hi is a very intelligent man. He speaks with great energy, is well acquainted with his subject, and his words carry conviction of truth to his hearers. * * * * I think everything bids fair for an early and satisfactory termination of this war."

"Rumors had reached me, some days previous, that Leschi, with a band of Nisqually Indians, was on this side of the mountains, and I was trying to communicate with him, when I found he had come in without any agency on my part. He came with Ow-hi and Te-i-as. He says he came over with about twenty warriors with their women and children. He is decidedly for peace. This man Leschi is connected with Ow-hi's people by marriage, and if peace is made, he is perfectly willing to go wherever I say—either to the Sound, or to remain with Ow-hi. I think he would prefer the latter and perhaps that will be the best disposition that could be made of him."

Governor Stevens persistently ignored Wright and pushed an expedition over the mountains into the country where these negotiations had taken place, but Colonel Shaw, whom Stevens had placed in command, had too much discretion to undertake to interfere, and passed on through the Yakima country to Walla Walla. Wright undoubtedly had orders to punish the volunteers if any such an attempt had been made.

In writing under date of August 17th, 1856, Colonel Wright uses this significant language:

"Governor Stevens has countermanded his requisition for two additional companies of volunteers, and those now in the field will be required forthwith to leave the country."

Other previous letters passing between Colonel Wright and General Wool, the commanding General, leave no doubt that as soon as the regulars could do so it was the intention to expel the volunteers by force from the Walla Walla country.

Prior to this the Colonel had written more in detail, steadfastly refusing the Governor's importunity to get possession of Leschi and other leaders of the Indians west of the Cascade Mountains.

July 25th, 1856, Colonel Wright wrote from At-ah-nam:

"I halted two days at Fort Natchess, at which place I was visited by a party of Nisqually Indians, who were temporarily living upon the upper waters of the Natchess. Eight of the principal men came in; the number of men, women and children in their camp is probably seventy. They are poor, having lost nearly all their horses and property when they crossed the mountains last winter. They are very anxious to return to the Sound, either to the reservation or any other point which may be decided on.

"At my camp on the Kittitas I left Nelson, Leschi and Kitsap, with a small party of Nisquallies. Leschi is the recognized chief of these people, including those on the Natchess. They are all desirous of returning to the Sound, provided they can do so in safety. With regard to the three named, I some time since received a letter from Governor Stevens, suggesting no terms should be granted them, but inasmuch as they came in and departed in security previous to that time, and appeared determined to be our friends, I would not take any harsh measures without having proof of their guilt."

Colonel Casey reported that three hundred Indians had given in their submission and had been sent to the reservations. Governor Stevens now took another course to coerce the military authorities into arresting

Leschi and delivering him over to his "Justice and Mercy," a phrase so often expressed by the Governor in his official letters. They knew perfectly well that it either meant the murder of these men or their incarceration, either of which as a matter of public policy as well as justice it was desirable to avoid. Later Colonel Casey wrote, Oct. 20th:

"Governor: For several weeks past there have been more than one hundred Indians, including women and children, encamped near this post. Your agents have taken no charge of them, and I understand decline doing so. I sent them to the reservation soon after they came in and was informed by Mr. Ford, your agent, several days after, that he had taken no charge of them and did not intend doing so. I received them again, in order to prevent any disturbance that might ensue from the strange conduct of your agents. * * * * Inasmuch as hostilities have ceased in this district, I do not consider that it is my province to take care of these Indians, and I respectfully request that you will relieve me from their responsibility. * * * *"

Governor Stevens promptly replied under same date:

"Although hostilities have for the present ceased on the Sound, yet in my judgment, the Indians at your post, most of whom have come from the east side of the mountains, are not in that condition of submission which makes it safe to incorporate them with the friendly Indians, nor will they be in that condition till the known murderers of that band are arrested for trial. * * * I have, therefore, to request your aid to assist me in apprehending Leschi, Quiemuth, Stahi, Nelson, and other murderers, and to keep them in custody awaiting warrant from the nearest magistrate, which being accomplished I will receive the remainder. * * *"

In October, 1856, Leschi came back near his old home and sent for Dr. Tolmie to meet him at a point near Fort Nisqually, which he did in company with Mr. Edward Huggins. What followed is related in the Doctor's own words, published soon after the event. I deem it best to rely on the accuracy of his statement rather than any of the many conflicting stories told.

Dr. Tolmie wrote:

"In the summer of 1856, Leschi, with the other chiefs made peace with Colonel Wright in command of the regulars in Yakima Valley, after which general pacification, and as the Indians phrase it, 'laying aside of guns and angry feelings' they lived for some time in friendly intercourse with the soldiers. In the fall of '56, the Nisquallies returned home and were placed on a reservation much more to their liking than that originally fixed upon.

"In October, Leschi came, and as I was the first white man he ventured to meet, he desired me to acquaint the Americans, that if they needed that assurance, he would cut off his right hand in proof of his intention never to fight them again. He expressed his willingness to surrender to Colonel Casey commanding at Fort Steilacoom, but that officer considered it most prudent that Leschi should, for a time, remain in the woods, as prejudice ran high against him. Soon after, tempted by a large reward, Sluggia entrapped Leschi by treacherous promises of complete reconciliation with the Olympia White Chiefs, and he was soon after imprisoned on the charge which has led to his condemnation."

The traitor "Sluggia" who betrayed him was a nephew of Leschi, and naturally would have his confidence. He was promised fifty blankets* if he would deliver Leschi into the hands of Stevens. Whether he received the promised reward or not I do not know, but that he finally received a reward is certain as he was killed by the hands of Yelm Jim (who is shown in the illustration), a friend of Leschi, and rolled over the bluff near where Leschi now lies buried.

---

*Office of Adjt. General, June 15th, 1856.—Capt. Ford: * * * It is necessary to procure a guide who knows the position of Leschi. If any of your Indians can be procured, promise fifty blankets to the man who will lead a party of soldiers to the camp.

(Signed)   JAMES TILTON, Adjt. General W. T. V.

By order of the Governor and Commander-in-Chief.

CHAPTER LVI.

The Two Trials of Leschi.

Leschi was betrayed on the 13th of November (1856), delivered at Steilacoom to Capt. Ford, who had charge of the reservation near by, on the 14th, and was taken to Olympia and delivered to Governor Stevens. The two men now again stood face to face, which had not occurred since that fateful day of December 26th, 1854. On that, or rather the following day, the reader who has followed this narrative will remember that Leschi first pleaded for a home, then threatened, and finally refused to sign a treaty that took his home from him and turned him out a wanderer without a spot where he could build a house or pasture his stock, or have a place to cultivate grain or vegetables, which for years had been his practice. The furrow in the field remained unfinished as it was on the evening of the 23d of October, 1855, when the two brothers took to the woods to avoid capture.

Since that fatal day, Stahi, the brother-in-law, had been killed in battle, and Quiemuth, Leschi's brother, brutally murdered in the Governor's office but a short time previous and the murderer not punished. Leschi had crossed the Governor's path and thwarted his aims as no man had dared to do, other than General Wool. Stevens' hatred toward the man was implacable.

It was not true that Leschi had waged a war of murder and rapine, as so often alleged by Governor Stevens in his official correspondence; it was not true that he had been treacherous and broken his promise made in the treaty, for he had made none; it was not true that Leschi had been the instigator of the war, as told over and over again by Stevens. Men intending to go on the war path, particularly Indians, are not likely to be quietly at home looking after their stock and have the plow running in the field until the evening of the day they flee from home. That was what Leschi and Quiemuth did. They were profoundly discontented with the turn affairs had taken and had canvassed their grievances a great deal, but had concluded that it was useless to contend. They knew the Indians could not succeed in the long run in a war with the American Government. All the Nisqually warriors said the same. "Then why did you go to war?" asked Mr. Mounts, the agent, who took charge of them when they returned. "We had just as well go to war and be killed as to be put off where we have no home and starve," came the answer. Mr. Daniel Mounts, who told the author his experience with these Indians, still lives* near the reservation. He is a steady, truthful man as all who know him will testify. He will verify this statement that it was sheer desperation that drove these Nisquallies into the war, because their homes had been taken from them and no suitable or adequate reservation allotted to them.

As mentioned, the two men stood face to face again. Both had been constantly in the public eye for over a year. Their acts had divided sentiment, and to an extent, parties. Stevens represented the Democratic party and had the partisan spirit of those days to back him, besides the patronage incident to the offices he held and distribution of funds so largely increased by the war, particularly under the Superintendency of Indian Affairs. "We are feeding 4000 Indians," Stevens wrote, but that did not tell how many contractors, petty agents and employees were feeding off the public crib. It had come to this, that if Leschi was right then Stevens was wrong; that if Leschi was proven guilty then Stevens would be vindicated, otherwise General Wool

---

*Mr. Mounts has recently died, and since this chapter was written.

would have his day in court. If Leschi and compatriots were not proven ruthless savages, murderers and criminals, what would become of all those official reports from Governor Stevens going forward with regularity to Washington? Leschi must be proven guilty or else Stevens would be discredited, and the contention of the regular army officers proven. As it was, the pressure had become so strong that Governor Stevens had been compelled to acquiesce and follow instructions from Washington, and give new reservations. Instead of 1280 acres of worthless land on the bluff, 18,600 acres had been set out for the Puyallup Indians alone under the Medicine Creek treaty. The Nisquallies had a new reservation allotted to them, precisely what Leschi had contended for from the first, including his home, but he was not allowed to enjoy it. He had fairly won these new reservations by his valor, but the irony of fate had decreed that while his people might enjoy the fruits of his suffering, he should not. Many who skulked and took no part in the war (like John Hiton and others), came forward to reap the benefits, while Leschi was thrown into prison to be tried for his life.

It was pathetic and should have moved the Governor's heart to pity, but it did not, and from his standpoint of vision, he could see nothing but the murderer staring him in the face; it was either that, or he, himself, was a ruined man, his party discredited, Wool vindicated, and the whole policy of the war he had himself proclaimed, condemned.

With indecent haste an express was sent to intercept Judge Chevoweth, whose term of court had just ended, to request him to convene a special term for the express purpose of immediately trying Leschi for the murder of Colonel A. B. Moses. Moses had been with the command of Captains Maloney and Hays in the Yakima country and was detailed, or volunteered, to accompany the express riders Tidd and Bradly coming ahead of the returning column.

To the surprise of everybody, Chenoweth did as the Governor requested, and a special grand jury was summoned to indict and a special petit jury to try him. On the 17th day of November (1856), this special court was convened at Steilacoom to try what was thought by many to be a foregone case—a mere matter of form.

We have to chronicle with regret the destruction by fire of the records of that trial* and are thrown upon our memory in part, bits of published notices in the newspapers of the day, and references in the Supreme Court records preserved.

It fell to the lot of the author to be drawn as one of the petit jurors that tried his case following an indictment quickly drawn and almost as quickly passed upon. This was my first experience as a juror and curiously enough my last case to try though now nearly fifty years have elapsed. The case had been tried outside the court and the prisoner found guilty. For months and months Leschi's name had been a household word. With the partisans of Stevens the story of his guilt had been told on every street corner, in every hotel or before the camp fire, until it was generally believed he was the monster murderer he was charged to be. There could be no fair trial in such an atmosphere of prejudice and false accusation told and retold a thousand times.

A painful duty devolves on me here to record the now unquestioned fact of the perjury of the chief, and, in fact, the only witness, A. B. Rabbeson. He was a too willing witness to be truthful, and had not been on the witness stand five minutes until the guilt of perjury showed so plainly reflected in his eyes that no one really believed he was telling the truth. His testimony on the second trial in Olympia, as published, is substan-

---

*The court and county records of Pierce County were burned April 5, 1859.

tially the same as I remember it on the first, at Steilacoom, except he was more guarded in his statements
and dwelt upon the question of time his party spent on
the prairie. This was important, as the reader will see,
as giving Leschi more time to get into the swamp ahead
of Moses and his companions.

By examination of the rough map made, by Lieutenant
Kautz, afterwards General in the Union army, and here
reproduced in all its crudeness, the reader will see the
utter impossibility of Leschi being at the two places
that Rabbeson testified he saw him. Lieutenant Kautz
made a careful survey of the only possible routes the
parties could traverse. By this it is shown that Leschi
would have had to travel twice as far to intersect the
road traveled by the express party and by a rough and
difficult trail, while the party would have the direct,
open wagon road to make the distance of 68 chains,
and by the trail Leschi would have had to travel 104½
chains.

The truth was that Leschi was not in either place
that Rabbeson swore he saw him, but was miles away,
as he said he was in his last words on the scaffold.

The unfortunate circumstance about this map was
that it was not ready before the trials were ended, the
conviction had, and the case gone to the Supreme Court
where evidence could not be received. The effort made
at so late a day was with a view of obtaining a pardon
from Governor McMullen, who had succeeded Governor
Stevens, if that were possible, otherwise to make an
appeal to the President.

Some years ago, while in a reminiscent mood and while
my memory was fresher, and be it said, more vigorous,
I wrote a short account of some incidents of the trial
and I hope the reader will pardon me for incorporating
these words as a part of my present narrative.

I was one of the jurymen to try him. William M.
Kincaid, familiarly known as "Father Kincaid," the

father of the numerous families of that name, of Sumner, was another. Albert Balch, of Steilacoom, was one, Sherwood Bonney was another;* also I. H. Wright. I cannot recall the names of any others of that historic jury. The secret ballot of the petit jury developed eight for conviction and four against. The balloting went on—eight-four, eight-four, eight-four—with pallor on the cheeks of more than one juror, for it was well known what the feeling on the outside was for vengeance. Finally, from ballots, the jurors passed to words and hot words at that—almost to the point of intimidation. That scene I shall never forget. The judge had charged that if the deed was done as an act of war the prisoner could not be held answerable to the civil law. Four of us so held and refused to convict. We came into court and asked to be discharged as no agreement could be reached, and were sent back again with instruction we *must* agree. What a travesty this upon justice, to pen up men and try to make them perjure themselves to agree. Two of the parties finally gave way leaving Father Kincaid and myself as the forlorn hope. It would have made no difference, though, whether another remained firm or not. Father Kincaid said, "I never will vote to condemn that man," and he never did. He and I stood out to the last against conviction and Leschi was saved for the time being. The jury was discharged and Leschi remanded into the custody of the military authorities at Fort Steilacoom for safe keeping until a regular term of court convened.

It is due to that grand old man, William M. Kincaid, that I should pay a tribute to his sterling character. Then, far past the middle age, he was the oldest man on the jury. He was at his best, mentally. A stout churchman and devout Christian he was ever liberal and had no contentions with his neighbors, either as to religious or political opinions or passing incidents. It could be

*Now 93 years old.

truly said that Father Kincaid did not have an enemy
in the whole settlement. He was not an aggressive
man, but one of deep convictions and nothing on earth
could swerve him from the path of duty as he saw it.
Although I had been close to him and thought I knew
him well, that night in the jury room dispelled the
illusion. . He was as firm as the rocks at the bottom of
the sea. He finally ceased to contend in words and sat
with head bowed as if in prayer, his only response a
slow shake of the head to the importunities of other
jurors. Would that there were many more such men in
the world as Father Kincaid, who many years since
went to his long home.

The judge, in his charge to the jury, had gone further.
He not only told us if the deed of killing Moses was as
an act of war the prisoner could not be held, but he also
indicated to us what constituted a condition of war.
I cannot, of course, pretend to quote his words, though
the incident has been so often discussed, his meaning
appears vivid in my mind almost as if his words had
been spoken but yesterday.

A declaration of war, he said. consisted of acts as well
as words, and that in Indian warfare a formal declaration was never expected and that with civilized nations
often omitted; that the fact of war between nations
often preceded a formal declaration, and that acts of
war in such cases shielded the person from individual
responsibility, and that if we found, at the time Moses
was killed, a state of war existed between our Government and the Indian tribes as such, then the prisoner
could not be held; otherwise, even if proven only an
accessory, we must bring in a verdict of guilty.

The argument in the jury room was that the Indians
were at war against our Government and that the United
States Government acknowledged the fact by sending
organized troops against them; that, taking the case
of the very man on trial before them, he and his people

had committed no depredations or acts of war prior to
the date acting Governor Mason had sent the Eaton
Rangers to make war on them; that these troops had
proceeded to his very home to forcibly carry him away,
and that from them he narrowly escaped capture by
hastily taking to the dense forests and secreting himself; that then and not until then, he fled and went to
Green River and was followed by this same troop of
nineteen armed men organized as volunteers; that four
days before the killing of Moses, one of these (McAllister), with arms on his person had been killed; that
three days previous the people on White River had been
massacred; that Capt. Hewitt's company of volunteers
had been organized prior to this and was on the point
of going into their country if not for war, then what
for? that Moses himself belonged with the military
arm of the Government and was on duty connected with
that service; that while it was true that Moses was with
the company that was making war on the Yakimas, yet
no such nice distinction ought to lie as it was a fair
presumption that his arm of the service was ready to
make war on the tribes west of the mountains as well.

The contention, on the other hand, was that Leschi
and those with him did not represent the tribe; that
they were marauders and nothing more. Governor
Stevens harped upon this in his official correspondence,
that the tribes, "as such," had not gone to war and
hence those engaged in hostilities were not entitled to
the rights of war. Stevens had grouped nine bands of
Indians under the Medicine Creek Treaty, and, in his
mind, called the group one tribe or nation, who, "as
such," had not gone to the war. More than half of the
Indians thus grouped by Governor Stevens in a purely
arbitrary manner to suit his convenience, did not go into
the war, but it can be said this fact should have no binding effect on tribes that did not enter into treaties "as
such" tribe. In fact, the treaty was made with indi-

viduals, members of the tribes, but in no wise representatives of the respective tribes. It was this point
insisted upon in season and out of season by the Governor and his partisans, as well as by many others who
were not his followers, that confused the public mind.

March 18th, 1857, Leschi was again placed on trial.
Subsequent to his first trial at Steilacoom, November
17th, 1856, the Territory had been redistricted to conform to a law of Congress restricting the holding of
court to three points in the Territory. This deprived
Steilacoom and Seattle of courts and compelled the
citizens of each to go to Olympia, which had been
selected as the one place in which court was to be held
in the Second Judicial District.

This was an unfortunate event for Leschi, transferring
the trial to Olympia, where the influence of the Governor had fanned the prejudice against the Indians
from the start, and where his official patronage was so
potent as to make certain an unbiased jury could not
be obtained or a fair trial had.

As on the former trial, Rabbeson swore that he left
Leschi on the prairie where his party had first encountered the Indians after several minutes talk with them;
that after riding three-fourths of a mile they struck
the swamp and were fired upon; that he took one of the
Indians who came out to be Quiemuth, but Leschi was
the one that fired at him; that the road traveled by his
party was three-quarters of a mile to the swamp *and
the trail three or four hundred yards*. If this had been
true Leschi could have left the prairie, taken the trail
and gotten into ambush in time to have fired on them,
as described. How utterly false his testimony was is
shown by the survey and map made by Lieutenant
Kautz, giving the distances in each case and reversing
the statement; that Leschi would have had to travel
104½ chains, while Rabbeson and his party traveled

but 68 chains, and that by the wagon road, while the other way was by a crooked, obstructed Indian trail.

The facts were the Indians had detailed seven men to keep watch in the swamp for the Eaton Rangers—a rear guard—and it was this party that killed Miles and Moses and not that met by Rabbeson on the prairie.

The unexpected ruling of Judge Lander who presided at the second trial, paved the way for conviction. The newspaper report, published at the time, shows the bent of the judge's mind:

"As no special instructions were asked for by counsel on either side, he dwelt principally upon what the Territory was required to prove before the jury could convict; that under our statute the jury must believe the defendant was present aiding and abetting, assisting or encouraging the commission of the offense charged.

"By our statute the distinction between principals and accessories was done away. All those present tendering assistance became principals, and if the jury believed, from the testimony, that Leschi was present so assisting, they must find him guilty. He also charged as to reasonable doubt."

The jury brought in the following verdict: "We, the jury, find the defendant guilty as charged in the indictment, and that he suffer death," whereupon, the prisoner was sentenced to be hung at Steilacoom June 10th, 1857.

Why no special instructions were asked for has never been explained, or why the survey and map made by Lieutenant Kautz were not in readiness to be offered in evidence did not transpire.

An application for a new trial was filed on the 20th, offering to provide this new testimony.

This was denied; an appeal to the Supreme Court taken, which could not be heard until the December term, and Leschi was again remanded to prison at Fort Steilacoom.

CHAPTER LVII.

Hearing Before Supreme Court.

Nine months, lacking a day, elapsed from the time the appeal taken from the findings of the trial court, the second trial of Leschi for the murder of A. B. Moses, before the case was determined in the Supreme Court. Chief Justice Lander being absent from the Territory, the two remaining Justices, McFadden and Chenoweth, constituted the court for the hearing of the case.

The opinion was rendered by acting Chief Justice McFadden and consisted of nearly seven thousand words, delivered December 17th, 1857, the following day after the close of the case. It was evident this elaborate opinion had been prepared in advance of the hearing.

As an introduction, Justice McFadden said:

"This case comes before us on a writ of error to the 2d Judicial District. The prisoner has occupied a position of influence as one of a band of Indians, who, in connection with other tribes, sacrificed the lives of so many of our citizens in the war, so cruelly waged against our people on the waters of Puget Sound.

"It speaks volumes for our people, that, notwithstanding the spirit of indignation and revenge so natural to the human heart, incited by the ruthless massacre of their families, that in the trial of the accused, deliberate impartiality was manifested at every stage of the proceedings.

"In the discussion of grave questions presented involving the life and personal liberty of the accused, we are anxious that none other than considerations of public justice, with due regard for the rights of the accused under the law, should influence us in the conclusions to which we may arrive. Whether the accused be guilty or innocent, it is to be regretted, for the sake of the accused as well as the future peace of the Territory, that a more summary mode of trial, one in accordance with the practice of the Government, and in perfect consonance with the rules of international law, had not been adopted."

It would be presumption in a citizen not versed in the law to criticise the legal conclusion of the highest judicial tribunal of his commonwealth, however much he might disagree with the court, but, when that body leaves the judicial consideration and branches off into political and speculative discourses, the lay members of the community not only have the right to protest but also may feel themselves entitled to criticise such supra judicial special pleading.

When the Honorable Court at the outset of the case notes that "the prisoner has occupied a position of influence as one of a band of Indians, who, in connection with other tribes, sacrificed the lives of so many of our citizens in the war," we are led to inquire what has that to do with the law in the case? The paragraph quoted shows he did not approach the subject with an unbiased mind, but when he warms up to his subject, "it is to be regretted for the sake of the accused" (why the accused?), "as well as the future peace of the Territory, that a more summary mode of trial, one in accordance with the practice of the Government and in perfect consonance with the rules of international law had not been adopted," we are led to inquire, since when did "the rules of international law" warrant "a more summary trial" to shoot or hang prisoners of war, for that was what his words meant if they meant anything.

It was the boast of the friends of Governor Stevens that Justice McFadden was in full sympathy with his policy of declaring martial law, which his words here fully bear out, and that summary punishment should be meted to the class to which Leschi belonged.

From the current literature of the day, as shown in the columns of the Governor's mouthpiece, the Pioneer and Democrat, the only paper published in the Territory at

that time, one would be led to believe there had been
conditions prevailing in Thurston County where men
and women were being shot down by the "ruthless savages" at every opportunity, and that a state of affairs
existed calling for the utmost exertion to meet the foe
and great caution to avoid the sacrifice of innocent women and children or unarmed citizens. No
such condition had existed. But one citizen had been
killed or in anyway molested in all of Thurston County;
one barn burned in that county in all the war from beginning to end, and we might say *at* the end, for
when White was killed and Glasgow's barn burned the
decisive battle with the regulars on White River had
been fought, the Indian forces scattered and discouraged.
The band that committed this depredation had withdrawn from the theater of war and never rejoined the
force again. When Leschi was first put on trial, the war
was ended, the troops disbanded, the Indians on their
new and magnificent reservations, the farmers were at
their homes, and peace reigned supreme over the land.

On the 18th of December (1857), Leschi was again
brought before the court for sentence.

The following note from that industrious seeker after
truth, George H. Himes, has given us an insight of the
closing scene.

"The last words of the Nisqually Chief Leschi in court.

"Upon my request in January, 1904, Col. B. F. Shaw related to me the circumstances concerning the sentence of
death passed by the Court of Washington Territory in
Olympia, in 1857, upon the Indian Chief Leschi, in substance as follows: (Note by George H. Himes.)

"By order of the Court it became my disagreeable duty to
interpret the sentence to Leschi, and I told him that the
Judges would listen to anything he desired to say. Leschi
then arose and said:

"I do not see that there is any use of saying anything. My
attorney has said all he could for me. I do not know anything about your laws. I have supposed that the killing of

armed men in war time was not murder; if it was, the
soldiers who killed Indians were guilty of murder, too. The
Indians did not keep in order like the soldiers, and, therefore, could not fight in bodies like them, but had to resort
to ambush and seek the cover of trees, logs and everything
that would hide them from the bullets. This was their mode
of fighting, and they knew no other way. Dr. Tolmie and
Quatlith, the red-headed chief, warned me against allowing
my anger to get the best of my good sense, as I could not
gain anything by going to war with the United States, but
would be beaten and humbled, and would have to hide like
a wild beast in the end. I did not take this good advice, but
nursed my anger until it became a furious passion, which led
me like a false Ta-man-u-ous. I went to war because I believed that the Indians had been wronged by the white men,
and did everything in my power to beat the Boston soldier,
but for lack of numbers, supplies and ammunition I have
failed. I deny that I had any part in killing Miles and
Moses. I heard that a company of soldiers were coming out
of Steilacoom, and determined to lay in ambush for it; but
did not expect to catch anyone coming from the other way.
I did not see Miles or Moses before or after they were dead,
but was told by the Indians that they had been killed. As
God sees me, this is the truth.

"Leschi then made the sign of the cross, and said in his
own Nisqually tongue,

"Ta-te mono, Ta-te lem-mas, Ta-te ha-le-hach, tu-ul-li-as-
sist-ah, which, being interpreted, means, There is the
Father, this is the Son, this is the Holy Ghost; these are
all one and the same, Amen.

"Quatlith was the Indian name for Col. Shaw."

The court then again pronounced sentence of death
upon the prisoner and the day of execution fixed for Friday, the 22d of January, 1858, being the earliest per-
missible date under the law of the Territory.

We will see, however, in the chapter following, that
this mandate of the Supreme Court was not carried out;
that Leschi was not hung on the date named and that a
new lease of life was vouchsafed to him.

CHAPTER LVIII.

Defeat of the Execution of Leschi.

A retrospective review will aid the reader to understand the narrative of events to be recited in this chapter. One might almost say the courts of the Territory had been denominated, at least in some counties, by unprincipled attorneys, who fattened on defending crime, not hesitating to procure subornation to accomplish their ends. In Pierce County this way to defeat the ends of justice had been made easy by the injection into the settlements of a class of discharged soldiers and Hudson Bay servants, many of whom were ignorant and some criminal in their tendencies. Previous to the time of which I write there had been scandalous miscarriage of justice in some cases by false swearing; in others by bribery of jurors (oftentimes only with whisky, and sometimes by both money and whisky). Many reputable citizens of Steilacoom were smarting from losses incurred through such means, almost always accomplished by one certain attorney, and at most, by three whom it came to be known would clear any criminal or defeat any suit however meritorious, for a cash fee in hand paid. Following this condition of affairs had come the proceedings of the Governor in breaking up the courts by the military arm of the Territory, sweeping the last vestige of civil jurisprudence from under the community. No breath of suspicion had attached to the judges of the courts, who were laboring assiduously to bring out better conditions, and, in fact, it was believed the worst had passed and that in the future we might look to our courts with more confidence of speedy justice.

When, on the evening of the 22d of January (1858), it bécame known the mandates of the Supreme Court had been defeated by a trick, the indignation of citizens generally was unbounded, and found vent in public meetings, resolutions, hot personal controversies and recriminations.

The reader will be well repair to peruse the story as told in the proceedings of a public meeting held in Olympia, on the evening of the day of this event.

MASS MEETING OF THE CITIZENS OF WASHINGTON TERRITORY HELD AT OLYMPIA.

"On Friday evening, the 22d inst., about two hundred citizens of Olympia and other parts of Washington Territory assembled **en masse** at the Public School house in said town, for the purpose of taking into consideration the unprecedented proceedings of the civil authorities and the military stationed at Fort Steilacoom, in relation to the culprit, Leschi, who was to have been hanged in the aforesaid county on the 22d inst., between the hours of 10 o'clock A. M. and 2 o'clock P. M.

Hon. Lewis Van Vleet, Chairman; J. T. Turner, Secretary.

"James M. Hunt was called on to state the object of the meeting. In response, Mr. Hunt said the object was to investigate the cause of the non-fulfilment of the sentence of the court in the case of the murderer Leschi, who was under sentence of death by the highest tribunal of the Territory, but through the high handed outrage prepetrated by the civil authorities of Pierce County, the connivance of the military officers at Fort Steilacoom, and particularly the disgraceful conduct of one James Bachelder, U. S. Commissioner, he, the culprit, Leschi, had escaped the ends of justice. * * * *"

"Committee appointed to report at an adjourned meeting on Tuesday.

"Hon. C. H. Mason addressed the meeting as follows: That upon his arrival at Steilacoom and before reaching the garrison, to which place he immediately repaired, he was met by a messenger who informed him that the sheriff of Pierce County was in custody of the commanding officer at Fort Steilacoom; whereupon, he used all dispatch in reaching the quarters of Col. Casey, when, upon finding that officer, the following conversation took place:

"Colonel, I understand that the sheriff of Pierce County is under arrest, and that by your order?

"To which he replied, "He is not, sir.

"May I ask you, sir, if it is true that you refused to furnish a guard to be present at the hanging of Leschi?

"Answer—It is not true! On the contrary I ordered a guard of twenty men to hold themselves in readiness to assist the sheriff, if demanded, and that he stood ready to surrender the prisoner, Leschi, upon demand of the proper officer with a legal warrant from the court.

"Can you give any information of his (the sheriff's) whereabouts?

"Answer—I cannot.

"Are you cognizant of the fact that the sheriff is under arrest by any authority whatever?

"Answer—I have been informed that he was arrested by civil process.

"Speech of Governor McMullen:

"Fellow Citizens: The majesty of the highest courts of our Territory has this day been trodden under foot, by the underground machinations of the civil authorities of Pierce County, and, if what I have learned to be true, also by the officers of the United States Army at Fort Steilacoom. The acts of these officers, both civil and military, fellow citizens, call for our unmitigated and unqualified condemnation. Active steps should be by you taken to ferret out and sift clearly, the causes that have led to this singular and extraordinary usurpation of authority, in preventing the ends of justice being meted out to one who has been sentenced to death by the Supreme Tribunal of our Territory. I would suggest, gentlemen, that the Legislative Assembly now in session, be requested to take such steps and adopt such measures as the exigencies of the case would seem to de-

mand at their hands, in bringing this unparalleled procedure to the notice of the proper department at Washington
City. Fellow citizens, it is your duty to see that the laws
of your country and the immutable doctrines of your sacred
constitution are upheld and sustained at every hazard. In
my official capacity as Executive of your Territory I shall
spare no means that I may be able to bring to bear in presenting this affair in an unprejudiced and impartial light to
the Secretary of War. *   *   *   *"

"Report of the committee appointed to investigate the proceedings at Steilacoom on Friday, January 22d, 1858, and report resolutions expressing the sense of the citizens on the
subject.

"The committee deem it their duty to state as a basis for
resolutions, the following facts: An indictment was found
against the Indian Chief Leschi, by a grand jury of Pierce
County, in November, 1856, charging him with the murder
of Col. A. B. Moses. At a special term of the District Court
in Pierce County he was tried on that indictment, having the
benefit of the best counsel. At that first trial the jury failed
to agree upon a verdict; consequently, he was tried again at
the March term, 1857, of the District Court for the Second
Judicial District, when he was found guilty of murder, and
accordingly sentenced to be hung on the 10th day of June
last. His case was then taken before the Supreme Court of
our Territory on a writ of error. Before the last named
court his case was argued elaborately, and he was again
sentenced to be hung at Steilacoom on the 22d day of January.

"A warrant was issued and delivered to the sheriff of
Pierce County commanding him to cause the execution to
be had. Between the time when the sentence was pronounced and the day fixed for its execution, the counsel and
the volunteer friends of Leschi made the most extraordinary efforts to secure his pardon or respite from our Governor. The counsel appeared before the Governor near the
place of confinement and re-argued the case, presenting its
favorable features with the utmost latitude, when no one
was present to uphold or defend the action of the courts.
Dr. Wm. F. Tolmie, the chief factor of the Hudson Bay

Company and Agent of the Puget Sound Agricultural Company at Nisqually, in Pierce County, addressed the Governor in an elaborate and powerful appeal in Leschi's behalf, in which he exhibits an ability in artful cunning and ingenious special pleading, worthy the representatives of an unlawful, illegitmate, foreign corporation. He goes entirely beyond the bounds of truth in his statements. His whole communication is characterized by a stubborn and selfish disregard for the laws of our Territory and the well being of our community.

"Lieutenant August Kautz of the U. S. Army at Steilacoom Barracks went to the ground where Leschi committed the murder, made a laborious survey of it, and, as we believe, by assuming the testimony of the material witness in the case to be different from what it is, made a cautious and cunning affidavit that it was impossible for Leschi to have been present when the murder was committed.

"Lieutenant Colonel Casey, of the army also, in his official capacity, addressed a letter to the Governor praying a respite for Leschi.

"Colonel Wright, another officer of the army, was appealed to and joined Tolmie and Casey in Leschi's behalf. Governor McMullen laid aside rules generally followed by an executive officer, and went to the military post at Steilacoom to give the prisoner more than a fair hearing. There he gave a patient audience to all the appeals of Tolmie, Casey, Kautz and all others who joined them, and considered them calmly and deliberately, as this committee believes, with an earnest desire to do justice in the premises and give the Indian the benefit of all doubts in his favor. When he had done this he came to Olympia, and announced his determination not to interfere with the sentence of the law. On Friday, the 22d inst., at 2 o'clock A. M., the Governor received the following letter from the sheriff of Pierce County:

"Steilacoom, W. T., Jan. 21st, 1858.

"Sir: This afternoon I called upon Colonel Casey, commanding Fort Steilacoom, with the request that he would furnish me with a sufficient guard to maintain the supremacy of the law in the execution of Leschi. He did not positively refuse, but informed me that if he was formally requested by some persons having authority he might or might not,' that he entirely washed his hands of the whole affair—that he considered it as murder at best,—that he and all the officers of the army entertained the same opinion. He also positively forbid me having him executed upon the Government Reserve. (So called.)

"I would request, if in your superior judgment, you deem it necessary, as I do, that a requisition or request to Colonel Casey, for a sufficient guard to protect me, be forwarded by the bearer of this communication.

"GEORGE WILLIAMS,

"Sheriff Pierce County, W. T.

"To His Excellency, Fayette McMullen, Governor, W. T:

"Upon the receipt of this letter Governor McMullen addressed a letter to Colonel Casey, desiring him to furnish the guard. Between the hours of 10 and 12 o'clock on Friday, the sheriff, George Williams, and his deputy and executioner, C. McDaniel, were arrested by Lieut. McKibben of the army, and Fred Kautz, the brother of Lieut. Kautz, upon a warrant issued by J. M. Bachelder, a U. S. Commissioner, and the sutler at the military post at Steilacoom. They, Williams and McDaniel, were taken to the town of Steilacoom, a mile or two distant from the post, where the sheriff remained until after the hour of 2 o'clock, which was the limit of time fixed for the execution. When Williams was in Steilacoom, and, as he said, under arrest, Secretary Mason requested Mr. Sealy to get the Death Warrant from him. Mr. Sealy proceeded to Steilacoom and demanded the paper. Williams refused to give it up 'without an order,' as he said. Mr. Sealy then asked to know by what authority he was detained there. Lieut. McKibben answered that Williams was under arrest and in his charge. Mr. Sealy then attempted to take Williams by force with a view of conveying him to the place where his duty required him to be. Lieut. McKibben, Dr. J. B. Webber and others interfered, and prevented Sealy from executing his design. Chas. McDaniel, the deputy sheriff and executioner, said he would not regard the arrest and demanded of Williams the authority (which was the Death Warrant of Leschi), that he might proceed with his duty. Williams refused to give him the paper.

"It is the fixed conviction of two truthful and reliable men who witnessed this affair that Williams remained under arrest willingly, and did not desire to be released. In consequence of this extraordinary and unprecedented conduct, the Indian Leschi was not executed in obedience to the sentence of the law.

"In addition to the above cited facts, the committee have gathered sufficient information to induce them to believe that this disgraceful scheme to prevent the execution of the law was concocted and carried out in the following manner:

"Frank Clark, an attorney at law, and one of the counsel for Leschi, procured an Indian to make an affidavit before J. M. Bachelder, the United States Commissioner, charging George Williams, the sheriff, and C. McDaniel, the executioner, with selling intoxicating liquor to Indians, in order to justify the infamous plot he was about to put into execution. We believe this, because he requested Dr. Webber and S. McCaw, Esq., to act as deputy marshals on the morning of that day, saying there were two persons to be arrested and he wanted it to be attended to; and because he offered to bet $100 on two different occasions that Leschi would not be hung on Friday.

"Bachelder, Williams, Fred Kautz and McKibben were cognizant of the plot. Our reason for this belief is the conduct of these individuals on that day.

"Entertaining these views, and with the foregoing facts before us, we would respectfully recommend the adoption of the following resolutions:

"Resolved, That we believe it is the duty of all good citizens to condemn publicly all outrages, and particularly is it the duty of everyone to publicly and privately denounce and condemn the disgraceful and disorganizing transaction at Steilacoom.

"Resolved, That the whole course of conduct exhibited by Dr. W. F. Tolmie in this affair has been a voluntary and unjustifiable attempt to interfere with the execution of the

laws of our Territory, with the bona fide citizens of which
he has no interest, sympathy or affiliation whatever, and
that his conduct merits and should receive the general condemnation of our whole people.

"Resolved, That we deem the conduct of Lieut. Col.
Casey, Lieut. Kautz, and all other officers of the United
States army, who have in this affair attempted to arrest or
interfere with the execution of the laws of the land, as entirely outside the line of duty, unbecoming public officers,
and calculated to bring disgrace upon our army and im-
measureable difficulties upon our people. Therefore, we do
condemn in the most unqualified terms all such conduct,
and earnestly hope the officers who are guilty of it may be
removed from our midst as soon as possible.

"Resolved, That such conduct on the part of officers
of the United States army exhibits a most unnatural and
unreasonable sympathy for the Indian, who was known to
have been engaged in the fiendish massacre of helpless
women and children on White River in the fall of 1855, and
that it is considered by this community good and sufficient
cause for their immediate removal from the Territory and
dismissal from the army.

"Resolved, That it is difficult and almost impossible to
find language sufficiently strong to express the feelings of
indignation entertained by this community toward George
Williams, the sheriff of Pierce County; J. M. Bachelder, the
United States Commissioner, and Frank Clark, the attorney
of the Indian Leschi. Their disgraceful acts on Friday last
were alike dishonest, disreputable and infamous.

"Resolved, That Fred Kautz and Lieut. McKibben, in
acting as the tools in the hands of dishonest officers, and
being used by them to carry out the most disgraceful violation of the law, have disgraced themselves and merit the
severest condemnation of the community.

"Resolved, That it would be unjust and unwise for this
meeting to adjourn without commending in the highest
manner the course of Capt. M. Maloney throughout this
whole affair, and we do therefore admire and highly esteem
his course of conduct.

"Resolved, That this meeting agrees most cordially with the sentiment expressed in the resolution adopted by a public meeting held at Steilacoom on the 22d inst., and we do hereby tender to those citizens engaged in that meeting our sympathy, and promise them a hearty and earnest co-operation in any attempt to bring to justice the perpetrators of this outrage.

"Resolved, That the publishers of the Pioneer and Democrat be requested to publish these proceedings.

"H. J. G. MAXON, Chairman."

It will be noticed that the chairman of this committee was the self-same H. J. G. Maxon, "who was known to have been engaged in the fiendish massacre of helpless women and children," the difference being that the location was on the Michel River and the number twice as great as the white people massacred by the Indians.

A like indignation meeting was held at Steilacoom on the evening of the same day, in which resolutions of like import were adopted, denouncing the act in most pronounced language and but slightly less offensively personal, but omitting any reference to the participation of the Indian Leschi in the massacre of women and children during the fall of 1855, for which he was not on trial, and in which the participants in the meeting did not believe he was guilty. In fact, the most of the citizens participating had, in no measured terms, denounced the persecution of Leschi, the declaration of martial law and forcible breaking up of our courts by the Territorial military authority under Governor Stevens, and most of them believed he was not guilty of the crime for which he was about to be executed, but the better element of the community had become tired of the persistent disregard of the law, which in this case was in great part by this disreputable and irresponsible set already mentioned.

I joined in those resolutions, and have always regretted that the name of Dr. W. F. Tolmie was included in the list of those condemned and denounced, for there is not the least doubt but what he did was from motives of pure humanity, if indeed he was concerned in the conspiracy at all.

The citizens had been scourged beyond description by the total disregard of law in their midst, and the prostitution of the machinery of the courts for the purpose of shielding criminals by some of the parties concerned in this outrage, and it had come to be believed that the time had arrived when such acts should no longer be tolerated, even if one innocent person should be sacrificed, for there had sprung up a dangerous coterie under the leadership of these parties that needed restraint in the interest of all.

One amusing aspect of the Olympia resolutions so vociferously calling for the enforcement of the law and denouncing the "disgraceful and disorganizing transaction" at Steilacoom, was that the meeting was made up in great part by the very men who had supported Governor Stevens in his "outrages" of trampling the law under foot, and who lauded the Governor to the skies for so doing.

CHAPTER LIX.

The Other Side.

To make the history of this transaction complete we must hear from the other side, first by a part of the very long letter from Frank Clark, the man, to my mind, who was responsible for the arrest of the sheriff and consequent defeat of the execution of Leschi, and Dr. William F. Tolmie, Chief Factor of the Puget Sound Agricultural Company at Nisqually, who had, like Clark, been bitterly denounced in the resolutions for his active efforts to save Leschi.

Clark was a man of bright intellect, with an active, fertile brain, but unscrupulous, and had become a terror to law-abiding citizens and a protector of criminals. He was so much feared by many well intending people that rather than incur his disfavor they would suffer a wrong to go unnoticed. But this time he had counted without his hosts. The outburst of denunciation was so general and so violent in the town (Steilacoom) where he lived, that for the first time I ever knew him to do so he felt it incumbent to plead in a public manner for justification of his conduct, which he did in a letter addressed "To the Citizens of Washington Territory," published in the *Truth Teller,* Feb. 3d, 1858, two numbers of which were issued for gratuitous distribution by the parties arraigned before the bar of public opinion, as outlined in preceding chapters:

"In placing myself before you in this communication," he wrote, "I would not be thought as influenced by considerations altogether selfish.

"The issue of the Pioneer and Democrat of the 29th ult. has just been placed in my hands. I there behold the names of good, truthful, honest men—men of whose friendship I feel proud—presented to you and to the world, as having been guilty of an act that reflects dishonor upon them. To them in the course of this article I shall refer.

"For myself, I shall take occasion to say that, in my judgment, no man can be dishonored but by his own acts.

"That time may develop to you every act of mine in the defense of the Indian Leschi, or that could in anywise affect his fate, together with my motives for the act, is my earnest hope.

"That if it does, I will then stand in your estimation as my conscience now places me—libelled and slandered for having faithfully discharged my duty to my country and my client, I know. Let us examine and see how the record stands:

"Leschi was indicted for the murder of A. Benton Moses. Moses was killed the day after the engagement between Captain Eaton's company with the hostiles,* and in the immediate vicinity of the encounter—was himself at the time among the force raised for service against the Indians. Of these facts I cannot be mistaken. When young McAllister came in from the Puyallup and brought intelligence of his gallant father's treacherous murder, that Connell was slain, and that Captain Eaton's company was then surrounded by a large force of savages, I immediately, with some eight others (all who could prepare themselves in time to go to the relief of Captain Eaton that evening), started for the place pointed out by young McAllister, where Eaton's party were surrounded. We proceeded some six or eight miles on our way, when we met Captain Eaton and company returning. We came back with them. The day following Dr. Webber and myself, at the request of Colonel Simmons, proceeded to the mouth of the Puyallup to endeavor to get the Indians, who were reported to be at that point, to come in. On our return we met Tidd at the house of Mr. Tallentire, and were informed of the death of Moses and Miles. We were also informed by him that Captain Maloney's command was returning, and would probably have an en-

---

*Clark is mistaken here as to dates. The Eaton Rangers were surrounded by the Indians on the 27th and escaped on the 28th, while Moses was not killed until the 31st of October.

gagement with the Indians in the vicinity of White River. Upon the receipt of this intelligence our people organized a company, and on the following day (Captain Wallace commanding) started to form a junction with Captain Maloney's command. I accompanied, and was the first who saw the corpse of Moses." * * *

Here follows a description of the horrors of the scene, the recovery of the bodies, and the natural indignation that would follow, not pertinent to this inquiry.

"With my knowledge of the facts, I am not surprised that upwards of seven hundred of our citizens signed a remonstrance against the extension of executive clemency to the Indian Leschi.

"And yet I know them to be generous, chivalrous and brave. But I know that a large majority of the signatures to that paper were placed there under a misunderstanding of the facts, and could not have been procured had the facts been properly understood. For instance, the fact is not generally understood by our people that the Indians entered into a truce with a high military authority. Yet such is the case. In the summer or fall of 1856 Leschi, with other Indians, laid down their arms to Colonel Wright and received from him assurance of protection against all harm for the part they had taken in the late war. Now, that the death of Moses was an incident of the war, I hardly think will be disputed. That the Indian and his people adhered to the conditions of the truce, and have not been guilty of its breach, history must record. I understand that some gentlemen deny that Colonel Wright had the authority, and that it is the generally received impression with our people that Colonel Wright could not legally make any such stipulations, and that the Government is therefore not bound by his acts in that behalf.

"But, let me tell you, he had that right, and upon that point there is no conflict of authorities. Vottel, Gratius, Ruthenforth, and all the elementary writers recognize the right of a subordinate commander to make a partial truce.

"Chancellor Kent asserts the same doctrine, and in speaking of truces says: 'These conventions rest upon the obligation of good faith, and as they lead to pacific negotiations and are necessary to control hostilities and promote the cause of humanity, they are sacredly observed by civilized nations.'

"Now, I do not believe that three out of ten who signed that remonstrance would have signed it with simply a knowledge of the foregoing facts." * * *

Here Mr. Clark introduces a long, ingenious story as to the probable truth of the charges made against him, and finally a flat denial.

"I will now meet the charge in direct terms: I deny it. I am as innocent of having procured an Indian to make an affidavit as either of those preferring the charges."

This was probably true, but did not relieve him from the well-founded suspicion of having procured some one who did procure the Indian to make the affidavit before United States Commissioner Bachelder that caused the arrest and detention of the sheriff whose duty it was to execute Leschi and to hold him until the legal hour for execution had passed. Nobody believed otherwise than that Clark was the man who concocted the scheme, but was shrewd enough to avoid direct responsibility for the result. Mr. Clark then proceeded to argue as to the danger of a new outbreak among the Indians in the event the Government broke faith with them, and finally recited an interview in July with several chiefs from east of the mountains who came over to intercede for Leschi:

"For the first time was I apprised that Leschi had made a truce with the authorities. I was told by the chiefs: 'We were present and cannot be mistaken as to the facts'" (which is fully confirmed by Colonel Wright over his own signature, printed elsewhere in this work). "'Leschi and his friends, when they went to see your white chief, Colonel Wright, were at war with the Bostons. They had arms and were not powerless. Colonel Wright spoke to Leschi and to us the words of a good father. He advised us to lay

down our arms and told us that we should not be harmed
if we did, for what had been done. We laid down our arms;
we placed confidence in the pledges of the white chief.' "

This was all true, and much more, in a very long,
adroit argument by Clark, which I am loth to consign
to oblivion, but the want of space forbids further extracts.

In some respects Clark was a very able man, though
by no means a deep thinker or profound lawyer. Yet
one great defect in his character marred his usefulness
to society. His rule that all means were justified to accomplish an end, while it gave him favor with the unscrupulous, kept him from attaining that position his
intellect otherwise would have warranted. He died
without a struggle in a passenger car while on his way
to Portland, nearly twenty years ago.

Dr. William F. Tolmie's letter, which was published
later (he being absent from home at the time of the occurrence so bitterly denounced by the citizens), throws
light as well upon some very interesting historical
events, while serving the purpose of illustrating the
"other side" of this controversy.

The Doctor had made an earnest plea before the Governor for the pardon of Leschi, and had tried to convince him that the ends of justice and of good public
policy would be promoted by such action, as shown by
extracts elsewhere, for while he had been denounced for
his "unjustifiable attempt to interfere with the execution of the laws of the Territory," he justified himself
in no uncertain words and then proceeded:

"The Hudson Bay Company's post at Nisqually was established in 1833, the summer of which year I spent here,
then obtaining my first insight into the peculiarities of Indian character. Since the summer of 1843 I have resided at
Nisqually permanently. In the summer of 1845 American
citizens, Messrs. Jackson (John R. Jackson), Ford (Sidney
Ford), Simmons (M. T. Simmons), Crockett and others

began to settle on the prairies between Cowlitz River and the shores of Puget Sound. Mention was soon thereafter made to the Indians that 'ere long they would be paid for their lands occupied by the whites, and, as the natives in turn came to inquire of me, the white man of their earliest acquaintance present, my oft-repeated explanations and injunctions for peace and good conduct on their part were the first instances of my interference. Till 1849 nothing of importance occurred to interrupt the harmonious relations existing between the whites and the Indians. American citizens arriving in the country, finding the natives peaceably disposed and friendly towards them—guilty only in rare and solitary instances of petty delinquencies, which were easily checked, and differing widely, as some citizens of the Territory subsequently found, from the wild, untamed savages of Queen Charlotte's and the west coast of Vancouver's Island. In those days I do not think there was a white man in the country who did not entertain kindly and compassionate feelings towards the Indians inhabiting the district now known as Pierce and Thurston Counties.

"In May, 1849, a sudden and, on our part, unprovoked affray took place here with the Snoqualmie Indians, then a comparatively savage and predatory tribe, but little acquainted with the whites, when an American citizen casually present, and a mere spectator, was shot dead by the Indians. In getting the perpetrators of this murder delivered up, I rendered very material assistance to the Indian agent of that period, J. Quinn Thornton, Esq., and to Captain B. H. Hill of the United States army, to whom, at Steilacoom, in the fall of '49, were delivered up by the tribe the six Indians who had here in May fired upon the whites, and the two most guilty of their number were soon after tried and executed at Fort Steilacoom.* * *

"In the summer of 1856, when Governor Stevens met the Nisqually, Puyallup and Nooscoop Indians near Steilacoom (known as the Fox Island Council), and changed their reservations, I was present by his special invitation and acted as interpreter."

The Doctor gave many other instances of his "interference" while acting in concert with the authorities for the public welfare, and not for private gain or personal aggrandizement (which were doubtless all true), and finished with a stirring appeal to his friends and old neighbors not to judge him hastily and unjustly.

All these letters, with other documents and defenses, were printed and circulated at private expense. No independent newspaper had been able to survive during the rule of the junta surrounding the Governor at Olympia, after the previous campaign of 1857, heralded as the triumphant vindication of the Governor by his election to Congress. During that campaign the opposition had given support to the *Washington Republican,* a campaign sheet which died with the campaign. This left the Governor's organ, the *Pioneer and Democrat,* again the only paper in the whole of the Territory. This paper received generous support from the junta, and not only published columns in support of the policy of the propagandists, centering in Olympia around the person of the Governor, but page after page appeared week after week in matter to strengthen their cause. And so, when Clark, Kautz, Tolmie or others wanted a hearing before the public, they must need publish a paper, which they did, two numbers, called the *Truth Teller.** This paper was "devoted to the dissemination of truth and suppression of humbug, edited by 'Ann Onymous,'" but the contributors wrote over their own names. Four copies only of this curious production are known to be in existence, illustrating, as they do, the iron hand that then ruled the Territory.

And yet, looking at the whole transaction in the light of what subsequently followed, and the motives governing the persistent persecution of this man Leschi, I have regretted the action taken in the meeting at Steilacoom. Here was the case, plainly stated: An innocent man

---

*See illustration.

was about to be hung under the forms of the law (a judicial murder, if ever there was one), condemned through prejudice and perjury, hounded to his death by a party who had caused his downfall, followed up by a political junta whose very political existence and continued power depended on the accomplishing of this man's death. These are plain words, but they are true. If Leschi lived, Stevens and his party were discredited, and they were afraid of him; and well they might be.

As to what Leschi would have done had he lived, we can only surmise. Of course, from the Governor's expressed point of view, he was a dangerous man to be at large, and would plunge the country again into war. Others believed his influence would have been for peace and for the advancement of his people. In one thing all were agreed—he had unbounded influence over all the Indians, whether they had been in the war camp or not, and his word would have been law. His fame extended far and wide.

For a man who dropped the plow handles and left the plow in the furrow, and the next day flew to arms to save himself from being carried off his farm a prisoner; who had committed no crime; who had pleaded for a home; who had afterwards felt the strong arm of the Government of thirty millions of people against his thirty-one Nisqually warriors; who, after the war, knew not only his home but more had been given to his tribe; who could see that now the great Government accorded his people even more than they had at first asked for—to my mind it cannot be doubted, if he could have lived, but that his voice would have been for peace and his influence upon his people beneficent and helpful.

CHAPTER LX.

Dr. Tolmie's Plea.

In an effort to obtain a pardon for Leschi, Dr. William
F. Tolmie wrote Governor Fayette McMullen:

"I have known Leschi since 1843, as a well-disposed,
peaceable Indian, of superior ability, respected by his tribe
and often referred to as an arbitrator in their disputes. Towards the whites he and his deceased brother, Quiemuth,
were, from our first settlement here in 1833, remarkably
friendly, and in early years they, on several occasions, rendered valuable assistance in suppressing thefts of horses
and cattle on the part of other Indians. Colonel M. T. Simmons, who was present, remembers how readily, in 1849,
the two chiefs volunteered their aid when we were in trouble here (at Fort Nisqually) with the Snoqualmies. Leschi,
I have learned, both from whites and Indians who were
present at the treaty making at Medicine Creek, in the
winter of 1854-55, protested vehemently there against the
reservation originally appointed for the Nisquallies at Seil-
seilootzen, on Nisqually Bay. I do not remember having
had any conversation with Leschi specially on this subject
till July, 1855, when one Sunday morning, accompanied by
another head man of the tribe, he came to state his grievances and ask my advice. He complained that he was kept
in continual apprehension and uneasiness, on account of
reports brought to him by Indians from Olympia, of his
being obnoxious to the agents there, and of their intention
soon to incarcerate, and perhaps hang him. He and his
companion then talked with great emphasis of the unsuit-
ableness of the reservation intended for them, and a passing Indian, approaching to listen, they reproached in bitter
terms for having failed at Medicine Creek to support their
protest. I reminded Leschi of the tale-bearing and lying
propensities of Indians in general, and added that, knowing
himself guiltless of offenses against either the property or

persons of the whites, he might go to Olympia and talk
without fear to Acting Governor Mason. He shared at this
time in the dread generally entertained by the Puget
Sound Indians that the buying of their lands was a prelude
to shipping them off in steamers to an imaginary dark and
sunless country; and the Indian agents of that day will remember how widespread and universal that apprehension
was—how an Indian, seemingly convinced of its absurdity,
would be back in a few days, as much alarmed as ever. In
August or September, 1855, I saw Leschi several times and
could perceive that the threatening reports from Olympia
still concerned him much. In October Governor Mason,
to whom I then, or in September, pointed out Leschi as an
Indian, in the event of hostilities, likely to be very useful to
the whites if with them, and formidable if the contrary,
hearing evil reports of him from Indian enemies, and I
believe from whites likewise, exacted a promise from Leschi
that he and his brother Quiemuth would forthwith move
with their families into Olympia; but the two brothers,
while yet uncertain whether to go or not, having notice
from Indians that next day a party of whites was coming
to seize them, fled in the night, leaving their families behind, and next day, when Captain Eaton and the rangers
reached their place of residence, the families were still concealed in the woods close by.

"Leschi has been greatly blamed for going off on this
occasion, but to any impartial person acquainted with the
circumstances of the case, and the condition of this country at the time, his conduct will seem natural enough. He
seems to have lingered in uncertainty till the last, and to
have gone off at length under the strong impulse of fear for
his personal safety. He maintains, and I have heard it from
others whilst he was yet at large, that Quiemuth and himself intended going direct from Nisqually to the Yakima
country, where they had numerous relatives, but were induced to remain at Green River by the threats of Kanasket
and Kitsap, chiefs there, to follow and assassinate them if
they persisted in going on. * * *

"My own belief, however, has always been that neither
Leschi nor Quiemuth would have taken up arms unless vir-

DR. WILLIAM F. TOLMIE

tually driven from their homes, as they were. Indeed, the latter had already commenced plowing his field for fall wheat when frightened into running away. Governor Mason urged these Indians to go to Olympia, in part for their own safety, as some whites were threatening them, but that to them was the lion's den.

"During the heat of the war Leschi has the credit of having twice interposed successfully between Kanasket and some defenceless white men, whose lives the latter sought, and again while Kanasket and Kitsap were absent attacking the town of Seattle, he got possession of and sent to Fort Steilacoom a captive white boy (George King), whose life with the Indians was constantly in danger.

"Leschi was also opposed to the commission of depredations in the abandoned settlements, and it was after a violent altercation with him on this account that Sluggia and others, disliking his severe discipline, moved to the upper Nisqually, whence issuing, they subsequently killed Northcraft and White at a later date. Leschi, returning from the Yakima valley, led off across the mountains the remaining stragglers, who had evaded the pursuit of the regulars and volunteers, and whose latest act of mischief was the burning of Glasgow's barn, by which, it must be admitted, he rendered the country good service."

No more truthful man lived in the community than Dr. Tolmie. He was a close observer, had the confidence of the brothers, Quiemuth and Leschi; had lived in close proximity with them for nearly a quarter of a century; could speak their language and knew, like no other white man could know, their past character and present impulses, and he has here told us the true story of these men.

Dr. Tolmie was a noble man, honorable in his dealings, courteous in his intercourse, and forbearing with his enemies. I knew him intimately and for a long time. It affords me great pleasure to be able to bear this testimony, in view of what transpired where his name was defamed because of his efforts to save Leschi's life.

CHAPTER LXI.

Final Sentence and Execution of Leschi.

Leschi, as we have already related, was under sentence for execution on Friday, Jan. 22, 1858, which sentence was not carried out, as related in a previous chapter.

The Territorial Legislature, then in session, the next day, Jan. 23, passed through both houses an act "That the Judges of the Supreme Court in the Territory be required to hold a special session of the Supreme Court on or before the first Thursday of February at the seat of government," and "that all laws and parts of laws in conflict with this act be, and they are hereby suspended until it may be executed."

The Secretary of the Territory was required to forward by express certified copies of the law to the Judges in the Territory, the Supreme Judge (Lander) being absent.

On Feb. 3, 1858, a further *ex-post facto* law was enacted by the legislature, which, stripped of its verbiage, baldly provided for amending the laws of the Territory to enable the authorities, under color of law, to hasten the execution of Leschi. Though not naming him, all knew that this was done specially for this case, and was in any event retroactive in its provisions.

Accordingly, the two Judges (Chenoweth and McFadden) held a special session as directed by the law, on the 4th of February, 1858, and remanded the prisoner to the District Court, where sentence was again pronounced (for the third time), that he be executed on the 19th of February, and appointing the Sheriff of Thurston County to carry out the mandate of the court.

The belief was prevalent that if sufficient time elapsed to hear from the President a reprieve would be granted. If the case should go over to the regular term of the court there would be time for this, although it would take three months to secure action and return of the paper. There was no doubt in my mind that a reprieve would have been granted had it not been for this precipitate action of the legislature and courts.

The Indians were unanimous in asking the Governor of the Territory, then Fayette McMullen, to pardon Leschi. At an assemblage of the Indians at the Squaxon reservation to receive their annuities on the 25th of December, 1,025 of those coming under the Medicine Creek treaty besought the Governor urgently, but without avail.

Chiefs Duke of York, from Port Townsend, and Seattle, of Elliott Bay, and "ten other principal men of different tribes, not subject to the treaty, spoke in behalf of Leschi to Governor McMullen, who was present, asking the Governor to pardon him," but all to no avail, as such action meant the political death of anyone who would intervene.

The unjust accusation of Major General John E. Wool that the citizens of Washington Territory had conspired to precipitate the Indian war with a view of speculating on the Government, had so inflamed the public mind that but few would listen to reason, and as Governor Stevens was industriously and energetically combatting that theory and laying the blame on the Indians, the general public came to believe that to secure their pay for supplies and time Wool must be discredited and Stevens vindicated, although they knew the treaties were the cause of the war; and it is safe to say, in their cooler moments after the events, nine-tenths of the people did not blame the Indians for resisting.

William Mitchell, of Olympia, Deputy Sheriff of Thurston County (Isaac Hays, the Sheriff, having left the Territory), appointed Charles Grainger of the same place as executioner, and twelve deputies as a posse to witness the execution and provide against any disturbance.

The commander of the fort (Steilacoom), Lieutenant Colonel Casey, refused to allow the execution to take place on the military reservation, denouncing the contemplated act in no unmeasured terms as murder. He, however, promptly delivered the prisoner to the Deputy Sheriff when convinced that the proper authority of the court had been exhibited.

A scaffold had previously been erected about a mile easterly from the fort, without the limits of the military reservation, in a sort of bowl-shaped depression in the prairie. It is said the spot can yet be located by the appearance of the ground thrown out in digging the post holes, but all else has long since disappeared, either through decay or by the hands of relic hunters.

The editor of the *Pioneer and Democrat,* always ready for an adventure, accompanied the Deputy Sheriff as one of the deputies to witness the execution, and wrote some facts and drew on his imagination to make a long newspaper article. The salient points contained in this article are in the brief description of the scene immediately preceding the execution. He wrote:

"Arriving at the place of execution, we found the gallows erected in a low gulch in the prairie. Here the unhappy man was assisted in dismounting and immediately led to the scaffold. At the foot of the ladder, looking up to the rope which hung suspended, with its sliding noose, he hesitated for a moment; but instantly collecting himself, he ascended with a firm step, as if he desired to show the white men how fearlessly an Indian can meet death. The prisoner evincing no desire to speak or make a confession, his arms were secured behind him, when, perceiving his life was drawing to a close, he bowed himself to the spectators, and for the space of some ten or fifteen minutes engaged in fervent prayer; said (in the jargon of the country), that he 'would soon meet his Maker; that he had made his peace with God, and desired to live no longer; that he bore malice to none save one man,' and upon whom he evoked the vengeance of heaven. Having concluded, the rope was adjusted, the cap drawn over his eyes, and at 35 minutes past eleven o'clock the drop fell, and Leschi, the brave in battle, was launched into eternity without having moved a muscle to indicate fear of death (by hanging) so dreadful to an Indian. He made no disclosures whatever and proved 'as true as the needle to the pole' to his confederates."

Charles Grainger, in a recent interview, said:

"I felt that I was executing an innocent man. I had had charge of Leschi for two weeks before he was taken to Steilacoom. He was cool as could be—just like he was going to dinner. I used to take his handcuffs off and let him eat. On the scaffold he thanked me for my kindness to him. He said that people had lied about him and had given false evidence. I asked him if he wished to say anything further. He said again that he was not guilty; that Rabbeson had lied when he said he saw him in the swamp, and that he would meet him before his God and he would tell him there he lied. He said he was miles away when Moses was killed. He said he would not be the first man that lost his life on false evidence. If he was dying for his people he was willing to die; that Christ died for others.

"After he made his speech he turned and thanked me again for my kindness to him while a prisoner under my care, and said that he had nothing more to say and that he was ready. He died without a struggle.

"It seems to me he talked for fifteen minutes, but spoke very deliberate and slow; but he made very few gestures while speaking and had a dignified way that made a lasting impression on my mind.

"Leschi was a square-built man, and I should judge would weigh about one hundred and seventy pounds. He was about five feet six inches tall. He had a very strong, square jaw and very piercing, dark-brown eyes. He would look almost through you, a firm but not a savage look. His lower jaw and eyes denoted firmness of character. He had an aquiline nose, and different kind of features than these Flathead Indians—more like the Klickitats. His head was not flattened much, if any at all. He had a very high forehead for an Indian.

"I saw Leschi in 1853 at McAllister's on the Nisqually. McAllister told me he was a good, faithful Indian. George McAllister and Joe Bunton both told me that Leschi met them on the way and helped them.

"He did not seem to be the least bit excited at all, and no trembling on him at all—nothing of the kind, and that is more than I could say for myself. In fact, Leschi seemed to be the coolest of any on the scaffold. He was in good flesh and had a firm step and mounted the scaffold without assistance, and as well as I did myself. I felt then I was hanging an innocent man, and believe it yet.

"There was a large crowd to witness the execution, but no women and but few Indians. Not a word was said, and no demonstrations whatever.

"Dan Mounts, who was then the agent at the Nisqually reservation, came with a two-horse rig to get the body. The Indians took him down very tenderly and put him in a box and kept the body for three days, but would not bury him in the same box."

CHAPTER LXII.

Reburial of Leschi.

Thirty-seven years after the execution and burial of Leschi, I attended the ceremonies paying tribute to the dead chief and his brother, Quiemuth, upon the occasion of the removal of their remains and reburial upon the Nisqually reservation, on a beautiful spot overlooking their former homes. The remains had been buried in a secluded spot and off the reservation, hence the movement for the reburial.

During the first week of July, 1895, the Indians began gathering on the Nisqually reservation, preparing for the great event. By the 4th of the month fully one thousand were in attendance. A special train of three coaches was run out from Tacoma, well filled with white people, to see these unusual ceremonies and hear from the lips of the natives of the virtues of the chief.

The service at the church on the reservation was conducted by the Indians and in their own language, so that but little of what was said could be understood, but that it was earnest and impressive was shown by the genuine grief manifested by attendants, and so impressed the white people that one might truthfully say there were not many dry eyes in the whole assemblage. Many of the Indians were on their knees, both Catholics and Protestants, and seemed to lose all thought of themselves or the surrounding spectators, and gave way without restraint to their grief.

Several eulogies were pronounced by Indian orators, the gist of which was that Leschi loved his home and that Governor Stevens tried to take it away from him,

and all the good land from the Indians, and if it had not
been for Leschi the Indians would have been without a
reservation they could live on.

The Tacoma *Ledger* sent a reporter, who wrote at
great length an account of what transpired, a part of
which follows:

"Slowly and impressively Henry Martin, a Nisqually Indian, arose and opened the services with a brief statement.
He was succeeded by John Swan, a Puyallup Indian, who
presided during the remainder of the ceremonies. The entire proceedings were conducted in the Indian tongue.
Hymns were sung, most of them to familiar gospel tunes;
prayers were made by members, and in a touching manner all the assembled Indians recited the Lord's prayer.
Then came the speeches. In their natural but their effective
oratory, the Indians told of their departed chiefs and the
deeds performed by them. Nearly all the remarks related
to Leschi and the events of the war in which he was so
tragic a factor. Governor Stevens, they said, never could
comprehend Leschi, and he could understand far less how
an Indian could so love his home as to fight for it when
told by a white man to leave. 'Governor Stevens tried to
cut down the reservations,' said George Leschi, during the
course of his remarks. 'The white men wanted our lands
and tried to move our people to the salt water, but Leschi
was our chief and he told the Governor our people would
not leave the land of our fathers. We did not want to go.
We had always lived here, long before the white men came,
and we wanted to die here. The Governor could not understand Leschi, and told him that he wanted our land and
our people must go to the salt water. It was then that Chief
Leschi went out, but he did not go out to kill.* He did not
want to do that. He only wanted to keep the Governor from
sending him and our people away from our homes. Then
Governor Stevens sent men out to bring him back, and it

---

*Dr. Tolmie said the same, that Leschi and Quiemuth both intended to go
east of the mountains, but were followed so closely by the Eaton Rangers
and met with so much opposition among the Indians that they were compelled
to remain.

RE-BURIAL OF LESCHI, 1895.

was when they tried to take him that war broke out and
James McAllister was killed.'

"This was the strain of all the speeches, most of them
dealing more in detail with the prowess of the two chiefs
on the field of battle. The character of Leschi was highly
eulogized, and his constant advocacy of the rights of his
people against the encroachments of the whites commented
upon at length.

"Upon the conclusion of the ceremonies at the church a
procession was formed to march four miles to the new-made
grave, in which the Indians all joined with their wagons,
buggies, or on horseback, with a few on foot, the whole
presenting an imposing spectacle, fully a mile long.

"At the grave but a simple, short ceremony was observed,
ending with a request that the Indians remain for consultation after the whites had dispersed."

If ever there lived a martyr for a just and righteous
cause, Leschi is one of them. He died that his people
might have a home where they could live, his supreme
effort sweeping away his whole fortune and finally costing him his life; he died in the defense of his home and
the homes of his people. He was possessed of the largest
fortune of his tribe. He freely sacrificed all during the
war and gained what he fought for, but was denied the
right to enjoy what he had won and lost his life, while
his tribe came into the inheritance won by his valor.

CHAPTER LXIII.

An After-Word.

At the eleventh hours my younger pioneer brother, Clarence B. Bagley, consented to write the chapter following, "In the Beginning." The old adage, "better late than never," however, applies, as we have here a chapter of our earliest history clustering around the old historic grounds of Fort Nisqually (shown in the illustration), drawn in great part from old original manuscript never before published and incidentally giving us an insight into the characters of the real pioneers of the Northwest "In the Beginning."

While I am profoundly thankful for the favor conferred by the writing of this chapter, nevertheless the readers of this volume, students of history, owe a greater debt of gratitude for the favor bestowed in the rescuing of these precious documents from possible oblivion, the more especially as the labor involved has been great and one of love for the preservation of historic records.

Mr. Bagley, shown in the illustration, one of the "Three Pioneer Boys," to the reader's right, needs no introduction to this community. It is, however, but just to say his life work of preserving historical data deserves substantial recognition at the hands of the citizens of this great commonwealth should he be moved to open up his treasure-store of historic records of which he is possessed.

In this group of the "Three Pioneer Boys" we have another, to the reader's left, Mr. Thomas Prosch, to whom I am also under great obligation for his unselfish, painstaking aid in the preparation of this work, by following my manuscript to round off the corners of a

THREE PIONEER BOYS

farmer author, who has had less than six months of school training. But he has gone farther than that in his helpful labor in the effort to make the work a standard of accuracy in historical statements. It is, however, but justice to Mr. Prosch to say that opinions and conclusions in this volume are wholly my own and for which no one is responsible but myself. In fact, we have disagreed as to some points in weighing testimony. What would a friend be worth, if you could not at some time have an honest difference with him? . It takes a good stout disagreement to thoroughly cement friendship; like the lovers' quarrel, that quickens the ardor and dispels the doubt.

In my chapter on names I give Mr. John W. Ackerson credit for applying the name Tacoma to the mill located on Commencement Bay in 1868, and in that way of indirectly naming the city of Tacoma. To this Mr. Prosch dissents, and because of his connection in the work as noted, I am moved to record his disclaimer.

To the central figure in the group of "Three Pioneer Boys" Mr. George H. Himes, now of the Oregon Historical Society, Portland, Oregon, but a Washington boy of early days, I am indebted for much valuable aid, and the great Northwestern commonwealth to a greater extent for his life work in building up that magnificent institution, the Oregon Historical Society, the pride of the people of Oregon and the hope of our historians.

I cheerfully print the following letter from Hazard Stevens, upon the request of the writer, although a letter substantially covering the same ground is printed elsewhere in this work without his request, and in fact without his knowledge. The loyalty of the son Hazard to the memory of his father, Isaac I. Stevens, is touching. To the father Hazard was like the "apple of his eye." I knew them both, but it is a matter of public knowledge that the Governor idolized the son, and, young as he was, always wished Hazard near him, in camp or on the plains, at home or on the battlefield, but he took pride in developing his manhood by sending him on missions of trust and danger, and right well did the son show the metal that was in him by his intrepid actions, that have become a part of our history for which we may be justly proud.

But is that any reason why I should pervert history? Is the loyalty of the son to the father or the father to the son any reason why the truth should not be told—why the acts of Governor Stevens, a public character, should not be criticised? I answer, no. The acts of a public man are public property—a part of our history—and the moment one swerves from telling the truth, that moment the work ceases to be the writing of history and becomes fiction. God forbid that I, through prejudice, should write aught against the patriot, Isaac I. Stevens. I am not conscious of any prejudice against the man Governor Stevens, while condemning his acts, knowing the great sorrow of his life, that really was the cause of leading him into such excesses, one of which, the attempt to deprive the Indians of their homes and allot them but sterile, heavy timber land instead, and but four acres at that to each Indian, as was done by the Medicine Creek treaty. The letter follows:

8 BOWDEN AVENUE,
Boston, Mass., January 28, 1905.

Hon. Ezra Meeker,
    Dear Sir,

Your letter of 13th requesting permission to reproduce in your forthcoming work the portraits of my father, General Isaac I. Stevens, and of Secretary Charles H. Mason, that appeared in my biography of the former, is received. I consent to your thus using them, and any other of the illustrations in the Life of Isaac I. Stevens that may assist you.

I only ask, as a matter of fairness, that you will publish this letter in your work, if you therein make the claim that

Leschi's name was forged to the Medicine Creek treaty, or if you claim that Governor Stevens called upon Kamiahkan to sign Looking Glass's name to the Walla Walla treaty on the strength of a carelessly written sentence in Vol. 2, page 54 of the Life. I have been informed that you make such claims in your MSS.

The sentence in question reads as follows; "Leaving his party to follow more slowly, he (Looking Glass) pushed on with a few chosen braves, crossed the Bitterroot Mountains, where for some distance the snow was shoulder deep on their horses, and, having ridden three hundred miles in seven days at the age of seventy, reached the council ground while Governor Stevens was urging Kamiahkan to give his assent to the treaty, for the governor, hearing the arrival of Looking Glass announced, seized the occasion to call upon the Yakima chief to sign the treaty in the name of Looking Glass, there being great friendship between these two."

The meaning I tried to express by this sentence was that Gov. Stevens called upon Kamiahkan in the name of Looking Glass, that is for the sake of Looking Glass, to sign the treaty himself. Carlessly I placed the clause, "in the name of Looking Glass" in the wrong part of the sentence. If transposed so as to read "to call in the name of Looking Glass upon the Yakima Chief to sign the treaty" there could have been no question. But if the context and all the circumstances make it so plain that of the thousands who have read the "Life" you are the only one who has discovered that Governor Stevens was guilty of such a mean and dastardly trick. It really seems too absurd to need contradiction. The Nez Percies were in favor of it. Governor Stevens supposed of course that Looking Glass, the Nez Perce war chief, would also be in favor of it, as in fact he was when his wounded vanity was appeased, when he signed the treaty with the other Nez Percy chiefs.

Your charge of the forgery of Leschi's name to the Medicine Creek treaty is contradicted by Col. Frank Shaw, the interpreter and myself, the only surviving witnesses. There were seventeen other whitemen who signed as witnesses, and not one of them ever made such a charge, although several became bitter political enemies of Governor Stevens. The charge is irreconcilable with Governor Stevens' whole life and character. No candid and disinterested man who will pursue the "Life" and note Governor Stevens great benevolence towards the Indians, and the great pains he took to protect them, improve their condition and start them on the road of civilization, could deem him guilty of such an act as you charge. You may be, and no doubt are sincere in your views, but your extreme prejudice has overcome all reasonable view and judgment. I remain

Very Truly,

HAZARD STEVENS.

And now, a word as to the witnesses mentioned in the foregoing letter. Hazard Stevens at the time was a rolicking boy of twelve, bent on seeing the sights and having a good time, and knew no more of what was transpiring or as to whether Leschi signed the treaty or not, than if he had at the time been in China or any other quarter of the globe. In fact, at the time, Leschi not having yet acquired notoriety, he would not have been readily recognized. Acting Governor Mason, one of the witnesses, did not know him by sight until after Doctor Tolmie pointed him out to him, six months after the council at Medicine Creek.

When Colonel Shaw, over his own signature, libelled his old-time pioneer neighbors by asserting they had caused the discontent among the Indians that culminated in the war, his statement was manifestly untrue, and known so to all the pioneers but the Colonel himself, blinded as he is by his partisan defense of the man who made him famous—and when he told Governor Stevens, "I can get the Indians to sign their death warrant," when asked, "Can you get the Indians to sign the treaty?" (the Medicine Creek treaty). This, to my mind, shows conclusively his unfitness to be called as a witness.

What possessed me to write, "At Oak Point we found Alexander Abernethy, former Governor of Oregon," as the reader will see by turning to page 35 of this volume, I do not know, unless it was that I had more in mind my plunge off the raft with my boots on and wondering if Jane was then and there to become a widow, than of writing accurate history. I knew that Alexander Abernethy had never been Governor of Oregon, but George Abernethy had, and so the slip of the pen, or aberation of mind or absence of brain action—something, I know not what—caused me to pen this erroneous statement quoted.

On page 249, in footnote, for "last proceedings," read "lost proceedings."

IN THE BEGINNING

By CLARENCE B. BAGLEY

FORT NISQUALLY, 1843.

CHAPTER LXIV.

In the Beginning.

By Clarence B. Bagley.

During the past two years it has been my good fortune to delve at will among the old records and correspondence of the early days at old Fort Nisqually, the earliest white man's home in what is now Western Washington. This has given me a clearer insight into the manners and customs of its people than any course of mere book reading.

To the citizens of the United States, to-day, it seems hardly possible that the English people could have honestly believed they had a just claim to any part of our present territory. In fact most of our people think we were cheated out of a large slice of territory when, by the treaty of 1846, our northern boundary was brought down from 54 deg., 40 min., to 49 deg.

On the other hand, no doubt of the ultimate settlement of this long-standing dispute between the two English speaking nations, by adopting the Columbia river as the natural boundary, appears in the old documents mentioned above, or in the published works of the Englishmen who wrote of this north-west prior to 1845.

This international dispute became a personal one between the American citizens of Old Oregon on one side, and the officers and adherents of the Hudson's Bay Company on the other. Since the wars of the revolution and of 1812 down to recent years it was a favorite pastime of the individual and collective Yankee to "twist the tail of the British lion," and the early immigrants from the valley of the Mississippi to the valley of the Willamette and the shores of Puget Sound kept alive the national custom. It is matter for wonderment that, in the face of so much braggadocio and bluster, the officers of that mightiest corporation of the 18th and 19th centuries maintained, as they did, so much of dignified forbearance, of kindly courtesy and of generous hospitality. To this every unbiased writer has given testimony from the beginning of American settlement in the early 'thirties.

A classic among the literature of life and travel in sub-artic regions, is "The Wild Northland," by General Sir William Francis Butler, K. C. B., it being a story of a winter journey with dogs, across northern North America, in the winter of 1872.

It is one of his notable characteristics to suddenly break away from the main narrative, with an interlude of gorgeous word-painting of some object of natural scenery or to discuss, more or less briefly, some public question, past or present. In one of these aberrations he remarked:

"From the base of the great range of the Rocky Mountains, the continent of British America slopes toward the north and east, until unbroken by one mountain summit, but in a profound and lasting dissolution, it dips its shaggy arms and icebound capes into a sea as drear and desolate.

"Long before a citizen of the United States had crossed the Missouri, Canadian explorers had reached the Rocky Mountains and penetrated through their fastnesses to the Pacific; and British and Canadian fur traders had grown old in their forts across the continent before Lewis and Clark, the pioneers of American exploration, had passed the Missouri. Discovered by a British sailor, explored by British subjects, it might well have been supposed that the great region along the Pacific slope, known to us as Oregon, belonged indisputably to England; but at some new treaty "rectification" the old story was once more repeated, and the unlucky 49th parallel again selected to carry across the mountains to the Pacific Ocean the same record of British bungling and American astuteness, which the Atlantic had witnessed sixty years earlier on the rugged estuary of the St. Croix.

"Unincumbered by the trappings of diplomatic tradition, Jefferson saw, vaguely perhaps, but still with prescient knowledge, the empire which it was possible to build in

that western wild; and as every shifting scene in the outside world's politics, called up some new occasion for boundary rearrangement, or treaty rectification, he grasped
eagerly at a fresh foothold, an additional scrap of territory,
in that land which was to him an unborn empire, to us a
half-forgotten wilderness."

The titled author of the foregoing is guilty of several
perversions of historical accuracy. Mackenzie was the first
British subject to reach the Pacific Ocean by an overland
trip, which he did on the 23d day of July, 1793, at the mouth
of an inlet called the Cascade Canal, into which the Salmon
river empties, and where was located one of the Hudson's
Bay Company's posts, Fort McLaughlin; but an American,
Kendrick, in the American ship, Washington, had sailed
around what was later called Vancouver's Island in 1789.
My edition of Meares' voyage, printed in 1791, has a large
map that gives the sailing route of Kendrick's ship clearly
marked on it.

In 1790 Gray discovered the Columbia river, and in 1805,
one hundred years ago, the American explorers followed the
course of one of the branches of that river from the Rocky
Mountains down to the Columbia and thence to the sea.
This expedition aroused the jealousy of the British government and trading companies. Its progress was watched
by agents of the British Association, and preparations were
made to anticipate the Americans in the settlement of this
part of the continent. A party of the North-west Company's
men was despatched in 1805 for this purpose, but failed to
cross the Rocky Mountains. In 1806, another party, led by
Simon Fraser, crossed the Rocky Mountains near the passage of the Peace river, and formed a trading establishment
on Fraser's Lake, in latitude 54 deg. This was the first
settlement or post of any kind made by British subjects west
of the Rocky Mountains. Other posts were formed, later,
in New Caledonia, as this country was called by the British
traders, but no evidence was ever brought out that any of
the waters of the Columbia, or the country through which

they flow, was ever seen by persons in the service of the North-west Company until 1811, when a party of said Company's men attempted to forestall Astor in occupying the mouth of the Columbia river. They arrived there July 15th of that year, but Capt. Thorne had sailed Astor's ship, Tonquiñ, over that river's bar the 24th of March, previous, and the large party it carried at once began a settlement which they called Astoria. They also founded another post at Fort Okanogan.

Because of the war of 1812 with England, these posts were abandoned and their goods sold to the North-west Company. In 1818, these posts were restored to the United States by the terms of the treaty of peace following said war.

In 1818, the North-west Company established a post near where the Walla Walla empties into the Columbia, and for perhaps fifty years it was called Fort Walla Walla, but, later, the place became known as Wallula, and Walla Walla was founded about thirty miles inland.

For many years there had been bitter rivalry between the North-west Company and the Hudson's Bay Company, but in 1821 they entered into partnership. Prior to this time the latter Company had no foothold on the Pacific Coast, but the new company took the name of the Hudson's Bay Company. In 1823, John McLaughlin was appointed to take charge of the Columbia district, and for a time he made his headquarters at Fort George, as Astoria was then called.

In 1825, attracted by the natural beauty of the place, surrounded by rich bottom lands and good grazing, nearby, Fort Vancouver was established on the present site of the City of that name on the north bank of the Columbia river about six miles above where the Willamette empties its waters. In 1827, Fort Langley was founded on the south bank of the Fraser river, about thirty miles from its mouth, and very soon a large amount of business was done between that post and Fort Vancouver, by way of the ocean and Columbia river, and up the Sound to Nisqually, and thence overland to the Columbia river and up that stream to Vancouver.

Lying in the northern angle formed by the Nisqually river and the Sound is one of the world's beauty spots. No grand park of human creation rivals its charm of undulating plain; its silvery lakes with pebbly beaches, nestling among detached or winding groves whose vivid green of oak, maple, alder and dogwood brightens the somber hues of the prevailing evergreens. The old gray oaks, with silver-threaded mosses pendant from every gnarled limb, are almost coeval with the snow-capped mountains off toward sunrise. Here and there big pines and firs, parents of the younger brood that crowd each other for breath of air and ray of sunshine, stand sentinel guard over all this loveliness. Evergreen cones are all about, whose lower branches caress buttercup, larkspur, violet, strawberry blossom and other sweet flowers amid the grasses at their feet and whose tops are already reaching to the shoulders of their progenitors.

On the crest of a hill overlooking the waters of the bay and the dozen islands that off toward the west seem to mingle with the foothills of the Olympics, one of the many little prairies boldly thrust itself over the almost precipitous hillside seventy years ago. To-day, it has been driven backward a full mile by a growth of firs that rise in the air a hundred feet, or more, and have a girth of that many inches at their bases.

Here, within a stone throw of the down sweep of the hillside, shrewd, hardy, brave and venturesome Archibald McDonald, one of the chief traders of the Hudson's Bay Company, erected the first white man's habitation on all this inland sea. There were the fort buildings, barns, blacksmith shop, cabins and other outbuildings, all inclosed within a strong and high stockade, with its bastioned corners. A little creek brought the waters of the lakes a few miles away down to the sea. The prairies extending north and east for miles were then covered with rich and luxuriant grasses, which in the next few years fattened many thousands of sheep and cattle.

Here is the first entry in the "Journal of Occurrences at Nisqually House":

"May 30th, 1833, Thursday. Arrived here this afternoon from the Columbia with four men, four oxen and four horses, after a journey of fourteen days, expecting to have found the schooner Vancouver lying here. She sailed the afternoon of the same day we started, with trading goods, provisions, potatoes, seeds, etc., bound for Nisqually Bay, where we have now determined, should everything come up to expectation, to locate an establishment. While on a trading expedition down Sound, last Spring, with eight or nine men, I applied about twelve days of our time to the erecting of a store-house 15x20 feet, and left Wm. Ouvrie and two other hands under him, in charge of a few blankets, a couple kegs of potatoes, and some small garden seeds, when I returned to the Columbia on the 20th of April. This is all the semblance of settlement there is this moment, but, little as it is, it possesses an advantage over all the other settlements we have made on the Coast. Mr. Yale, in consequence of a note to that effect, sent him from home by Indians, six weeks ago, forwarded, the other day, four men out of thirteen left with him at Fort Langley, middle of February, which now makes our total number at Nisqually House eleven hands. I have with me, at this moment, Dr. Tolmie, a young gentlemen lately arrived from England as surgeon for the Company, and bound for the Northern Estate in the Vancouver, but did me the pleasure of his company across land this far."

It is not often that we find in the early records such exact statements of fact and dates as the above.

The summer of 1833 was mostly consumed in the erection of buildings and stockade and making a wagon road down the steep bank from near the fort to the landing.

The main building was 55 feet long, 20 feet wide, with walls 12 feet high. The sills, posts, studding, and floor beams and flooring were hewed out of logs; and, as all the men were inexperienced, at this kind of labor, the task was severe and long continued. The buildings were all covered with large pieces of cedar bark held in place by timbers. The outer enclosure was about 250 feet long and 200 wide, and at the corners four bastions, constructed of squared oak logs, were erected.

In the early part of winter a saw pit was fitted up where boards were sawed out by hand—a laborious process well known to frontiersmen as "whip-sawing.' These boards were used for doors, shelving, gates and rough furniture. An immense chimney, constructed of sticks plastered with clay, served to warm the chief officer's living room.

Their first vehicles were home made, and almost wholly of wood. Wheels, round disks sawed from oak logs, axles large and of oak, with wooden linch pins. Whoever has heard the frightful noise emitted by these primitive carts or wagons when in motion has never forgotten it. A modern electric car, driven around an ungreased curve, for a second or two wails and screams somewhat after the fashion of these old-time "go-carts," but every motion of the latter served to announce its sufferings. These carts were hauled by oxen and served to transport the company goods up and down the beach road, to bring in the grain from the fields and to bring in the immense quantities of fuel consumed within the precincts of the station.

An entry of July 21, 1833, Sunday, shows somewhat of the attitude of the officers at the station in their dealings with the Indians, and of the wish to set a good example before them. It is, "No skins traded today, the Indians having been informed, last night, that we intended in future not to trade on Sunday."

Dr. Tolmie records in his diary the following: "Today, the Indians assembled in front of house to the number of seventy or eighty, male and female. With Brown as interpreter, who spoke in Chinook, Heron and I explained the Creation of the world, the reason why Christians and Jews abstained from work on Sunday; and had got as far as the Deluge in sacred history, when we were requested to stop, as the Indians could not comprehend things clearly."

Miss Jennie W. Tolmie wrote a few days ago, giving me the foregoing. She adds: "My father was much interested in missionary work; in fact, at one time, he thought of leaving the H. B. Co., and becoming a missionary. I remember driving to Nisqually from Tacoma, many years ago, and stopping at a farm house where an old, white-haired man was leaning over the gate. When my aunt, Mrs. Edward Huggins, told him who we were, he said 'your father taught my wife the Lord's Prayer.'"

The foregoing is the first mention I have found of religious instruction being given to the Indians in this Northwest. The missionaries did not arrive until later—the Methodists in September of 1834, nearly a year later, the Presbyterians and Congregationalists and Episcopalians in 1836, and the Catholics in 1838, so these lone gentlemen on the shores of Puget Sound were the pioneer preachers in "Old Oregon."

Thereafter, for a long time, the Sunday record shows that the Indians assembled regularly to listen to religious instruction.

"Sunday, Dec. 22d, 1833. Cold, frosty weather. Several Indian families came in as usual to get some religious instruction. I began to give them some instruction soon after my arrival, which they treated with much indifference; but, have at last succeeded in altering their savage nature so far that they not only listen with attention to what I tell them, but actually practice it."

"Sunday, August 10, 1834. The natives assembled and requested me to point out to them what was proper for them to act in regard to our Divine Being. I told them that they should endeavor to keep their hands from killing and stealing, to love one another, and to pray only to the Great Master of Life, or, as they say, the Great Chief who resides on high. In fact I did my best to make them understand Good from Evil. They, on their part, promised fair, and had their devotional dance, for without it they would think very little of what we say to them."

This simple narrative of the beginning of a great work, that of the teaching the natives Good from Evil, and that is the whole law, that too by laymen spending long years of exile in a savage land, is an eloquent testimony to the manly virtues of Doctor William F. Tolmie and Francis Herron. It was penned before Lee, Whitman, Spalding, Hines or Eells had taken up the same work in the valleys of the Columbia and the Willamette, and it has remained hidden in old, worm-eaten diaries and record books for more than seventy years. The writers and all their associates and the simple-minded people they sought to elevate in moral life have been dead for many, many years.

Little is known of Mr. Herron. He was transferred to another post and died early in 1841.

Dr. Tolmie had much freedom of action, not being confined to the daily routine of life at the station; so, late in the summer, he made a trip to Mt. Rainier, the first by a white man, and it will be seen that to him belongs the credit of discovering its glaciers. His daughter, mentioned elsewhere, copied for me from her father's diary the part relating to this "botanizing expedition" as follows:

August 27, 1833. Obtained Mr. Herron's consent to making a botanizing excursion to Mt. Rainier, for which he has allowed 10 days. Have engaged two horses from a chief living in that quarter, who came here tonight, and Lachalet is to be my guide. Told the Indians I am going to Mt. Rainier to gather herbs of which to make medicine, part of which is to be sent to Britain and part retained in case intermittent fever should visit us when I will prescribe for the Indians.

Aug. 28. A tremendous thunder storm occurred last night, succeeded by torrents of rain. The thunder was very hard, and the lightning flashing completely enlightened my apartment. Have been chatting with Mr. Herron about colonizing Whidby's Island, a project of which he is at present quite full—more anon. No horses have appeared. Understand that the mountain is four days' journey distant—the first of which can only be performed on horseback. If they do not appear tomorrow I shall start with Lachalet on foot. .

Aug. 29. Prairie 8 miles N. of home. Sunset. Busy making arrangements for journey, and while thus occupied, the guide arrived with 3 horses. Started about 3, mounted on a strong iron grey, my companions disposing of themselves on the other two horses, except one, who walked. We were 6 in number. I have engaged Lachalet for a blanket, and his nephew, Lashima, for ammunition to accompany me and Muckalkut and Poyalip (whom I took for

a native of Mt. Rainier) with 2 horses to be guide on the
mountain and after leaving the horse track, and Quilliliaish,
his relative, a very active, strong fellow, has volunteered to
accompany me. The Indians are all in great hopes of killing elk and chevriel (deer), and Lachalet has already been
selling and promising the grease he is to get. It is in a
great measure the expectation of finding game that urges
them to undertake the journey. Cantered slowly along the
prairie and are now at the residence of Nuckalkut's father's,
under the shade of a lofty pine, in a grassy amphitheatre,
beautifully interspersed and surrounded with oaks, and
through the gaps in the circle we see the broad plain extending southwards to Nisqually. In a hollow immediately
behind is a small lake whose surface is almost one sheet
of water lillies about to flower. Have supped on sallals;
at dusk shall turn in.

Aug. 30. Sandy beach of Poyallipa River. Slept ill last
night, and as I dozed in the morning was aroused by a stroke
across the thigh from a large decayed branch which fell
from the pine overshadowing us. A drizzling rain fell during most of the night. Got up about dawn, and finding
thigh stiff and painful thought a stop put to the journey,
but after moving about it felt easier. Started about sunrise,
I mounted on a spirited brown mare, the rest on passable
animals, except Nuckalkut, who bestrode a foal. Made a
north-easterly course through prairie. Breakfasted on bread,
sallal, dried cockels and a small piece of chevreil saved from
the last night's repast of my companions (for I cannot call
them attendants). The points of wood now became broader,
and the intervening plain degenerated into prairions. Stopped about 1 P. M. at the abode of 3 Lekatat families, who
met us rank and file at the door to shake hands. Their
sheds were made of bark resting on a horizontal pole, supported at each end by tripods, and showed an abundance of
elk's flesh dried within. Two kettles were filled with this,
and after smoking, my Indians made a savage repast on the
meat and boullion, Lachalet saying it was the Indian custom
to eat a great deal at once and afterwards abstain for a time;
he, however, has twice eaten since 11. Traded some dried
meat for 4 balls and 3 rings, and mounting, rode off in the
midst of a heavy shower. Ascended and descended at different times several steep banks and passed through dense
and tangled thickets, occasionally coming on a prairion.
The soil was throughout was of the same nature as that

of Nusqually. After descending a very steep bank came to the Poyallipa. Lashima carried the baggage across on his head. Rode to the opposite side through a rich alluvial soil plain, 3 or 4 miles in length and ¾ to 1 in breadth. It is covered with fern about 8 feet high in some parts. Passed through woods and crossed river several times. About 7 P. M. dismounted and the horses and accoutrements were left in a wood at the river's brink. Started now on foot for a house Nuckalkut knew and after traversing woods and twice crossing the torrents "on the unstedfast footing" of a log, arrived at the house, which was a deserted one, and encamped on the dry part of the river bed, along which our course lies tomorrow. The Poyallipa flows rapidly and is about 10 or 12 yards broad. Its banks are high and covered with lofty cedars and pines. The water is of a dirty white colour, being impregnated with white clay. Lachalet has tonight been trying to dissuade me from going to the snow on the mountains.

Aug. 31. Slept well, and in the morning two salmon were caught on which we are to breakfast before starting. After breakfast Quilliliaish stuck the gills and sound of the fish on a spit which stood before the fire, so that the next comer might know that salmon could be obtained there. Have travelled nearly the whole day through a wood of cedar and pine, surface very uneven, and after ascending the bed of river a couple of miles are now encamped about 10 yards from its margin in the wood. Find myself very inferior to my companions in the power of enduring fatigue. Their pace is a smart trot which soon obliges me to rest. The waters of the Poyallipa are still of the same colour. Can see a short distance up two lofty hills covered with wood. Evening cloudy and rainy. Showery all day.

Sunday, Sept. 1. Bank of Poyallipa river. It has rained all night and is now, 6 A. M., pouring down. Are a good deal sheltered by the trees. My companions are all snoozing. Shall presently arouse them and hold a council of war. The prospect is very discouraging. Our provisions will be expended and Lachalat said he thought the river would be too high to be fordable in either direction. Had dried meat boiled in a cedar bark kettle for breakfast. I got rigged out in green blanket without trowsers, in Indian style, and trudged on through the wood. Afterward exchanged blanket with Lachalat for Ouvrie's capot, which has been on almost every Indian at Nusqually. However, I found it more convenient than the blanket. Our course lay up the river, which we crossed frequently. The bed is clayey in most parts. Saw the sawbill duck once or twice and I fired twice, unsuccessfully. Have been flanked on both sides with high, pineclad hills for some miles. A short distance above encampment snow can be seen. It having rained almost incessantly have encamped under shelving bank which has been undermined by the river. Immense stones only held in place by dried roots, form the roof and the floor is very rugged. Have supped on berries, which, when heated, with stones in kettle, taste like lozenges. Propose tomorrow to ascend one of the snowy peaks above.

Sept. 2. Summit of a snowy peak immediately under Rainier. Passed a very uncomfortable night in our troglodite mansion. Ascended the river for 3 miles to where it was shut in by amphitheatre of mountains and could be seen bounding over a lofty precipice above. Ascended that which showed most snow. Our track lay at first through a dense wood of pine, but we afterwards emerged into an exuberantly verdant gully closed on each side by lofty precipices. Followed gully to near the summit and found excellent berries in abundance. It contained very few Alpine plants. Afterwards came to a grassy mound where the sight of several decayed trees induced us to encamp. After tea I set out with Lachalat and Nuckalkut for the summit which was ankle deep with snow for ¼ mile downwards. The summit terminated in abrupt precipice Northwards and bearing N. E. from Mt. Rainier the adjoining peak. The mists were at times very dense but a puff of S. W. wind occasionally dispelled them. On the S. side of Poyallipa is a range of snow dappled mountains, and they as well as that on the N. side terminate in Mt. Rainier. Collected a vasculum of plants at the snow, and having examined and packed them shall turn in. Thermometer at base 54 deg., at summit of ascent 47 deg.

Sept. 3. Woody islet on Poyallipa. It rained heavily during night, but about dawn the wind shifting to the N. E. dispersed the clouds and frost set in. Lay shivering all night and roused my companions twice to rekindle the fire. At sunrise accompanied by Quilliliaish went to the summit and found the tempr. of the air 33 deg. The snow was spangled and sparkled brightly in the bright sunshine. It was crisp and only yielded a couple of inches to the pressure of foot in walking. Mt. Rainier appeared surpassingly.

splendid and magnificient; it bore, from the peak on which I stood, S. S. E. and was separated from it only by a narrow glen, whose sides however were formed by inaccessible, precipices. Got all my bearings correctly today, the atmosphere being clear and every object distinctly perceived. The river flows at first in a northerly direction from the mountain. The snow on the summit of the mountain adjoining Rainier on western side of Poyallipa is continuous with that of latter, and thus the S. Western aspect of Rainier seemed the most accessible. By ascending the first mountain through a gully on its Northern side, you reach the eternal snow of Rainier and for a long distance afterwards the ascent is very gradual, but then it becomes abrupt in the sugar loaf form assumed by the mountain. Its eastern side is steep on its Northern aspect. A few small **glaciers** were seen on the conical portion; below that the mountain is composed of bare rock, apparently volcanic, which about 50 yards in breadth reaches from the snow to the valley beneath and is bounded on each side by bold bluff crags scantily covered with stunted pines. Its surface is generally smooth but here and there raised into small points or knots, or arrowed with short and narrow longitudinal lines in which snow lay. From the snow on western border the Poyallipa arose, and in its course down this rock slope was fenced in to the eastward by a regular elevation of the rock in the form of a wall or dyke, which, at the distance I viewed it, seemed about four feet high and four hundred yards in length. Two pyramids of rock arose from the gentle acclivity at S. W. extremity of mountain, and around each the drifting snow had accumulated in large quantity, forming a basin apparently of great depth. Here I also perceived, peeping from their snowy covering, two lines of dyke similar to that already mentioned.

Sept. 4. Am tonight encamped on a small eminence near the commencement of prairie. Had a tedious walk through the wood bordering Poyallipa, but accomplished it in much shorter time than formerly. Evening fine.

Sept. 5. Nusqually. Reached Tekatat camp in the forenoon and regaled on boiled elk and shallon. Pushed on ahead with Lachalet and Quilliliaish, and arrived here in the evening, where all is well.

"Lachalet," so often referred to here was the hereditary chief of the Nisqually tribe and a man of importance with the Hudson's Bay and Agricultural Companies for many years. At his death the tribe refused to allow his sons to succeed him and remained without a chief until about 1854 when Governor Stevens appointed Quiemuth and Leschi chiefs of the tribe, which appears to have willingly accepted their leadership.

Early in November, 1833, Doctor Tolmie sailed on the Cadboro for Fort McLaughlin, to which place he had started when he came to Nisqually. In a few days Mr. Herron, who was then in charge, started with two boats laden with goods, tools and provisions to establish a post on the large prairie on Whidby Island, that had been selected for that purpose at an earlier date. They were overtaken by a gale of wind and narrowly escaped being swamped, but finally got ashore, though the boats became separated. This led to a return to the Fort. A higher sort of servant had been left in charge, but during the short absence of the chief trader matters had got into such bad shape the plan of establishing the other post was abandoned for the time being, and, in fact, was never revived.

June 9, 1834, Mr. Heron writes in the journal, "About 2 p. m., we heard a couple of cannon shot; soon after I started in a canoe with six men, and went on board the Llama, with the pleasure of taking tea with McNeil, who pointed out two Chinese he picked up from the natives near Cape Flattery, where a vessel of that nation had been wrecked not long since. There is one still amongst the Indians, inland, but a promise was made of getting the poor fellow on the Coast by the time the Llama gets there."

As a matter of fact, these were Japanese, and the third man was rescued later. They had lost command of their junk and drifted before the storms across the ocean and driven ashore near Cape Flattery. They had many companions, but only these escaped. Later, they were sent to China, and an effort made to get them home to Japan, but as this was long before that country was thrown open to other nations, it is generally thought they never reached their native land.

June 11th, "All the outfit safely landed and received safely in store. The cattle were also got out; they are very wild and wicked; one of the cows wounded one of the men, William Brown, in the groin and nearly killed a couple more. The cattle received are three cows with their calves, and a bull." These came from the Company's farm at Vancouver. This was the beginning of an industry that in later years attained immense proportions, so much so, that at times cattle were slaughtered by the hundreds for their hides alone.

Soon after the establishment of Fort Vancouver, the Company had driven what were always called in early days, "Spanish" cattle, overland from the Mexican settlements in California. This breed was slim, active, hardy, long-horned, vicious, and poor milkers, but they bred like rabbits, almost, and it did not take long for the owner of a few cows to have a large herd around him. In a few years the Company sent numbers of these cattle to their posts in the interior of the Columbia basin, where they throve amazingly. After a time it was found that Nisqually was better fitted for their herds and flocks than the more exposed eastern stations and it was decided to make a transfer. An old manuscript in the handwriting of A. C. Anderson, gives the following:

"After harvest in 1841, I set out with a party of men to receive a number of cattle transferred from the Hudson's Bay Company to the Puget Sound Agricultural Company from the posts of Nez Perces, Colville, and Okanagan. We crossed the Cascade range over the northwest shoulder of Mt. Rainier, by the Sinahomish pass, (Now, I think the Snoqualmie pass—Edward Huggins.) We followed an Indian trail, but expended a good deal of labor in parts to render it passable for our return. Met the party conducting the cattle low down on the "Yachimah" river, on the Swanapun branch. Hired some Yachimah Indians to assist in driving. Left the greater portion of the party to herd the cattle near the verge of the mountains so as to recruit. Returned to Nisqually with a man to procure provisions and further assistance. Met the party and returned with them, bringing the cattle through to the Nisqually plains, with some loss, by estrays on the way, some of which, if not most of them, probably, afterwards reached the same locality, following on the trail of the herd. In October, I had orders to proceed to Vancouver. A large herd reached Nisqually just as I was leaving. Others were on the way. A large number of ewes were introduced at the same time. These were the results of purchase made that summer in California by Chief Factor, now Sir James Douglas. They were driven up by land via the Umpqua and Willamette valleys. I cannot state the numbers, leaving Nisqually as I have said just as they were arriving. There were a good many swine, used chiefly for provisioning the people. No settlers in the country at this time, and only the Wesleyan Mission, under Dr. Richmond, near the present site of the Fort, with the aid and concurrence of the Company. The dairy was conducted by an Englishwoman, whose husband superintended the farming operations."

Here is one of the troubles of these old books and papers. They give enough to whet one's curiosity, and then leave out so much that would have been interesting and oftimes valuable information. How easy it would have been for Mr. Anderson to give the numbers of that first drove over the mountains. It must have been an immense one to require so much help, for when cattle have been driven together for a few days, they follow the leader, with very little attempt at scattering. Two of us, A. S. Mercer and I, drove over from near Salem, Oregon, in 1863, first to Portland, then by steamer to Monticello, at the mouth of the Cowlitz river, and from there to Seattle, by land, more than two dozen cows, without any loss, or serious difficulty. There must have been several hundreds and, probably, thousands in that early day drove.

In later years the Agricultural Company had on Nisqually Plains from 5,000 to 8,000 head of cattle and from 6,000 to 10,000 sheep, also 300 head of horses. It required from fifty to seventy-five men to take care of these, and they were a motley crew—English, Scotch, Canadian-

French, Kanakas, half-breeds and Indians. Of the latter the Company employed but few, as all the records show they were considered too worthless and dishonest to be entrusted with much responsibility.

As early as 1841, they were milking two hundred cows and had several hundred more on the range. After their importations from California they set to work to improve their breed, and imported some of the best from England. At that time they were also farming on a large scale, using the servants of the Hudson's Bay Company for that purpose, who were bound by contracts to do all kinds of work required of them, civil or military.

For many years they had the supplying of all the forts and stations of the Hudson's Bay Company on the Pacific Coast, and also furnish the Russians of Alaska with grain, butter and cheese, at one time as high as fifteen thousand bushels in one year. They also exported to England hides, horns, tallow, and wool, thereby giving cargoes to the vessels that brought out the supplies needed for the use of the employees and for traffic with the Indians. which would otherwise have gone home comparatively empty, as the annual shipments of furs required but little space, though immensely valuable in themselves. At that time their stock required little feed other than they picked up on the range and of course it was quite a profitable business for the Company.

The flocks of sheep soon became of the best breeds, mostly merino, as large importations of blooded animals were made from England. As early as 1844, nearly seven thousand pounds of wool were shipped, and in ten years later this went up to over thirteen thousand pounds. This year, 1854, it was found that the sheep had become too numerous for the pasturing capacity of the Nisqually Plains, and there being a large demand for improved breed of sheep, in the Willamette valley, Doctor Tolmie, then in charge at that place, decided to get rid of a few thousands, so he started with a band of 3600, going as far south as Eugene in the valley, disposing of them to the farmers as he went along. The doctor was absent on this trip about four months, and the venture proved very profitable, as the sheep brought good prices. I can remember that the farmers of the Willimette valley bought very freely of merino sheep brought out from Vermont and sold at from one hundred to one hundred and twenty-five dollars per head, and of short-horn cattle from Kentucky at from two hundred and fifty for cows to five hundred dollars per head for bulls, the latter having been brought out by Gen. Gaines, who had been Governor of the Territory under an early Whig administration.

There was one part of the yearly work where the Indians did the most of it; that was in the washing and shearing of the flocks. It was made a sort of holiday time, similar to modern hop-picking. The men did the washing, and assisted in the packing of the wool, and the women did the shearing. The work was done in a primitive way. The women would work in pairs. A man would catch a sheep and carry it to the women, who would be seated on the floor of a large store room, called the shearing-house, with an Indian mat under them. One would take the fore part and the other the hind part of the animal, whose legs were tied to prevent it from struggling too much or getting away. Some of the workers were skillful and others the reverse, in the latter case the poor brute would be badly mangled.

Much has been written of the cattle and sheep of the Company destroying the indigenous and highly nutritious bunch grass of the Nisqually Plains. I do not think this indictment will lie. If there ever were a set of men who did things on a methodical and prudent scale, it was these early Hudson's Bay people, so long as they were in control of affairs there. It was their custom to keep their sheep in bands of about five hundred, each band under the charge of two men, which were under the supervision of a white shepherd, who resided at an out-station. Each of these had from two to four of these bands to care for. The sheep were carefully parked every night, and the parks or corrals moved every two or three nights, thus keeping the ground enriched, and at the same time from being overpastured to the injury of the grass. Although this grass was a "Bunch grass," it was different from that so-called east of the Cascade Mountains which leaves fully half of the ground bare. It covered the ground completely, making a thick sward, which, even in the hot months did not dry up, but was of a bluish-green color. After the white settlers secured most of these lands this intelligent care of the grazing ended. In the 'seventies there were probably not less than thirty thousand sheep scattered over the prairies, as well as thousands of other stock, and as they were there during the spring and summer the grass had no chance to seed and was soon eaten down to the roots so that the hot summer sun and drying winds killed it out completely in a few years, and a growth of worthless grass and weeds has taken its place.

The cattle, during the later years of the occupation by the Company, became very wild, and were shot by its employees, by the settlers, and by the Indians, so that it became almost impossible to handle them. In fact many of them became as wild as deer, and it took a skillful hunter to get a shot at them. They would hide in the woods in the daytime, and come out cautiously at night to feed on the prairies, and it became the custom to hunt them at times of bright moonlight.

The farming and stock-raising operations of the Hudson's Bay Company and the Puget Sound Agricultural Company had such an important effect in securing the early occupation of the country west of the Cascade mountains and north of the Columbia river, and also in affording the early American settlers means of subsistence for several years until they had become self-supporting, that a detailed explanation of the origin and operations of the latter is important.

The older corporation was generally known as the Hudson's Bay Company, but its legal title was the "Governor and Company of Adventurers of England trading into Hud-

son's Bay." Its sole business was to secure furs and peltries, both by traffic with the Indians, and by maintenence
of a large force of trappers and hunters in its own employ.

The idea of forming a company, having for its object the
raising of flocks and herds for commercial purposes was
first mooted in the Spring of 1833, and introduced to the
Company by Chief Factor Archibald McDonald. The site
of operations then proposed was in Sacramento valley, California, under a contemplated grant from the Mexican government. Later, the extensive pastoral and agricultural
country around Nisqually and the Cowlitz was preferred
because of their nearness to Vancouver, the headquarters
of the Company's operations west of the Cascade mountains.
This tract was then lying unoccupied and was believed by
the company people to belong to Great Britain. Objections
were raised to the Hudson's Bay Company entering on the
business, as it was thought it would be likely to interfere
with the legitimate business of that Company, the fur trade.
There were, however, many advantages that might accrue
to the company in the prosecution of their ordinary business
by an association of the kind proposed, with adequate capital, if independently conducted, therefore the directors
of the Hudson's Bay Company in London agreed to lend
that Company's cooperation.

A prospectus was accordingly issued in London in 1838,
a copy of which lies before me as I write. It is engraved
in artistic style, and occupies four pages of foolscap size.

Its introduction is as follows: "The soil and climate of
the Country of the Columbia River, particularly the district
situated between the head waters of the Cowlitz River,
which falls into the Columbia River about 50 miles from the
Pacific and Puget's Sound, being considered highly favorable for the rearing of Flocks and Herds, with the view to
the Production of Wool, Hides and Tallow, and also for
the cultivation of other Agricultural produce, It is proposed":

Then follow twenty clauses giving the purposes of the

proposed organization, its name, capital stock of 200,000 pounds sterling, in shares of 100 pounds each, that until the sovereignty of the country involved should be determined the main office and entire management of the affairs of the Company should be retained in London, naming John Henry Pelly, Andrew Colvile and George Simpson agents with full powers to conduct and direct the business, providing for yearly meetings of the proprietors of the Company, rules of voting and sales of stock, that the superintendent of the Agricultural Company should always be an officer attached to and interested in the Hudson's Bay Company, that no person in the employ or taken into the district of the Agricultural Company should in any way trade in furs or peltries, that all such employees should be subject to dismissal and removal from the district, and that such persons should be in every respect subject to the like conditions, restrictions and regulations imposed upon the servants of the Hudson's Bay Company, that whenever any part of the district should become British territory the Company should apply for a grant of the land, and then the said Puget's Sound Agricultural Company should be incorporated, and finally, whenever the holders of not less than three-fourths of the whole stock should so decide the Company should wind up its affairs and dissolve.

A reserve of the privilege of purchase was made in favor of those already out here, and many availed themselves of this privilege. The regulation about the superintendent insured a man experienced in the management of the native tribes. It was also agreed that such breeding stock as could be spared for the purpose should be transferred at stipulated prices from the Hudson's Bay Company's farms to the new Company, and all seeds and grains for the agricultural requirements.

The post at Nisqually was transferred to the Agricultural Company about 1842, and the Cowlitz Farm was established exclusively by the latter Company, both with the provision that the older Company should have all the furs and peltries.

Restrictions were made as to the purchase of the stock, no one person being allowed more than twenty shares, the Governor being allowed that many and from him down a graduated scale to the lowest clerk, who could only take one share.

Of course there was some friction between some of the members of the two companies, each party complaining that the other was getting the advantage, but the two companies gained immense profits for twenty years or more.

The following extracts from the old Hudson's Bay Company journal, for the year 1839, give all that I have been able to find regarding the selection of the site for the Indian Mission at Nisqually. It is understood that Rev. Jason Lee came over to the Sound the preceding year and decided to have a mission at this place as soon as the increased number of missionaries then expected should arrive.

April 10, 1839. This evening the Rev. Mr. (David) Leslie and brother (William H.) Willson arrived with an intention of making at this place a small Missionary Establishment for converting the Indians around.

Thursday, 11th—Showed a spot of ground north of the small river for building house for the mission, as desired by Mr. Douglas.

Friday, 12th—Took a ride out near the Poolapa river (Puyallup) with the two gentlemen strangers. They were delighted with the country.

Sunday, 14th—The Indians of the place have been brought into the big house, and Mr. Leslie told them of the purpose of their mission, that is, that they intended to settle here if they, the Indians, wished it for the purpose of giving instruction in religion, and learning their children to read.

15th—* * * Mr. Leslie has gone home and Mr. Willson is left to begin building.

17th—* * * This day the first tree was cut down for the missionary building. Mr. Willson gave the first blow and I the last.

18th—Mr. Willson was arranging our grindstone for grinding his broad axe.

21st, Sunday—About 11 o'clock a. m., Mr. Demers, the Roman Catholic priest arrived from the Cowlitz and brought letters from Vancouver.

25th, Thursday—Eighty-nine men, women and children of the Sawayewamish (Snohomish) have come in to see the priest.

28th, Sunday—* * * Seven children baptized by Mr. Demers.

29th, Monday—* * * This afternoon, Miss Helen Mc-Donald and Miss Margaret Riedout Orriber were both baptized by Mr. Demers, and after the latter was married to her old husband, Joseph Pin. (Note by Edward Huggins—The first marriage was a civil ceremony, quite legal, tho'.) At seven o'clock, Miss Helen McDonald was married to William Kittson, (Chief Trader in charge) without much ceremony, the latter being a Protestant and former a Roman Catholic. The rites were performed in a civil manner. Witnesses Mr. William Holden Willson, a brother of the Missionary Society and Joseph Pin.

May 6th—* * * Mr. Willson has lost his Indian. The scamp received pay in advance, and shammed sickness in order to pay a visit to his friends, with whom he has gambled a part of his gains.

Here the record ends. It is known that Willson got the building so it could be occupied and then returned to the Willamette valley.

In 1878, a book of "Historical Sketches of the Catholic Church in Oregon, during the past forty years" was issued under Church auspices, and in it are some references to the Nisqually and Cowlitz Missions from which the following are extracts:

"The first mission to Cowlitz was begun by the Vicar General on March 17, 1839, and continued until the 1st of May following. Arriving at the settlement on the evening of March 16th, the Vicar General was accommodated by Mr. Simon Plamondeau with a room for his own use and also an apartment 18x25 feet to be used as a chapel. Besides the four farmers and their families forming the colony, there were a large number of servants, employed on the farms of the H. B. Co., some of them having wives. * * *

"The news of the arrival of the missionary at Cowlitz caused numerous delegations of Indians to came from remote distances in order to hear and see the "blackgown." Among these delegations was one led by a chief named

"Tsla-lacum," (Steilacoom) whose tribe inhabited Whidby Island, Puget Sound, 150 miles from the Cowlitz Mission. After a journey of two days in canoes to Fort Nesqualy, and an arduous march of three days on foot, across streams and rivers and by an exceedingly rough trail, they reached Cowlitz with bleeding feet, famished and broken down. Their object was to see the "blackgown" and hear him speak of the great spirit. As soon as they were refreshed the Missionary began to speak to them of God, of the Incarnation and Redemption. But the great difficulty was how to give them the idea of religion so plain and simple as to command their attention, and which they could retain in their minds and carry back with them to their tribe. In looking for a plan the Vicar General imagined that by representing on a square stick, the forty centuries before Christ by 40 marks; the thirty-three years of our Lord by 33 points, followed by a cross; and the eighteen centuries and thirty-nine years since, by 18 marks and 39 points, would pretty well answer his design, in giving him a chance to show the beginning of the world, the creation, the fall of angels, of Adam, the promise of the Savior, the time of his birth, and his death upon the cross, as well as the mission of the Apostles. The plan was a great success. After eight days' explanation, the chief and his companions became masters of the subject; and, having learned to make the sign of the cross and to sing one or two canticles in Chinook jargon, they started for home well satisfied, with a square rule thus marked, which they called Sa-ha-le stick. That plan was afterward changed from a rule to a large chart containing the great epochs of the world, such as the Deluge, the Tower of Babel, the Ten Commandments of God, the 12 Apostles, the seven sacraments and precepts of the Church; these being very useful to enable the missionary the teaching of the Indians and whites. It was called the "Catholic Ladder."

"About the 8th of April, 1839, Rev. D. Leslie, a Methodist minister, arrived at Cowlitz, en route to Nesqualy where he intended establishing a mission among the Indians. This information at once prompted Vicar General at once to despatch an Indian express to Father Demers at Vancouver, asking him to proceed at once to Nesqually in order to plant the true seed in the hearts of the Indians there. Father Demers left immediately and reached his destination in six days, during which he was drenched with cold and continuous rain. He was welcomed by Mr. Kitson, the commander of the Fort; a house was appropriated for the purpose of a chapel, and he at once entered upon the subject of his arduous journey. The Indians flocked from all sides to see the great chief of the French and receive his instructions. An unforeseen incident, however, came near preventing the mission begun under such favorable auspices. The commandant was unwilling to allow a vast crowd of Indians to enter the fort, and ordered them to stay outside of the palisades. One of the Indians, bolder than the rest, dared to force an entry and was pushed back rather roughly by Mr. Kitson, hence the beginning of a riot, which might have become fatal, if the appearance of the Missionary had not appeased that untamed multitude. * * *

"Father Demers was then obliged to go out of the Fort to teach the Indians, who, during the whole time of the mission, gave evidence of their most perfect docility to their advice. The first mass was celebrated in the presence of the commander and other persons of the Fort. Among the throng there were counted Indians of 22 different nations. * * * After having given orders to build a chapel, and said mass outside of the Fort, Father Demers parted with the Indians, blessing the Lord for the success of his mission among the whites and Indians, and reached Cowlitz on Monday, the 30th, with the conviction that his mission at Nesqualy had left a very feeble chance for a Methodist mission there. Brother Willson, whom Minister Leslie had left orders with to build a house, on a certain piece of land, must have been despondent at being witness to all he had seen.

"From his Mission at Wallamette falls, the Vicar General went, on May 6th, 1841, to the Clackamas tribe, which he had already visited in March, at the Wapeto lake. The usual daily exercises were continued at the ringing of the bell for nine days. Bro. Waller came and called him an intruder. His Evangelical ladder was brought near the Catholic one; the Indians pronounced themselves in favor of the latter; twelve lodges were gained. Being obliged to return to St. Paul on the 15th, Rev. M. Demers, being at Vancouver came to replace him. He continued the mission for two weeks, giving some days to the Wallamette tribe and the rest to that of Clackamas. It was on that occasion that Wesamus, the Corypheus of Bro. Waller was gained.

"From the Clackamas, Father DeMers returned to Vancouver, to administer to the Brigades of the north and south, after which he went home to teach catechism. And as the Colville mission was being omitted this year, because of Father DeSmet being expected to come down that way, and it had been resolved that Father DeMers would go this year to the Sound, he started on August 11th, went to Nesqualy and thence to the bay. He visited many tribes, besides those seen by the Vicar General; he traveled from one nation to another, accompanied by Chief Tslalakum and many other great chiefs. His traveling was a triumphant one, surrounded sometimes by six hundred and other times by 3000 Indians, who, hostile to each other, were peaceable in the presence of the "blackgown." He often passed whole days in teaching, with a ladder 10 by 2½ feet, these poor Indians so desirous of heavenly things, and continuing late at night to sing, pray and hear the harangues of the chiefs repeating what they had learned. * * * From the bay he passed to Fort Langley on the Fraser river. There were new triumphs among the Kawitshans. There ended his mission, and on Sept. 27th he was at home, having made 765 baptisms, and been 44 days absent.

"In the beginning of June Commodore Wilkes left Vancouver on a visit to the Willamette valley, and took dinner with the Vicar General at his residence at St. Paul. He told him that on seeing a cross on Whitby Island, he called it the "Cross Island." The Vicar General having promised Father DeMers that he would visit Cowlitz during his absence, started June 14th, for that place. On returning he gave a mission of 14 days at Vancouver. It was on that occasion that Commodore Wilkes, assisted with several officers of his staff and Dr. McLaughlin, at High Mass and Vespers on a Sunday. It was a solemn day. The following Sunday, though the Commodore was absent, the ceremony was not less solemn. A house was raised in March, at St. Paul, 62 by 25 feet, to serve as a hall for the people on Sunday and a lodging for the priest.

"The next mission to be made was that of the Cascade tribe which had never been visited by the "blackgown." Tamakoon, its chief, had already been a convert since 1839, at the sight and explanation of the Catholic Ladder. He had met, many times, the assaults and efforts of the Methodist preachers, but all in vain; he remained unmoved. He was glad to see "le plete" arrive on September 17th. His tribe contained 150 to 200. * * * Tamakoon received

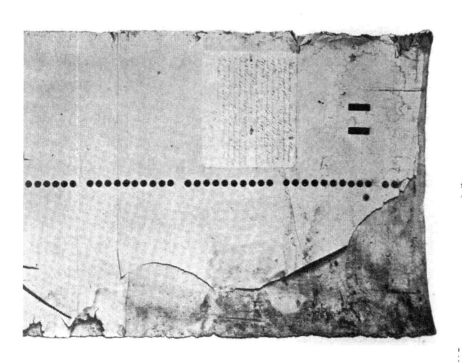

a bell and a Ladder to be used on Sundays. He was able to speak on it for several hours. Thirty-four children were baptised."

This "Catholic Ladder" was well designed to accomplish the purposes for which it was prepared. In all matters foreign to their daily life and material wants the natives were as simple as little children, and the ladder was an object lesson, where the eye as well as the ear served to fix the subject under discussion in their minds. In the hands of the zealous and exceedingly capable men sent out to engage in the work of christianizing the Indians, it was a highly effective agent in the conversion of those who had not hitherto come under instruction, and in proselyting those who had already listened to the teachings of the Methodist, Congregational and Presbyterian missionaries.

The Indian of this region was a materialist—that is he knew nothing that his bodily senses did not teach him. His gods and spirits all had visible forms.

The Catholic priests appeared in their black gowns and carrying with them the emblems of their service; they were received with great respect by the officers of the Hudson's Bay Company, and gladly welcomed by the employees who were nearly all Catholics. The Hudson's Bay Company was the highest corporeal power known to the Indians. Its officers enunciated the law and enforced it with iron hands in all that came up between the Company and the natives. Any wrong doing that affected the company was punished surely and swiftly. For these reasons, when the Indians saw what deference was shown to the priests by those whom they, the Indians, looked up to as "Tyees," whatever the priests said to them was naturally accepted with greatest respect. The ceremonials of the Church service were attractive to them, and, together with the emblems on the chart as explained to them served lastingly to fix in their memories the lessons expounded to them.

The "ladder" from which the illustration is made is one of the first prepared. It has been among the papers and documents at Fort Nisqually more than sixty years, and is still in fairly good condition. The material is strong paper, pasted on strong white cloth, and the illustrations were evidently prepared with a small paint brush, the color being probably India ink. The first was used at the Cowlitz Mission by Rev. Father Blanchet in July, 1842. Thereafter copies of it were in constant use among the Indians all over the North-west until in 1860 an engraved edition was issued, of elaborate form with a vast amount of historical matter in print and in pictorial form. The method of using it was also printed, and will appear further on.

The parallel black bars represent the four millennial periods—First, from Adam to Noah; second, from Noah to Abraham; third, from Abraham to the completion of the Temple; and fourth, from that time to the time of the general peace under Augustus Caesar. The dots represent the thirty-three years of the Christ at Jerusalem, and then the eighteen bars bring the time down to the year 1800. Lastly, the dots represent the years to 1842, when this "ladder" was prepared.

In each of the first thirty centuries mention is made of some leading scriptural character. In each of the next ten centuries important events in Jewish, Babylonish, Persian and Greek history are noted briefly. In the eighteen centuries of the Christian era the spread of the Romish church among the nations of the earth is given. The circles and other figures at the bottom of the chart are emblematic of the days of creation, and of the angels in heaven, and of the devils in hell.

Going up the forty centuries are the emblems of the leading characters in biblical history, of the ark, the tower of Babel, Sodom and Gomorrah, Mount Sinai, Solomon's Temple, Old Testament, Star of Bethlehem, etc.

Between the lower and upper ladders many events of Jesus' time on earth are noted. The large house at the left is St. Peter's Basilica at Rome. The black branch leading off at the right near the top is the stream of "New Chief

Heretics," from Luther to Joseph Smith, and the three upright bars under it are the three chief heretics, Luther, Cal-
vin and Henry the Eighth.

Here follows the method of using the Catholic Ladder:—

1. Begin by running up from the bottom to the top, the
column of the ages, through which the world has lasted.
Immediately after, point out, in succession, the epoch of
the 4,000 years, that of 33 and that of 1860. Having done
this you will point out the mysteries of the Holy Trinity,
of the Incarnation and of the Redemption, so as to teach
the learner how to distinguish them by their names.

2. After this, you will point out, at the foot of the column of the centuries, the image which relates to God, and
say all that we know of His divine attributes and divine
perfections, namely: His Eternity, His Immensity, His
Providence, His Power, &c., &c., &c. You will then proceed to explain the great mysteries.

3. From speaking of the power of God, you will pass on
to the Creation in a period of six days, adverting to the
sanctification of the seventh day, which God reserved for
Himself and consecrated to rest. Further on, you will refer
to the creation of the Angels, which took place, in the opinion of St. Augustin, when He made the light on the first
day of creation. Then speak of the rebellion of the wicked
angels, a short time after their creation, their fall into hell,
created at the moment of their rebellion; as also of the
faithfulness of the pure angels, and of their reward in
Heaven.

4. You will subsequently point out the tree of knowledge of good and evil. You will state God's command not to
touch its fruit; also the envy and the madness of the cursed
enemy of man at the sight of the happiness of Adam and
Eve; the resolution which he took to work out their ruin
and to drag them into the pit along with himself and his
rebellious followers; his temptation of the first pair, under
the form of a serpent; the wiles of the devil in that work
of temptation; the disobedience of our first parents, but a
short time after their creation; the rejoicing of the devils
when they saw Adam and Eve, with all their posterities,
involved in one and the same condemnation by the justice
of God: the promise of a savior, through the means of another woman (Mary, the Virgin Mother, most pure and
immaculate), who was to crush, that is to baffle the power

of the serpent, the devil, by bringing into the world the promised Savior, in order to repair the guilt of the first woman.

5. From this point you will proceed to the fulfillment of the promise, pointing out, in a merely cursory manner, the intermediate events, and especially so to the beginners, whose attention should be distracted as little as possible from the thread of historical facts, but rather made to dwell on the principal object. The rest is but accessory, and may be brought in, further on, with some measure of advantage.

6. When you have reached the period of 4,000 years, you will begin to give a historical sketch of religion, from the birth of Jesus Christ down to our days. You will refer to the 33 years of his life; to the apostles; to Calvary; to the sacraments; his promise to the church; his death; his Resurrection and Ascension; to the mission of the Apostles; the coming of the Holy Ghost; the conversion of the Nations of the earth to the Catholic faith down to the present day. Having done this, you will proceed more fully to explain the various points which had been only touched upon in the reference to the chart.

7. Having concluded this sketch of religion, you will pass to the explanation of the symbols of the Apostles, of the commandments of God and of His church, of the Lord's prayer, angelical salutation and sacraments, which embrace the whole of the Christian doctrine, or all that is to be believed, done, and asked and received for salvation. But before you touch this branch of your duty, do, in regard of those prayers, what you had done in respect to the historical sketch of religion; that is, give a general character of them and of each of them; tell by whom, how, and under what circumstances they were composed or uttered; and teach your beginners to retain the title of the sum of the things or articles contained in them. For example:

1. In relation to the Apostolic creed: By whom and when it was composed; say all that is embraced in it, was, in substance, received from the lips of Jesus Christ; that there is one article respecting the first of the three persons of the Godhead; that there are six articles relative to the second person, and one touching the third, and so on.

2. Touching God's commandments: By whom, when, and how they were given out and uttered; that there are three which refer to God, and seven which refer to our neighbor. Sum of them: God, His holy name, His holy

day; honoring father and mother; not to kill, not to commit impurity, not to steal, not to lie, not to covet impurities, not to covet another's goods.

3. Touching the commandments of the church: By whom and for what purpose they have been established; the sum of them: Festivals, Mass, Confession, Communion, Fasting and Abstinence, and Church Dues.

4. Touching the Lord's prayer: By whom and at whose request it was uttered; three petitions which relate to God, and four which relate to ourselves.

5. The Hail Mary or Angelical Salutation: By whom it was addressed, and so on.

6. Touching the Sacraments: By whom and for what purpose instituted; their names; two of them which blot away sin; three of them which can be received once only, and the definition of them all.

To this general statement you may add later, with profitable results, particular and more substantial details.

Revs. Jason and Daniel Lee, uncle and nephew, were the first missionaries to reach Oregon, having arrived overland in the fall of 1834. They were accompanied by two lay members of the Methodist church, P. L. Edwards and Cyrus Shepard. Their first field of labor was near the present city of Salem, Oregon.

In September, 1836, Rev. H. H. Spalding and wife and Dr. Marcus Whitman and wife and W. H. Gray arrived overland at Walla Walla. These were the first American women to arrive in Oregon. They were sent out by the American Board of Foreign Missions.

In May, 1837, a considerable reinforcement to the Methodist mission arrived by water around Cape Horn. They were Dr. Elijah White and wife, Mr. Alanson Beers and wife, and Misses Ann Maria Pitman, Susan Downing and Elvina Johnson, and William H. Willson. This latter gentleman will appear often in our story, later.

In September, following, Rev. David Leslie, wife and three children, Rev. H. K. W. Perkins, and Miss Margaret Smith, the second Methodist reinforcement, also arrived by water.

Early in 1838, it was decided to commence a second mission at The Dalles, on the Columbia river. The Umpqua, Killamook, Clatsop, Chenook, Nezqually, and many other tribes were destitute of missionaries, and an effort was made to supply them. The Society passed a resolution advising Jason Lee to make a visit to the United States to represent to the Missionary Society and the public generally the true condition of the country and of the Indians, and soliciting men and means for the missionary work in Oregon.

In March, 1838, with two white and two Indian companions, he started overland for the East. He arrived in New York in November, but delivered a great many addresses in Illinois and at other points along his route, about Oregon, as a missionary field and as a home for settlers. A few weeks later, the Board passed a resolution to send to Oregon five additional missionaries, one physician, six mechanics, four farmers, one missionary steward and four female teachers.

During the summer of 1839, Jason Lee, attended by William Brooks and Thomas Adams, the two Indian boys whom he brought with him, traveled quite extensively through the New England and Middle States, holding missionary meetings in all the important places, and collecting funds for the Oregon mission. His success was unparalleled, and an interest was excited throughout the land amounting to enthusiasm. Crowds thronged to see and hear the pioneer missionary beyond the Rocky mountains, and the Indians who accompanied him. Liberal collections were taken up in almost every place, and these, with the appropriations of the Board for the purchase of goods, amounted to forty thousand dollars—an immense sum in those days, and sufficient to provide all kinds of tools for agricultural and mechanical purposes, and the necessary articles for the construction of a saw-mill and grist-mill for the use of the mission.

October 10, 1839, the ship Lausanne set sail from New York harbor with a missionary party of fifty-two persons, thirty-six adults and sixteen children, on board. They were gathered from Massachusetts, Connecticut, New York, Maryland, North Carolina, Illinois and Missouri. There were eight ministers of the gospel, all Methodists, with the exception of Rev. Sheldon Dibble, who was a Presbyterian on his way to his field of labor in the Sandwich Islands. The others were Jason Lee, A. F. Waller, Gustavus Hines,, J. L. Parrish, L. H. Judson, J. H. Frost, W. W. Kone, and J. P. Richmond. With the latter we have most to do in this story. The first five died in the harness in Oregon, after shorter or longer terms of service. Frost, Kone and Richmond worked a few years and then went away, never to return.

While lying in New York harbor, the infant son of Richmond and wife was christened "Oregon," in honor of the country to which they were bound.

The ship came by way of Cape Horn and the Hawaiian Islands, and the voyage was not disturbed by any disaster or unusual event. May 21, 1840, the good ship crossed the Columbia bar in safety, but it required ten days more to thread the channels and get off the numerous shoals between Astoria and Fort Vancouver, the early day Mecca of every voyager to Oregon by land or sea, be he Methodist, Presbyterian, Catholic, English, American, French, or any other faith or nationality. Dr. McLaughlin extended the hospitalities of the place to the whole party as long as they desired to remain.

June 13th, a meeting of the members of this mission was called to select the stations for work of the newly arrived missionaries. J. H. Frost was sent to Clatsop, near Astoria, W. W. Kone and Gustavus Hines to Umpqua, A. F. Waller to the station near Salem, and John P. Richmond to "Fort Nez Qualy, on Puget's Sound."

Cotemporaneous missionary books and records are almost completely silent as to the work of Mr. Richmond at Nisqually and of the duration of his stay at that point. Elwood Evans also ignored this event almost completely. Evans

was, during his long life in the North-west, the great overshadowing authority regarding early local historical matters.   Nature lavishly endowed him with a broad and com-
prehensive mind, a retentive memory and a graceful flow of
language.   He was a voluminous writer, an eloquent speaker, a learned counsellor and an active politician.

From the time the first Americans made their permanent
homes in Oregon antagonisms arose toward the Hudson's
Bay Company, which widened and deepened as years rolled
on, and Americans became more and more numerous.   It
is a fact that needs but to be. stated to be accepted as true,
that down to our late war with Spain American sentiment
was largely unfriendly toward the "British." The individual
Englishman, Scotchman or Irishman rarely came in for a
share of this dislike, until, collectively, they became British.
The hostility was stronger in the west than on the Atlantic
seaboard.   As a consequence, when the true pioneers came
to "Old Oregon" and found the Hudson's Bay Company the
dominant power all over the great New West it was looked
upon as a hereditary enemy.   It was the representative of
British power and the advance agent of British colonization
schemes, therefore the antagonist of all that was American.
That company and its foster child, the Puget Sound Agricultural Company, had large holdings on the shores of Puget
Sound.   Americans here all felt that these companies were
intruders, that they had no rights that an American citizen was called to regard.   There were, from time to time,
disputes and lawsuits between the representatives of these
companies and the settlers; the adjustment of the boundaries at the time of the treaty of 1846, later of the water
boundary in the San Juan Archipelago, and finally of the
immense and unreasonable claims for compensation made
by those companies for their lands in Pierce and Cowlitz
counties.

In all these, Mr. Evans was concerned as lawyer and ad-
viser in opposition to the companies, and, as it was popular
to "twist the lion's tail," it was quite natural for all that he

said or wrote to carry with it a strong bias against them. The allotment of large tracts of land for sites for early missions had also led to many contests in the land department and the courts between the settlers and the missionaries, resulting in a quite general sentiment that the latter were in the wrong. In these controversies Mr. Evans was often engaged. For these reasons, perhaps, much of his writings had a vein of unkindness or uncharitableness running through them toward the Hudson's Bay Company and the early missionaries. It is to this I ascribe the fact that he ignored almost entirely the work and lives of the Hudson's Bay people and the early missionaries on Puget Sound.

In the past two years I have devoted a great deal of time to the congenial task of assembling into a more or less connected story the history of this first missionary effort west of the Cascade Mountains. Old newspapers and still older letters, and recent letters from the children of these first missionaries have all contributed something.

Mrs. Abbie J. Hanford furnished an article or interview that appeared in the Seattle Weekly Chronicle of July 12, 1883, as follows:

"John Cornelius Holgate was born in Trenton, Butler county, Ohio, October 15, 1828. He moved with his father's family to Van Buren county, Iowa, in 1839. Being delicate and suffering greatly with the ague, he was often confined to the house, and became very fond of reading to and with his sister. Their favorite books were the adventures of explorers and hunters in the far west. Among the various books of adventure which they read two greatly pleased them. They were the journals kept by the Pike's exploring expedition, and a book by one of the men who was in the expedition of Lewis and Clark, whose name was Gass. What pleased them most was the fact that the climate of the northwest Pacific Coast was shown to be so healthful by the experience of all the men who visited it. Although a child, young Holgate determined to see for himself that wonderful, and at that time, unknown country, which all who visited it described with such admiration. He formed a very glowing idea of the country in Iowa, from the descriptions written by Pike, but he was satisfied that the remote northwest was far superior to anything he could hear or read of. He never altered his determination until his ambition was accomplished, and he saw for himself Puget Sound. He was so well pleased with the country as he found it that he always regarded it as the most beautiful, healthful and attractive one he had ever seen. In 1847 he crossed the plains with a party of Quakers commanded by Llewellyn. He drove the wagon which brought the first fruit trees to Oregon. It was loaded with trees from a nursery at Salem, Henry county, Iowa. Among others they brought from that nursery a fir tree for which they refused $5 for on their way across the plains, thinking, from all he could hear, that it would be very valuable and rare tree in Oregon. When they arrived they were much surprised to find great forests of fir throughout many portions of the northwest, and of course their fir tree was of no value. While Holgate was in Oregon he met with numerous adventures in the Indian wars. One night he, with a party of others who were looking for Indians that had carried away the horses of settlers, found the Indians in a position where it was dangerous to attack them as a body. Young Holgate volunteered to go into the Indian ambush alone and cut the fastenings of the horses so they could run out to the Hudson's bay men who were with him. He told them he was the youngest and of the least value to the party, and if he was killed few would miss him. The Indians saw him and were very much surprised to see "tenas" boy go alone, and they reserved their fire, expecting to see the entire party follow him. Fearing that if they fired at him the whites would charge them after they had wasted their ammunition on the boy they continued to reserve their fire until the youth was beyond the range of their guns and out of danger. Thus he succeeded in driving off the horses and delivering them to his own party. He then became a general favorite, and afterwards did many other daring deeds, so that the officers of the Hudson's Bay company in Oregon became greatly attached to him, and often related to him stories of the great attractions offered by the country further north and west. They described the country about Puget Sound as being very far superior to any other country in America in every way, and gave him details of its many attractions.

"In November, 1847, the Rev. Dr. Whitman, his lovely wife and nine other Americans were atrociously murdered by a band of perfidious Cayuse Indians at Whitman's mis-

sionary station not far distant from the present city of Walla
Walla, Washington Territory, (then in Oregon). This led
to the Indian war with the Cayuses and other tribes. Among
the Oregon volunteers was a pale youth yet in his teens
who had recently arrived in the Willamette valley. During
the campaign he was distinguished for his bravery, but at
the close of the winter he was stricken down with the
measles. Through his severe illness he was kindly cared
for by an old officer of the Hudson's Bay company, who took
strange interest in his youthful protege, on learning he had
worked his way with comparative strangers to this far off
land in search of that healthful and beautiful clime his
glowing imagination had pictured on the shores of the
Pacific. The officer delighted to tell his eager listener of
the wonderful beauty and healthfulness of that great inland
sea, Puget Sound; of its magnificient harbors, its surpassingly beautiful scenery, its timber—the grandest on the continent, its fertile valleys, its fish and its hidden treasures of
coal, iron and other minerals. Young Holgate thought where
all these advantages were combined would be built, at some
future day, a great city. He (young Holgate) was so impressed with the descriptions he had heard he determined to
see the wonderful country for himself as early as possible.
Accordingly, in the summer of 1849 he traveled entirely
alone from Portland, Oregon, across the country to Tumwater, at the head of Puget Sound. There he was hospit-
ably entertained for a few days by Col. M. T. Simmons,
the first American settler north of the Columbia river, who,
with his family, came and located that place in October,
1845.

"Here Holgate employed an Indian to take him down the
Sound in a canoe. After spending about two months in
cruising around, exploring the country he staked out a
claim, which he intended to make his future home, near the
head of Elliot bay, about three miles distant from the present city of Seattle. While on this cruise, in order to make
his stock of crackers and dried beef last as long as possible,
he subsisted principally on fish, clams, berries, game and
camas (a bulb which the Indians use, and when dried substitute for bread.) On his return to the Willamette valley
he gave such glowing descriptions of the country he had
visited, that a number of persons determined to go there before locating south of the Columbia river. In September,
1851, a number of persons selected claims and settled on the

Dwamish river, whose mouth is at the head of Elliot bay. A Mr. Maple took the claim selected by Mr. Holgate, who had not yet returned to the Sound. He afterward came and located nearer the town. On the 26th of September, 1851, J. N. Low, Lee Terry and D. T. Denny arrived at Alki point, five miles distant from Elliot bay, where Low and Terry located and established a trading post, and soon after laid out a town, which they called New York, to which was facetiously added the Chinook word "Alki," meaning after while. Afterward, as its population drifted away to Seattle, it lost the New York, but has retained the name of Alki point. On the 5th of November, 1851, the schooner Exact, Capt. Folger, sailed from Portland, Oregon, for Puget Sound and Queen Charlotte island, with passengers for the sound and a party of gold miners for the island. On the 13th of November she arrived at Alki point and landed A. A. Denny and family, and also three other families. On the 15th of February, A. A. Denny and two others located claims on the east side of Elliot bay. On the 31st March, 1852, Dr. D. S. Maynard arrived, who also located a claim on the east side of Elliot bay, adjoining the others. On the 3rd day of April they moved on to their claims, having previously surveyed the harbor. In May a town was laid out to which they gave the name of "Seattle," (a word of three syllables, accented on the first,) in honor of the Indian chief of that name who owned and occupied the townsite, who was much respected by the early settlers, and to whom he was greatly attached, and continued to be their firm friend until his death. His death occurred about ten years after the war, and in compliance with a request he had previously made, that all the "tyees," (that is leading citizens) of the country attend his funeral, an oration commemorative of his many virtues and greatness was delivered on the occasion by his son Jim Seattle.

"The funeral of Jim Seattle took place at the "Old Man House" reservation, near Port Madison. A number of the citizens of Port Madison were present at the ceremonies and followed the body to the grave. The ceremonies were performed in the chapel at the reservation, an old Indian (Louchy or Jacob, in English), leading. The following speech was made during the service: "People of Port Madison, we are glad to see you here today. Many years ago you came here to assist in the burial of the father of the deceased. We are thankful to good white men who are not

afraid to come and mix with the poor Indians. Before the
white men came the Indians were ignorant and did many
things that were not right, but now they hope, with the
assistance of good white men, to become better and more
civilized every year. The Indians on the reservation are
members of the Roman Catholic church, and perhaps there
are some present who were brought up in that religion. If
there are, we hope that you will assist us with your prayers."
The leader then waved a small white wand and all began to
chant. At the close of the chant the crucifix was borne on
high, the women forming and marching two abreast, the
men next in the same order and then the coffin. At the grave
the women walked in single file, passing the head of the
grave, into which they each threw a handful of dirt. The
leader then threw the first shovel of earth on the coffin and
the ceremony was closed.

"In October, 1852, H. L. Yesler arrived in Seattle and the
settlers so adjusted their claims as to enable him to hold
a claim, including the site he had selected for a steam saw-
mill then en route from Ohio. This was the first steam
saw mill built on Puget Sound. The first lumber was cut in
March, 1853. Large accessions were now made to the settlements, and large sums of money were realized from the sale
of piles, lumber, pickled salmon and cranberries shipped to
San Francisco. Cutting piles was very profitable, persons
engaging in this business realizing $20 per day, as they were
in great demand for filling the city front of San Francisco
at that time. The valleys of Duwamish and White rivers
were settled up for a distance of twenty miles from Seattle.
The little valley of Black river was settled up, and a saw-
mill built on the river, which was afterwards burned by the
Indians. King county now seemed to be very prosperous,
the inhabitants little dreaming of the calamities soon to
overtake them. Farms were rapidly improved, orchards
planted, cottages built and schools organized. A little church
was also built in Seattle. Universal health, peace and prosperity seemed to prevail."

At that time Rev. John P. Richmond was living at Tyndall, Bon Homme county, Dakota, where he had gone in
1874. By some means the foregoing article came under his
notice, and in a short time he sent a letter to Seattle from
which several extracts are taken, as follows:

"The writer of this does not wish to be invidious, nor
to pluck from the brow of Col. Simmons and Mr. Holgate
any laurels to which they may be entitled, but as he sup-
poses that in giving an historical sketch of the settlements
in Washington Territory, accuracy is desired by any who
may wish or attempt to do it, he feels it his duty before he
leaves this for the eternal world, to contribute his knowledge as to the first settlements on Puget Sound, and north
of the Columbia river. In order to do
this understandingly, he makes the general declaration as to
the main facts, first, and then details of the events as they
occurred, in consecutive order. In the first place, the writer
of this declares that the Rev. John P. Richmond, M. D., and
his family were the first full-blood white settlers on Puget
Sound and north of the Columbia river; that his son, Francis Richmond, now superintendent of schools for Bon
Homme county, was the first full-blood white child born
in Washington Territory, and west of the Rocky Mountains; that a Mr. Willson and a Miss Clark were the first
white couple united in matrimony in Washington Territory. Now for the facts, in consecutive order, leading to
the residence of the writer of this communication, near
Puget Sound. He is now in his 73d year, having been born
in Maryland, August 7th, 1811, and at his advanced age
does not wish to arrogate to himself any honors to which
he is not entitled. He was educated and graduated as a
physician fifty years ago in Philadelphia, and subsequently
became a minister in the M. E. church. In 1839 he was in
charge of the Methodist church in the city of Jacksonville,
Ill., when he received notification through Rev. Dr. Bangs,
of New York, that Dr. Richmond was appointed a missionary and physician to Oregon. As soon as practicable, he
and his family made preparation to start for that destination. They ascended the Illinois river as far as practicable,
and thence by land traveled to Chicago, then a village,
thence by steamer through the chain of lakes to Buffalo;
thence by the Erie canal to Troy; thence via Albany to New
York City. In the month of October, 1839, they sailed from
New York in the ship Lausanne, via Rio Janeiro, in Brazil,
Cape Horn, Valparaiso in Chili, to Honolulu, in the Sandwich Islands. After remaining some weeks at Oahu they
sailed for the Columbia river, and debarked at Vancouver
late in the spring of 1840. There they found much hospitality from Dr. McLaughlin and James Douglas, his as-

sistant, who were in charge of the Hudson Bay Company's operations in Oregon. The writer of this learned that Mr. Douglas afterward became Sir James Douglas, who recently died in British Columbia. After a brief sojourn at Vancouver Dr. Richmond and family of wife and four children, the youngest born on the way and named Oregon, accompanied by Mr. W. H. Willson, a carpenter to build a house, and Miss Clark, from Connecticut as a teacher, descended the Columbia in a boat furnished by the gentlemen of Vancouver, to the mouth of the Cowlitz river ascended that stream some distance, then mounted horses, the ladies having provided sidesaddles in New York, the luggage on packsaddles, and the children in the arms of the assistants, who were Canadian voyageurs and servants of the Hudson Bay Company, and traveled by land from the Cowlitz river to Puget Sound, having crossed on the way the Chehalis and Nisqually rivers, and arrived at Fort Nisqually, a stockade inclosure near the head of Puget Sound, in the summer of 1840, antedating Mr. Simmons' settlement by five years. At Nisqually they found Mr. Kitson, with an Indian family in charge. He was succeeded by Mr. Anderson in 1841. There they found also a small but very neat steam vessel, owned by the H. B. Co., under the command of an American, Captain McNeil, having also an Indian family. The vessel was called the Beaver and was the first vessel that plowed the Pacific waters, and which plied regularly between Nisqually and Sitka, then owned by Russia. The house occupied by Dr. Richmond and family was erected on the open plain or prairie, contiguous to a small rivulet, running thro' a ravine, from a chain of small lakes in the interior of Puget Sound—about three quarters of a mile from the stockade and the same distance from Puget Sound. Soon after they had settled in their house, the writer of this solemnized the marriage ceremony which united Mr. Willson and Miss Clark, and who were the first couple married in Washington Territory. They left for the Willamette Falls in 1841. During '41 the American Exploring squadron under Capt. Wilkes, U. S. N., arrived at Nisqually and lay at anchor for some months, making surveys and observations, and measuring the altitude of Rainier and other mountains.

"The writer of this had a son born to him in 1842, as before stated, and whose birth and baptism entry was made then and there in his family register, which reads as follows:

"Francis Richmond, son of John P. Richmond and America, his wife, was born at Puget's Sound, near Nesqually, Oregon Territory, on the 28th Feb., Anno Domini, 1842, and was baptized by the Rev. Jason Lee, superintendent of the Oregon Missions." The writer of this was engaged to remain for ten years in Oregon, and intended to remain his lifetime at Puget Sound, but domestic affliction and other circumstances cut short his stay to four years. As it is, he retrospects with much imaginary gusto the time when he and his family lived exclusively upon oysters and other shell-fish, brought by Indians from the Sound, for three weeks, with a pine box for a table, carried there on a pack-horse, with tin plates and some iron spoons for table accouterments. He wishes, very frequently, for some of those luscious shell-fish. Dr. Richmond and family returned to Illinois, via Sandwich and Society Islands, Boston, New York and the lakes to Chicago."

Francis Richmond, at this time of writing, lives at Tyndall, South Dakota, and considerable correspondence has passed between him and the writer.

The first white child born within the limits of "Old Oregon" was Marcel Isadore Bernier. Marcel Bernier, the elder, was one of the many fearless and venturesome trappers who roamed all over the vast stretch of country beween the Rocky Mountains and the Pacific Ocean, wherever furs and peltries could be obtained to eke out a precarious livelihood. He and his wife were whites, Canadian French, not half-breeds as many of those who knew them on their farm in Lewis county thought them.

The child Marcel, was born on the site of the old fort on the bank of the Spokane river, November 10, 1819, more than eighty-five years ago. As a lad he was white, with curly hair, and light blue eyes. At eleven years of age he was sent to school at St. Boniface, Red River, Manitoba, where he grew to manhood. In 1841, the oft-mentioned Red River Colony came to Nisqually and settled for a time, and among them were Marcel Bernier, wife and Isadore. In 1844, the latter married and took a claim on Newaukum Prairie, not far from the present line of the Northern Pacific

Railroad. He died December 27, 1889, a few days after the admission of Washington as a state, having thus been born here soon after the war of 1812, becoming a resident of this country prior to the organization of the Provisional Government of Oregon, and living here through all the years of Washington's territorial existence. He was the senior "Native Son."

The first American white child born within "Old Oregon" was a daughter of Dr. Marcus Whitman and wife, but she was drowned when two years old, the next was Eliza, daughter of Rev. H. H. Spalding and wife. She became Mrs. Warren, and a few years ago was still living in Eastern Oregon; the third was a son of Rev. Elkanah Walker and wife, Cyrus H. Walker, near the present site of Spokane, December 7, 1838.

In 1841, Sir George Simpson, the governor of the Hudson's Bay Company, came overland on a tour around the world, and reached Nisqually in September of that year. Some time after a party of immigrants from the Red River region also arrived. This migration has been generally ascribed to the influence of Governor Simpson, and claimed to be a part of a deep laid scheme to people this western country with citizens of Canada and Great Britain to prevent its falling under the control of the Americans. Sir George mentions this party several times, but nowhere have I been able to find in his journal that he had anything to do with inducing or ordering its members to start to this country, though, when he overtook them, on the way, he gave them good advice as to their route of travel and place to settle. He remarks:

'There were twenty-three families, the heads being generally young and active, though a few of them were advanced in life, more particularly one poor woman, upwards of seventy-five years of age, who was tottering after her son to his new home. This venerable wanderer was a native of the Saskatchewan, the name of which, in fact she bore. She had been absent from this the land of her birth for eighteen years; and, on catching the first glimpse of the river, from the hill near Carlton, she burst, under the influence of old recollection, into a violent flood of tears.

"As a contrast to this superannuated daughter of the Saskatchewan, the band contained several young travelers, who had, in fact, made their appearance in this world since the commencement of the journey. Beyond the inevitable detention, which seldom exceeded a few hours, these interesting events had never interfered with the progress of the brigade; and both mother and child used to jog on, as if jogging on were the condition of human existence.

"Each family had two or three carts, together with bands of horses, cattle and dogs. The men and lads traveled on the saddle, while the vehicles which were covered with awnings against the sun and rain, carried the women and young children. As they marched in single file, their cavalacade extended above a mile in length. The emigrants were all healthy and happy, living in the greatest abundance and enjoying the journey with the highest relish."

The Governor came down the Columbia river to Vancouver, and spent several days in and about that place, then down the Columbia and up the Cowlitz and overland to the Sound. He says:

"After crossing the 'Squally river, we arrived at Fort Nisqually, on the evening of our fourth day from Vancouver. (Sept. 4th.) Being unwilling to commence our voyage on a Sunday, we remained here for six and thirty hours, inspecting the farm and dairy, and visiting Dr. Richmond, an American missionary, stationed in the neighborhood. The surrounding scenery is very beautiful. On the borders of an arm of the sea, of about two miles in width, are undulating plains of excellent pasturage, presenting a pretty variety of copses of oak and placid lakes, and abounding in Chevreuil (deer) and other game.

"The sound yields plenty of fish, such as salmon, rock cod, halibut, flounders, etc. The dogfish and shark are also numerous, some of the latter having been caught here this summer of five or six feet in length.

"Near the Fort there was a small camp of 'Squallies, under the command of Lackalett, a good friend of the traders. The establishment is frequented also by the Clallams, the Paaylaps, the Scatchetts, the Checaylis, and other tribes, amounting in all, the 'Squallies included, to nearly four thousand souls."

John Flett was a member of this Red River brigade of 1841, and after the treaty of 1846 he became an American citizen of fine character, and was well known among the pioneers until his death a few years ago. To most of those who were with the H. B. Company during the early years of American settlement, but, in later years, were naturalized as citizens of this country, the emphasis laid upon "American born," "first American child," etc., was annoying, so when Flett saw Mr. Richmond's letter, he called upon Elwood Evans, and they prepared an article that was published in the Daily News, of Tacoma, Feb. 2, 1884, sharply criticising the clerical writer. Most of this would be of little present interest, except the closing paragraphs, in which he says:

"I cannot account for the desire of the reverend gentleman to see an Indian in every family but his own, unless he had Indian on the brain. He fills two news columns, but never gives us a word about his mission work. I hope he will come out with a historical sketch of the work on the Nisqually Plains. I have never had the first Indian to tell me that he knew the gentleman as a missionary. Several knew him as a "Boston," living on the stream on the north side of the small brook near the place of Edward Huggins, Esq., who now owns old Fort Nisqually.

"I have a bible that Mr. Richmond gave me in 1841, that I prize much. It has been my companion for many years. I wish I could present the public something that the first missionary left in the country besides this book."

In all kindness, I feel like approving what Mr. Flett said. I have been trying for two years to find out something about the missionary work at this point, but there is nothing left to find out. The fact is that the religious work of the early missionaries among the Indians was a complete failure at Nisqually, at Salem, at The Dalles, at Wailatpu, at Lapwai, and everywhere else. The Methodists were the first to recognize this fact and to accept its consequences. They abandoned their outlying posts, and concentrated their work in the Willamette valley, among the white people and soon had flourishing churches and schools that have done effective work for good for more than sixty years.

A copy of Flett's letter was sent to Dr. Richmond, and in April the latter's reply appeared in the News, and occupied over three columns. Much of this is not available for use here, though several paragraphs help make up the record. The Doctor says:

"It was not as a missionary that I wrote to the Seattle Chronicle to correct some errors as to the first American family settled on Puget Sound, and north of the Columbia river, now embraced in Washington Territory. Neither do I feel under any obligations to report my operations for John Flett's edification, or for that of anybody else. It was done more than forty years ago, when I addressed the missionary board at New York for more than three hours at two sessions, Bishop Hedding presiding at the first and Bishop Morris at the second, with Dr. Charles Pitman as secretary of the board, after which my report and operations in the Oregon country were unanimously approved. That matter was concluded to my satisfaction. I have never undertaken to vaunt my achievements in the Puget Sound region, or anywhere else.

"Very few persons seem capable of comprehending the logic or the pure purposes of the board of American Missions in sending a large force of men and women into Oregon at an early day, commencing with or during Gen. Jackson's administration, and continued more or less until the settlement of the controvening claims of the United States and the British government to the occupancy of that territory in 1846, on the 49th degree of north latitude. The question was held in abeyance by the treaties of joint occupancy until that year, and until then the Hudson Bay Company, and the subsidiary organization called the Puget Sound Agricultural Company, had stretched their army more or less all over the Territory, and were urging the British Government to hold fast to their pretensions. Hence the Puget Sound Agricultural Company had enlivened the plains back of Puget Sound with flocks of sheep and herds of cattle, with their concomitants of shepherds, shepherd dogs, herders, dairy farms, and servants to conduct them. On the Willamette river they had their superannuated servants planted upon the best of the soil and founded or commenced the building of Oregon City, at Willamette Falls. I met with a number of French Canadian settlers on the plains above the Willamette Falls in 1841, every one of whom had families, had Indian wives and half-breed children, and they were all subject to the Hudson Bay Company's authority. It was in pursuance of the same policy that brought here the "seventeen families" or colony referred to by John Flett, settled in the neighborhood of Puget Sound, under the direction of Sir George Simpson, in 1841.

"In 1827 a treaty between the governments of Great Britain and the United States, as a temporary compromise agreed to a joint occupancy, which could be terminated by either party, by giving twelve months' notice. This occurred during the administration of John Quincy Adams. Under this condition of things the Hudson Bay Company had free sway—their jurisdiction was acknowledged by all their servants and employees. They had British or Canadian laws, with officers and magistrates to enforce them. Dr. McLaughlin assumed to reign as an autocrat, and exercised both judicial and executive functions in that part of the Hudson Bay Company's dominions. On the other hand American settlers had the protection of no law until they themselves created a provisional government, and my old friend, Geo. Abernethy, connected with the Methodist mission, was appointed or elected first Governor in Oregon by American citizens. From the time that Mr. Jason Lee and his nephew, Daniel, were sent into that region, the missionary society of the Methodist Epispocal Church were laboring to establish a foundation deep and wide for the enterprise, the civilization, and above all the christianity that should be developed by proper influences to operate upon the immigrants who were expected to follow, and who did follow them in a few years. In the meantime they were to use every appliance available for the betterment of the condition of the Indian aborigines. My part of the work was to represent American citizenship and American enterprise in the same capacity in the region of Puget Sound. I had no complaints to make against the deportment of the gentlemen of the Hudson Bay Company, whom I encountered, in the matter of hospitality. But I wish to be distinctly understood that in all cases they received their compensation, and I was never a subject of their charity, and generally I could not but be impressed with the conviction that I was regarded as an intruder. On the contrary I could

not divest myself of the conviction that I was treading upon
American soil, and had all the indefeasable rights belonging
to an American citizen in his own country, and acted accordingly, in view of the circumstances surrounding me.
Hence when I was introduced to Sir George Simpson I
could not but feel that he was trying to snub me as his inferior, and too insignificant personage for his dignified notice. I did not much wonder at it, because he appeared to
be surrounded by a body of sycophants. While I was willing to accord to him all his titular honors, I could not feel
he was my superior in any respect, and I was forced to the
conclusion that he was an aristocratic snob, who, while
occupying a dignified position, probably possessed more
money than brains. Of all the officers of the Hudson Bay
Company with whom I became acquainted I was the most
favorably impressed by the courteous manners and intelligence of Sir James Douglas.

"He also happened to know Capt. McNeil of the steamer
Beaver, and that I might have well have affirmed that his
family were white. I was intimately acquainted with Capt.
McNeil for several years; he often ate at my table, and
on one occasion he brought with him two or three very interesting half-blood children, and requested me to baptize
them, which I did. His wife was a full-blood Indian from
somewhere on the North-west coast, and was comely in
appearance, but rather pendulous in her movements. I
apprehend that Mr. Flett knew very little about Capt. Mc-
Neil. Mr. Flett appears to have made a new discovery in
ethnology, that as soon as a white man mingles his blood
with an Indian woman, their progeny are transformed immediately into whites, and they must be recognized as a
white family. I never was an admirer, much less an advocate of miscegenation, particularly the mixture of the Cau-
cassian with the lower races of the human family—but I
have regarded with less reprehension the mingling of the
white with the Indian blood. In a long, varied life I have
encountered it among the Cherokees in Mississippi, among
the Indians in Oregon and also in Dakota where white men
thus associated are designated squaw men. Where I have
encountered these relations I have regarded them with as
much leniency as possible, and when expedient, I have invariably urged legal marriages. As to the marriage of Mr.
Willson and Miss Clark, I still hold that theirs was the first
marriage of full blood whites, and of American citizens in

REV. JOHN P. RICHMOND, WIFE, AND SON FRANCIS, 1840.

Washington Territory. The second marriage of the same description I solemnized on board ship in Baker's Bay, between Mr. Rogers, connected with the American Board of Missions, and Miss Leslie, a daughter of Rev. David Leslie, Methodist missionary in the Willamette Valley."

The following paragraph is by Mr. Frost, in an old book entitled, "Ten Years in Oregon, by Lee and Frost," both of whom are mentioned elsewhere. It says:

"On the 1st day of September, 1842, we were highly gratified with a visit from my old and tried friend, the Rev. Dr. Richmond, and Mr. Whitcomb, whose families were on board of the Chenamus, which was lying at Astoria, and on board of which they had taken passage to the United States. The Doctor had become satisfied that the prospects of usefulness among the Indians would not warrant his longer continuance in the country. This I am fully convinced was the true state of the case: and, besides this, he had suffered much in consequence of family affliction. I should be very happy to have recourse to his journal, so that I might have the pleasure of laying before our readers some of the scenes through which he had passed while at Nisqually, where I left him, just taking possession of the post assigned him, in the summer of 1840; but this privilege is denied me in consequence of the distance which now separates us."

From this same book it appears that the trip made by Richmond in 1841, as mentioned in his letter above, was to attend the session of the annual church conference.

Rev. John P. Richmond, M. D., was born on the 7th day of August, 1811, in the City of Middleton, Maryland, and died August 28th, 1895, aged 84 years and 21 days.

The subject of this sketch was a remarkable man, and lived an eventful life. He was the lineal descendant of John Richmond, of England, who emigrated to Virginia late in the 16th century, and all along down the list of descendants are to be found men of learning and of distinguished characteristics, among them, Rev. Leigh Richmond and the distinguished Dean Richmond of New York City.

Doctor Richmond was the son of Francis Richmond, by his wife, who was a member of the distinguished Stottlemeyer family, of Maryland. His youthful aspirations were to become a physician, and at the age of twenty he was graduated from a noted medical college in Philadelphia, then under the management of the celebrated Dr. McFarland, but his religious conversion soon following he took a course in theology and at the age of twenty-three he held a license to preach from the Methodist church. About this time he was united in marriage to Mrs. America Talley, widow of the lately deceased Rev. A. Talley, M. D., superintendent of the Choctaw Missions. She was a native of Alabama, and a member of a Walker family.

Possessed of strong physique, indomitable will and large Christian zeal, Dr. Richmond elected to enter the itineracy of the Illinois conference. The father of the writer, Rev. Daniel Bagley, about six years later, entered this same work in this same field, in another branch of the Methodist church and underwent the same hardships and experiences here recounted of Dr. Richmond. Assigned to a timbered portion of the state, almost a wilderness as yet, often no road to follow except that outlined by blazed trees, his circuit embraced a large territory. On horseback, with saddlebags, fording streams and swimming torrents, making the round once in three weeks, and preaching twenty-six times, he never then or ever afterward failed to meet his appointment if it was a human possibility. Upon one occasion, in particular, after having swum the swollen Snye Cartye, he was so unfortunate as to lose his saddlebags, and was towed to land by holding on to his horse's tail, yet, arriving on time, he preached his sermon while his clothes were drying on him.

Of course, the promotion of such a man was rapid, and shortly afterward we find him stationed at Jacksonville, from whence, in 1839, he was sent to the Oregon Board of Missions in the capacity of physician as well as missionary.

After returning from that field of labor to Illinois, he was stationed at Springfield, Quincy, and other points, ex-

ercising his gifts with telling effect. His regular labors in
the ministry ended in 1854, but he continued to preach at
intervals on suitable occasions so long as his physical and
mental powers remained intact. While in the ministry he
was a tower of strength, a mighty force, inferior in ability
to but very few of his distinguished associates.

He was held in high esteem by Peter Cartwright and was
his family physician for some time.

His constituency always loved to honor him in later years.
He served in the Senate of Illinois, while Abraham Lincoln
sat in the lower house; he was speaker of the lower house
while the present Chief Justice Fuller, and ———— Morrison and John Logan occupied seats in that body; he was
chosen by the Electoral College of his state to cast its vote
for President in 1856; was chosen a member of two constitutional conventions of the state and for eight years was
superintendent of schools.

Dr. Richmond and family left their station at Nisqually
in the last days of August, 1842, having been there a little
more than two years. They returned overland to the Cowlitz river over the same rugged trail they had followed in
1840, thence down the Cowlitz and the Columbia to the
ship that carried them home by way of the Sandwich Islands and Cape Horn, so that while their actual stay at
Nisqually was a little more than two years, nearly four
years were consumed in their missionary trip.

A few days after they left the Indians burned their cabin.
I have before me a letter from Doctor McLaughlin, dated
at Vancouver, 23rd Sept., 1842, to Angus McDonald, in
which are detailed instructions about the Company's cattle
at Nisqually. He closes by, saying, "I am sorry to hear
that the Indians have burnt Dr. Richmond's house. Every
endeavor ought to be made to give the perpetrator a good
fright so as to prevent others doing the same thing; I say
to give them a good fright, as I would not wish we found
out who did it, as we would not be justified, perhaps, in
giving him corporeal punishment, and if we knew who it

was, and did not do so, it might induce the Indians to do the like again; our policy, therefore, is not to find who did it but to make a noise about it so as to frighten the Indians from doing the like."

No reason for this destruction of the cabin ever came to light. Many of the Indians were Catholics, and it may have been sectarian fanaticism on the part of some of them, but the following incident often related by Doctor Richmond and his wife, furnishes a more probable reason for the incident:

There was an Indian who became infatuated with bright, black-eyed baby, Francis, and first made efforts to obtain possession of his person by traffic, and, failing in this, he proceeded to abduct him. As the Indian afterward explained, his object was to adopt the little fellow into his tribe. One day, Doctor Richmond had gone to the Fort, the mother was in the main room busy with domestic duties, the baby was in the cradle in the outer room or shed, and the other children were off on a ramble. The mother heard a rustling and a slight cry from baby and hastened to the room to find the cradle empty and the outside door open. Glancing through the open window, she saw the Indian with the baby in his arms, making off over the prairie toward the Sound. With her to see was to act. She seized a loaded rifle, which was ever at hand, sprang to the outside door and drew a bead on the Indian, but if she was quick, the Indian was equally so, for he saw her in time and turning held up the baby between him and her, and continued to retreat backward. This, no doubt saved his life, as Mrs. Richmond was a dead shot with the rifle. At this moment she saw her husband on a rising ground coming from the Fort, and making a sign which he recognized, he started on the run. The mother left the house in pursuit of the retreating Indian, the pursued and the pursuer keeping about the same relative distance until the latter came to one corner of the palisades of the Fort, when the Doctor coming up behind him knocked him down with the cane which appears in the illustration. The mother handed the gun to the father and picked up the baby. The Indian sprang up and seized the cane, but, after quite a scuffle, the Doctor recovered possession of it and again knocked his antagonist down, after which he took the gun back to the house for the mother and then went back to the Fort and reported the circumstance to the officers. Search was made for the Indian, and after much time spent he was found concealed under a large mat. His head and face were badly bruised and swollen, and, the Doctor interceding for him, he was let off with light punishment. When the Richmonds were embarking for their return home, this same Indian was discovered prowling around suspiciously, and was taken in custody to the Fort, but, no doubt, later wreaked his revenge so far as possible by the destruction of the house.

In Doctor Richmond's letters and in every book written by the early missionaries—of which I have seven or eight, long out of print and exceedingly rare—the writers acknowledge and emphasize their great obligations to the officers of the Hudson's Bay Company at their many posts for their generous hospitality, uniform courtesy, and considerate acts of continuing kindness. Still, all through their writings runs a vein of ill concealed resentment, or of open unfriendliness. At this late day, this seems little short of blackest ingratitude; but, to one familiar with the affairs of that period, there seems some excuse for it.

While not all the officers of the Company were Catholics, still the influence of the entire organization was favorable to that Church. Nearly every subordinate was a Catholic, and, so far as I can find out, all the wives and daughters of high and low degree were members of that Church. Its priests were welcomed as friends and companions; with them it was not a matter of hospitality or of courtesy, but wherever the "Blackgowns" went they found an open house and a seat of honor at the table and by the fireside. As said elsewhere, this had great influence upon the minds of the Indians, and in the vicinity of every Hudson's Bay Company post, the Catholic missionaries left few if any converts for the other churches. Besides this sectarian condition of affairs, opposing political interests arose. The Catholic priests and the Hudson's Bay people were all foreigners, and all opposed to the organization of a civil government in Oregon at the time the missionaries and the free American settlers began their efforts in that direction.

Doctor Richmond says in his letter that he had no complaint of the gentlemen of the Hudson's Bay Company in the matter of hospitality, but that he paid for all he received and was never a subject of their charity. This is, perhaps true, but ungracious; besides he could not be ignorant that he and his family were under the protection of the Company, that they could not have remained safely in their lonely cabin but for this protection, and that under direction from Governor McLaughlin those in charge of Fort Nisqually did much for them that money alone could not pay for; that only thanks and gratitude could be offered as a recompense.

In a letter to A. C. Anderson, of October 17, 1840, the Governor says, "You will please supply Dr. Richmond with five bushels of pease and four barrels of flour." In another of May 8th, 1841, "You may continue to break in and milk as many cows as you can. It is not so important to milk them for a long time as to break in so that next year we may establish several dairies at the place. You can lend six broken-in cows to the Methodist Mission for the season, and after sometime when their calves are big you will let them go and give the missionaries others in their place," February 1, 1841, "Please hand the accompanying pamphlets to Rev. Dr. Richmond with my compliments, and after perusal I beg he will return them to you, and you will please send them back by first opportunity."

Here was the head of the Hudson's Bay Company's affairs on the Pacific coast, with stations scattered all over the area much larger than "Old Oregon," because it reached northward to the Russian Possessions, with all the complex interests of that giant power to oversee, a domination kingly in its extent, and undisputed everywhere; but this man was not too busy or too indifferent to forget the comfort of a lonely family of an alien race over on the shores of Puget Sound. Volumes could not more surely prove the grandeur of character, or the simple loveableness, of this prince among men, John McLaughlin.

Again, a few years later, but for this same kindly spirit of unselfish charitableness, it would have gone hard with the advance guard of true pioneers who established American settlements about the headwaters of Puget Sound. They might not have starved, but they would have gone hungry and poorly clothed, and felt the hardships and privations of the first few years far more than they did but for the aid so often extended to them at Fort Nisqually.

July fourth, 1841, was a notable day at Nisqually, as it was celebrated in genuine Yankee fashion, the first event of the kind on the Pacific Coast, and, probably, west of the Missouri river. Capt. Wilkes declared a holiday, and the crew were given a whole day of frolic and pleasure. He purchased an ox of the Company, which they were allowed to barbecue, and they also made their own arrangements for the celebration.

The place selected was near one of the small lakes lying to the eastward, and from that time it has been known as American Lake. Here they slaughtered their ox and spitted him on a sapling large enough to support its weight, the ends of the spit resting in the forks of other small trees that had been set in the ground for the purpose. A trench, perhaps four feet deep, and large enough to hold the carcass, was dug. In this a large fire of dry wood that gave off little smoke, was maintained, and over this the carcass was turned slowly until thoroughly cooked.

All was activity and bustle on the 5th, as the 4th fell on Sunday. Before nine o'clock all the men were mustered on board in clean white frocks and trousers, and all, including the marines and music, were landed shortly afterward, to

march to the scene of festivity, about a mile distant. The
procession was formed at the observatory just at the brow
of the hill, whence all marched off with flags flying and
music playing. Two brass howitzers were also carried to
the prairie to fire the usual salutes. When the procession
reached Fort Nisqually, they stopped, gave three cheers,
and waited, sailor-like, until it was returned. This was
done only by a few voices, a circumstance which did not
fail to produce many jokes among the seamen. On reaching the ground, various games occupied the crew, while
the officers also amused themselves in the same manner. At
the usual hour, dinner was piped, when all repaired to partake of the barbecue. By this time the Indians had gathered from all quarters, and were silently looking on at the
novel sight, and wistfully regarding the feast which they
saw going on before them. At this time a salute was fired,
when one of the men had his arm most dreadfully lacerated
from the sudden explosion of the gun. This accident put a
momentary stop to the hilarity of the occasion, but men-of-
wars-men were familiar with such scenes, and the interruption did not last long. The amusements of the morning
were now exchanged for that of horse racing, a sport always
in favor with Jack ashore. Of course they had many tumbles off the wild horses provided by the Indians of the
place, for a consideration. There were many tumbles, but
no one was injured.

In 1846, the British war vessel, Fisgard, lay a long time
at anchor in Nisqually bay, and horse racing was one of the
chief amusements of the men-of-wars-men at that time. A
regular race course was laid out in the small prairie north
of the Fort, which had been then moved to the site so familiar to early day settlers, and now known as "Huggins'
Place." It was a half mile around, flat and smooth, with
grand stand, etc., all complete. Indians came from east of
the mountains with their race horses, and betting at these
races was the only way the sailors had to spend their money,
that and riding horses.

Doctor Richmond delivered the oration which was one of the features of the old-time celebrations, but the record fails to say who read the Declaration of Independence. Here are a couple of extracts from the Doctor's address:

"The average man, faithful to the lines of human reason and experience, and unconsciously inclined to attribute to Deity thoughts similar to his own, often makes most grave and hazardous ventures with respect to the will and the designs of Providence. Upon Fourth-of-Julys, especially, we are irresistibly impelled to entertain the belief that the whole of this magnificent region, so inestimably rich in the bounties of nature, and susceptible of measureless development, is destined to become one of the physical ingredients of our beneficent Republic. The time will come, though you and I may not live to realize it, when these hills and valleys will have become peopled by our free and enterprising countrymen, when yonder towering mountains will look down upon magnificent cities, fertile farms, and smoking manufactories. Every succeeding Fourth of July there will gather together hosts of freemen to recall the glorious past of their country and to renew their fidelity to the maxims of the fathers of the Republic as embodied in that grand state paper which has been this day eloquently and effectively read to us.

"Still further than I have ventured to define, the eye of the philosopher may penetrate the future to view its wonderful and inevitable developments. It may see the sure and steady advance of our dominion to the frozen regions of the North and to that narrow strip of land which connects this continent with its sister of the South; when, in this "New World" there will have arisen into boundles wealth and power the grandest nation which, in all the annals of mankind, will have appeared upon the earth.

"Your names and mine may not appear among the records of the future historians of this region; but those of our descendants will appear. Where our work will end theirs will begin, and we may be sure that as we would now define for them their careers, so they will perform their parts in the grand pageants of American Patriotism.

"Providently instructed by their knowledge of the past of nations of the deadly dangers therewith, the illustrious founders of the Repubilc declared against the union of church and state; and this doctrine involved both the fact and the theory, both the reality and the suggestion; but what I now venture to say I am sure will be considered as no violation of any of the doctrines of the fathers. While it would be untrue to claim that Christianity was the founder of civilization, knowing as we do that the greatest of all past civilizations was just expiring when Christ appeared, yet it is undeniably true that the world's civilization of today is indissolubly connected with the religion of Christ; and neither could survive the fall of the other. This permits me to say of our mission in this remote region that, by bringing to these savage children of the wilderness the truths of Christianity, we encourage in them that future development of character which will fit them to act creditably their destined parts as citizens of the Republic."

Late in the summer of 1838, there left New York harbor the first National Maritime Exploring Expedition fitted out by the Government. It consisted of five vessels, under the command of Charles Wilkes, who afterward became noted by reason of his capture of the English ship Trent, and taking out of her the Confederate commissioners, Mason and Slidell, who were on their way to Europe on business of the Confederacy. The work of this expedition was so well done that it is a matter of national pride to this day. There were. two ships of war, the Vincennes and Peacock, the brig of war, Porpoise, and two tenders that had been pilot boats and renamed Sea Gull and Flying Fish. The corps of scientists consisted of nine men noted in their several fields of work in their day. There were eighty-six officers and five hundred and ninety seamen.

They were directed to examine the region about the Rio Negro on the southerly coast of South America, to explore the southern Antarctic to the southward of Powell's Group, to proceed southward and westward in the Southern Pacific as far as Captain Cook had gone in any of his voyages, to survey the Navigator's Group, the Feejee Islands, and select a harbor there, and in 1840, to proceed to the Sandwich Islands, where a government store-ship was to meet them. Thence they were to direct their course to the Northwest

Coast of America, making such surveys and examinations, first of the territory of the United States on the seaboard, and of the Columbia river, and afterwards along the Coast of California, then Mexican territory, with special reference to the bay of San Francisco, as could be accomplished by the month of October of that year. This was only a small part of the work that was planned for accomplishment.

Pursuant to these orders Capt. Wilkes found himself sailing up the Straits of Fuca May 1, 1841. They first stopped at Port Discovery for a few days, but on the 11th of that month they dropped anchor at Nisqually, near where the steamer Beaver was undergoing repairs, in command of Capt. McNeil, while A. C. Anderson was in charge of the Fort. The latter gave the party a warm reception, and offered it all the assistance in their power. Capt. Wilkes remarks, "Nothing can exceed the beauty of these waters, and their safety: Not a shoal exists within the Straits of San Juan de Fuca, Admiralty Inlet, Puget Sound, or Hood's Canal, that can in anyway interrupt their navigation by a seventy-four- gun ship. I venture nothing in saying there is no country in the world that possesses waters equal to these. The shore, here, rises abruptly, to a height of about two hundred feet, and on top of the ascent is an extended plain, covered with pine, oak, and ash trees, scattered here and there so as to form a park-like scene. The hillside is mounted by a well constructed road, of easy ascent; from the summit of the road the view is beautiful, over the Sound and its many islands, with Mount Olympus covered with snow for a background. Fort Nisqually, with its outbuildings and enclosure, stands back half a mile from the edge of the table land."

The Porpoise, with two of the Vincennes' boats, under Lieutenant-Commandant Ringgold, were directed to take up the survey of Admiralty Inlet. The launch, first cutter and two other boats of the Vincennes, under command of Lieut. Case, were sent to survey Hood's Canal. Another party intended for land explorations, was formed under the command of Lieutenant Johnson of the Porpoise. Eighty days were allowed for the operations of this party, which it was intended should cross the Cascade mountains and the Columbia river, and up that valley to Fort Colville, thence south to Rev. Spalding's Mission at Lapwai, on what was in the early days called the Kooskooskie river, thence to Walla Walla, and thence returning by way of the Yakima river, and over the mountains to the place of departure. This was the first party of Americans to cross the Cascades, though the Hudson's Bay people had used the mountain route for several years earlier. They found the Indians had a regular trail over the range, passing to the northward of Mount Rainier, when they first settled at Nisqually.

An observatory was established on the brow of the hill, a few rods north of the roadway, and within hail of the ships. The remains of the observatory remained until a few years ago when the proposed new railroad across from the Sound to the Columbia river was surveyed and mostly graded, when at this point the grade entirely obliterated the old landmark.

Captain Wilkes also arranged for another land party, headed by himself with four companions. Their intended route was across the country to the Cowlitz, and down that stream and the Columbia river to Astoria, then back to Vancouver, and up the valley of the Willamette, and then up the Columbia river to Fort Walla Walla.

While these preparations were making he visited and received visits from the white people at the station. He mentions receiving visits from Chief Factor Anderson and Captain McNeil, and from Doctor Richmond and Mr. Willson. Of the two former he remarks, that both reside in the Fort; both are married to half-breeds, and have several fine children. He also visited Dr. Richmond, and says:

"Here I found Mrs. Richmond and Mrs. Willson, the former of whom has four fine, rosy and fat children, whose appearance speaks volumes for the health of the climate. This mission was but recently established; so far as respects its prospects, they are not very flattering. The location of the mission-house, on the borders of an extensive and beautiful prairie, can scarcely be surpassed, and would be admirably adapted for a large settlement, if the soil was in any respect equal to its appearance. At the season when we arrived, nothing could be more beautiful, or to appearance more luxuriant than the plains, which were covered with flowers of every color and kind."

After visiting the missionary stations in the Willamette valley and elsewhere, he gives a summary of his observations. The writer became acquainted with the condition of affairs in the Willamette valley only ten years after Captain Wilkes was there and by frequent interchange of views with others who were well acquainted with other parts of the mission work at that time and subsequent thereto, as well as a careful perusal of practically all that has been published regarding the same, he quotes, with his approval, what the Captain said at that time, as follows:

"We were exceedingly desirous of obtaining information as to the future plans of these missionaries as to teaching and otherwise forwarding the civilization of the Indian boys, but from all that we could learn from the missionaries, as well as lay members, my impression was, that no fixed plan of operations had been digested; and I was somewhat surprised to hear them talking of putting up extensive buildings for missionary purposes, when it is fully apparent that there is but a very limited field for spiritual operations in this part of the country. The number now attached and under tuition are probably all that can be converted, and does not exceed the number attached to the mission. I was exceedingly desirous of drawing their attention to the tribes of the north, which are a more numerous and hardier race, with a healthy climate. It is true that a mission has been established at Nisqually, but they are doing nothing with the native tribes, and that post is only on the borders of many larger tribes to the northward. As the holders of a charge, committed to their hands by a persevering and enlightened class of Christians at home, who are greatly interested in their doings and actions, they will be held responsible for any neglect in the great cause they have under-

taken to advance, and in which much time and money have
been spent.

"That all may judge of the extent of this field of missionary labors, I will enumerate the numbers of Indians within
its limits. Nisqually, two hundred; Clatsop, two hundred
and nine; Chinooks, two hundred and twenty; Kilamukes,
four hundred; Callapuyas, six hundred; Dalles, two hundred and fifty: say in all in this district, two thousand Indians; and this field is in part occupied by the Catholics,
as I have before stated. Of these, the Methodist missionaries have under their instruction, if so it may be called,
twenty-five at the Willamette station; at the Dalles, and
occasionally on the Klackamus river, are the only places
where divine services are attempted. I would not have it
understood that by these remarks I have any desire to throw
blame on those who direct or are concerned in this missionary enterprise, or to make any imputations on the laborers;
but I feel it a duty I owe my countrymen, to lay the truth
before them, such as we saw it. I am aware that the missionaries come out to this country to colonize, and with
the Christian religion as their guide and law, to give the
necessary instruction, and hold out inducements to the
Indians to quit their wandering habits, settle and become
cultivators of the soil. This object has not been yet attained in any degree, as was admitted by the missionaries
themselves; and how it is to be effected without having
constantly around them large numbers, and without exertions and strenuous efforts, I am at a loss to conceive. I
cannot but believe that the same labor and money which
have been expended here, would have been much more ap-
propriately and usefully spent about the Straits of Juan de
Fuca, who are numerous, and fit objects of instruction."

The nomenclature of the waters from Port Townsend
southward to the heads of Budd's Inlet and of Hood's Canal
is almost entirely the result of this survey and exploration
of Wilkes, while of the waters to the northward it is almost
all that of Vancouver in 1792, though the Spanish explorers
of an earlier day established some names that still remain.

To the party under Lieut. Commander Ringgold fell the
task of surveying from the Narrows down east side of Vash-
on's Island, thence northward on both sides of the Sound,
particularly all the bays that would afford shelter for ves-

sels, not only as harbors but for temporary anchorage. Under these orders the bay in front of what is now Seattle was surveyed and sounded and named after Samuel Elliot, midshipman of the Vincennes, which is probable or in honor of Chaplain J. L. Elliot of the same vessel who left the expedition at San Francisco in October, 1841. Captain Wilkes says:

"The first bay at the bottom of Admiralty Inlet was termed Commencement Bay. Into this falls the Puyallup, which forms a delta, and none of the branches into which it is divided are large enough for the entrance of a boat. The Indians were at this season of the year to be found on all the points, and were the same filthy creatures that have been before described."

"Port Orchard is one of the most beautiful of the many fine harbors on these inland waters, and is perfectly protected from the winds. The sheet of water is extensive, and is surrounded by a large growth of trees, with here and there a small prairie covered by a verdant greensward, and with its honeysuckles and roses just in bloom, resembling a well-kept lawn. The woods seemed alive with squirrels, while tracks on the shore and through the forest showed that the larger class of animals were also in the habit of frequenting them."

William Holden Willson and Miss Chloe Aurelia Clark were united in marriage at Nisqually, August 16, 1840. To the writer this is a coincidence, for his parents, Rev. Daniel Bagley and Miss Susannah Rogers Whipple, were married the day preceding, or August 15, 1840. My father was sent out by the Board of Missions of the Methodist Protestant church, and we arrived in Salem, on the townsite laid off by Willson, and named by him after the Massachusetts town of that name, September 21, 1852, where we found him and his wife occupying a fine home, the Doctor having already acquired considerable wealth at that early day. The two families became well acquainted, and a strong friendship grew up between the Doctor and my father. The Doctor gave my father a lot for a church site, and also sold him two lots on which our first home on the Pacific Coast was erected. On the church lot a substantial church was

erected, of good seating capacity, and it was used by my
father much of the time until we came to Seattle in 1860.

Mr. Willson was born in Charlestown, New Hampshire,
April 14, 1805, being of English ancestry. Later he lived
in Massachusetts for a number of years, learning the trade
of a carpenter, and afterward became a ship-carpenter.
About 1834, he began the study of medicine as opportunity
offered, there being no regular medical college near him at
that time. As mentioned heretofore, Dr. Elija White arrived in Oregon at the head of a considerable missionary
party, among whom was Mr. Willson.

They sailed from Boston, July 28, 1836, on the ship Hamilton, for the Sandwich Islands, arriving there late in the
winter. They were compelled to remain there five months
before an opportunity offered to get passage to the Columbia
river. In the latter part of April, 1837, they sailed on the
brig Diana, and arrived at Vancouver about a month later.

Dr. White, in his "Ten Years in Oregon," gives some of
the characteristics of his sailing companions. Of Willson,
he says he was five feet, ten inches in height, cheerful,
sympathetic, and affectionate, fond of relating old sea-
stories, for he had been quite an experienced whaler. A
peculiar characteristic, and a strange one for a man, was
an almost childish partiality for cats; and as there were
none on board, he made a pet of a beautiful kid, whose head
he would comb for an hour together, talking to it the while
as though it was a human being."

Mr. Willson at once set to work to get the goods of the
party up the Willamette river, and continued to lead an
active life in the work of the Mission, especially in the
mechanical department, where there was always plenty to
do.

He did not take part in the earliest steps toward the formation of the provisional government in Oregon, in 1841, as
he was then at Nisqually, but at a meeting at the Oregon
Institute, February 2, 1843, he was present and was one of
six to outline a plan of procedure, and to notify the people

of a meeting appointed for the first Monday in March, following. Not much was accomplished at that appointed meeting, but at one held at "Champooick," May 2, 1843, an organization was effected. Dr. J. L. Babcock was chosen chairman, and Messrs. Gray, LeBreton and Willson, secretaries. A list of officers was named, consisting of supreme judge, clerk of court, sheriff, three magistrates and three constables, and a treasurer. Joe. Meek, whom Mrs. Victor has immortalized in her book "River of the West," was chosen sheriff, and William H. Willson, treasurer.

In February, 1844, an affray between an Indian desperado and six of his companions and a party of whites took place at the Willamette Falls, or Oregon City. The leader of the Indians was killed and several others wounded, and three whites wounded slightly, as it was at the time supposed, but two young men, LeBreton and Rogers, died the next day from the effects of poisoned arrows, and our friend Willson, after considerable suffering, recovered without permanent injury. A few days later a meeting was called of which Mr. Willson was chairman, at which it was decided to organize a volunteer company of mounted riflemen, to co-operate with other companies, to bring to justice all the Indians engaged in the affair mentioned above, and to protect the lives and property of the settlers against similar assaults in future.

One of the first acts of the first Oregon legislature is dated December 24, 1844, and grants to "L. H. Judson and W. H. Willson, and their successors, the right to construct a mill-race from the northern branch of the Santiam river to the eastern branch of the small stream which runs to and drives the mills at Chemeketa, formerly owned by the Methodist Espiscopal Mission."

The first woolen mill in Oregon, and, I think, the first on the Pacific Coast, was built on the banks of this little stream, later called "Mill Creek." Our home was a few hundred feet from it, and it was rich in numerous "swimming holes," where the small boys of those early days disported themselves in safety until they had "learned to swim," when they went to the Willamette river to spend all the spare time their hard-hearted parents would allow them from their tasks at home and their books at school. It was in this "crick" the writer learned the art of natation. Our old friend, M. M. McCarver, the founder of Tacoma, was speaker of the first legislature, of which there was but one house, and he signed the bill granting said "charter," as it was then called.

Willson was one of the Loan Commissioners of the Provisional government in 1848, to raise funds to prosecute the Indian war, which was undertaken to punish the Cayuses for the murder of Doctor Whitman and his wife and nearly a dozen others the preceding year at Waiilatpu. He was also a member of the Oregon Exchange Company, which coined $57,500 in five and ten dollar pieces in 1849, at Oregon City, known as "Beaver" money, from the figure of that industrious animal, proper emblem for those days, that was stamped upon the coins. This was the first coinage in American territory on the Pacific Coast. The writer saw a good many of these coins in his boyhood days but they are now quite rare, and highly prized by their fortunate owners. They were made of the natural gold, and in consequence, were a light yellow in color, and being very soft quickly wore off smooth if long in circulation.

March 15, 1842, the "Oregon Institute" was established near Salem, under the management of the Methodist Church. After some delays and considerable negotiation a large building that had been put up for an Indian mission school, was secured. It stood near the present site of the Willamette University, a few hundred feet south of the present state Capitol building in Salem. For more than sixty years this institution has done a grand work in educating and training the youth of our sister territory and state. Thousands of young people, and those who are no longer young, are proud to remember the time spent within the walls of the "Old Institute" and its successor, the University. Prof.

F. S. Hoyt, who returned in early days to his old home in Kentucky, was one of the early instructors there, Rev. Isaac I. Dillon and wife, who were well known on Puget Sound, a few years ago, also taught there; T. M. Gatch, for years President of the State University, in Seattle, was professor of foreign languages and mathematics there more than forty-five years ago, but one of our Nisqually friends of the long ago, Mrs. Chloe A. Willson, was the first teacher, and therefore upon her devolves the lasting honor of being the first teacher of an American school for white children west of the Rocky Mountains. The school at that time was conducted as a boarding school, most of the pupils coming from a distance and living at the institution.

Mr. Willson took an active part in the affairs of the institution for many years, it being intrusted to him, personally, to secure the title to the grounds, which he did by means of the Donation Claim act; and in this connection a vexatious and long-standing dispute arose with the school board, that is not pertinent to this story.

He had completed his medical studies on shipboard, on the long voyage out from Boston, under the instruction of Dr. White, himself an educated and skillful physician and surgeon, and about 1843, he became Doctor Willson and entered into active practice, continued until a few years before his death, which occurred April 17, 1856. Mrs. Willson lived until June 2, 1874, having spent her later years with her daughter in Portland, who married a well-known business man of that city, H. K. Gill.

Thus the man who laid the foundation for the first American home by the beautiful waters of this inland sea, also helped to lay the foundations broad and deep of the great sister commonwealth that lies just across the "Oregon" of Thanatopsis.

To Michael Simmons, Colonel by courtesy, he having held that rank in the Independent Oregon Company in 1841, while crossing the plains, and to all old settlers, "Mike," belongs the honor of being the leader of the first permanent

American settlers on Puget Sound. In July, 1845, he, George Wanch and William Shaw and a party of others come over from Vancouver to the Sound. In August they made a canoe trip down as far as the north end of Whidby Island, returning by the east side of that island, and then going back to their families at Vancouver. A new party was organized, consisting of M. T. Simmons, and family, James McAllister and family, David Kindred and family, Gabriel Jones and family, George Bush and family, and Jesse Ferguson, Reuben Crowder and Samuel B. Crockett. They had to cut a road from the Cowlitz Landing to the prairie near the present town of Centralia. This consumed two weeks and made it near the close of October before they reached the site of Tumwater, at the head of salt water above Olympia. Simmons was attracted by the water power of the Deschuttes, then called The Shutes.

In 1846, he built there a grist mill which would grind wheat but not bolt it. The stones were chiseled out of granite boulders found on the beach. In 1847, Simmons, Frank Shaw, Edmond Sylvester, A. B. Rabbeson, Gabriel Jones, Jesse Ferguson, John Kindred and A. D. Conifix built a saw mill near the lower part of the falls at the same place, and this was the first mill of the kind on Puget Sound.

At the time of the re-organization of the Provisional Government in July, 1845, the territory north of the Columbia river was formed into Vancouver district. James Douglas, then one of the Board of Control of the Hudson's Bay Company, James Forrest, officer in charge of the P. S. Agricultural Company's Affairs at Cowlitz Farms, and Colonel Simmons were named as the first three commissioners or county judges. Lewis county was organized that winter and embraced all the territory north of the Columbia and west of the Cowlitz rivers, and at the succeeding election in June, 1846 Doctor William F. Tolmie, chief Trader at Nisqually, was elected the first representative. Thus, it will be seen that the Hudson's Bay Company officers were in control of affairs of the young community, as well as of its business affairs; in fact, but for this Company these pioneer settlers would have been on the verge of starvation much of the time for several years.

Often, I come across ill-natured remarks regarding its treatment of the early settlers, and the descendants of these early settlers have been among the offenders in this particular. No greater falsehoods could have been told. It is claimed that Dr. McLaughlin and the other officers of the Company endeavored to dissuade Simmons and party from coming to the Sound. This may be true. It would be quite natural, and no matter of criticism. The trading, farming and stockraising operations of the two companies were large and immensely profitable, and it was quite natural they should desire to retain them, but when it became apparent that Simmons and party had decided to come, instead of showing any ill nature or pique the good Doctor set to work to aid them in many ways. He gave orders on Forrest at Cowlitz, and on Tolmie at Nisqually to furnish them on credit with several hundred bushels of grain and ten or a dozen head of cattle at twelve dollars per head. For years this system of credits was continued to all who proved worthy of it, and in addition the Company made work for them it could very well have left undone.

James McAllister was the first to take a claim away from the prairies near Deschuttes. He was, also, among the first to be killed by the Indians in the war of 1855-6. With the consent of the Indians, he took his claim in the Nisqually bottom, not far from the council ground of the tribe of that name.

Mrs. Hartman, daughter of James McAllister wrote several years ago a long article from which are selected the following paragraphs:

"We had all kinds of game, which was more plentiful than the tame stock now, fish and clams, dried and fresh, the Indians showing us how to prepare them, but we never succeeded in learning the art of drying them. We were successful in drying fruits, the Indians' mode requiring no sugar. For vegetables we had lackamas, speacotes, and

numerous other roots. We children learned to like the
Indian food so well that we thought we could not exist without it. We kept a supply as long as we could get it, but I
have not seen any for many years.

"In 1846, mother disliking to stay alone while father was
building, he laughingly told her he had seen two big stumps
side by side, and that if she would live in them he would
take her with him. Mother told him she would go, so father
scraped out the stumps and made a roof, and mother moved
in with her six children. She found it very comfortable,
the burnt out roots making such nice cubby-holes for stow-
ing away things. Mother continued to live in her stump
house until father built a house, the work being necessarily
slow, for father had but few tools."

To one familiar with the big cedar stumps of Nisqually
bottom, this charming little story will not seem improbable.

This home was not far from Nisqually, and one day Mrs.
McAllister went to see Mrs. Huggins, and at that time gave
an account of the hardships of the trip to the Sound. They
grew short of provisions so that the children were crying
from hunger, somewhere on the Cowlitz trail, between the
Company's store near the mouth of that stream where Monticello afterward stood and the Cowlitz Farm. Here Mr.
John Work, father of Mrs. Huggins, met them on his way
to Fort Vancouver from Fort Simpson, away up on the
North-west Coast, where he had an important post. Mr.
Work was a tender hearted man and appreciated the pitiful
condition of the poor mother and her children. He promptly
unloaded his packhorse and gave Mrs. McAllister all that
was left of the plentiful supply of provisions he had secured
at Nisqually, enough to last them until they could reach the
Company's farm at Cowlitz. This kindness Mrs. McAllister
had not forgotten, and showed much pleasure in telling of it
to his daughter. Somebody put a story afloat a few years
ago that it was the noted Indian Leschi who had performed
this generous deed.

A letter from Peter Skeen Ogden and James Douglas, of
July 3, 1846, makes the first mention of the shingle business I have found, and it shows that the Company had pur-

chased shingles previous to that date. Here is the paragraph: "If it would be any accommodation you may ship the shingles on hand at Nisqually and all the last year's salmon at Victoria to the Sandwich Islands by the Rosalind, paying one and one-half dollars per barrel for the salmon or per thousand shingles; or, if there be any opportunity of selling the shingles to advantage you are at liberty to dispose of them." Simmons, McAllister and party arrived in October, 1845, and already the shingles made by them had begun to accumulate in July, 1846.

A summary of these purchases after February, 1847, taken off the old books of the Company by Mr. Huggins, shows an aggregate of 1150 thousand, for which not less than three dollars per thousand and from that to ten dollars were paid. As it is practically a roster of the settlers in that region at that time, I give the names: T. M. Glasgow, William Packwood, Joshua Melvin, Gabriel Jones, George Bush, M. T. Simmons, Jesse Ferguson, James McAllister, William O. Bush, Charles Eaton, Maurice Jones, Franklin Shaw, Benjamen Gordon, ———— Williamson, Tyrell & Melvin, Jonathan Logan, Evans, Gordon & Buchanan, Redwood Easton, Henry Evans, A. M. Poe, Samuel Davis, David Kindred, L. A. Smith, Samuel Crockett, D. D. Kinsey, Edmund Sylvester, A. B. Rabbeson, George Shazer, George Brail, C. Obrist, Joseph Broshears, Lewis Jones, Luther M. Collins, John Bradley, Joseph Borst, A. T. Simmons.

In 1885, the writer bought of Schwabacher Bros. & Co. good shaved shingles at two dollars and twenty-five cents per thousand, and on them the firm made a good profit and, the makers made good wages. This shows that the early settlers had no reason to go hungry, when they could make from five to fifteen dollars per day shaving shingles. Of the amount named above James McAllister is credited with two hundred and twenty thousand, or nearly one-fifth the whole number, and for 35½ thousand he was paid at the rate of ten dollars.

Doctor Tolmie inaugurated this traffic and nothwithstanding large shipments were made to the Sandwich Islands and to other places at times the stock on hand reached large proportions. Along in 1849, he grew apprehensive the Company would suffer loss. He wrote to James Douglas, then his superior officer, telling him the condition of the business and asking orders as to whether he should reduce the price or discontinue buying them. Mr. Douglas replied, "We must assist these poor people and cannot see them suffer for want of the necessaries of life." He instructed Doctor Tolmie to continue buying shingles at the old price of three dollars, as it would in the long run turn out all right. A market would be found for the shingles somewhere and he was confident the Company would suffer little or no loss by the transaction.

Sure enough, in the beginning of 1850, the Sound country began to feel the effects of the mining of gold in California. In March the brig Sacramento, Capt. Alex. Monat, an old Hudson's Bay Company employee, arrived at Nisqually seeking a cargo of piles, lumber and shingles. He paid Luther M. Collins, then of Nisqually but later one of the first settlers in King County, three dollars each for one hundred and five small piles and Doctor Tolmie thirteen dollars per thousand for 121 thousand shingles.

Capt. Monat obtained a limited supply of lumber from the little Tumwater mill, and for a time the prices ranged from sixty to one hundred dollars per thousand.

The changed condition of affairs was not altogether in favor of the settlers. To be sure labor was largely in demand at big wages. Good axmen were paid five dollars per day, and whatever produce the struggling settlers had to spare brought them large prices. To offset this, breadstuffs and provisions generally, went up to famine prices. Flour reached forty to fifty dollars a barrel, and the demand outran the supply on this Coast, therefore shipments from New York and Boston were made around the Horn, and often when these barrels were opened the contents would be musty or sour.

How fairly the Company dealt in regard to prices of articles out of its store, the following list of advances made to the American settlers from Nov. 7, 1845, to December 31, 1846, the period immediately following the arrival of Simmons and party, will show. The reader must not forget this was the only place these goods could be secured, in all this North-west, except at some other post of the Company. These prices average twenty-five per cent. below those of today for similar articles, and were about one-half the rates prevailing in Oregon when we arrived there in 1852:—Six axes at one dollar, twenty-five cents; one drawing knife at 90 cents; 28 bushels of oats at 50 cents; 43 bushels of pease at 90 cents; 213½ bushels potatoes at 25 cents; 71½ bushels wheat at 80 cents; 1½ bushels of buckwheat at 60 cents; 12½ lbs. black wool at 16 cents; 8 bullocks at eighteen dollars; 2 mares at thirteen dollars and fifty cents; 25 lbs. salt-pork at ten cents; 2½ doz. quinine powders at 50 cents; 98 lbs. coffee at 25 cents; 62½ gals. molasses at 55 cents; 90 lbs. brown sugar at 12½ cents; 11½ bushels of salt at 70 cents per bushel; 13¼ lbs. Congo tea at 70 cents; ¼lb. Epsom salts at 16 cents (this charge was four cents); 60 lbs. 30d Rose nails at 4 cents; 40 lbs. 20d clasp nails at 4 cents; 16 lbs. 10d clasp nails at 13 cents; 32 lbs. nails for bark covering at 2 cents per lb.; 4½ doz. Kirby hooks at 6 cents; 7 lbs. gunpowder at 30 cents; 15 lbs. ammunition (lead) at one cent per lb.; 15½ lbs. twist tobacco at 40 cents; 84 1-3 lbs. leaf tobacco at 26 cents; one tin kettle $1.80; one gimlet four cents.

With plenty of time and space at my disposal, I should use a great deal more of the old records and letters Mr. Huggins has placed at my disposal, but it is out of the question. The original letters that follow have more or less bearing upon matters referred to in this sketch, and at the same time will give the reader of today an insight to the manner of doing business out here at the times when they were written. Nearly every one of these was sent by special messenger from Vancouver to Nisqually. The messenger came down the Columbia and up the Cowlitz rivers by canoe and from the Cowlitz Farm on horseback. It took from four to seven days for the trip one way, and no doubt cost from fifteen to twenty dollars for each express.

Mr. A. C. Anderson,   Vancouver, 21 July, 1841.

Dear Sir:—I forward with this a letter for Commodore Wilkes, which you will please deliver and retain the Indians till you see the Commodore as he may, perhaps, wish to send an answer.

I found the letter I wrote to Mr. Yale from Nisqually had been put up with those for this place. I now send it and if the Cadboro has been with you, as I presume, you will endeavor if possible to send it by Indians to Mr. Yale.

I say nothing about the work at your place as I have already mentioned my views in my former communication; but I must observe that I hope you will take particular care that the cows are not so much milked as to injure the calves, as our main object is only at present to tame the cows, and raise as many calves as possible.

I am, dear sir, yours truly,

JOHN McLAUGHLIN.

P. S.—Vizena's things will be sent him by a subsequent opportunity. There is an Indian woman, Madam Tetrean, lawfully married to one Tetrean; but who ran away and left him, and this woman has lived with Vizena here, but if she goes to Nisqually you will not allow her to live with him.

J. McL.

My servant left a pair of my suspenders and a pair of trousers of mine at Nisqually.

JOHN McLAUGHLIN.

Mr. A. C. Anderson,   Vancouver, 22d Feby., 1841.

Dear Sir:—I have to inform you that the Cowlitz, Capt. Brotchie, is arrived and by her we have accounts that Messrs. Francis Heron, Alex. Stewart, and A. K. McLeod are no more; but I am happy to be able to inform you that Europe is at peace.

I am, dear sir, yours truly,

JOHN McLAUGHLIN.

Vancouver, 31 March, 1841.

Mr. A. C. Anderson,

Dear Sir:—This will be handed to you by the Revd. Jason Lee, whom I beg to introduce to your polite attentions, and request you will be so good as afford him such assistance as he may require.

I am, very truly,

JOHN McLAUGHLIN.

Vancouver, 5 July, 1843.

To Angus McDonald,

Dear Sir:—This will be handed you by Dr. Tolmie, to whom you will please deliver the charge of Nisqually and all papers and information connected with the place; and when Dr. Tolmie can dispense with you, you will come here.

I am, yours truly,

JOHN McLAUGHLIN.

Vancouver, 26 March, 1843.

Dr. Tolmie,

Dear Sir:—Yours of the 18th reached this today, with the accompanying letters and will be forwarded with our last express.

I am happy to see you are removed to the new Fort, which in every way is the most convenient situation for you, besides being one of the most pleasant situations in the Indian country.

I was aware, a long time ago, of the difficulty of getting work done as it ought, nay impossibility of doing so, but situated as we are it is impossible to get along without them (Indians), though I am fully aware they are the dearest and worst servants we have, yet we never can get enough of others to make us independent of them. The best is, as you know, for Mr. Heath to do is to humour them; if he begins by being strict he never will get on with them. I hope he is satisfied with the stock. Pray are the sheep poor or in good condition?

I am certain there have been more cattle killed at Nisqually than we are aware of, and here also. I hope you will be able to find out who shot at the steer that was wounded.

Yours truly, JOHN McLAUGHLIN.

Vancouver, 27th Sept., 1845.

Dr. Tolmie,

Dear Sir:—This will be handed to you by Col. Symonds, (Simmons) who is going with some of his friends to settle at the falls at the Chute River. He has applied to me to get an order on you for grain and potatoes, but I presume you have not more than you need for your own use. If you have any to spare please let him have what he demands and charge it to home (Vancouver). Col. Symonds and his friends passed the winter in our vicinity. They have been employed by us in making shingles and procuring logs. They have all conducted themselves in a most neighborly, friendly manner, and I beg to recommend them to your kind assistance and friendly offices.

I am, yours truly,

JOHN McLAUGHLIN.

———————

Vancouver, 9 Oct., 1845.

Dr. Tolmie,

Dear Sir:—The Cadboro is to proceed in tow of the steamer to Nisqually, and both are to be employed till further orders in taking cattle and sheep to Fort Victoria. It would be desirable to send forty head of oxen, which will be fit to kill next year, and a thousand of the finest wool sheep with their rams, and two hundred wethers, which I mention that you may know our views. It will be necessary that one of your most experienced shepherds go with the sheep. I merely mention these in case of Mr. Douglas not knowing your instructions about them already.

As the steamer is limited in her time it will be necessary every precaution be taken that she be detained as little time as possible at Nisqually, as if we can get more than that quantity to Victoria, so much the better.

I am, yours truly,

JOHN McLAUGHLIN.

———————

Fort Vancouver, 26 Sept., 1846.

Dr. Tolmie,

Dear Sir:—Mr. Simmons having applied to us for a supply of flour, you will please to order about thirty barrels from Fort Victoria, for the purpose of supplying that demand, and you may take shingles, at the usual price, in payment, always taking care not to allow him nor any of his people to get involved in debt.

We have given Mr. Simmons a crank and other irons for a saw mill, of which Mr. Forrest will send you an account and the weight, such irons being charged by the pound, and you will carry it to his account, at the rate of twenty cents per pound.

We have promised to take shingles from Simmons' people for the coming winter at former prices; they have spoken to us about getting sheep and cattle on shares and also for purchase, but we have given them no encouragement to expect a compliance with their wishes on that point.

As soon as the steam vessel arrives, she will be employed as last year in transporting cattle to Fort Victoria, and you will please to make the necessary preparations for that purpose.

Accompanying you will receive notes of hand as follows: —David Kindred, $6.74; Gabriel Jones, $82.93; M. T. Simmons, $53.43; James McAllister, $24.31, being the amount of their Vancouver accounts when they left this place last year. As soon as they have paid the amount due, you will return these notes to the drawers. Charge no interest on the notes, as they have been making payments on their accounts for many months past, and the sum is so small that the interest is not worth charging.

With best wishes, yours truly,

PETER SKEEN OGDEN,
JAMES DOUGLAS.

This letter is the handwriting of James Douglas.

———

Fort Vancouver, 22d May, 1846.

Dr. Tolmie,

Dear Sir:—We have just heard through Mr. Jackson, the Sheriff, that you had lately been over to Newmarket, and announced your intention of presenting yourself, at the approaching election, as a candidate for the county of Lewis, a most satisfactory piece of intelligence, as until it reached us, we were uncertain whether you had taken any steps towards the attainment of the object recommended in our letter of the 11th April. We are informed that all the Americans of Newmarket are disposed to give their suffrages in favor of Mr. Jackson, whom we firmly believe to be a good worthy man; and were it not for other considerations we should have no objection to their choice; but you know it would not be proper or appear right to the world, that we who possess a prevailing influence, and hold so large a share of the property of the County should allow a fragment of the population to represent and legislate for the interests of the whole.

The election is to take place on Monday the first day of June, and the polls to be opened by the judges of election, at the several precincts, as stated in the letter of the Clerk of Court, which Mr. Jackson will forward; say, one at Mr. Forrest's house, Cowlitz, one at Mr. Simmond's house, Newmarket, and one at Mr. Tolmie's house, Nisqually. The poll is merely a register of the voters' names, to be kept by the Judge of Election, to which office I have appointed Mr. Heath of your precinct.

The pollbook should be returned to this place under seal, as pointed out in the "Election Notice" on the fourth page of the 7th number of the Oregon Spectator herewith.

The number of qualified voters at Nisqually is 16, as per statement herewith. Besides their votes for the return of a member of the legislature, you will also submit the proposed amendment in the land law; and take the sense of the people as to the manner of electing Judges of County Courts, whether by the people or by the House of Representatives. On the first point, we intend to oppose the amendment of the land law, as it is, in all circumstances, dangerous to tamper with and make inroads on fundamental institutions, and more so in a new country, where things have not assumed a settled form, nor had time to take hold on the affections of the people. The law in its present state is certainly not perfect, neither is the amendment calculated to improve it.

On the second point, the sense of this county is decidedly in favour of the Judges being elected by the people, in their several counties. These things we mention for your information, trusting that the feeling in your county will be found akin to that of ours.

We think that a majority of the suffrages of the people at the Cowlitz will be given in your favor, as we intend to lend you all our influence.

Referring you to the accompanying number of the Oregon Spectator, we remain, dear sir, yours truly,

PETER SKEEN OGDEN.
JAMES DOUGLAS.

Fort Vancouver, 4 Novr., 1846.

To Dr. Tolmie,

Dear Sir:—We have to acknowledge your letter of the 23d Octr., with the accompanying documents, which were found correct and satisfactory. A bill against the Fisgard, for postage of Captain Duntze's letters to Fort George, was forwarded to you some time ago, of which we can discover no traces in your documents, from whence we fear it has been entirely overlooked, and not brought forward in your statement with Mr. Rames. Pray examine into that matter and let us know the result. The amount of the bill was $18.53.

The Barque Toulon arrived lately in the river with very important intelligence from the Sandwich Islands. It appears that the Oregon Boundary is finally settled, on a basis more favorable to the United States than we had reason to anticipate. We forward with this copy of communication from Sir George Seymour, Commander-in-Chief in the Pacific, to our agents at the Sandwich Islands, which contains all that is at present known to us relative to the Boundary Treaty. Business will, of course, go on as usual, as the treaty will not take effect on us for many years to come.

You will please get as many shingles ready to ship by the Columbia as possible, which may be shipped by the Beaver to Victoria, as we have not yet a sufficient cargo for both ships. Inform the shingle makers of this, and that they will be allowed 4 dollars a thousand for all they can deliver between this and the sailing of the ships, but the old prices only will be paid afterwards.

You will please to send six men or engaged Indians immediately to clear the road in the two points of wood between the Nisqually River and Bute Plain, which are nearly impassable for loaded horses; another party will be employed at the Cowlitz end of the Portage, under Mr. Sangster, who will afterwards proceed to Nisqually to relieve you for a time as your presence here will be required on or before the first day of December, to attend the Legislature, and you will please to take your measures accordingly, using every exertion to be here by the time specified.

With best wishes, yours truly,

PETER SKEEN OGDEN.
JAMES DOUGLAS.

The first term of court held on Puget Sound was convened at Steilacoom on the last Monday in October, 1849, the Oregon chief justice Bryan, presiding. This was brought about by a tragedy that took place under the walls of Fort Nisqually. In May of that year one hundred or more Snoqualmie and Skeywamish Indians visited Fort Nisqually with the ostensible purpose of ascertaining whether the reports in circulation among them of the cruel treatment of a member of their tribe, a sister of Patkanim, who had married a Nisqually Indian named Wyamoch, were true or not. These Indians were among the most warlike of the native tribes on the Sound, and the other tribes to the southward of them feared them greatly.

At the time of the advent of the Snoqualmies, a large number of the Nisquallies were camped near the Fort, and these sought protection within its palisades. The Fort had been moved from its original location near the brow of the hill to what is still known as the fort in 1842-3, the new location being far more advantageous for many reasons, the chief of which being its proximity to an abundant supply of pure, running water. The original fort was surrounded by a high and strong stockade, but when the transfer was made it was omitted. When the news of the massacre of Whitman and party was received, coupled with the probability of a bloody war to punish that crime, the Hudson's Bay people felt compelled to erect a stockade around the post then occupied. The Indians looked upon this action with disfavor, but a strong force was employed, most of them with arms by their sides during the progress of the work. The palisades were about twenty feet high; at the north-west and south-east corners were large and very strong bastions, constructed of squared timbers twelve inches in diameter, impregnable to any attack of Indians armed only with their old-fashioned muzzle-loading guns. The bastions were three stories high, and armed with small cannon and small swivel guns. A dozen muskets and a good supply of ammunition were always kept in each of the bastions ready for immediate use.

About noon the visiting Indians, fully armed, came up and took position in front of the water gate on the north side. It has always remained an open question whether their original purpose was an attack on the Fort or upon the Nisqually Indians, but, presumably, was the latter, with the intention of carrying off all the women and property they could get within their clutches. Two armed men were placed at the gate, and all the whites outside the enclosure, of whom there were several Americans, were called to come in the gate. At this, several of the Snoqualmies rushed for the gate, but were warned to keep away. Several shots were then fired and one Indian killed and two others wounded.

For some reason two Americans, named Wallace and Lewis, did not come into the enclosure when the alarm was sounded, although they had plenty of time. They, perhaps thought as they did not belong to the Fort they would not be harmed, but if so it was a fatal mistake, as Wallace was shot dead, and Lewis wounded in the arm.

The Indians found the Fort too strong and well defended for them to capture, so they made off as rapidly as possible.

This disturbance led to the sending of a company of artillery around from Fort Vancouver to Steilacoom, this being the first advent of United States soldiers here. They were under command of Capt. B. Hill.

On August 7, 1849, J. Q. Thornton, sub-Indian Agent for Oregon Territory, arrived at Fort Nisqually and immediately proceeded to investigate the facts connected with the killing of Mr. Wallace. He sent messengers to Patkanim, and advised him to arrest the chief offenders and bring them

to Capt. Hill at Fort Steilacoom. He also offered a reward
of eighty blankets if this were done within three weeks.
Patkanim succeeded in inducing the tribe to give up six
of its members, Kussass, Quhlawot, Stullhahya, Juttain,
Wyah and Qualthlinkyne. These were delivered to Capt.
Hill, and by him turned over to Joe Meek, the United States
Marshal. All six were indicted, but only the first two were
convicted, and they were executed. Three of the others
were mixed up in the affray but had no part in the killing,
while the sixth was found not to have been on the ground,
but had been brought along, he being a slave, whom the
guilty chiefs hoped to place in their stead, to become a scape-
goat.

The result of this trial and execution had a good effect
upon the Indians. The whole Snoqualmie tribe was present
at the execution; also a vast gathering of Indians from other
tribes on Puget Sound, and they were made to understand
that under the United States laws they would be punished
for every murder they committed, and that no satisfaction
would be accepted short of all who participated in the murder of white people. Judge A. P. Skinner was appointed
United States District Attorney by Judge Bryant, to conduct the trial, and David Stone was appointed Attorney
for the defense. They had traveled two hundred miles from
their homes, camping in the woods on the way, as did nearly
all concerned in the trial. They all had to travel in canoes,
batteaux, and on horse back, and of course the journey was
one of hardship and fatigue. Many of the grand and petit
jurors had to travel like distances and by the same methods.
The total expense of holding this first term of court for the
trial of these Indians was $1899.54, and the value of the
blankets given as a reward $480 more, making in all
$2379.54.

One of the numerous farms of the Company was rented
for the use of this military company. It had a considerable
number of comfortable buildings on it that served the purpose of the company for some time. The United States paid

the Company a yearly rental of six hundred dollars for nearly twenty years for the use of this place. When the companies were finally paid for their holdings in Oregon and Washington a mile square enclosing this farm became a military reserve, and when it was abandoned as a military post it was sold to the Territory of Washington for a small sum, and was then devoted for the uses of the Territorial Hospital for Insane. The old quarters for the officers and soldiers were adequate for this purpose for many years, or nearly to the time of admission to statehood. This is where the present Hospital for Insane is situated. The first brick building was begun, I think, in 1886.

Prior to the advent of American settlers here the Puget Sound Agricultural Company encouraged independent farmers to settle near Nisqually, and in 1844, Mr. Heath came over from Vancouver with letters of recommendation from Gov. McLaughlin, and he leased this farm and occupied it for many years, in fact, I think, until the coming of the American soldiers.

William W. Miller was the first surveyor of customs on Puget Sound, and Nisqually being the only port at that time, he roomed and kept his office in the house built by the Company on the beach, and took his meals at the Fort on top of the hill. He had an excellent metallic boat and kept a crew of four or five men to use in traveling about the Sound. One of these, named Pocock, but who went by the name of Wilson, later, was one of the two men killed at the time of the Indian attack on Seattle.

General Miller afterward married the daughter of Judge O. B. McFadden. His widow, Mrs. Mary M. Miller, and their two sons have long been residents of Seattle, and the sudden death of Penfield Miller, one of these sons, is still fresh in the memories of hundreds of loving friends in this City and his early home in Olympia.

To the casual reader it will, no doubt, seem strange that so many extracts from other sources should have been included in this sketch of early events, but to the historian and those interested in historical matters the reason will be manifest. The time and labor bestowed upon the gathering of this matter from a hundred sources would have sufficed for the production of many times the amount of matter collected here. In one sense this sketch is "original history," for no large part of it has ever appeared in print, and much of the selections were found only after wide and diligent search in long forgotten newspapers or in old time books long out of print. So much in explanation—not in apology.

The number of those who have lived on Puget Sound fifty years or more is small and rapidly growing less. Among them is my friend Edward Huggins, who lives on the site of Fort Nisqually, where he came a young man five and fifty years ago. He occupies a unique position, connecting, as he does, the old regime and the new.

To him I am indebted for countless favors in the matter of historical information. Old papers and old records have been placed freely at my disposal, and in addition by correspondence he has given me historical material that I have been able to use but in small part in this sketch. He is a veritable mine of information regarding early days.

My first recollections of him began about 1866, when I went to live in Olympia and for years frequently saw him riding between that place and his home at Nisqually.

Mr. Huggins was born in Southwark, a borough of London, England, June 10, 1832. Beginning school at an early age he continued until in his fifteenth year when he entered a broker's office within a stone's throw of the Hudson's Bay Company's office in Fenchurch street. Through the influence of Mr. Benjamin Harrison, one of the directors of that company, he obtained a situation in its service, and on the 10th of October, 1849, he sailed from London on the Company's ship, Norman Morrison, for Fort Victoria, Vancouver Island, and arrived at his destination late in March, 1850.

James Douglas was then in charge at that place, and sent

EDWARD HUGGINS, 1850.   FIFTY-FIVE YEARS AT FORT NISQUALLY.

the youth to Nisqually, where he arrived by the little trading schooner Cadboro, April 13, 1850. Dr. Tolmie was in charge at that place. He set the new arrival at work in the Company's store or "trade shop," as they called it. Settlers were few and Indians numerous, so most of the trade was with the latter. At that time the Company's business was much hampered by the loss of most of its white employees, who had been attracted to California by the gold excitement. It had then about seven thousand cattle, ten thousand sheep and three hundred horses. Nearly all the white men, with the aid of a large crew of Indians had to take care of the stock, while the store business fell largely upon young Huggins. He quickly learned the Chinook jargon and a smattering of the native language, and young as he was became very serviceable. Here he continued until after the breaking out of the Indian war in 1855, when the servants of the Company who looked after the live stock became frightened and abandoned their posts. Mr. Huggins volunteered to head a party and take charge of the stock. He picked up a cosmopolitan crew of English, Irish, Scotch, Canadians, Kanakas, Indians, half-breeds and one negro, and went to the Company's farm at Muck, about ten miles east of the Fort. They had no great fear of the Indians, except a band of renegades who had separated from the main body of hostiles and committed two murders and many depredations. The party remained at the farm until several years after the war ended. On the 21st of October, 1857, Mr. Huggins and Miss Letitia Work were united in marriage and they resided at Muck for about two years.

Mrs. Huggins was the daughter of John Work, Esq., who has been mentioned elsewhere, and who attained high rank early in the service of the Hudson's Bay Company. Three others of his daughters became the wives of Chief Factors William F. Tolmie, Roderick Finlayson and James A. Grahame. The latter afterward became Chief Commissioner.

In common with all the employees of the Company Mr. Huggins looked forward to advancement in the service but it was long in coming. Fort Nisqually was under the control of the Agricultural Company and the parent company failed to give him his steps. At one time he was ordered to go to Fort Kamloops, on Thompson's river, but this was soon countermanded, as it was felt his life at Nisqually had made his services valuable in the negotiations then pending regarding the compensation to be made by the United States for the Company's holdings in Washington Territory.

In July, 1859, a little more than twenty-six years after his first arrival there, Dr. Tolmie and his family left Nisqually and moved to Victoria, where he subsequently made his home. James Douglas, one of the Board of Management of the Western Department of the Hudson's Bay Company, having accepted the appointment of Governor of the Province, Dr. Tolmie succeeded him on the Board. Mr. Huggins thus succeeded to the charge of Nisqually and with his family at once removed from Muck.

In June, 1870, the Puget Sound Agricultural Company surrendered the rights it claimed under the treaty of 1846, and Mr. Huggins was again ordered to get ready to move to a post in the interior of British Columbia, but his family had been increased by six sons, all still young, and he and his wife decided that the difficulties and perhaps dangers of the new post were so great that he had best resign from the Company's employ, which he accordingly did.

He had become a citizen of the United States several years before, and as was quite natural, determined to remain upon the place where he was then living and enter it as a pre-emption claim. This quarter section included the principal buildings of the old fort and the best of the land nearby. He expected to have to pay something for the buildings, but the Commission appointed later to appraise them reported they were so old they would be valueless to move off the land, and so they finally came to him without compensation. They consisted of the historic building in which he still lives, that was put up in 1854, a smaller squared log dwelling house erected in 1843, and a lot of other out-buildings that show in the illustration. It took a long time to settle the many questions and conflicts arising out of the Company's claims in Pierce County, and in common with many others Mr. Huggins was long in getting the patent to his land claim. Later he bought other lands until he had about one thousand acres in a body, but of such sandy and gravelly nature as to be of small value, except for grazing. Here for many years he continued farming, stockraising and trading a little in furs, but the latter business gradually dwindled away to nothing.

In the 'seventies he was given the unsolicited honor of a nomination for county commissioner on the Republican ticket and was elected by an overwhelming vote. He was re-elected twice to the same position, and in 1886, while serving as chairman of the Board was nominated for county auditor. The Democratic candidate was very popular and it seemed Mr. Huggins was the only man who could defeat him at the polls. A warm canvass ensued but Mr. Huggins was elected by a small majority. He then moved to Tacoma with his wife and the younger members of the family, while the elder boys remained at Nisqually to care for the farm and stock. He was re-elected two years later, and after serving the four years he rested awhile and then became a member of one of the leading banks of Tacoma, in a short time becoming its vice-president. Here he remained until failing health compelled him to give up active work, when he and his family moved back to the old farm that is a part of the most historic spot in all Washington, save Fort Vancouver on the banks of the Columbia. Here he and his wife are living quietly in their declining days, in the enjoyment of the respect and love of all who know them.

There is almost a virgin field for the historian and the story writer on Puget Sound. But little has been written of pioneer days following the arrival of the first American

colony on the banks of the Deschutes, and still less of the
years preceding, when the Hudson's Bay Company was the
only representative of civilization. For three decades, at
least, the few white people braved constant dangers, encountered numberless hardships and endured ever-present
privations, with stoical fortitude. They traversed pathless
forests, crossed towering, rugged mountains, swam swollen
rivers, and navigated all parts of this inland sea as far as
Vancouver Island, the Fraser River, Queen Charlotte
Island, or the mouth of the Straits of Fuca in an open canoe,
often but one white man and an Indian crew.

Of McLaughlin much has been written, and he richly
deserves the tardy justice that later writers have done him;
but there were other strong men of whom the reading public
knows but little. James Douglas, Peter Skeen Ogden, William Fraser Tolmie, Archibald McDonald, John Work and
many others, who built the posts and conducted the important operations of the Hudson's Bay and Puget Sound
Agricultural Companies were no ordinary men, and they
all left their impress upon the times of which I have endeavored to write in this sketch. It is a difficult matter to
obtain the information that is still extant of them and their
work. They were emphatically men of action, and most of
them left few personal papers. Their history was that of
the companies they served all the best years of their lives,
and most of this history is still locked up in the musty
vaults of the Company in Victoria or London, or has been
borrowed and never returned by a noted California Historian.

It is one of my ambitions to get access to the old Hudson's Bay records kept at Vancouver, Nisqually and Langley, and then add to and amplify what I have here set out.

During the preparation of this volume a mass of material bearing on the life and achievements of the heroic pioneer women of the Northwest has come under my notice not available for the work in hand.

I am moved to continue the collection of this material, which I have found scattered in the homes of pioneers, and to embody it in bound volumes of manuscript, for the use of future historians; or, perhaps, if my life and health are spared, to use it myself to tell the story of the marvelous heroism of these sturdy matrons, whose lives were lives of sacrifice, and whose deeds deserve a better recognition in recorded history than has been accorded them.

I invite all who are interested in this work to send me the experiences and incidents of the fore-mothers as handed down to the later generations by precept or example—anything that will serve to illustrate the lives of these matrons of "ye olden times," and throw light on their manners, customs, dress, religion, work; in a word, that will give us an insight of their daily lives, of their trials and achievements.

To the matrons themselves, a word. Where the hand is not stayed by infirmity, I conjure you to take this work in hand personally; but where for any reason it is not practical, then exercise the old-time authority once more and see to it that the youngsters (?) do it without delay, even though they may be grandmothers or grandfathers.

Seattle, 1905.   *E. MEEKER.*

Ezra Meeker, Oregon Trail Pioneer, Dies

Memorial Association Head Succumbs at 97: Lost For-~~~~ Failure

londyke

Trek of
Airplane

Associated Press from
Underwood & Underwood

Ezra Meeker

3 (P).—Ezra Oregon Trail one of the eers of the e this morning eral months. old.
to life unly sheer will nd relatives had been at Detroit hospital re returning had grown n his condition vas impossi- spital.

ecember 29 eer was recent improvement momentarily ould recover ninety-eighth He was in k end and were about here was a ank rapidly. pointed bed prevented in time to tion. It was ed since he election in

and three sborne and Seattle, and f Peshastin.

held here be in the Wash., where 1909.

Crosne, Siebold; music in '52

Ezra Meeker, pioneer of the West and contemporary of Kit Carson, Jason Lee and Marcus Whitman, first crossed the Oregon trail in 1852. His greatest apparent interest in life during the present century has been the preservation for posterity of this pathway.